MASTERING **LANDSCAPE**

PHOTOGRAPHY

DAVID TAYLOR

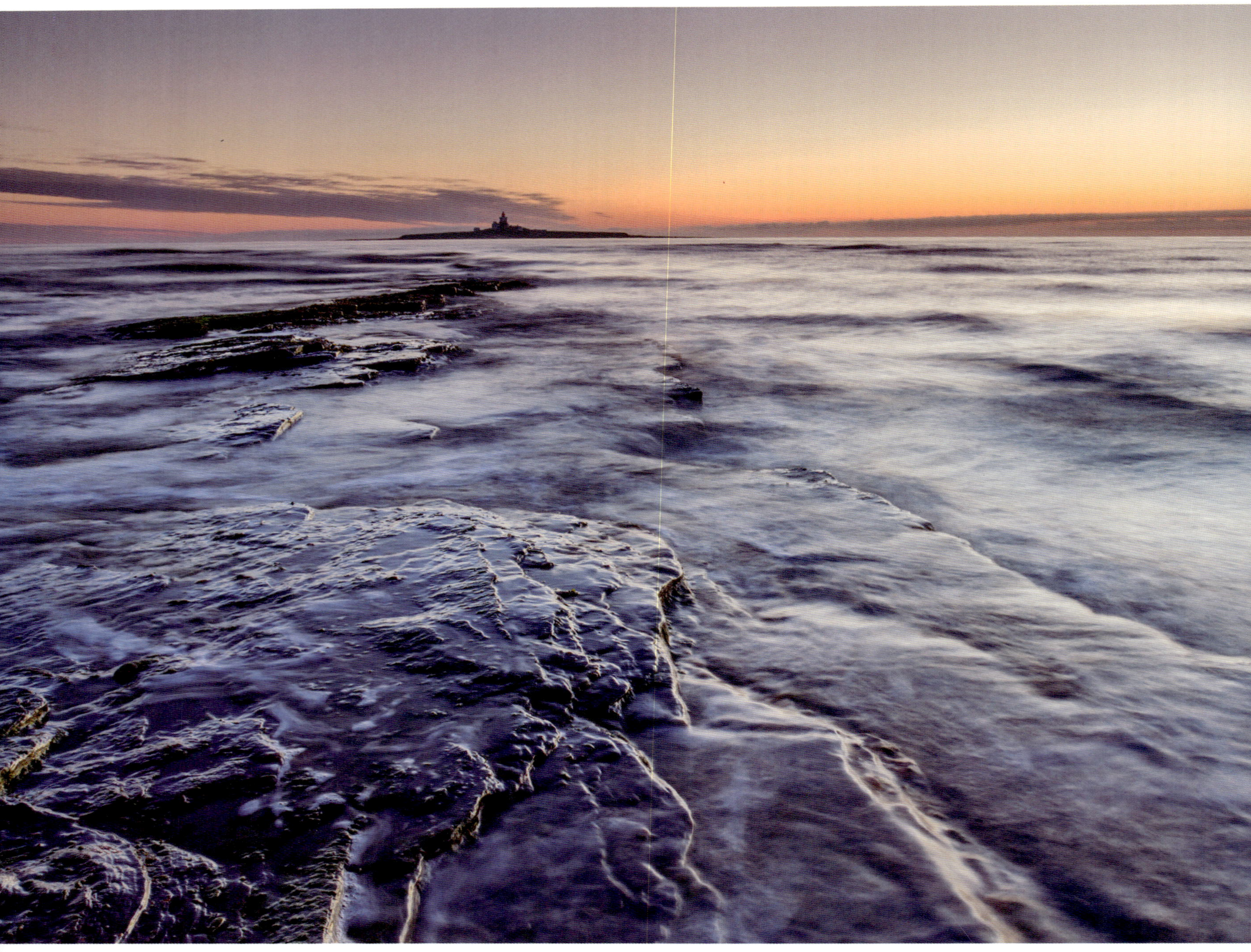

Above: One of the pleasures of shooting landscape images is that you can spend time doing something pleasurable in a beautiful location. You also have a concrete reminder of that moment as a keepsake, in the form of your photograph.

MASTERING **LANDSCAPE**
PHOTOGRAPHY

DAVID TAYLOR

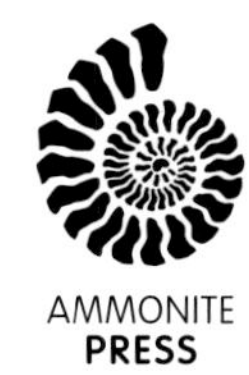

AMMONITE
PRESS

First published 2014 by
Ammonite Press
an imprint of Guild of Master Craftsman Publications Ltd
Castle Place, 166 High Street, Lewes, East Sussex, BN7 1XU, UK

Reprinted 2017

ISBN 978-1-78145-084-0

British Library Cataloging in Publication Data: A catalog record of this
book is available from the British Library.

Editor: Chris Gatcum
Series Editor: Richard Wiles
Designer: Robin Shields

Typeface: Helvetica Neue
Color reproduction by GMC Reprographics
Printed in China

Contents

Introduction

Photographers often go through two stages as they start to explore photography. The first stage is relatively simple to define: it's the learning stage. This is when the technical issues involved in making photographic images are grappled with and mastered.

The second stage is slightly subtler. It requires the photographer to ask himself or herself a philosophical question: what kind of photographer am I? If the answer is "landscape photographer," then this is the book for you.

Defining Skills

All photographers need to know the basic technical skills of the craft. However, as strange as it may seem, this is actually the easy bit, as there's a logic behind things such as exposure or focusing. Even if they seem mystifying initially, these skills can be learned.

Less easy to define are the skills that need to be learned once you've decided what sort of photographer you are. A wedding photographer needs to have the same basic photographic skills as a landscape photographer, but that doesn't mean that one would be able to do the other's job. Wedding photographers need to be able to get the best out of people and to have the patience and organizational skills of a saintly general. I'm full of admiration for wedding photographers—it's not something I'd wish to do on a regular basis, if ever!

A landscape photographer, however, needs to understand how the landscape is affected by the weather, the seasons, and the light falling upon it. Navigational skills are also useful for finding potential subjects, but above all, empathy for the natural world is essential. Without that I don't think a landscape photographer can make images that will inspire others. Ultimately, to be fulfilled creatively, a landscape photographer has to move beyond being a mere technician to find his or her own artistic voice.

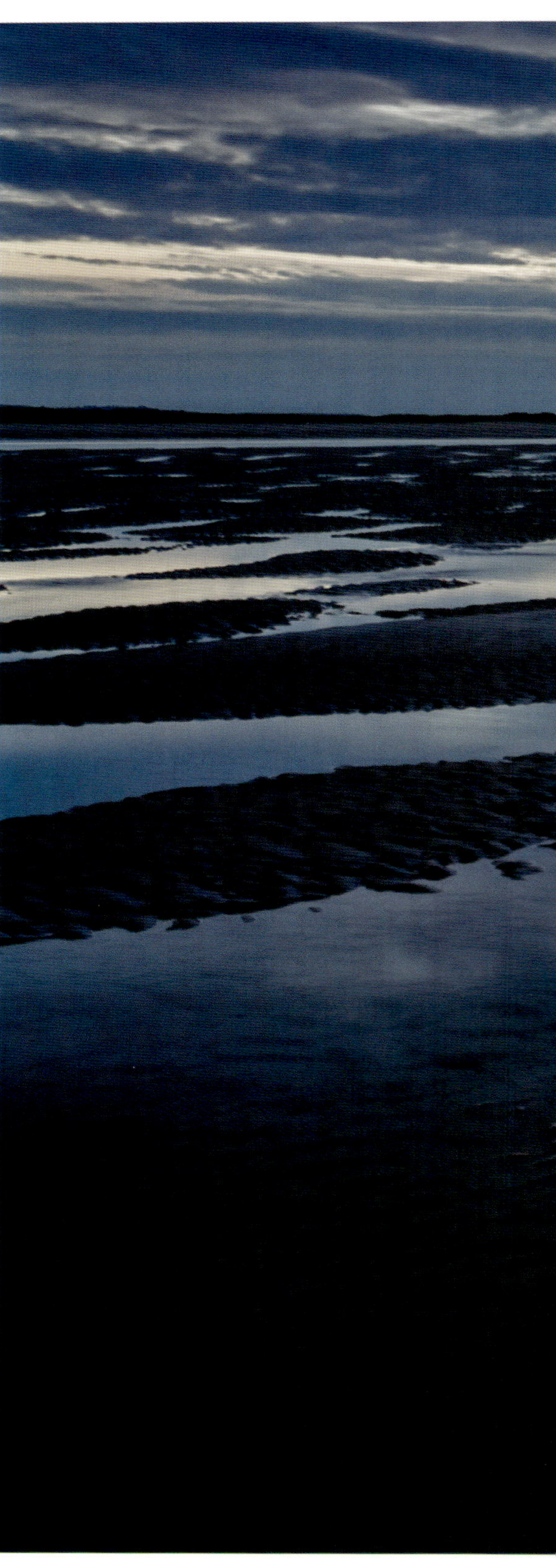

Right: One aspect of landscape photography that I find endlessly fascinating is the way the light changes throughout the day, affecting the mood of an image.

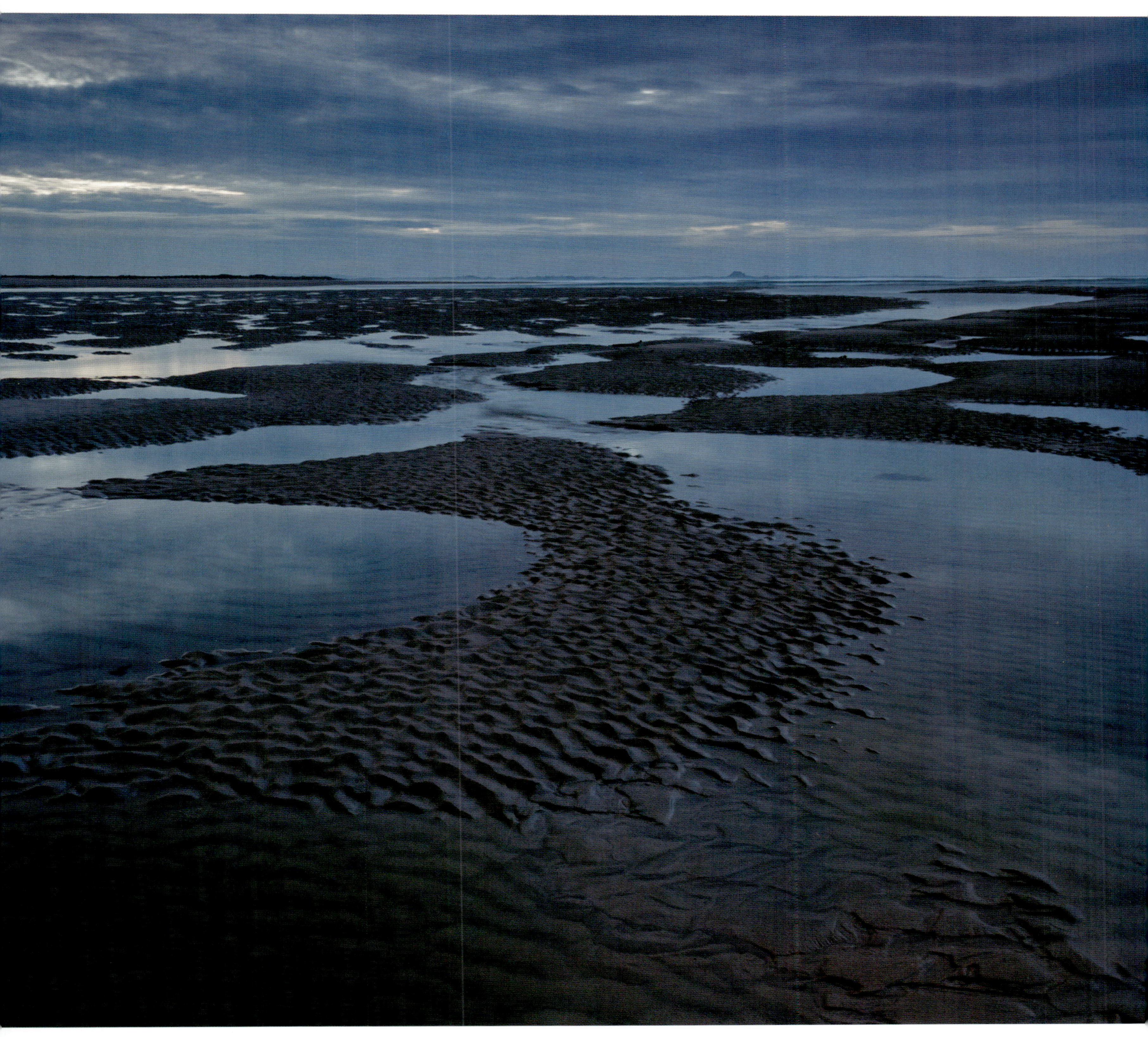

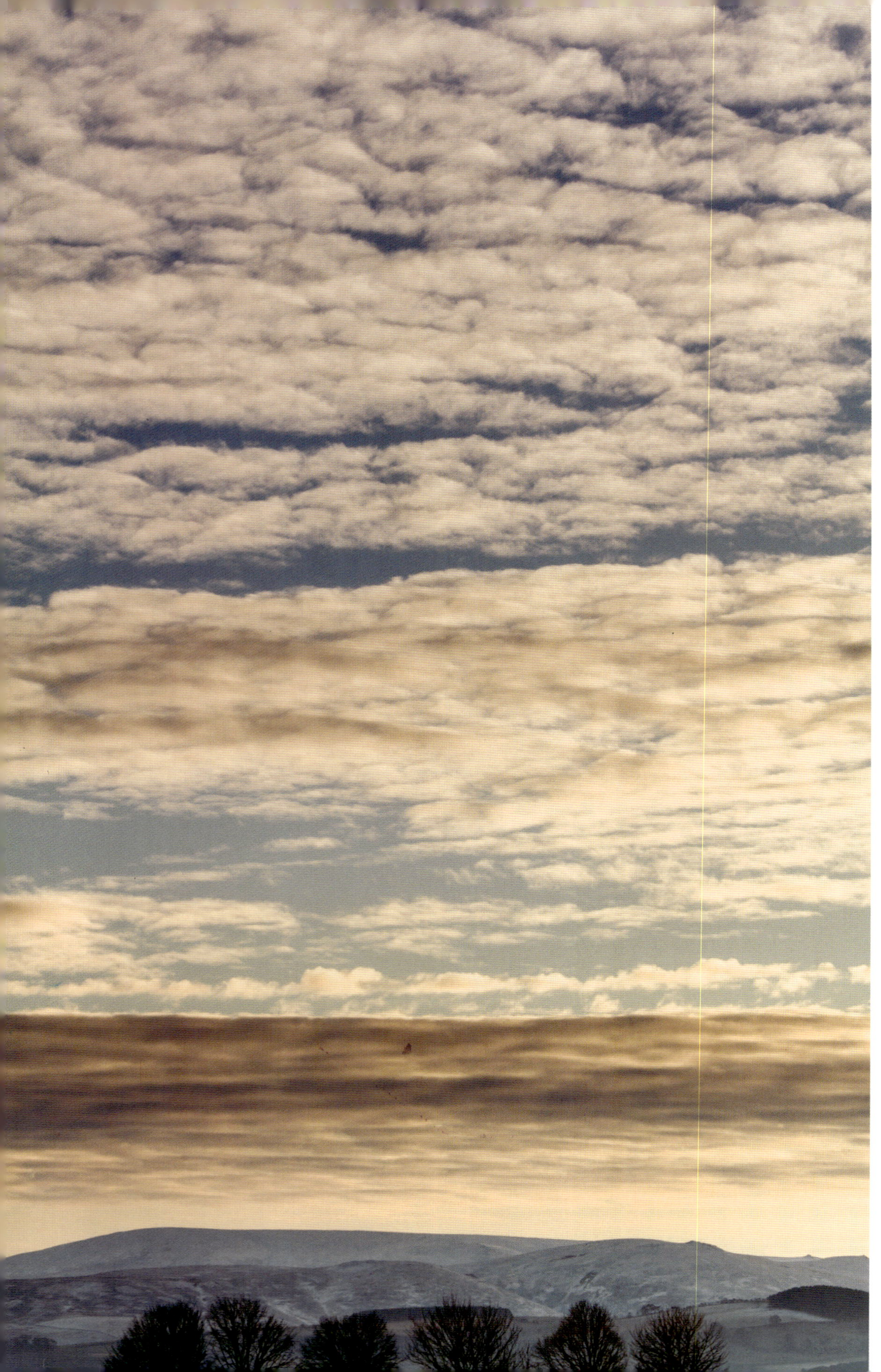

Slowing Down

Landscape photography gives you permission to temporarily cut yourself off from the modern world. Being out in the landscape early in the morning or late in the evening means you're often on your own, with only your thoughts for company. These are all good things: creativity requires a certain amount of peaceful contemplation to flourish. It's incredibly difficult to be creative in a noisy, busy office if others constantly disturb you.

It is important to allow yourself time at your chosen location without feeling a desperate panic to shoot. This means arriving in good time so you can wander around, take in the atmosphere, and allow your subconscious to get to work. In fact there's something to be said for not shooting for at least ten—even 20—minutes after you arrive.

It's all too tempting to fire your camera like a machine gun, hoping that if you shoot often enough you will create at least one worthwhile image. Don't give in to that temptation. A few good images will always be more satisfying than scores of mediocre ones.

This is another good reason to arrive in good time: if you've got time to think and to contemplate, you'll panic less and shoot fewer images. An even more compelling reason to slow down is that every image you shoot will have to be assessed and either rejected or processed at some point in the future. Overshooting will expand the time this takes, and this could be time better spent outdoors shooting instead!

Left: Walking can be incredibly helpful to the creative process, particularly if you take time to look around you as you walk. This image was shot on an afternoon's stroll because I did just that.

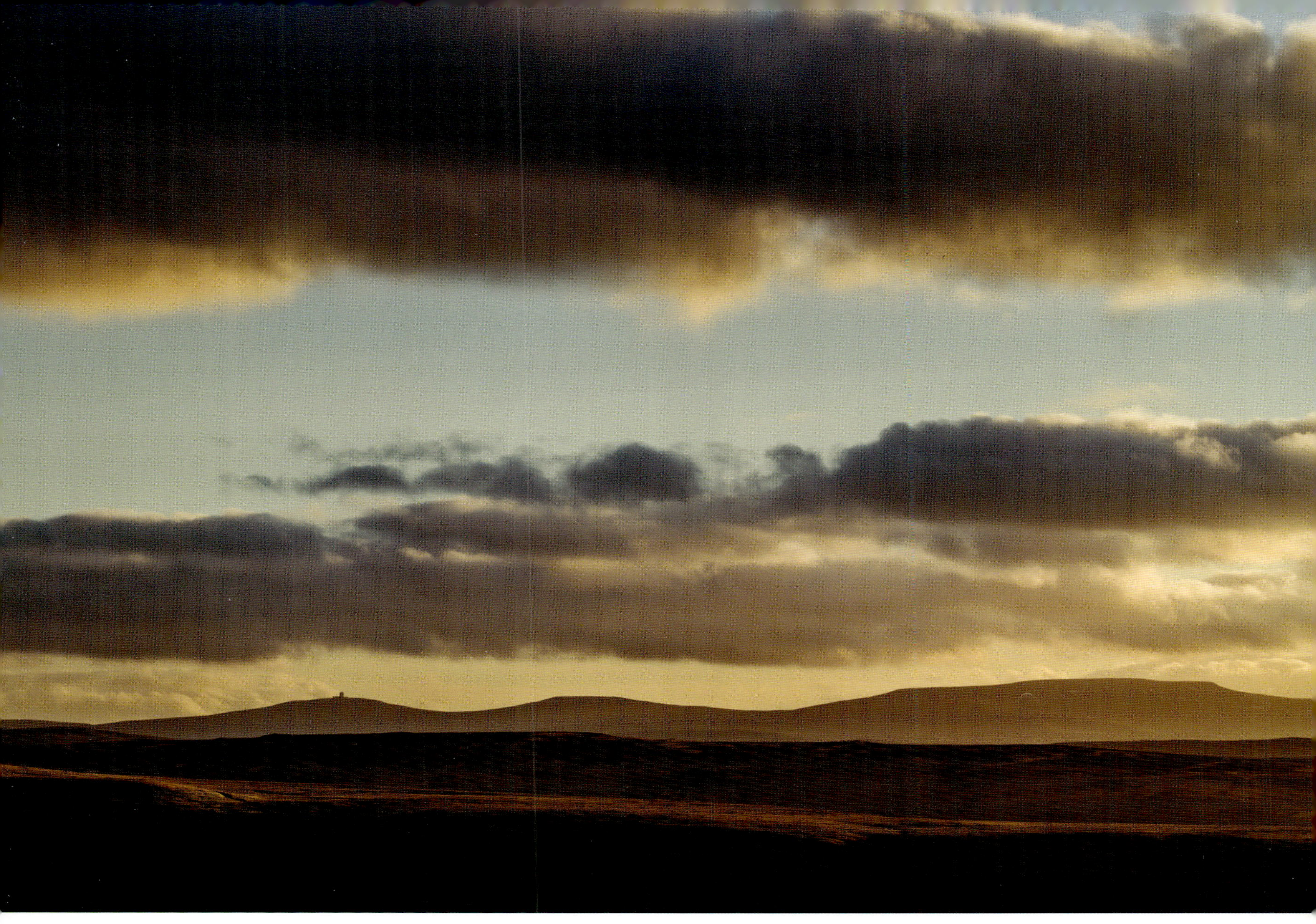

Above: Landscape photography isn't an immediate social experience in the way that portrait or wedding photography is. The pleasure of sharing comes later, when you show your images to friends, family, or via social media. And your work should be shared: spreading the wonder of the natural world will encourage others to explore it for themselves.

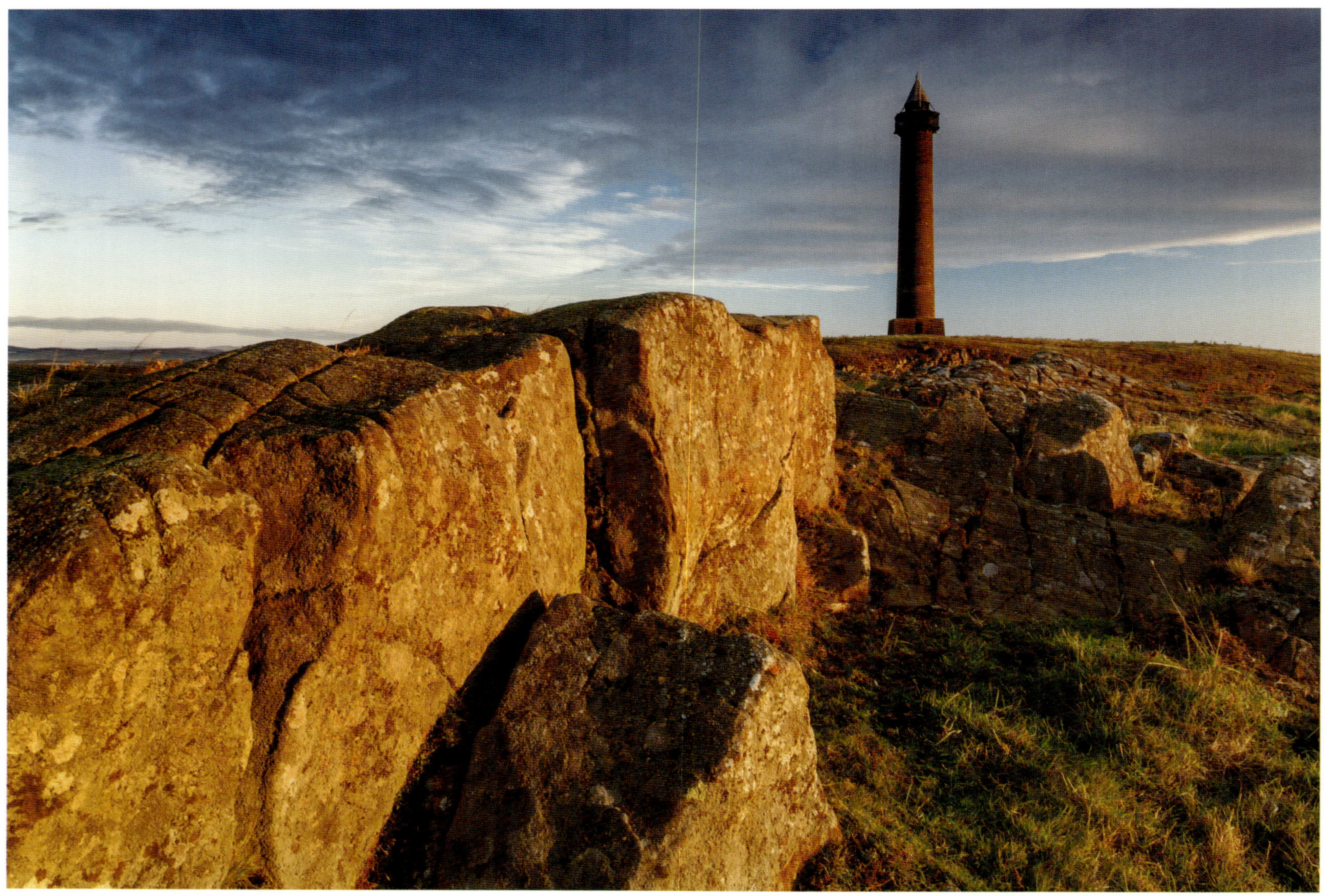

Heroes & Heroines

Landscape photography as a genre is almost as old as photography itself. This means that we have our pick of nearly two centuries of images to look at and learn from, and everyone should have heroes and heroines to inspire them. The Internet has made this easier, of course, but there's arguably nothing better than curling up with a book about landscape photography and taking in the work of others. For me, this is a particular treat on dark, wintry evenings when the weather isn't cooperating and inspiration is lacking.

The work of a really great photographer, more often than not, still seems like magic to me. I sometimes look at a particularly inspiring image by one of my photographic heroes and can't see immediately how the trick was done. How did the photographer see the shot in the first place? What exposure settings were used? Were filters involved? What time of day or year was the image made? In a negative frame of mind this could be intimidating, but I think it's wonderful, as it means there's still something new to learn or some

previously unknown technique to try. Hopefully this book will reveal aspects of landscape photography that you were unaware of, and inspire you to put them into practice.

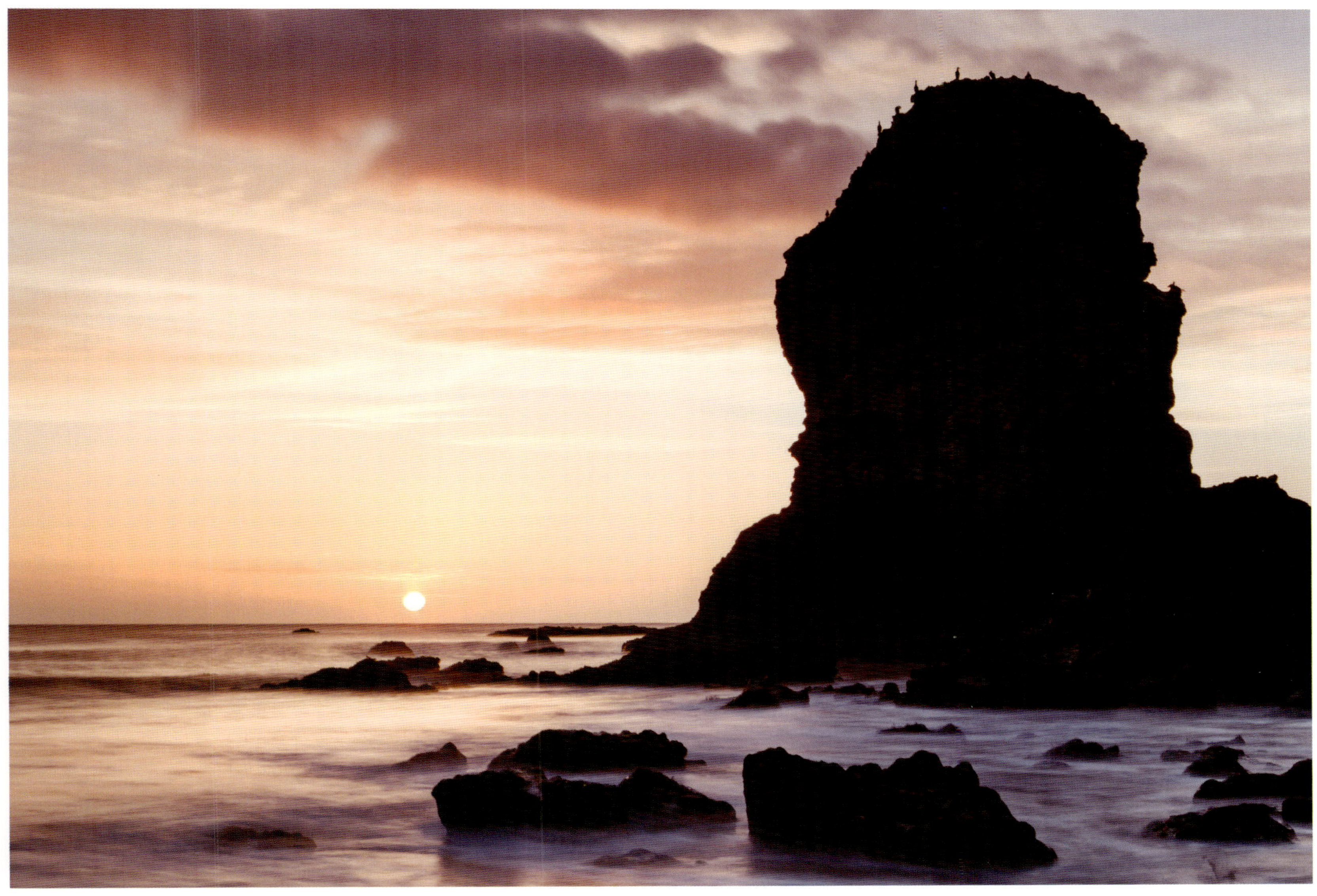

Left: Landscape photography sometimes requires determination. The natural world can't be relied upon to act according to your needs. This shot required several attempts on separate mornings before I got the result I was after.

Above: Landscape photography involves certain sacrifices. Being out and about before dawn is one of those sacrifices. Fortunately, the reward of a spectacular sunrise generally makes the effort worthwhile.

Chapter 1
Equipment

All you really need to be a landscape photographer is a camera, a lens, and a memory card: once you have those three items you can begin in earnest. However, there are other pieces of equipment that will expand the range of images that you can create or that will help to keep your equipment safe from the elements. This chapter is a guide to cameras, lenses, and those other bits and pieces that may initially seem like a luxury, but will ultimately come to be considered essential.

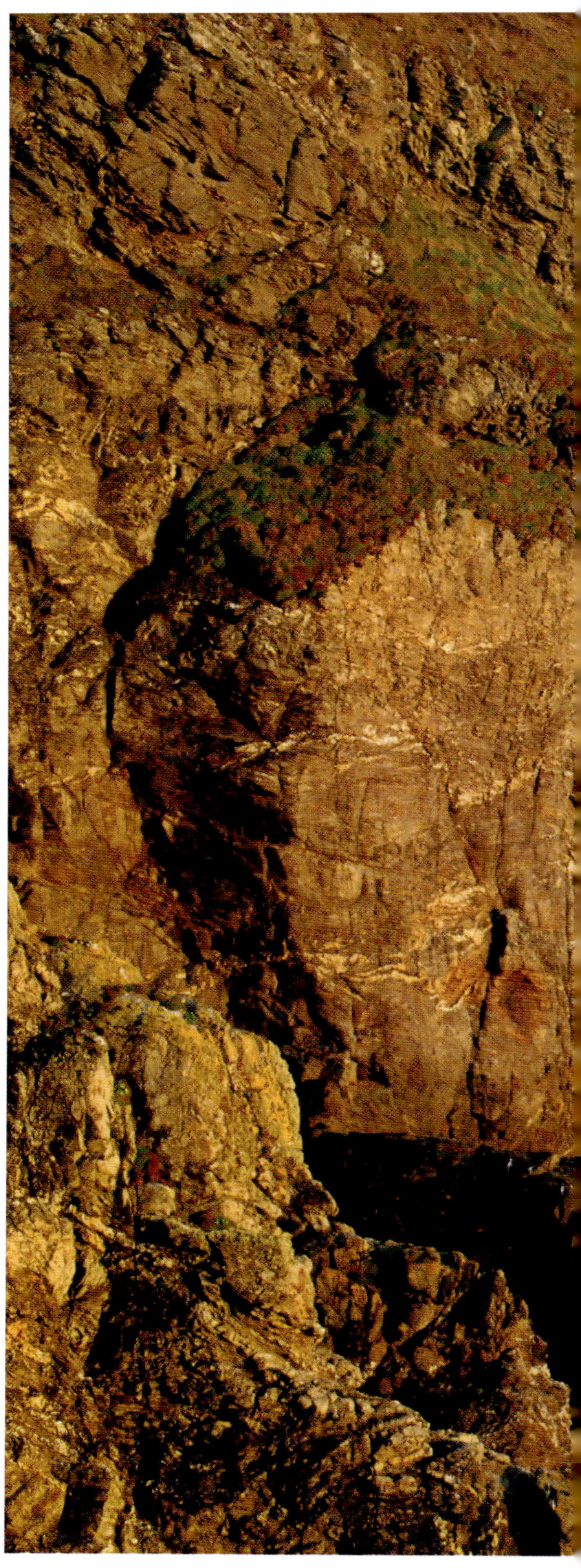

Right: This image was shot with a medium-format film camera in the pre-digital era. Some modern digital cameras can produce files that match the resolution of medium-format film in a body that is the fraction of the size and weight. This is a welcome development for landscape photographers who often have to carry their equipment over long distances.

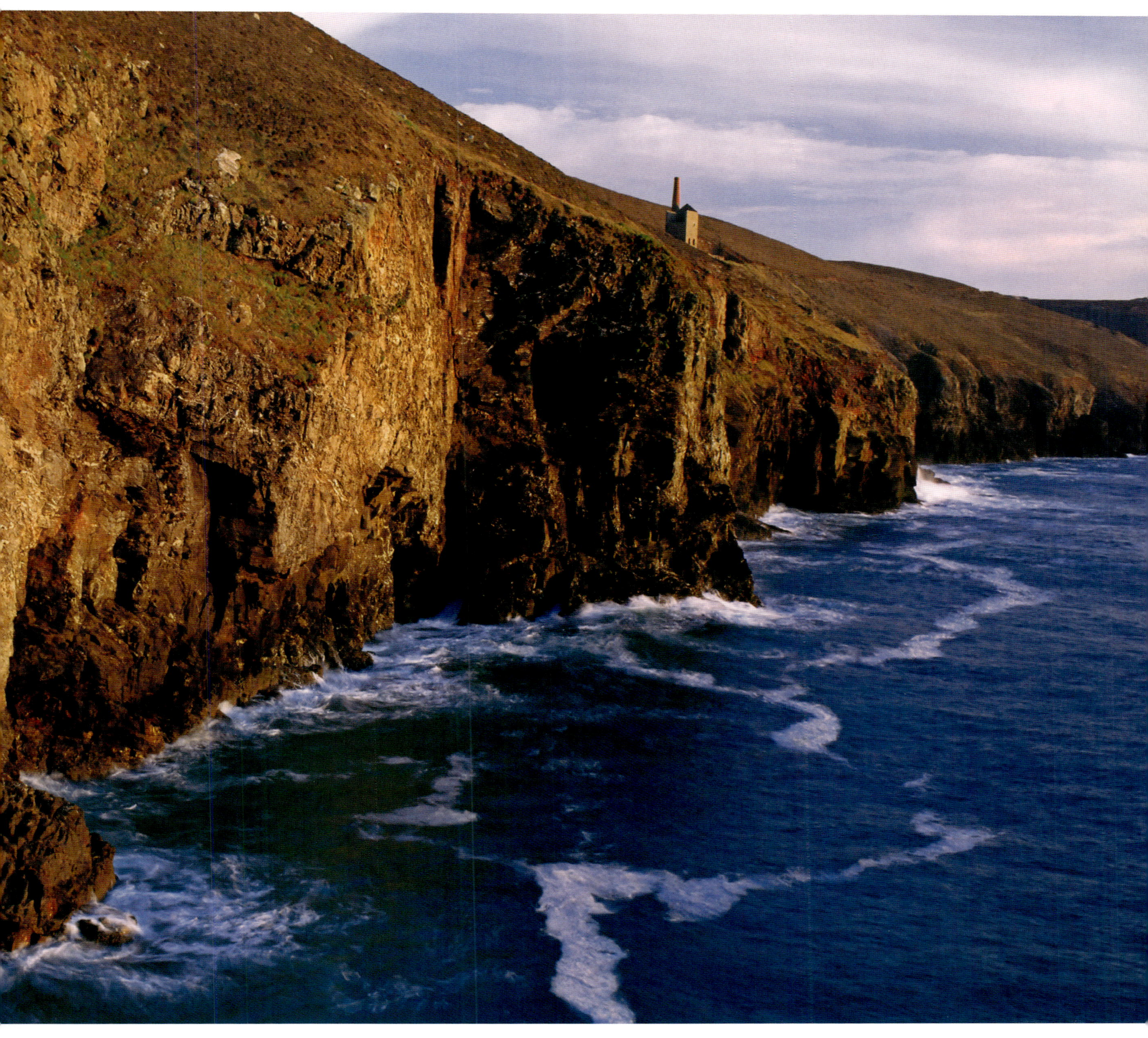

Cameras

Whether it's built into a cell phone or a fully fledged DSLR, virtually any camera can be used to shoot landscapes. However, just because you can take landscape photographs with any camera, that doesn't mean it's suited to that role.

Compact Cameras

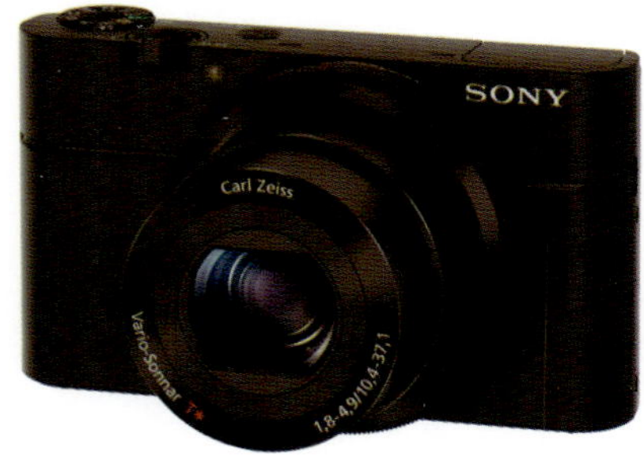

Above: Sony's Cyber-shot RX-100 is a highly regarded compact camera.
© Sony

Compact cameras (a broad term that covers cell phones, bridge cameras, and everything in between) typically use small digital sensors. Although the technology improves constantly, these cameras suffer from a lack of dynamic range and high image noise. Working in low light is often frustrating because of these issues, and an often-limited shutter speed range doesn't help either. Another disadvantage of this type of camera is that its capabilities are essentially fixed. Although some compact cameras allow you to add a hotshoe-mounted flash, it's often difficult to use other accessories, such as filters.

However, one big advantage of compact cameras is that the size of the digital sensor requires the use of short focal length lenses, even for telephoto-type images. This means that only moderate apertures are required to achieve extensive depth of field. This makes it easier to achieve front-to-back sharpness (an often desirable quality in a landscape image) than it is with a camera with a larger sensor. The downside is that it is more difficult to use a shallow depth of field to isolate a subject from its surroundings.

Another good thing about a compact camera is that it is easy to carry around. The best camera in the world is the one you have with you when you need it, and for that reason alone a compact camera is worth considering as a backup (or even as a primary camera, as long as its limitations are understood). There are several images in this book shot with compact cameras, including the one above: can you spot them?

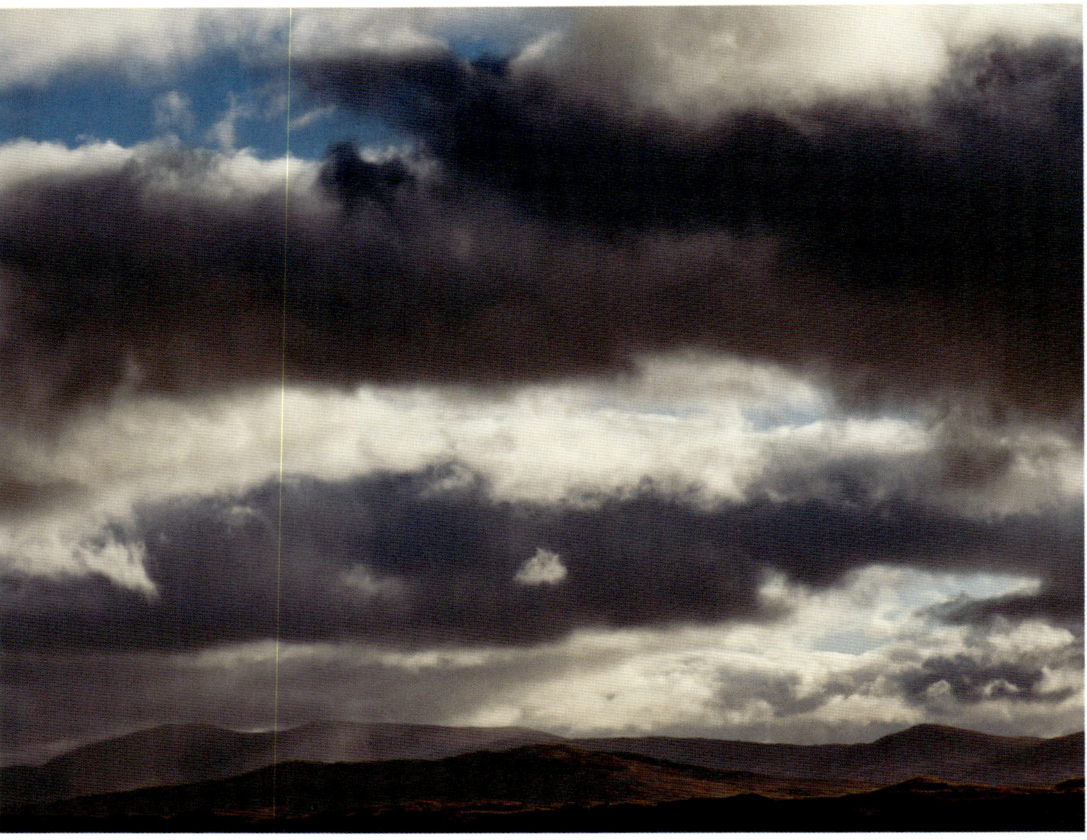

Above: Compact cameras are ideal for keeping in a jacket pocket or car for those times when spontaneity is required. They also make good "visual notebooks," allowing you to work out compositional ideas for shooting later with a larger, better-specified camera.

System Cameras

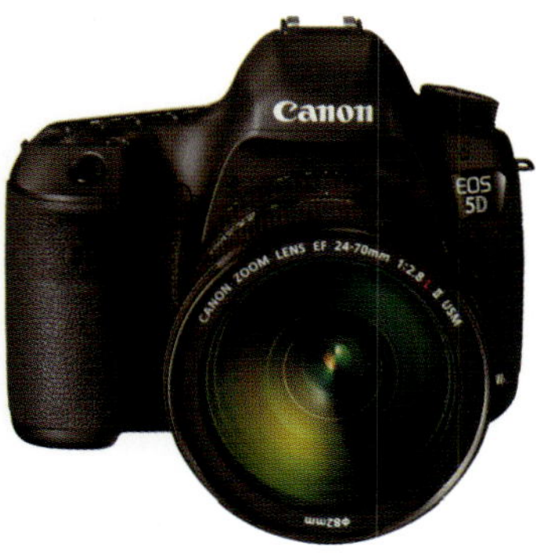

Above: The Canon EOS 5D MkIII is a full-frame DSLR that is popular with landscape photographers because of its rugged, weather-sealed body.
© Canon

A system camera is one that allows you to swap lenses, and in much broader terms lets you fit other accessories, such as a hotshoe-mounted flash, filters, and so on. This makes a system camera expandable, so its capabilities can grow and evolve with your needs.

Single lens reflex (SLR) cameras are the most common type of system camera, often abbreviated to DSLR (Digital Single Lens Reflex). This type of camera uses an angled mirror to direct the image directly from the lens to an optical viewfinder, via a pentaprism. The mirror in this arrangement blocks the sensor, so when an exposure is made, the mirror swings out of the way until the exposure is complete (in live preview or Live View mode the mirror is swung permanently out of the way and doesn't return to its original position until Live View is deactivated).

The appeal of a DSLR is that you see exactly what the camera "sees," but the downside is that this view is blocked during the exposure. Unless you step away from the camera you won't know whether the scene has changed during the exposure until the image is reviewed on the LCD. Nikon and Canon are the two heavyweights of the DSLR world, followed by venerable camera manufacturer Pentax, and Sony (based on the Minolta standard that was originally developed in the 1980s).

However, in recent years there has been something of a revolution and DSLRs are no longer the only type of system camera available. Mirrorless cameras (also known as Compact System Cameras or CSCs) have ditched the mirror in favor of a live feed to an LCD screen (either on the back of the camera or to an electronic viewfinder/EVF). Although it's arguable that LCDs and EVFs don't currently offer the quality and clarity of an optical viewfinder, the technology is improving all the time.

The appeal of a mirrorless system camera is that this type of camera tends to be smaller and lighter than a DSLR. Any saving in weight is welcome for landscape photographers who need to walk any distance with camera equipment.

The most mature mirrorless system uses the Micro Four Thirds standard and is produced by a consortium of camera and lens manufacturers (chiefly Olympus and Panasonic, although Sigma, Tokina, and Voigtländer are also members). However, other mirrorless systems are available, including Fujifilm's X-mount range and Sony's Alpha SLT and NEX systems.

Sensor Size

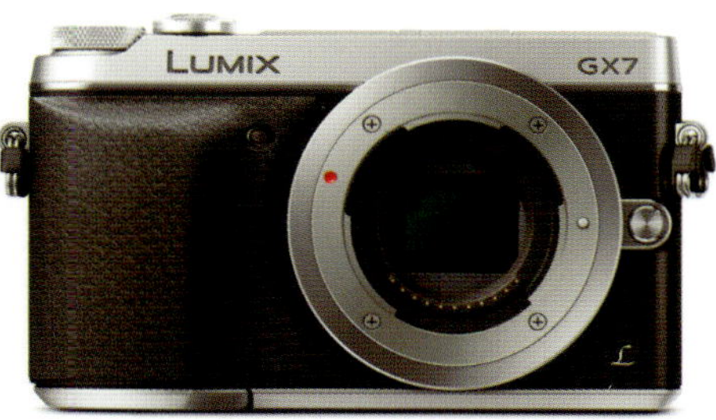

Above: The Panasonic Lumix GX7—a Micro Four Thirds camera with a very useful EVF.
© Panasonic

The element of a digital camera that perhaps makes the biggest difference to its performance is its sensor: specifically, the size of the sensor. A larger sensor allows the individual light-gathering photodiodes on the imaging chip to be larger in size, which in turn means the photodiodes can gather more light during an exposure. The practical upshot of this is that larger sensors theoretically have a greater dynamic range and produce cleaner, less noisy images than smaller sensors.

There are three common sensor size standards, which in descending order of size are: Full-frame, APS-C, and Micro Four Thirds. The size of a full-frame sensor matches the 35mm film standard (36 x 24mm); an APS-C sensor is approximately 30% smaller in area (around 24 x 16mm); and Micro Four Thirds is 50% smaller than full frame (17.3 x 13mm). Cameras with smaller sensors are typically smaller, lighter, and less expensive than those with a larger sensor.

Lenses

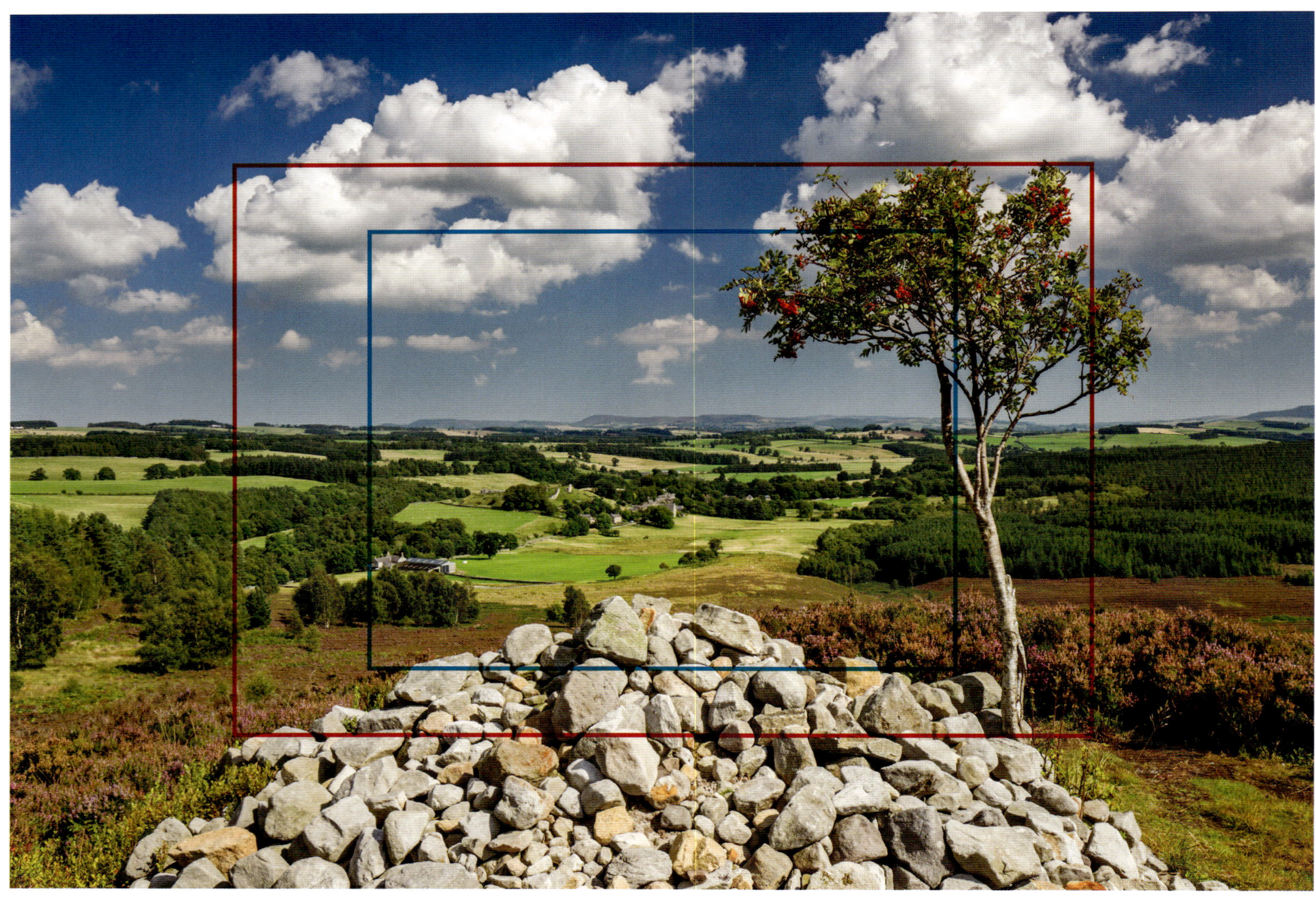

Focal Length

There is a good argument to be made that the lens is far more important than the camera. Digital cameras are relatively ephemeral items, which are often replaced as technology improves. A good lens, however, is for life. This is borne out by the fact that pre-owned lenses retain a significantly higher resale value (compared to their purchase price) than used digital cameras.

Lenses are described in terms of their focal length, which is a measurement of the distance from the optical center of the lens to the focal plane when a subject at infinity is in focus. There are two types of lens: prime lenses, which have a fixed focal length, and zoom lenses that cover a range of focal lengths.

Above: This image was shot using a 28mm lens on a full-frame camera. If the same lens were fitted to an APS-C camera the angle of view would be restricted to the red box. If fitted to a Micro Four Thirds camera, the angle of view would be within the blue box.

Regardless of the type of lens, focal length affects a number of factors. The most obvious of these is the angle of view, which is the angular extent of an image projected by the lens onto the sensor: the shorter the focal length, the wider the angle of view.

However, it's important to understand that the size of the sensor inside a camera also affects the angle of view. On a full-frame camera, a 28mm wide-angle lens has an angle of view of 75°, but on an APS-C camera the angle of view from the same lens would be 54°, due to the smaller sensor size. This means the lens is effectively not as wide: an 18mm lens must be used on an APS-C camera if you want to match the angle of view of a 28mm lens on a full-frame camera. To avoid having multiple naming conventions, lenses are described in terms of their "35mm equivalent" focal length.

To confuse things, it is worth noting that another effect of focal length—depth of field at a given aperture—does not change, regardless of the type of camera a lens is fitted to.

Wide-angle Lenses

Wide-angle lenses are the type most closely associated with landscape photography. As the name suggests, wide-angle lenses take in a wide angle of view. Until relatively recently, a 28mm focal length (approximately 18mm on an APS-C camera or 14mm on Micro Four Thirds) was regarded as the limit of wide-angle imagery, but 24mm is now seen as the new norm.

An odd quirk of wide-angle lenses is that the spatial relationships of near and far parts of a

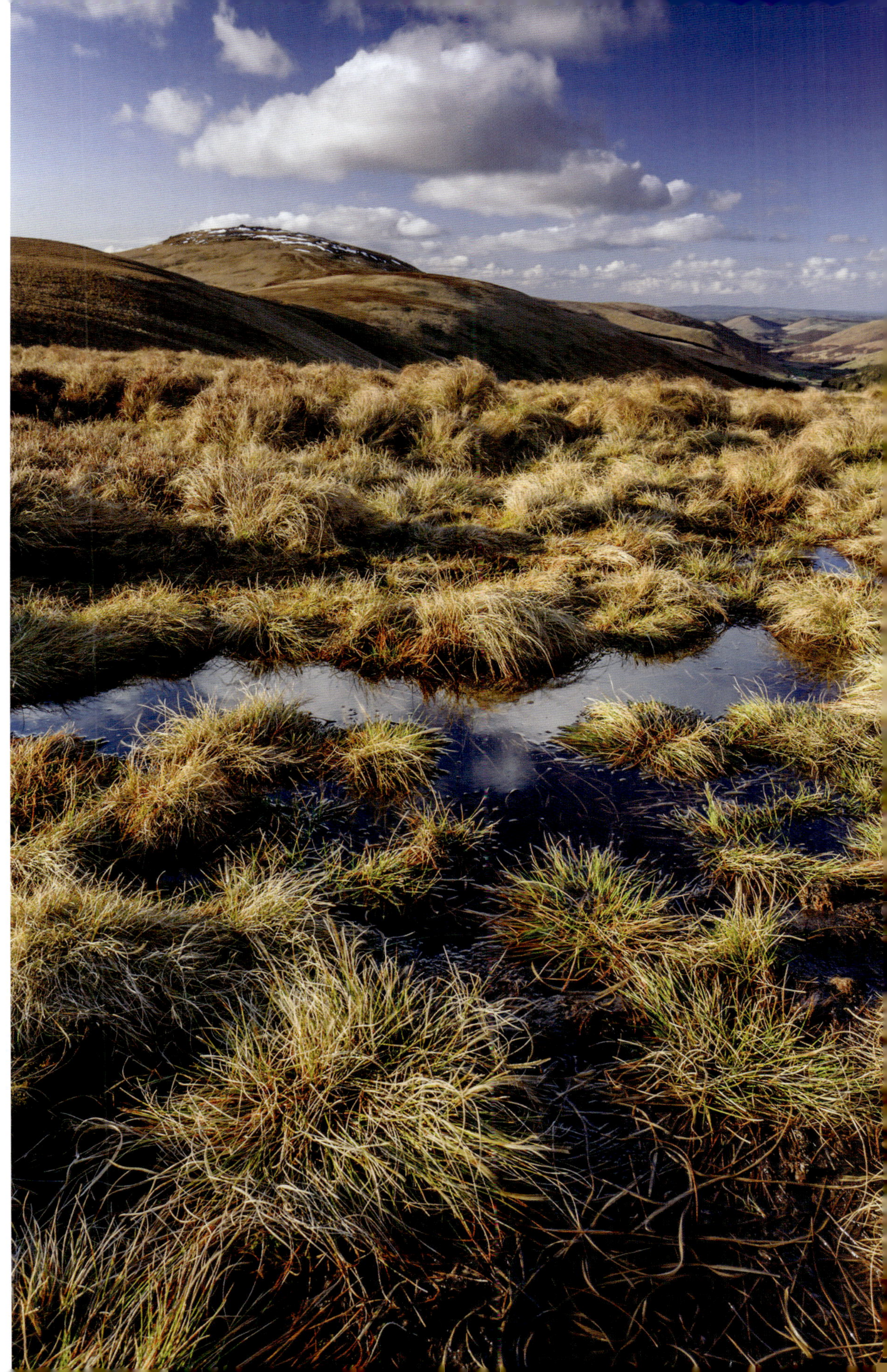

Right: Wide-angle lenses effectively convey a sense of open space. However, this often means setting the camera close to the ground to fill the foreground.

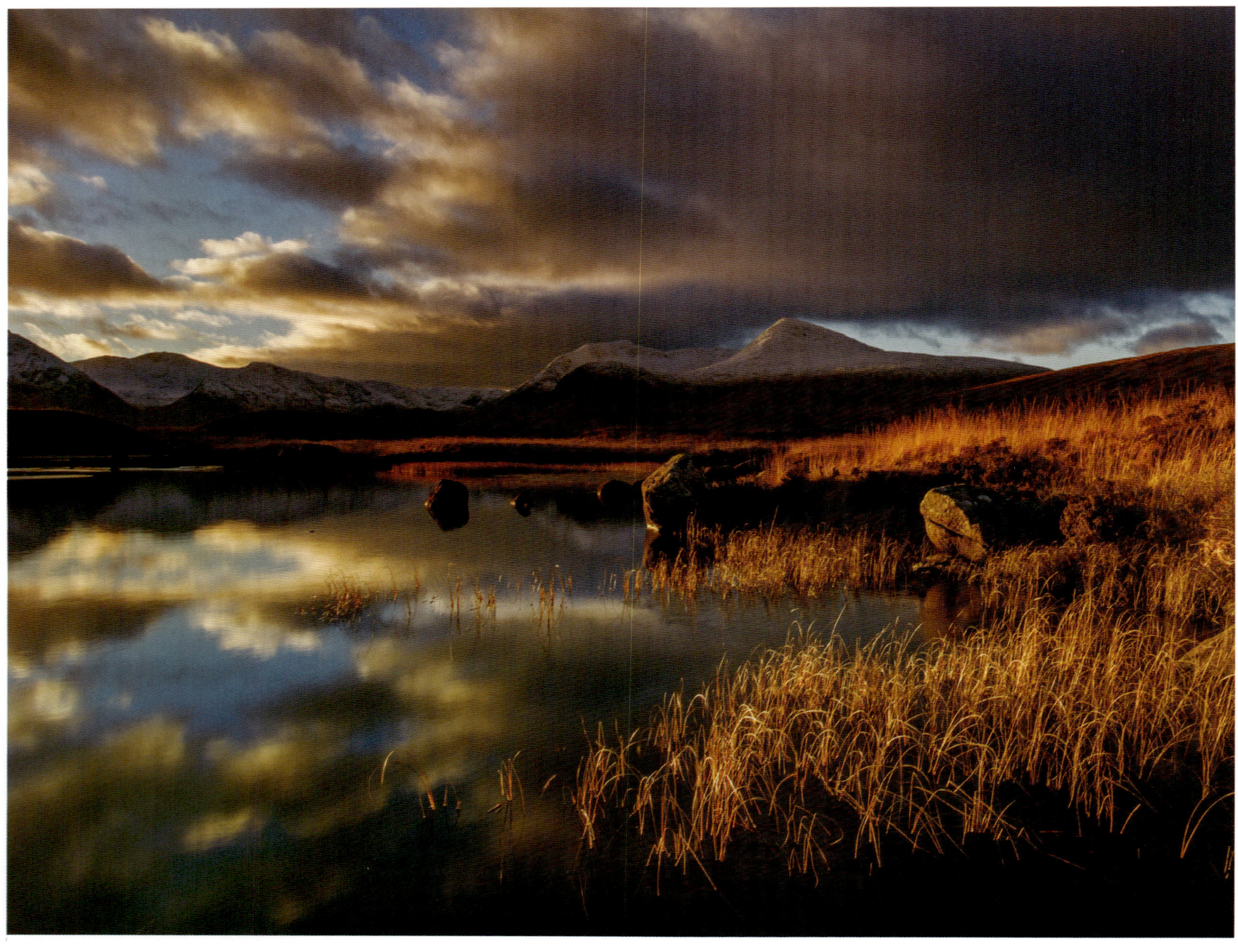

scene are exaggerated, and the wider the lens, the greater this exaggeration is. Extreme wide-angle lenses can therefore be difficult to compose with. It's all too easy to create empty looking images in which the various elements of the shot don't seem to have any logical relationship due to their apparent distance from each other.

The key to using wide-angle lenses is to think carefully about the foreground and how this can be made interesting in your photograph. It is often a case of getting in close to fill the foreground with your intended subject.

Another characteristic of wide-angle lenses is that they have inherently greater depth of field at any given aperture than longer focal length lenses. This makes it relatively straightforward to achieve satisfactory front-to-back sharpness (see chapter 2 for more on depth of field).

Above: Shot using an APS-C camera with a zoom lens set to 13mm, I only needed a modest aperture of f/11 to ensure front-to-back sharpness.

Standard Lenses

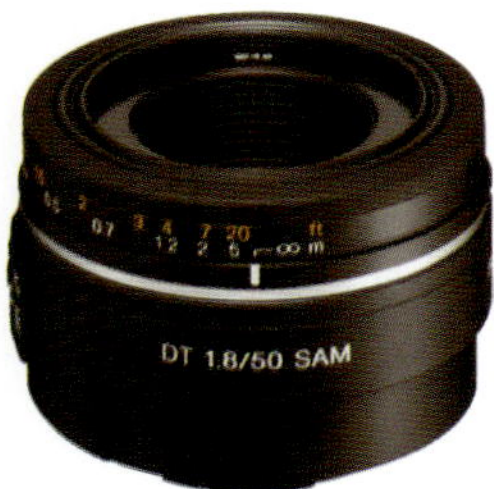

Above: Sony's DT 50mm f/1.8 SAM lens is small and light, with a fast maximum aperture.
© Sony

The definition of a standard lens is one with a focal length that matches the diagonal measurement of the camera's sensor. The lens regarded as the standard for full-frame cameras is 50mm (although, strictly speaking, 43mm is closer to the diagonal size of the sensor). On APS-C cameras the standard focal length is 28–35mm (depending on the precise sensor size) and on Micro Four Thirds it is 24mm.

Another name for a standard lens is a "normal" lens, which is a clue to its appeal. Standard lenses create images with a very natural look that closely matches the way that we see the world. Unfortunately, standard lenses are often overlooked for this reason, as they don't have the visual impact of either a wide-angle or telephoto focal length. However, if you want to take an unfussy, documentary approach to landscape photography this is the focal length to use.

Primes vs. Zooms

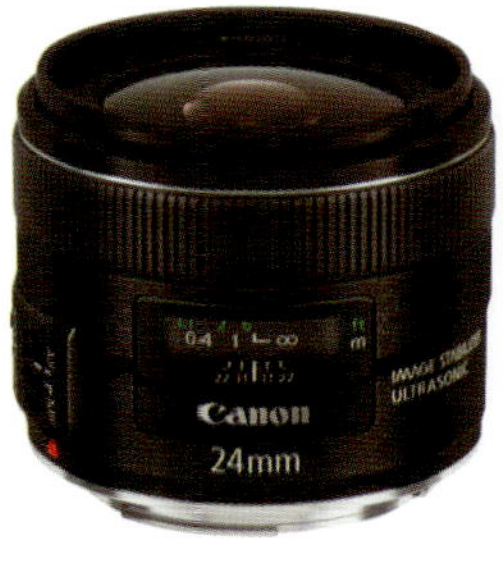
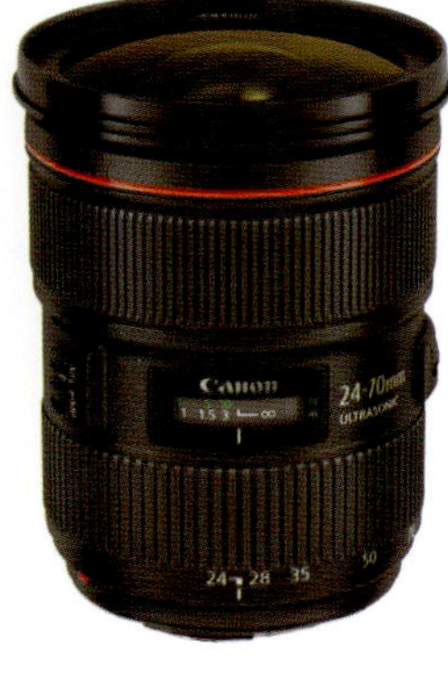

Above: Canon's 24mm f/2.8 prime lens and 24–70mm f/4 zoom both offer wide-angle focal lengths that are ideal for landscape photography with a full-frame camera.
© Canon

Zoom lenses are by far the most popular type of lens in terms of sales, and it's not hard to see why: the ability to change focal length without changing the lens makes a zoom far more convenient for everyday shooting.

However, for landscape photography prime lenses are worth considering for a number of reasons. It was once a truism that zooms were far inferior optically to primes, and while modern lens designs have reduced the gap considerably, the difference is still there.

Prime lenses also tend to have wider maximum apertures than zooms. As landscape photography often requires the use of smaller apertures for depth of field reasons the advantage isn't immediately obvious. However, a lens with a large maximum aperture makes a viewfinder brighter, which helps with focusing (manually or if relying on the camera's AF system) in low-light conditions.

The disadvantage of prime lenses is that you often need three or four lenses to cover roughly the same focal length range as a single zoom lens. This means carefully considering which primes to pick. The "classic" wide-angle lenses are 28mm and 35mm and these are good first choices for landscape work. A standard lens is also a useful addition to the collection for images with a more natural perspective. After that, your personal style would dictate which lenses would be most useful.

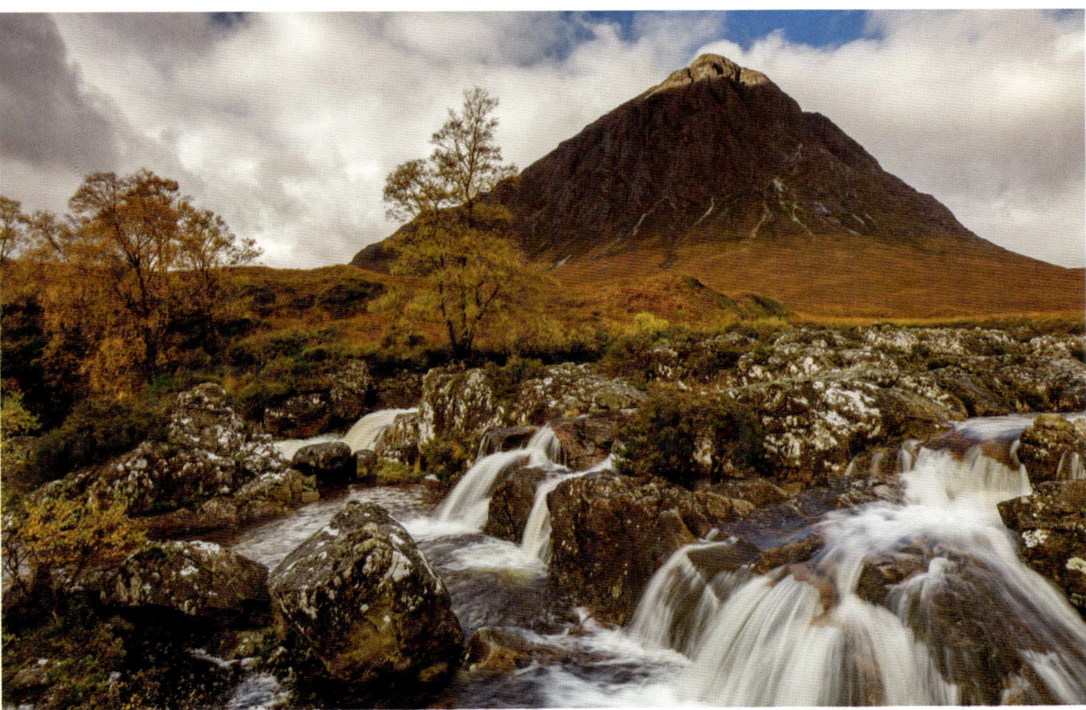

Above: Using a 20mm focal length allowed me to include a great swathe of foreground in this shot. The downside is that the mountain in the background doesn't dominate the scene in quite the same way that it did in "real life."

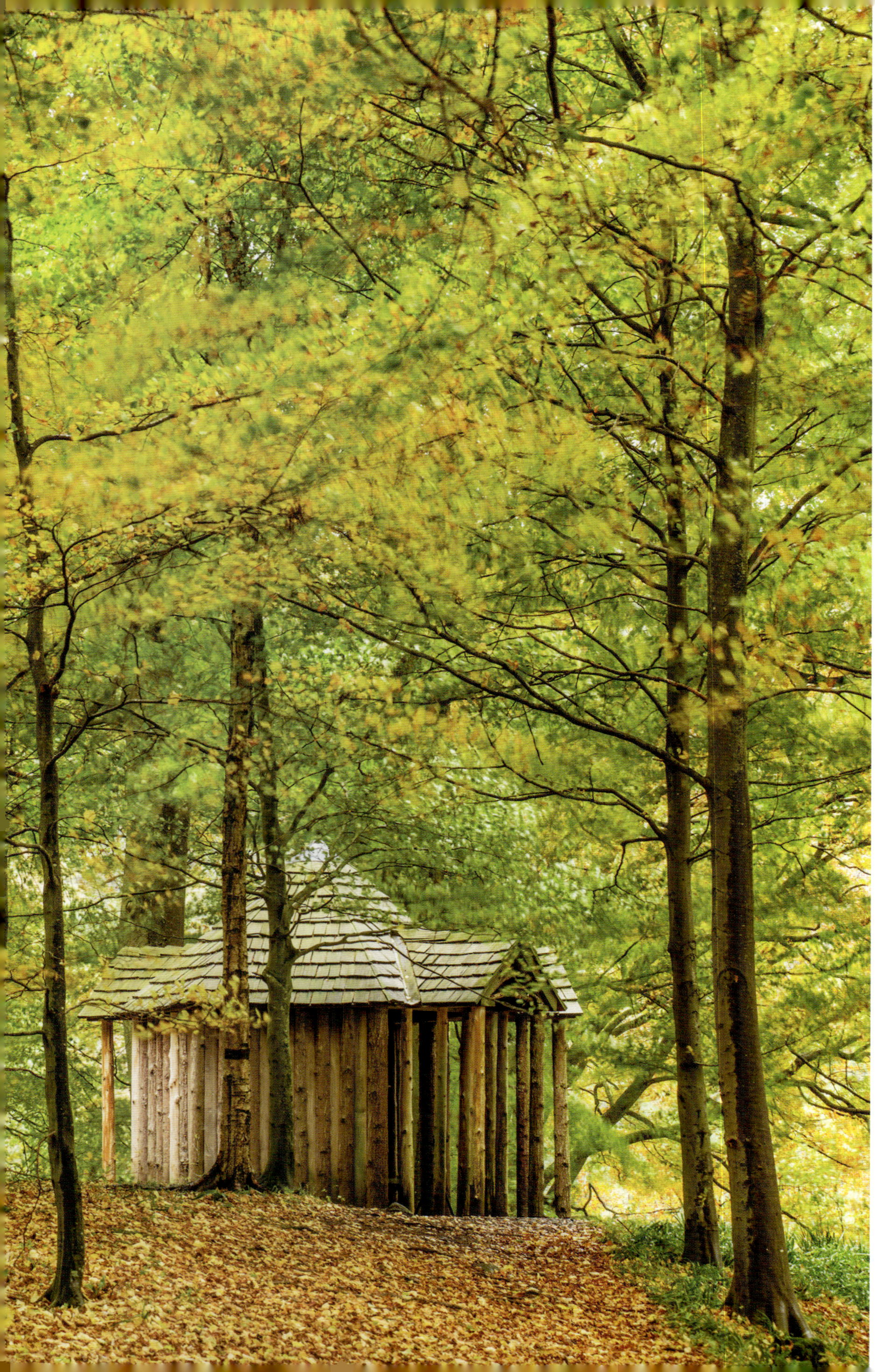

Telephoto Lenses

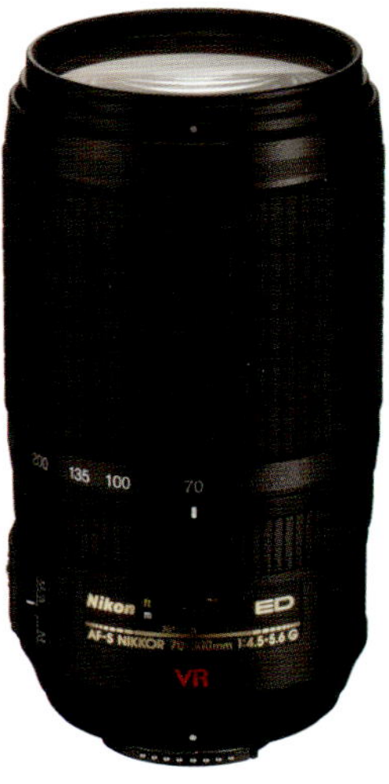

Above: A telephoto zoom such as Nikon's 70–300mm f/4.5–5.6 is useful for filling the frame with distant details. © Nikon

A telephoto lens is essentially any lens that has a longer focal length than "standard." On full-frame camera systems this covers a focal length range from approximately 70mm upward.

Telephoto lenses are often seen as being more appropriate to nature photography than landscape. This is because telephoto lenses magnify the image projected onto the sensor, making distant objects appear larger (as well as restricting the angle of view). However, telephotos do have a place in the landscape photographer's camera bag, as they are useful for isolating details in the landscape and for techniques such as differential focusing (see chapter 2).

Left: The flatter perspective of a telephoto lens is ideal for architectural details in the landscape. The need to step back from the subject with a telephoto lens reduces the risk of converging verticals.

Tripods

A tripod is essential for landscape photography. Although certain types of shot can be achieved by handholding the camera, there are far more that cannot. Choosing a tripod involves weighing up a number of factors: weight, stability, and cost. Which of these is most important to you is very much a personal choice.

A heavier tripod will be more stable, but will be less easy to carry around for long periods of time. The lightest (and least expensive) tripods are typically made of plastic, but these generally aren't stable for anything but the smallest cameras.

Metal tripods are far more stable, but also far heavier. Metal tripods are typically made of aluminum and are good value, although metal can be very cold in the depths of winter!

Carbon-fiber tripods are generally the most expensive, but offer superb stability for less weight than a metal tripod.

Regardless of the material it is made from, the ideal height for a tripod is to have it reach eye level without the use of the center column. Unfortunately, height adds weight, so that's another factor for consideration.

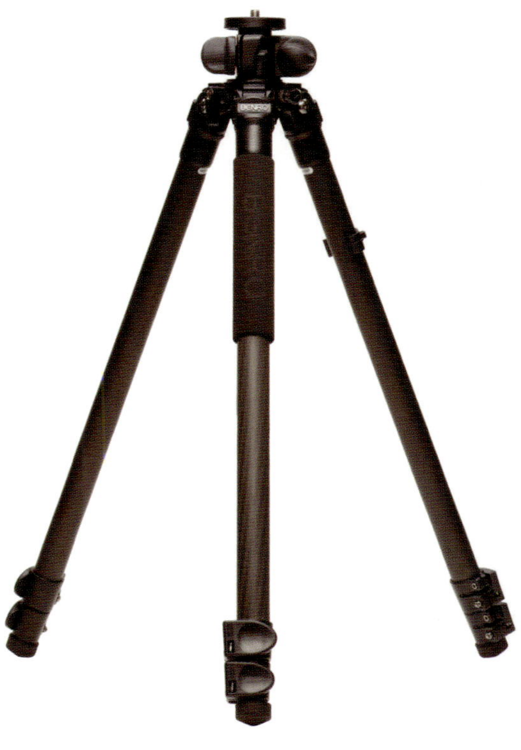

Above: Benro Versatile C2970F carbon-fiber tripod. © Benro

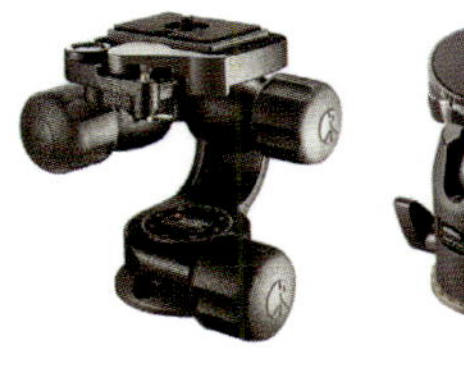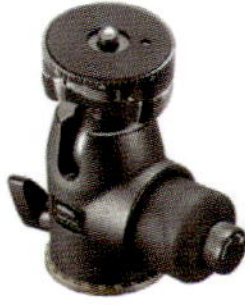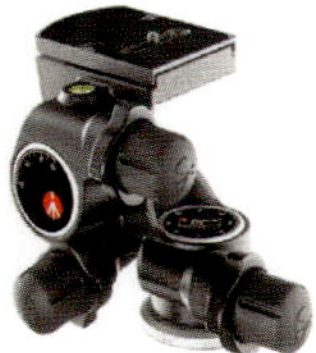

Above: Examples of a three-way head (left), ball-head (center), and geared head (right). © Manfrotto

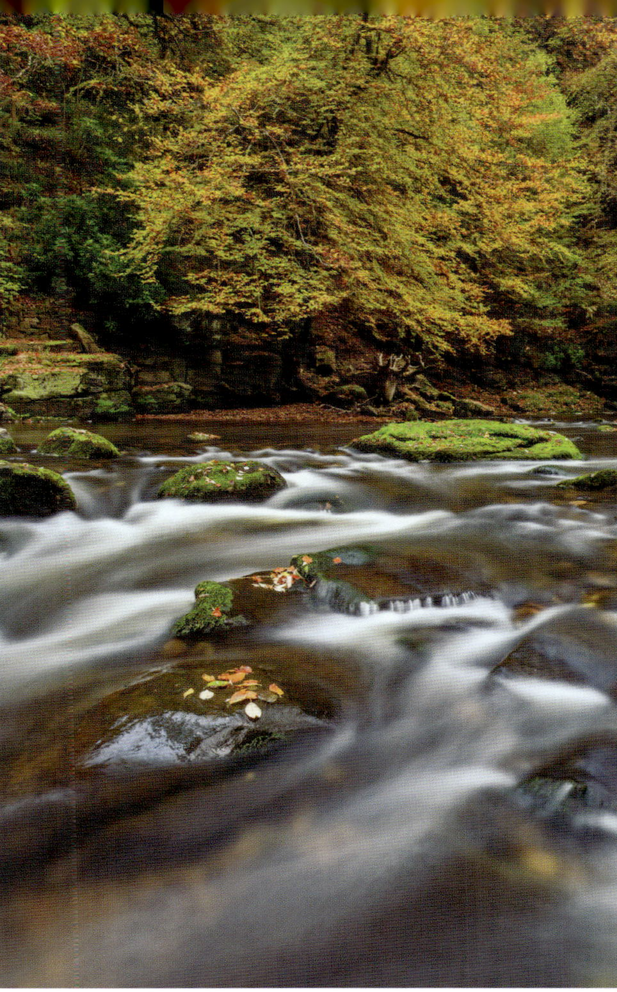

Above: The primary role of a tripod is to stabilize your camera in low light, when you can no longer handhold your camera without risking camera shake. Woodland, particularly on overcast days, can be darker than expected due to the tree cover reducing the ambient light level.

Tripod Heads

Some tripods have a fixed head, while others require a separate head to be fitted. The latter type is more expensive (and it adds a further layer of complexity to your decision making), but it does give you the flexibility to "mix and match" tripod legs and heads to suit your needs.

There are three common types of tripod head: three-way heads, ball-heads, and geared heads. A three-way head can be moved and then locked in three different axes, while a ball-head uses a ball-and-socket joint that can be unlocked and pivoted freely to the required position. Ball-heads have an excellent weight-to-strength ratio, but they can be tricky to make fine adjustments to.

A geared head is similar to a three-way head, but the three directional controls don't need to be locked into position—they move and stay in position by turning geared knobs. Of the three head types, a geared head offers the greatest control over positioning, but it's far more expensive and heavier than the other two.

NOTE

An invaluable feature on a tripod head is a quick-release plate. This allows you to quickly mount and release your camera from the head, saving valuable time and effort when it comes to setting up and packing away.

Other Accessories

There are other accessories that won't necessarily make a difference to the quality of your landscape photos, but will make the process of shooting them easier.

Camera Bag

Like a tripod, the camera bag you choose is very much a personal decision. The size you require will largely depend on the amount of camera equipment you need (or may one day need) to carry. The most comfortable type for use all day is a rucksack-style bag with two straps worn over your shoulders. This type of bag distributes the weight more evenly across your shoulders than a bag with a single strap.

Camera bags with padded straps are more comfortable than those with simple cloth straps, and another welcome feature is a waist strap. When fastened, a waist strap relieves weight from your shoulders and helps your posture—this can make a significant difference to your comfort levels during a day of heavy use.

A camera bag will need to protect your camera equipment from the elements, so one that's waterproof will be of more use than one that isn't. A well-designed camera bag will have zips that are protected from water ingress too.

A good camera bag should have removable dividers inside that allow you to configure the interior space to your needs. It's important to think carefully about how you divide that space: ideally you should distribute the weight evenly around the bag and if you have a heavy telephoto lens try to place this centrally.

One way to look at a camera bag is as a toolbox for your camera equipment. A good habit to acquire is replacing equipment in exactly the same place in the bag. If you can find something in your bag immediately, it will save valuable time when you're out shooting.

Remote Release

A remote release is an underrated piece of equipment that allows you to fire the shutter without touching the camera at all. This helps to avoid knocking your camera accidentally or even subtly moving it to the detriment of your composition. There are two types of remote release: wireless and cable.

Wireless releases use an infrared beam to communicate with the camera. This means there is no physical connection to the camera at all. The drawback is that they often have a limited range and they can be awkward to use if the sensor on the camera is in an inconvenient place. Some cameras are now equipped with WiFi, which can allow you to view a live image on a smartphone if you have an appropriate app. You can then focus and fire the shutter using the phone as a wireless release—the result is then sent to the phone.

Cable remote releases plug into the camera. The simplest type of cable release screws into the shutter-release button and fires the shutter mechanically. This type isn't widely supported now, with the exception of cameras from Fujifilm and Leica, and the retro-styled Nikon Df.

Instead, most cameras use proprietary electronic remote releases. These range from simple releases that only have a shutter-release button, through to more sophisticated types that feature built-in intervalometers. The latter function is useful for automatically shooting long sequences of images that can be used to create timelapse movies or blended images such as star trails. At the very least a remote release should allow you to lock the shutter open for use with your camera's Bulb mode.

Camera Care

Landscape photography involves taking your camera out of its protective bag and using it in all sorts of environments and weather conditions.

There are many aspects of the landscape that can prove detrimental to a camera. Sand is highly abrasive and can damage moving parts if it finds way into your photography equipment (the crunching sound of sand inside the zoom ring of a lens is something you don't want to hear). Water is also a problem, especially salt water, which will gradually corrode metalwork in your equipment if it isn't cleaned off in good time.

However, a camera that isn't used isn't worth having. Ultimately a camera is a tool, and using a tool means there is a risk of damage. The key is to minimize that risk as much as possible, so you can enjoy your landscape photography without worrying unduly.

Water

One common selling point of modern cameras is the level of built-in weatherproofing. This typically means that rubber seals and gaskets are fitted around dials, buttons, and flaps to prevent water from finding its way inside the camera. It doesn't mean that a camera is entirely waterproof—it couldn't be used underwater without damage—but short exposure to rain or mist shouldn't affect it. The weak point is generally the lens mount, although some lenses (typically the more expensive in a manufacturer's range) have rubber seals around the mount to prevent the ingress of water.

Keeping a soft cloth in your camera bag will allow you to dry your camera should it get wet (although you'll need to remember to take the cloth out of your camera bag and dry it later). Salt water needs to be wiped away with a slightly damp cloth and then dried to remove any salt residue (sea spray is a particular hazard as it's often fine and barely noticeable). A packet of silica gel kept in your camera bag will help to absorb moisture and condensation, although it too will need to be dried out or replaced every so often.

If working in wet conditions is something you enjoy then it's worth investing in a protective cover for your camera equipment that will protect it from even the heaviest downpour.

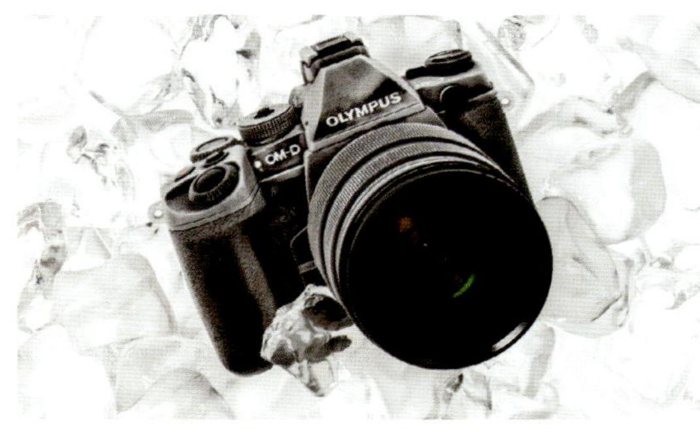

Above: The Olympus OM-D E-M1 has been promoted heavily as a rugged, weatherproof camera designed for outdoor use.
© Olympus

Dust

One big improvement seen in recent years is self-cleaning sensors on system cameras (it's not necessary on cameras with a fixed lens). This has reduced the need to blow away dust that invariably lands on a sensor. Self-cleaning sensors work by vibrating the anti-aliasing filter fixed to the front of the sensor, literally shaking the dust from the front of the sensor.

However, it's not a perfect solution. Wet, sticky particles (such as pollen) can adhere to the sensor's surface and remain there no matter how many times the self-cleaning mechanism is activated. At this point, your sensor will need to be cleaned manually. The most common method (and the one that I prefer) is to lightly run a swab impregnated with cleaning fluid over the sensor.

Sensor cleaning solution is typically alcohol-based so that it evaporates without leaving a smear. For more stubborn marks, however, a detergent-based solution is preferable. Although it's initially a slightly nerve-racking experience, manually cleaning a sensor isn't an onerous task. It can also save you valuable time in postproduction, as it reduces the need to remove unwanted spots in your images.

Of course, prevention is generally better than cure. The risk of dust or sand entering your camera can be reduced by minimizing lens swapping as much as possible (which is a good argument for using zoom lenses rather than primes). If you do need to swap a lens, try to shelter your camera from any breeze.

Finally, because of the increase in depth of field, dust will be more visible at small aperture settings. Using the largest aperture possible to achieve the desired depth of field is highly recommended.

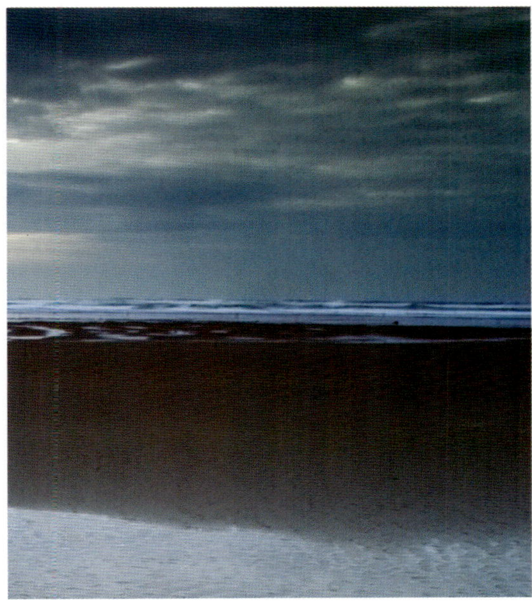

Above: Modern built-in sensor-cleaning systems are extremely effective. This image was shot on an older digital camera without such a system. I've never had the will to sit and clone out all the dust in the image.

Chapter 2
Exposure

In photography, the word "exposure" has two definitions. To "make an exposure" is to create an image by letting light reach a light-sensitive surface (which is usually either a sheet of film or, more commonly now, a digital sensor). However, the meaning of exposure that's relevant to this chapter is the act of measuring the exact amount of light that's necessary to make a successful image. Modern cameras have made this a far more automated process than it once was, but this doesn't mean that exposure should be left entirely to a camera. Exposure can be as creative a part of photography as selecting a pleasing composition. By taking control of exposure you'll find your landscape photography far more rewarding and successful.

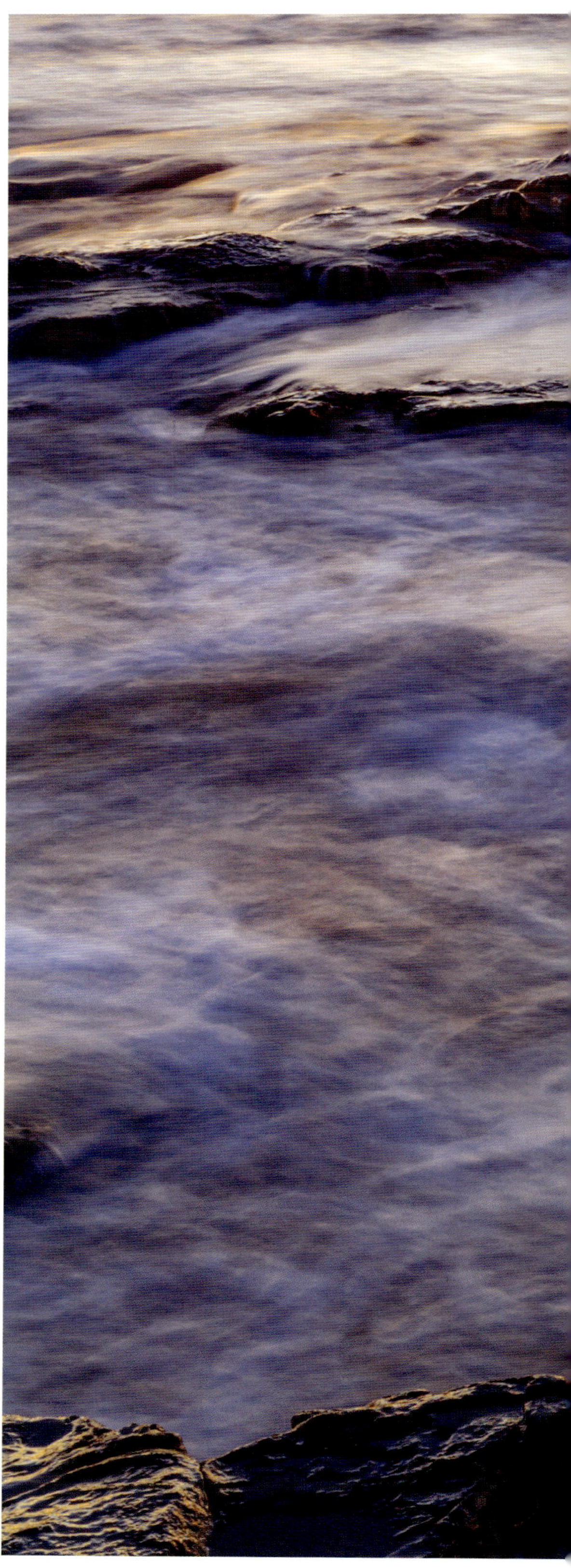

Right: One of the key issues with photography is that a camera—whether film-based or digital—can't record the range of brightness levels that the human eye can perceive. Exposure can therefore be a compromise: this backlit scene required an exposure that didn't lose the bright highlights, but this meant sacrificing some detail in the shadows.

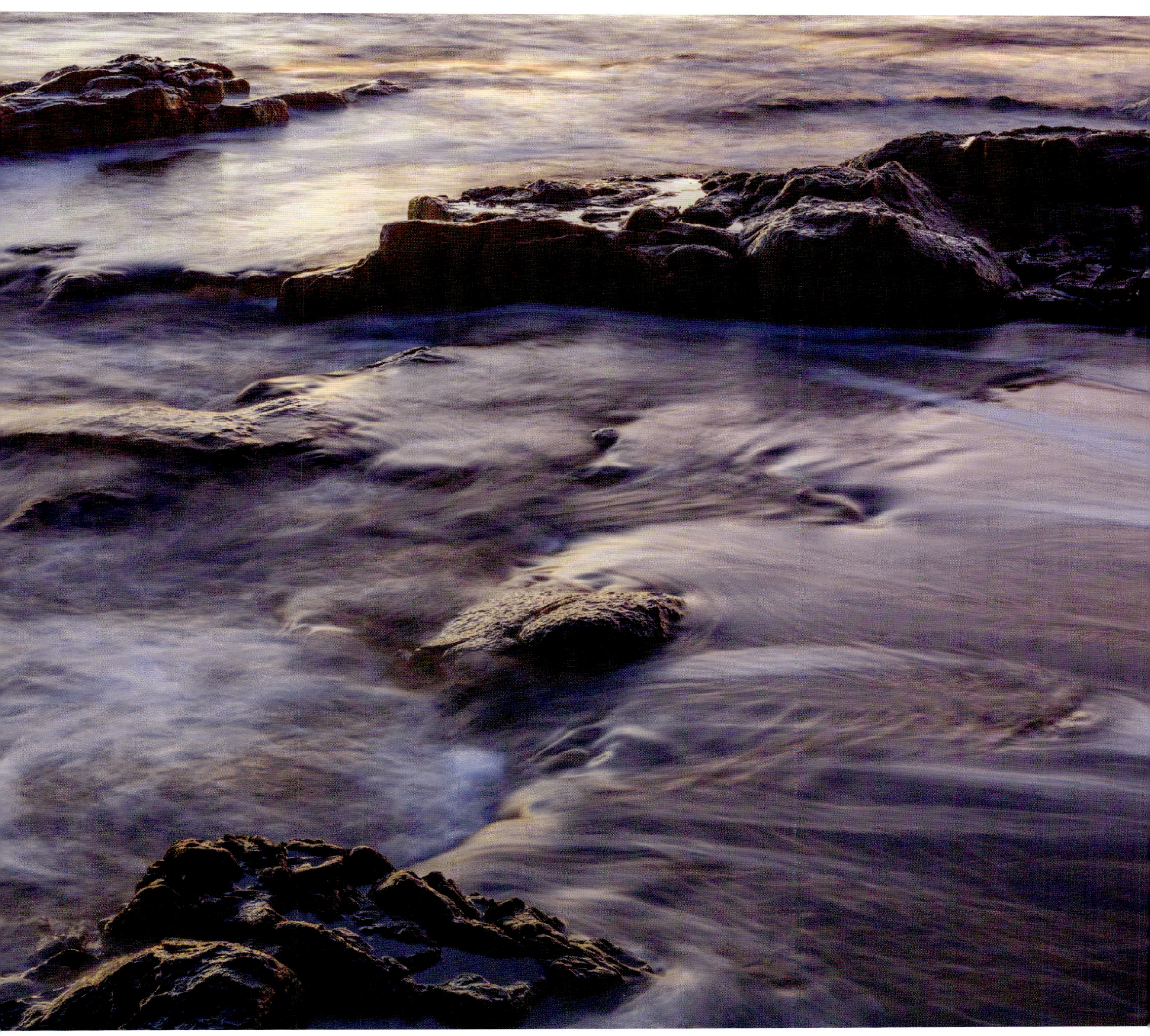

First Principles

The simplest camera is a pinhole camera. This is a box with a precisely placed pin-sized hole that allows light inside. If you place a light-sensitive surface inside the box, opposite the pinhole, you can make a surprisingly sharp photographic image (a pinhole camera doesn't need a lens as the hole itself focuses light).

However, there's a bit more to it than that. A light-sensitive surface (either film or a digital sensor) requires a precise amount of light to make an image. Too little and the image will be dark and muddy, referred to as underexposure; too much and the image will be too light, or overexposed.

How much light is required for an exposure is determined by the ISO. The higher the ISO value, the less light is required in order to make an acceptable exposure.

Lens-based cameras have two controls that between them allow you to vary the amount of light reaching the sensor. The first control is the shutter, which can be opened and closed for a period of time known as the shutter speed. The second control is the aperture. The aperture is an iris inside a lens that can be varied in size. By adjusting the length of the shutter speed and the size of the aperture a precise amount of light is allowed to reach the sensor to form an image. The act of controlling the amount of light needed to form an image is known as "setting the exposure."

The length of time the shutter needs to be open for, or the size of the aperture that's needed, is determined by the ambient light level. In order to measure the light levels you need a light meter.

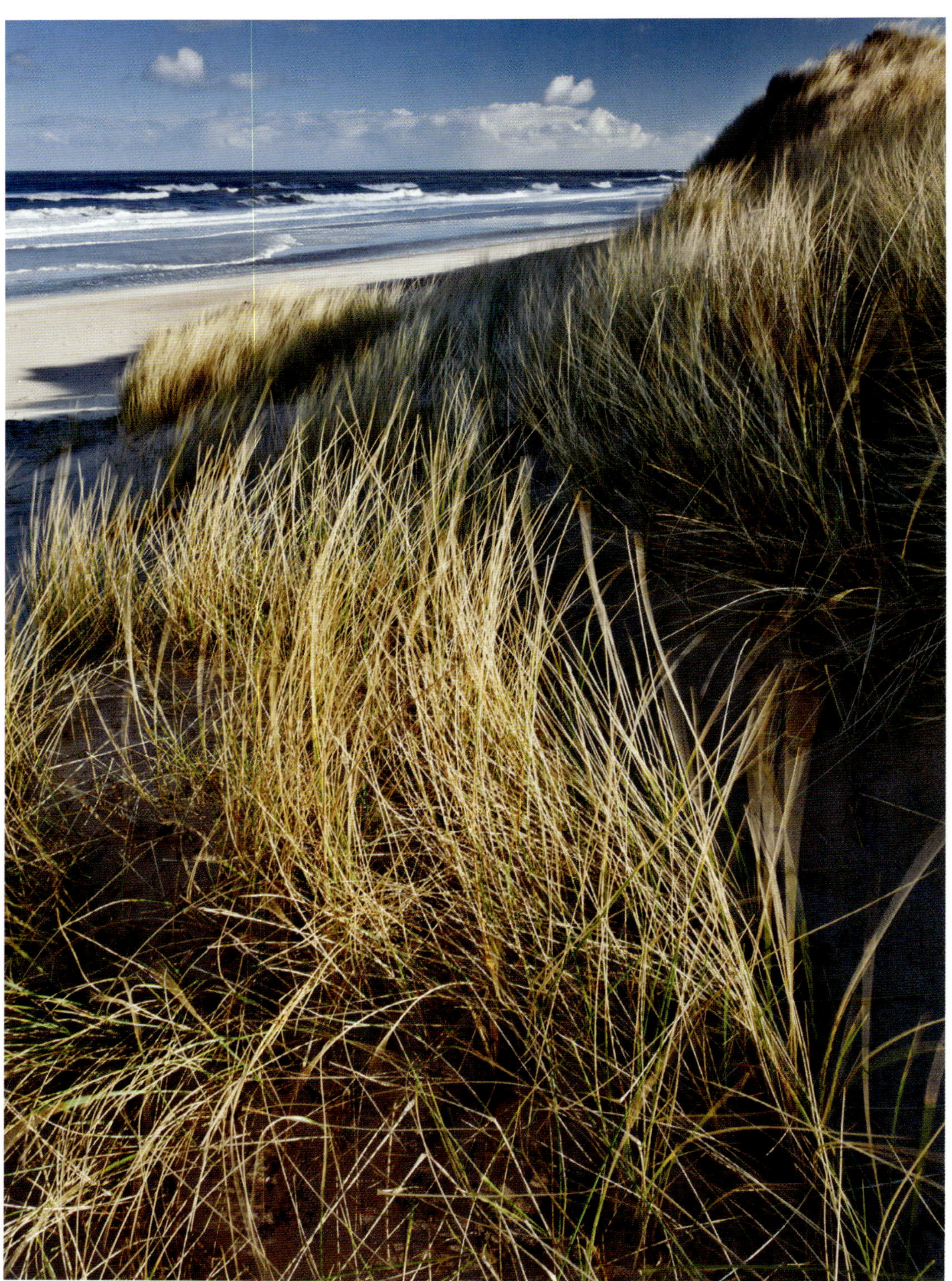

Right: Shutter speed, aperture, and ISO are linked, so if you change one, you must also change one or both of the other two in order to maintain the same level of exposure overall. This image was shot using a shutter speed of 1/15 sec., an aperture of f/16, and ISO 100. I could have shot it with a shutter speed of 1/30 sec., but to maintain the same exposure overall I would have needed to set the aperture to f/11 or increase the ISO to 200.

Exposure Meters

There are two basic types of light meter: incident and reflective. An incident light meter is a small, handheld device that measures the amount of light falling onto a scene. A reflective meter—the type that's in your camera—measures the amount of light reflected by the scene. It's a subtle, but important difference.

A reflective meter makes the assumption that the scene being metered has an average reflectivity, reflecting approximately 18% of the light that falls onto it. This equates to a mid-gray tone. A typically average scene, with no bright highlights or deep shadows, will usually be assessed correctly by a reflective meter. Problems arise, however, when a scene has a higher- or lower-than-average reflectivity. This can happen more often than you'd think in landscape photography.

In a scene that is predominantly light-toned—a landscape covered in snow, or a sandy beach, for example—reflective meters tend to underexpose. This is because the light tones are darkened to bring them closer to the midtone ideal. The opposite is true when metering scenes that are predominantly dark toned: in these situations reflective meters tend to overexpose.

To a certain extent this isn't too disastrous when shooting Raw. As long as the highlights aren't burnt out or the shadows blocked, the exposure can be adjusted in postproduction (although extreme adjustments should be avoided if possible).

If you're shooting JPEGs or using a higher ISO there is less room for maneuver, so it is more important to get the exposure right in-camera. Using the histogram on your camera is a very objective way to check exposure.

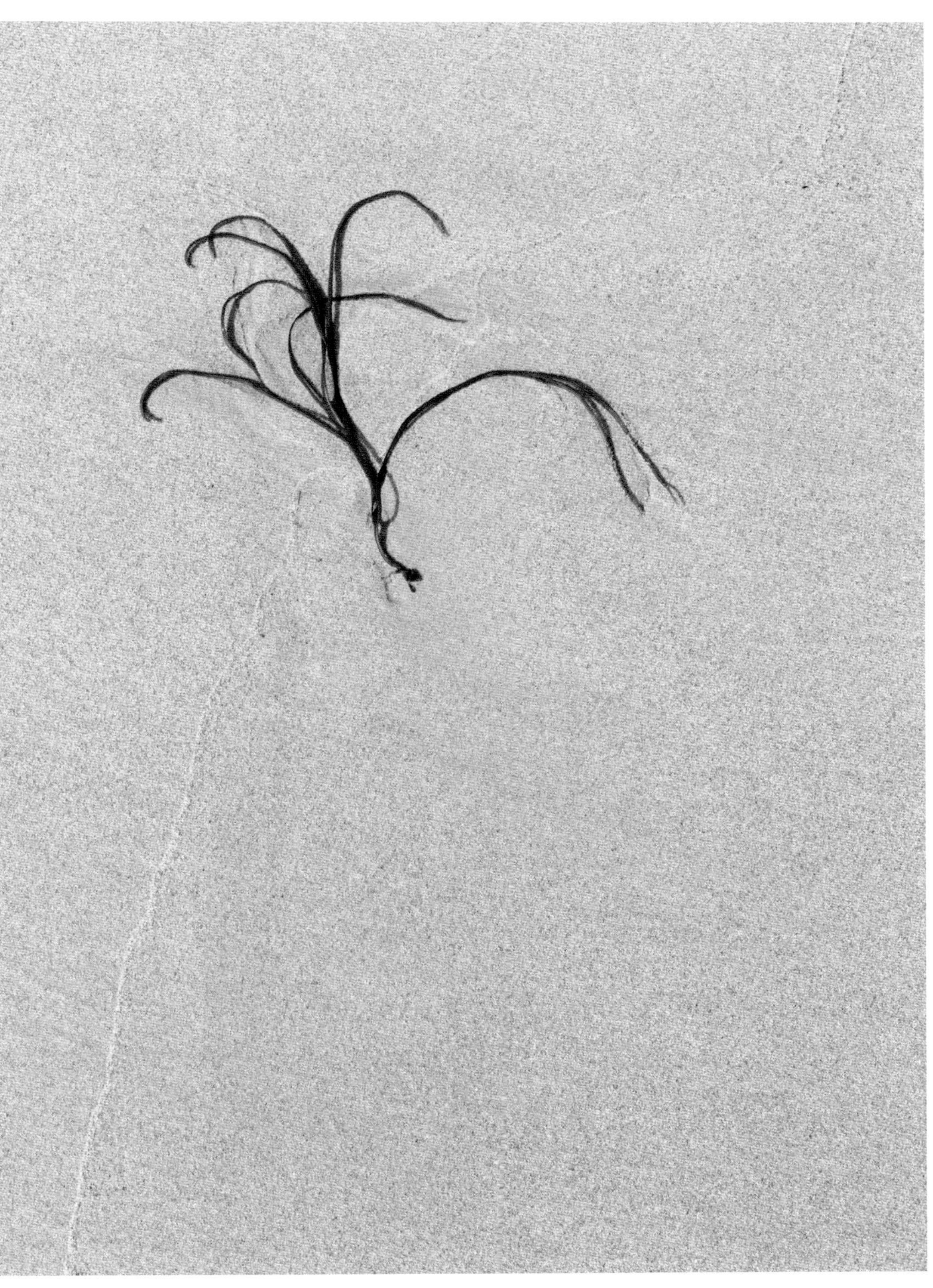

Right: This is the sort of shot that can fool a reflective meter, but wouldn't fool an incident meter. The light tones of the sand caused my camera's meter to underexpose, so I had to dial in +1.5 stops of positive exposure compensation to achieve the correct exposure.

Metering Modes

Cameras typically offer three different metering modes. Although each works using the principles of reflective metering, they can produce radically different exposures depending on the scene being metered. It's worthwhile experimenting with the different modes to find out the advantages and disadvantages of each.

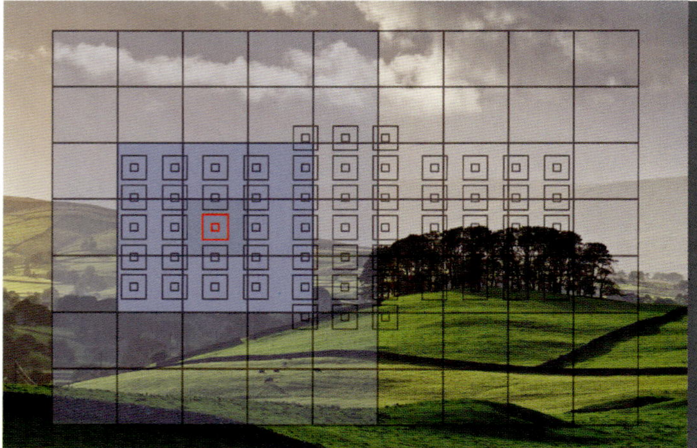

Evaluative metering (also described as matrix, multi-area, or multi-pattern metering) is generally the default setting on most cameras, and is often the only mode available in more automated shooting modes. Evaluative metering works by dividing the image into a grid of cells or zones. When metering is activated these zones are measured separately. The camera calculates the final exposure by combining the readings from the different zones and weighting the result according to the type of scene it thinks is being shot and the point of focus. Although in-camera "scene recognition" sounds slightly magical, it's based on the distribution of tones: a lighter strip along the top and a darker strip along the bottom would indicate a landscape; a circular patch of light tones might indicate a face, and so on.

Evaluative metering is usually accurate, but it's not entirely foolproof. It can be fooled if your point of focus is lighter or darker than average, for example, and it can also be thrown by the use of filters such as graduated ND filters.

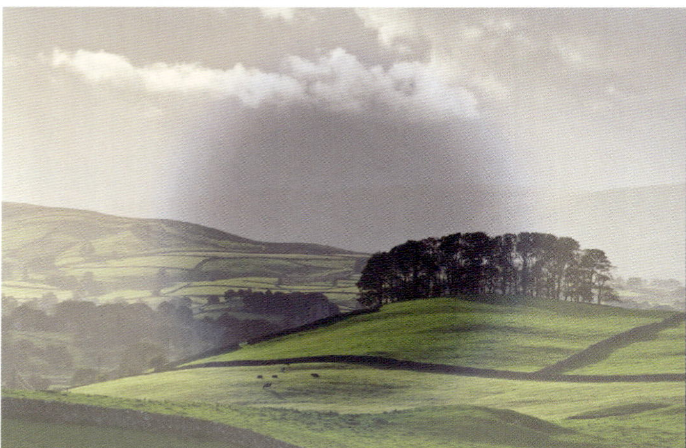

Center-weighted metering has largely been superseded by Evaluative metering, but it is still an option found on most cameras. When set to Center-weighted metering the camera meters the entire scene, but biases the exposure toward the center of the frame. How great this bias is will depend on the camera, although 60% isn't an unreasonable assumption. Although it is less "intelligent" than Evaluative metering, Center-weighted metering is arguably more consistent, as it ignores information such as the focus point when determining the exposure.

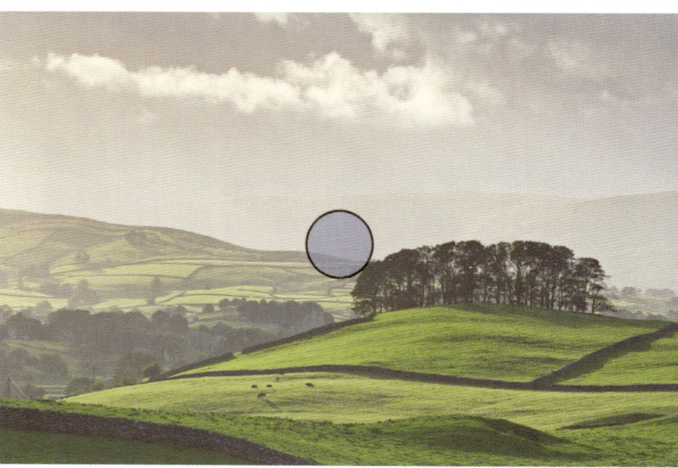

Spot metering measures a very small section of a scene, typically 1–5% of the image area. The spot metering area is usually at the center of the image, although some cameras allow you to link it to the active focus point instead. Spot metering gives you more control over exposure than Evaluative or Center-weighted, as you can choose precisely where in a scene the camera meters from. This means you can ignore lighter or darker elements that could affect exposure, and meter only from midtone areas such as stone, grass, or blue sky.

Exposure Modes

Almost all cameras allow you to select different exposure modes, which determine the level of automation when setting exposure. Some of these modes are highly automated, to the point where all you have to do is frame your shot and press the shutter-release button, with the camera setting the shutter speed, aperture, and ISO automatically. These modes essentially trade creative control for spontaneity, but to get the best out of your camera it is better to learn how to use the less automated exposure modes that follow.

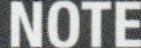

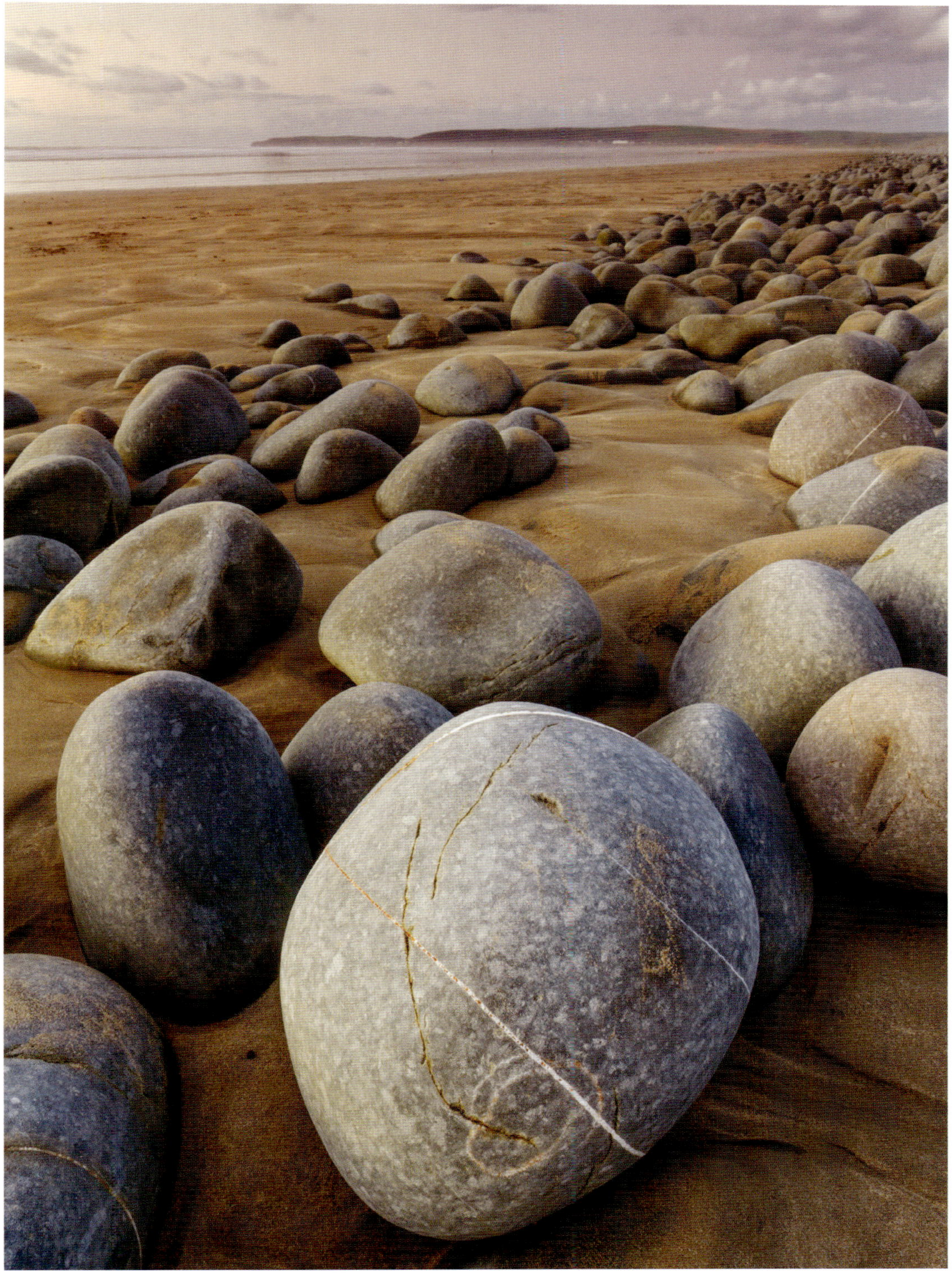

Right: A lot of landscape photography requires you to think carefully about depth of field and make sure that your images are sharp throughout. Aperture Priority and Manual are the exposure modes that give you the greatest control over depth of field.

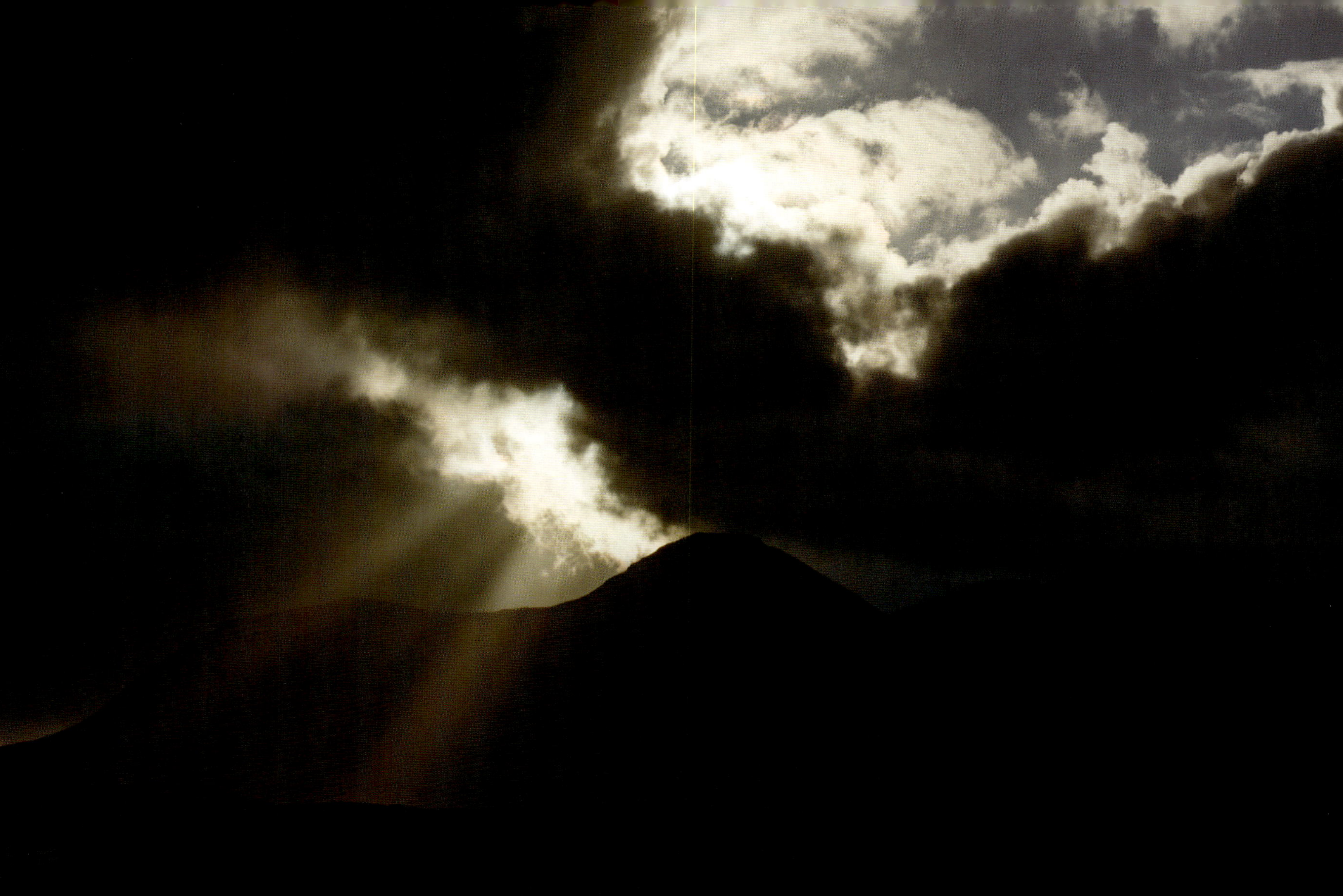

Programmed Auto (or **P**) is an automated exposure mode, where the camera chooses both the aperture and shutter speed. However, **P** allows you to override the camera's exposure decisions, either by applying "programme shift" (in which you alter the selected aperture and shutter speed combination), or by applying exposure compensation. **P** also allows you to set the ISO, which controls the level of light required for a correct exposure.

Shooting using **P** is a valid way of working, but the camera may "forget" your shifted exposure settings after a certain period of time. This can catch you out if you're not paying attention.

Shutter Priority (**S** or **Tv**) is a semi-automatic exposure mode in which you set the shutter speed and the camera selects the aperture. **S** is particularly useful when shooting moving subjects, as it allows you to control how movement is captured in the image.

Aperture Priority (**A** or **Av**) is also a semi-automatic mode. In this mode you set the aperture and the camera sets the shutter speed. The drawback to **A** is that in low light the shutter speed is likely to be slow. However, as long as you're aware of this (and are ready with a tripod) **A** is recommended for landscape photography.

Above: Bracketing is invaluable if you're shooting in difficult lighting situations and it's not immediately clear how an image should be exposed.

Manual (**M**) puts you in full control of exposure. You have to set both aperture and exposure, although your camera's meter can be used as a guide to the correct exposure. The drawback with **M** is that the exposure settings don't change until you alter them. If the lighting levels change, or you fit light-sapping filters, you must remember to change the exposure settings or incorrect exposure will result.

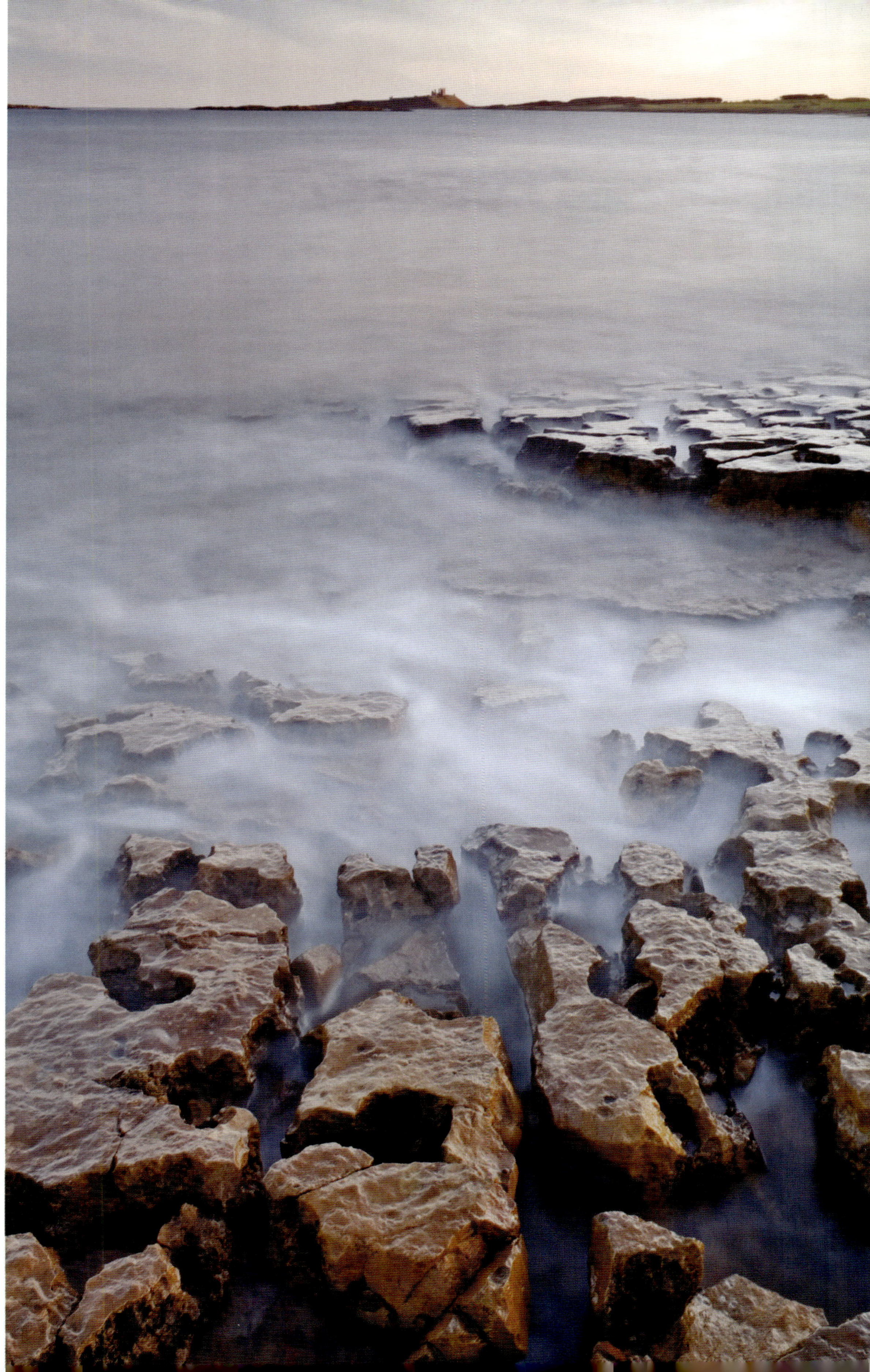

Right: There's no right or wrong answer as to which
exposure mode to use—it usually depends on the subject
you're shooting and personal preference. I typically use
Aperture Priority for my landscape photography, as it gives
me control of depth of field. However, I'd switch to Shutter
Priority for more action-orientated images.

Aperture

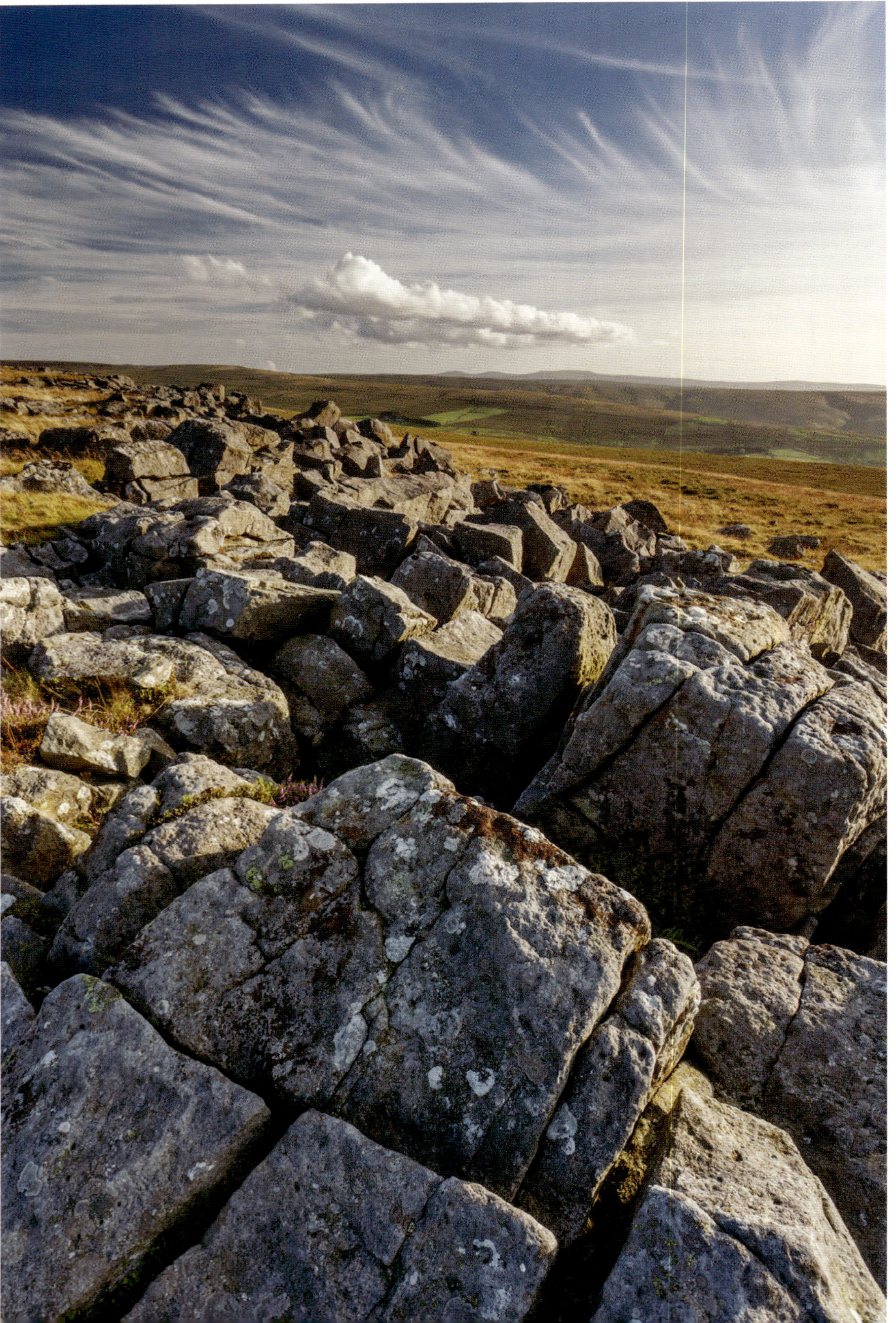

The size of the aperture within the lens is measured in f-stops (represented as f/ and a suffix number). The range of available apertures varies between lens types, but prime lenses tend to have wider maximum apertures than zooms, making them "faster" (a lens with a relatively small maximum aperture is referred to as a "slow" lens).

The f-stop value describes the diameter of the aperture as a fraction of the focal length: at f/4, the diameter of the aperture would be 25mm on a 100mm lens, at f/8 it would 12.5mm, and so on.

A typical range of f-stops on a lens is f/2.8, f/4, f/5.6, f/8, f/11, f/16, and f/22. In this range f/2.8 is the maximum ("largest" or "widest") aperture and f/22 is the minimum ("smallest") aperture. When reading the sequence above from left to right each f-stop represents a halving of the amount of light that passes through the lens. When reading from right to left, each f-stop indicates a doubling of the amount of light that passes through the lens. This is referred to as a difference of one "stop."

There are two methods used to set the aperture on a lens. Some lenses have aperture rings that can be turned to set the aperture (Nikon D lenses and Fuji X-mount prime lenses allow you to use aperture rings in this way), but the most common method (and sometimes the only option) is to change the aperture using a dial on the camera.

Left: Achieving front-to-back sharpness often means using relatively small apertures. Here, an aperture of f/16 was required to make sure that the depth of field extended from a distance of three feet in front of the camera to infinity.

Depth of Field Preview

Most camera systems hold the lens open at the maximum aperture until the moment of exposure: it is only when the shutter-release button is pressed down fully that the aperture is set to its selected value. This has the advantage that the viewfinder is always at its brightest and it also allows the camera's AF system to operate more effectively. However, the scene through the viewfinder is seen with minimal depth of field.

To overcome this, some cameras have depth-of-field preview buttons. Pressing this button temporarily closes the aperture to the selected value, allowing you to see the effect the chosen aperture has on depth of field. The drawback is that the viewfinder will darken (considerably if you're using a small aperture), so you need to give your eyes a few seconds to adjust to the lower light levels.

The same is true when viewing a Live View image. Typically, the image won't darken as the camera will try to maintain a consistent level of brightness on the LCD, but the display can become grainy and slightly slower to refresh if you move the camera. This is because the camera is amplifying the image signal to compensate for the reduction of light when the depth of field preview button is held down. Despite this drawback, in low light it is often easier to see the effects of aperture on depth of field in Live View, rather than through the viewfinder.

Minimizing Depth of Field

There are two basic approaches to depth of field: you either minimize it, or you maximize it to ensure front-to-back sharpness. Like many aspects of photography, there is no definitive right or wrong answer, so the approach you take will largely depend on your subject.

Using minimal depth of field will help you isolate your subject from its surroundings. We tend to avoid looking at out-of-focus areas in an image, so if there's only one sharp area in a photograph we tend to look there exclusively. In this way, depth of field can be used to direct the viewer's attention. Another reason to minimize depth of field is to simplify an image: by rendering a distracting background out-of-focus, an image is immediately easier to "read."

To effectively minimize depth of field you need to use a telephoto lens (the technique isn't suited to wide-angle lenses). The lens should then be set at its maximum aperture (the faster the lens, the less depth of field there will be). Finally, focus precisely on your subject (for this reason the technique is also known as "differential focusing"). The closer your subject is to the camera, the more out of focus the other areas of the image will be.

Maximizing Depth of Field

Using a lens' minimum aperture will give you the greatest depth of field possible, but slightly ironically, your images will be less sharp than you might expect. This is because, optically speaking, a lens typically offers its peak performance at 2 or 3 f/stops down from the maximum aperture. Beyond that point images start to exhibit the effects of diffraction. When light strikes the edges of the aperture blades it's randomly scattered (or "diffracted"), which causes a noticeable softening of an image. The smaller the aperture used, the greater the softening, despite the overall increase in the depth of field.

Therefore, to maximize image quality it's not a good idea to use a lens' smallest aperture setting unless it's unavoidable. This immediately raises the problem of depth of field and how to maximize it using larger apertures. Fortunately, this is where the "hyperfocal distance" comes to the rescue.

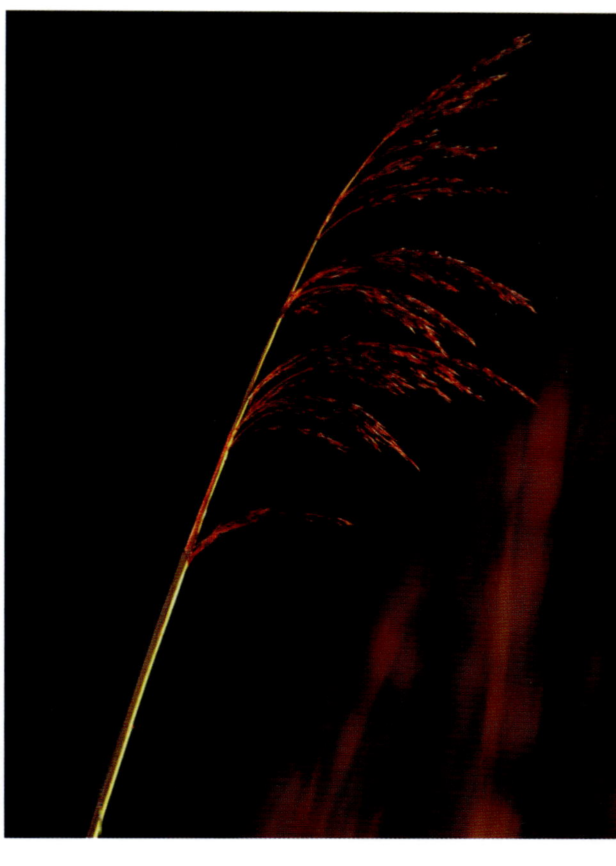

Above: Differential focusing is suited to simple, single subjects, rather than more complex ones. The visual quality of out-of-focus highlights is determined by the lens, which is referred to as a lens' "bokeh."

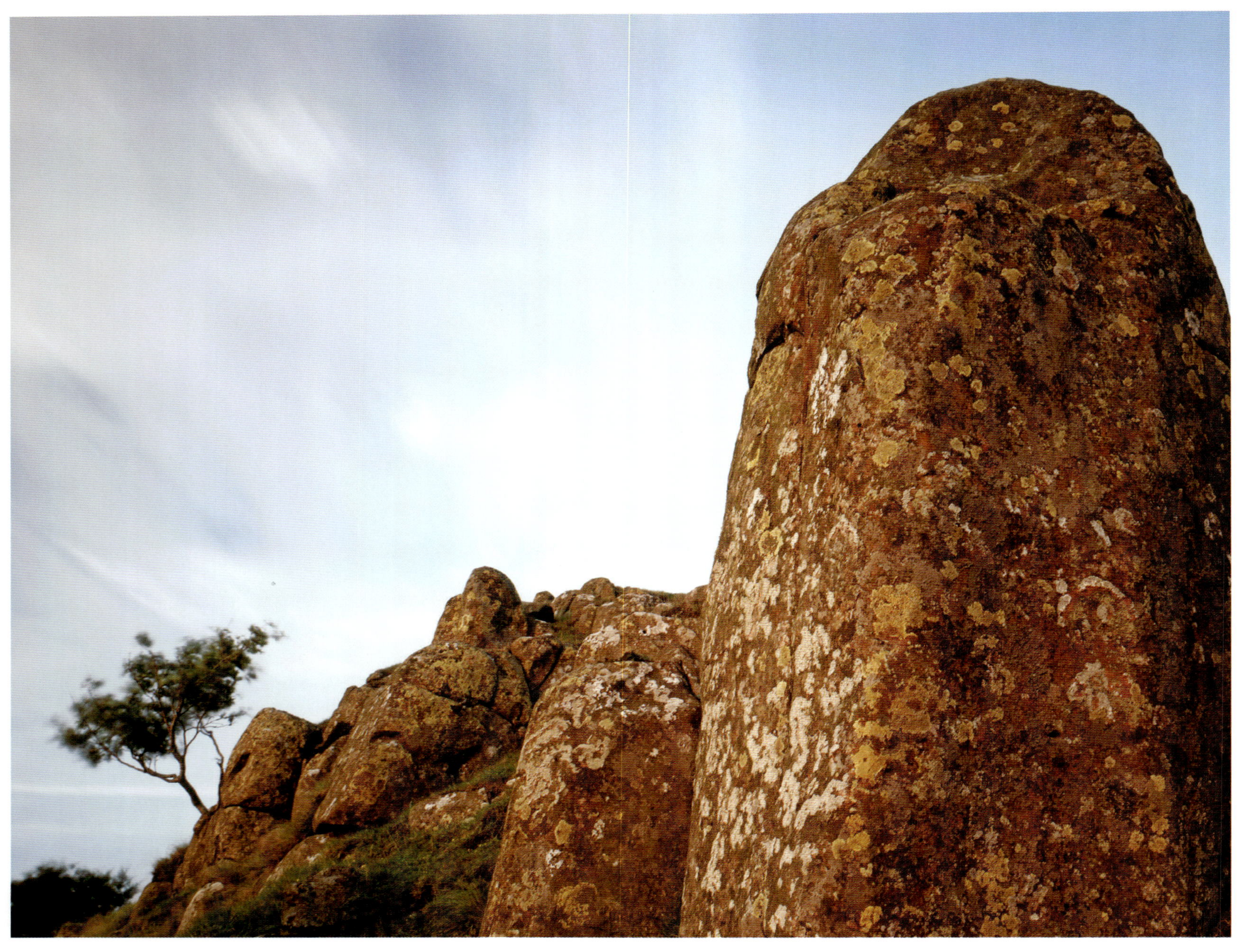

By setting the focus point at the hyperfocal distance, an image will be sharp from half that distance to infinity. Focusing precisely at the hyperfocal distance and using the largest aperture that will comfortably cover the required depth of field will reduce the risk of diffraction.

Prime lenses often feature a depth-of-field scale that helps you work out the hyperfocal distance. You first need to set the desired aperture. After that, move the focus ring so that ∞ is aligned with the selected aperture mark on the lens barrel (on the left side of the lens for Nikon lenses and on the right for Canon lenses). The focus point will now be set at the hyperfocal distance. However, setting the hyperfocal distance means that the focus point isn't necessarily where your subject is, so your subject may appear to be out of focus in

Above: The more three-dimensional your scene, the more care you need to take with the aperture setting and your point of focus.

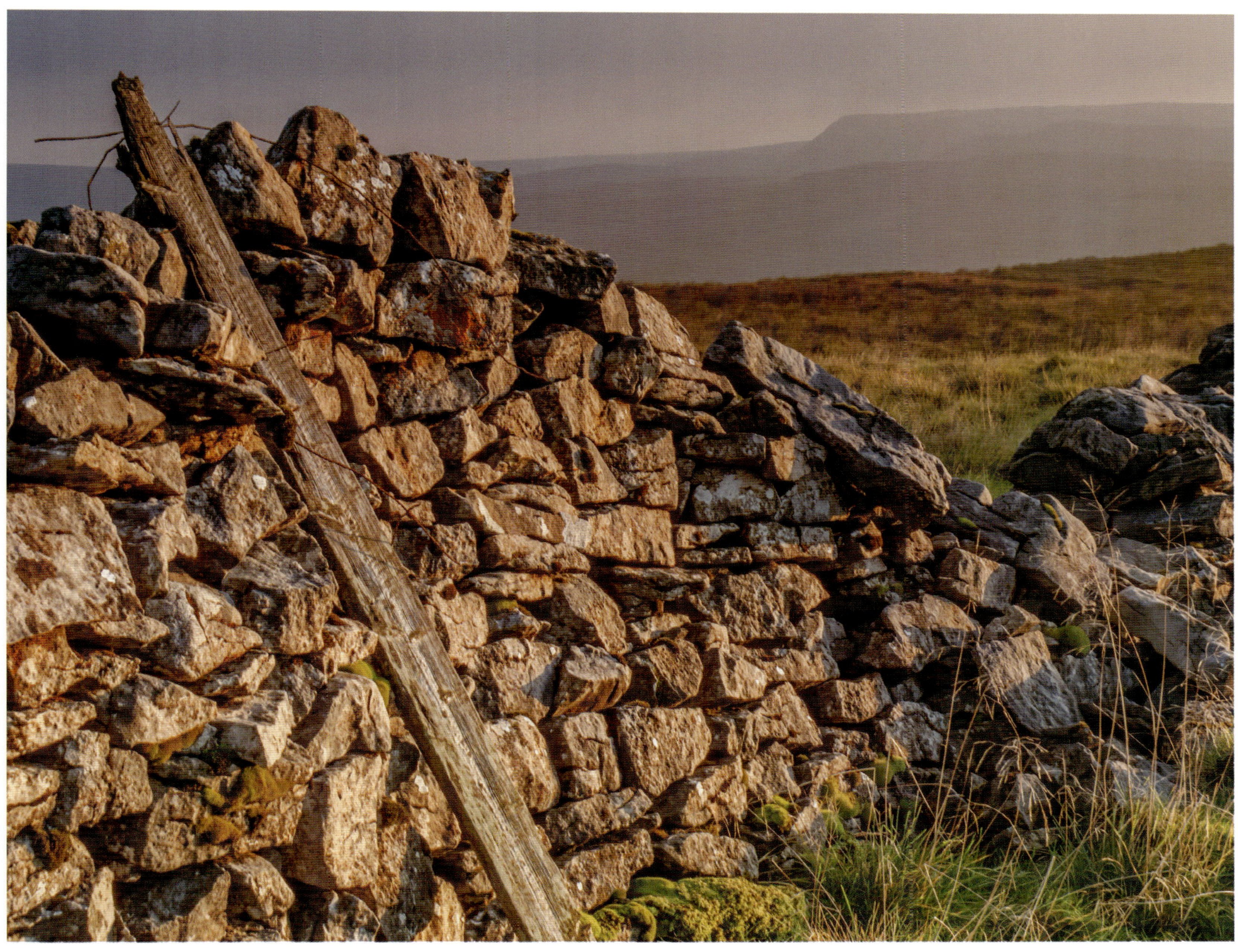

the viewfinder. This is normal, and if you press the depth-of-field preview button your subject should snap into focus.

Zoom lenses tend not to feature a depth-of-field scale, making it slightly more difficult to set the hyperfocal distance. However, on the following pages are two sets of hyperfocal distance charts. To use the charts, set the focal length on your lens and switch it to manual focus. Set the focus

distance at the hyperfocal distance (HD) and then set the requ red aperture. The depth of field will now extend from the Near point given in the chart, through to infinity (∞).

Above: Compact cameras (with their smaller sensors) are more diffraction limited than system cameras. Fortunately, because compact cameras use very small focal length lenses the aperture generally doesn't need to be set to minimum to achieve front-to-back sharpness. This image, shot on a Canon PowerShot camera, only required an aperture of f/7.1 to maximize sharpness.

Hyperfocal distance (in meters): APS-C sensor

14mm focal length

f/2.8		f/4		f/5.6		f/8		f/11		f/16	
Near	HD	Near	HD	Near	HD	Near	HD	Near	HD	Near	HD
1.83	3.66	1.3	2.59	0.92	1.84	0.65	1.3	0.29	0.57	0.2	0.41

18mm focal length

f/2.8		f/4		f/5.6		f/8		f/11		f/16	
Near	HD	Near	HD	Near	HD	Near	HD	Near	HD	Near	HD
3.05	6.09	2.13	4.26	1.52	3.05	1.07	2.13	0.78	1.55	0.53	1.07

24mm focal length

f/2.8		f/4		f/5.6		f/8		f/11		f/16	
Near	HD	Near	HD	Near	HD	Near	HD	Near	HD	Near	HD
5.41	10.8	3.79	7.58	2.71	5.41	1.89	3.79	1.38	2.76	0.95	1.89

35mm focal length

f/2.8		f/4		f/5.6		f/8		f/11		f/16	
Near	HD	Near	HD	Near	HD	Near	HD	Near	HD	Near	HD
11.5	23	8.06	16.1	5.76	11.5	4	8	2.9	5.9	4	2

50mm focal length

f/2.8		f/4		f/5.6		f/8		f/11		f/16	
Near	HD	Near	HD	Near	HD	Near	HD	Near	HD	Near	HD
23.5	47	16.4	32.8	11.7	23.5	8.2	16.4	6	12	4.1	8.2

85mm focal length

f/2.8		f/4		f/5.6		f/8		f/11		f/16	
Near	HD	Near	HD	Near	HD	Near	HD	Near	HD	Near	HD
68	135	48	95	34	68	24	48	17	35	12	24

135mm focal length

f/2.8		f/4		f/5.6		f/8		f/11		f/16	
Near	HD	Near	HD	Near	HD	Near	HD	Near	HD	Near	HD
171	340	120	240	85	171	60	120	43	87	30	60

Hyperfocal distance (in meters): Full-frame sensor

21mm focal length											
f/2.8		f/4		f/5.6		f/8		f/11		f/16	
Near	HD	Near	HD	Near	HD	Near	HD	Near	HD	Near	HD
2.6	5.2	1.8	3.6	13.	2.6	0.9	1.8	0.67	1.3	0.45	0.9

24mm focal length											
f/2.8		f/4		f/5.6		f/8		f/11		f/16	
Near	HD	Near	HD	Near	HD	Near	HD	Near	HD	Near	HD
3.4	6.9	2.4	4.8	1.7	3.4	1.2	2.4	0.9	1.7	0.6	1.2

28mm focal length											
f/2.8		f/4		f/5.6		f/8		f/11		f/16	
Near	HD	Near	HD	Near	HD	Near	HD	Near	HD	Near	HD
4.63	9.27	3.28	6.58	2.32	4.65	1.65	3.29	1.17	2.34	0.83	1.66

35mm focal length											
f/2.8		f/4		f/5.6		f/8		f/11		f/16	
Near	HD	Near	HD	Near	HD	Near	HD	Near	HD	Near	HD
7.3	14.6	5.1	10.2	3.6	7.3	2.5	5.1	1.9	3.7	1.3	2.5

50mm focal length											
f/2.8		f/4		f/5.6		f/8		f/11		f/16	
Near	HD	Near	HD	Near	HD	Near	HD	Near	HD	Near	HD
14.9	29.8	10.4	20.8	7.4	14.9	5.2	10.4	3.8	7.6	2.6	5.2

85mm focal length											
f/2.8		f/4		f/5.6		f/8		f/11		f/16	
Near	HD	Near	HD	Near	HD	Near	HD	Near	HD	Near	HD
42.6	85.2	30.1	60.3	21.3	42.7	15.1	30.2	10.7	21.4	7.56	15.1

150mm focal length											
f/2.8		f/4		f/5.6		f/8		f/11		f/16	
Near	HD	Near	HD	Near	HD	Near	HD	Near	HD	Near	HD
132.7	265.3	93.8	187.7	66.4	132.7	47	93.9	33.2	66.4	23.5	47

Shutter Speed

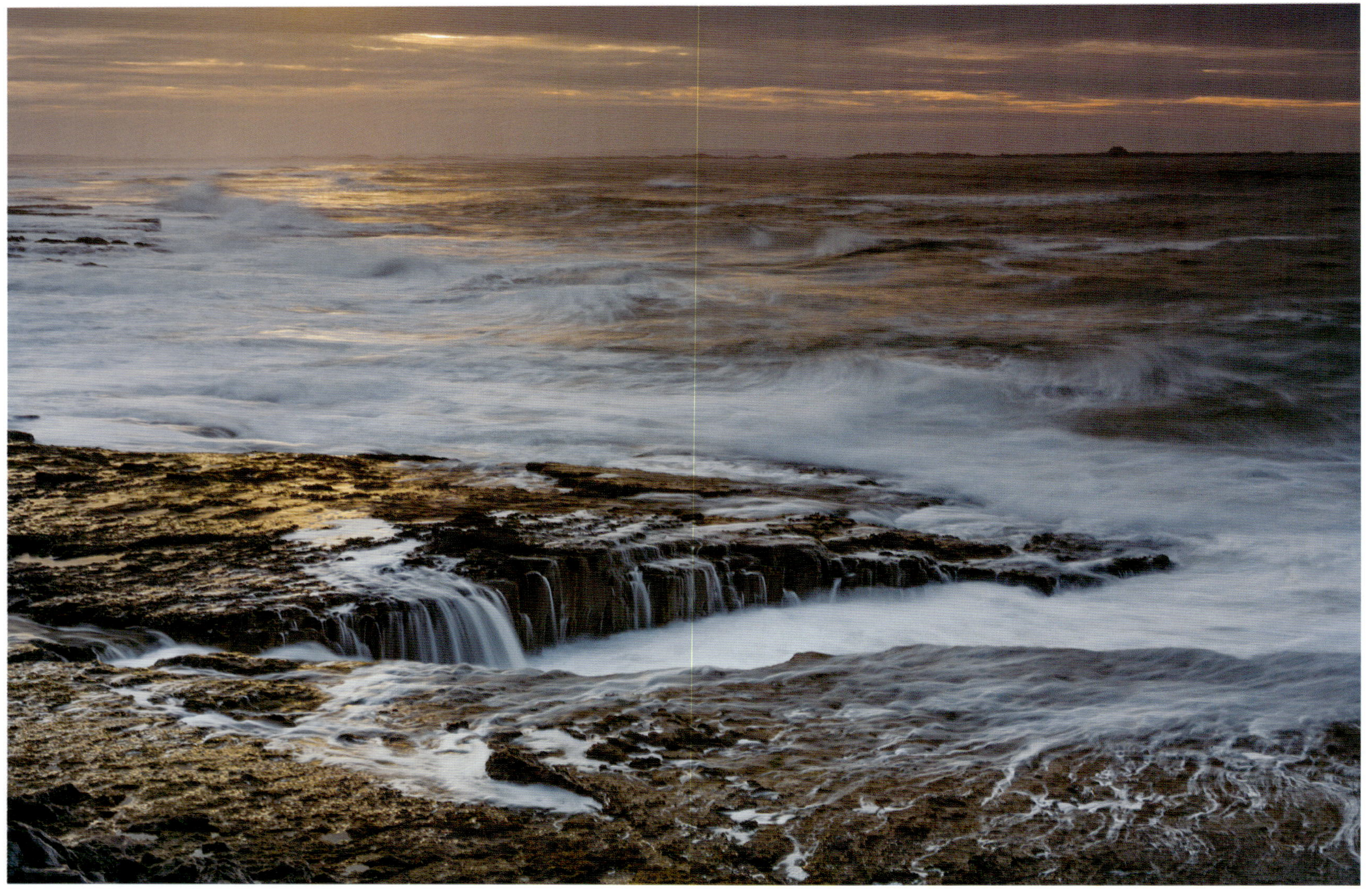

The range of shutter speeds available is dependent on the camera, although a typical range on a DSLR is 1/4000 sec. to 30 seconds (compact cameras are generally more limited at both ends). In addition to this, some cameras also have a Bulb mode that allows you to hold the shutter open for as long as required (or for as long as the camera battery holds out).

Between these two extremes the shutter speed can be varied by set amounts: 1/2000 sec., 1/1000 sec., 1/500 sec., and so on. As with aperture, the difference between these values is referred to as one "stop." If you increase the shutter speed by one stop (from 1/1000 sec. to 1/2000 sec., for example) you halve the amount of light that reaches the shutter. Decreasing the shutter speed by one stop (from 1/1000 sec. to 1/500 sec.) doubles the amount of light reaching the sensor.

If your subject is static then the shutter speed you use is relatively unimportant. However, when

Above: The shutter speed you use should be determined by how you want movement recorded in an image. However, this often involves compromise. For this coastal image I had to use an ND filter to slow the shutter speed sufficiently to avoid using my lens' minimum aperture.

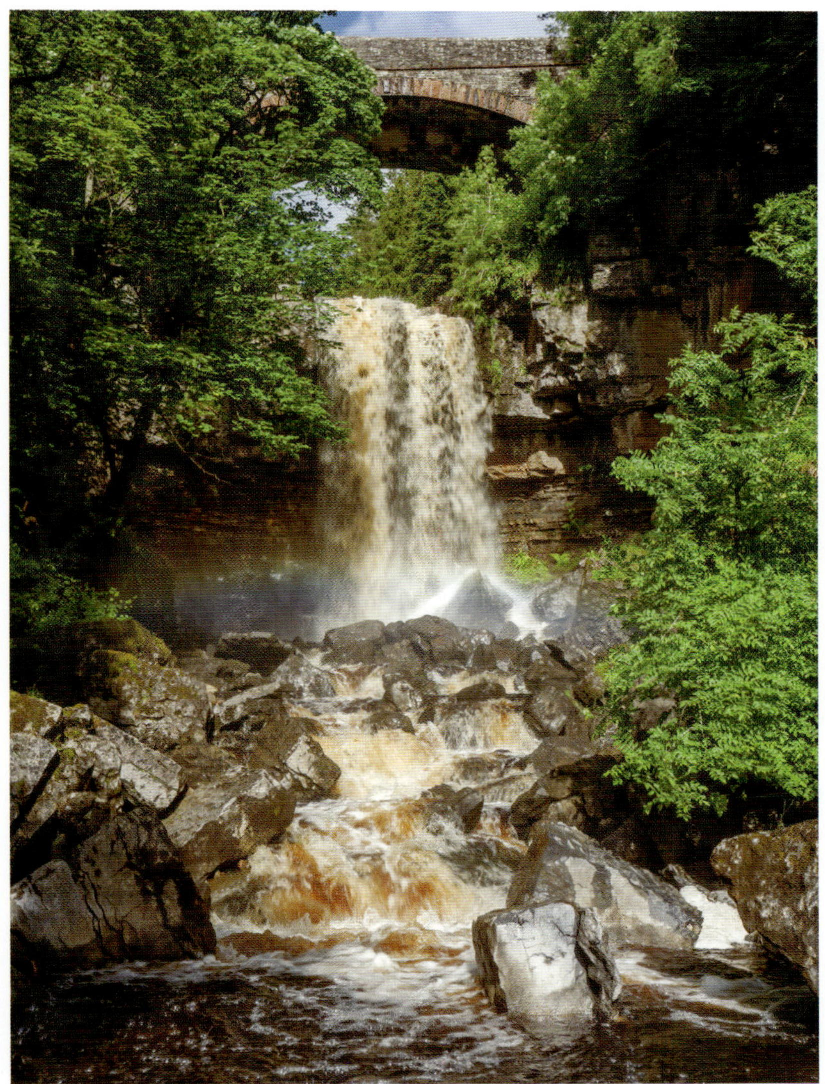

Above: The shutter speed for this waterfall shot was 1/50 sec. For the size of the subject in the frame and the speed of the falling water this is an oddly "in between" sort of value. The water is neither "frozen," nor sufficiently blurred, so the result feels strangely indecisive.

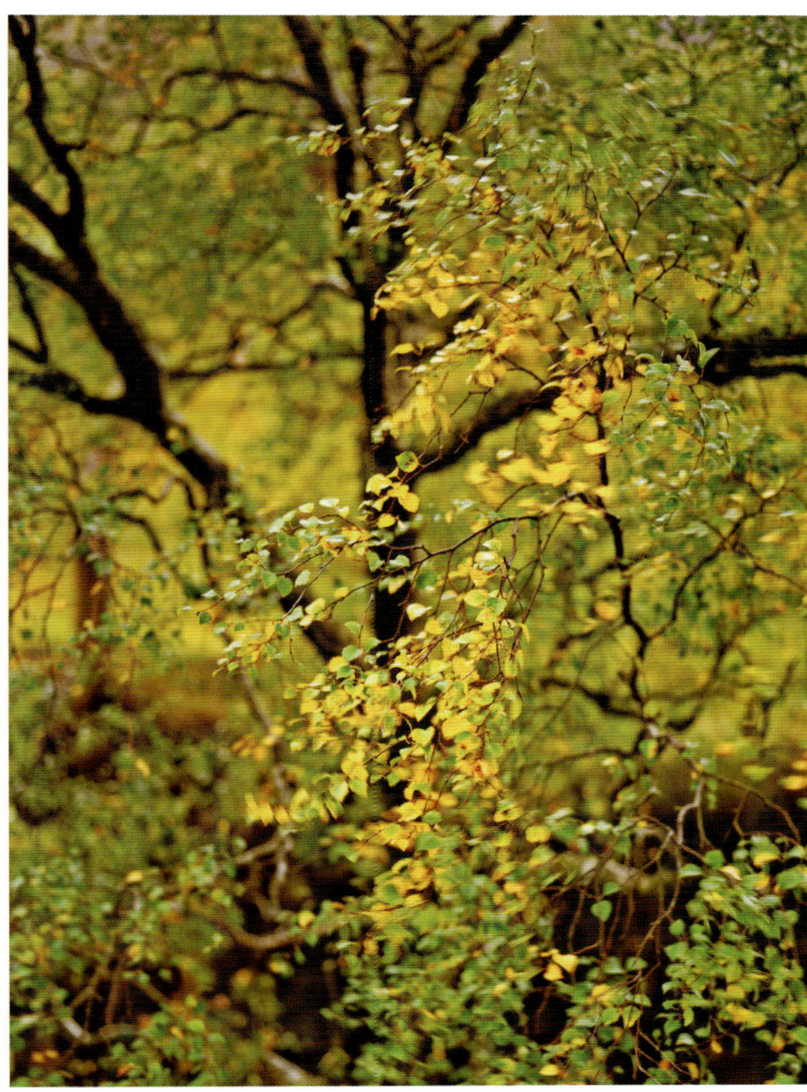

Above: If a faster shutter speed is required (such as here to avoid losing detail in wind-blown leaves), you can either raise the ISO, which will increase image noise, or you can use a larger aperture and compromise depth of field. I chose the latter option for this image.

you introduce movement into a scene the shutter speed you use will determine how that movement is captured in the final image. The faster the shutter speed, the more frozen any movement appears (although the closer the moving subject is to the camera, the faster the shutter speed needs to be in order to freeze movement). Conversely, the slower the shutter speed, the more that movement is rendered as a blur in the image: if you use a sufficiently long shutter speed your moving subject may disappear from the image entirely.

ISO

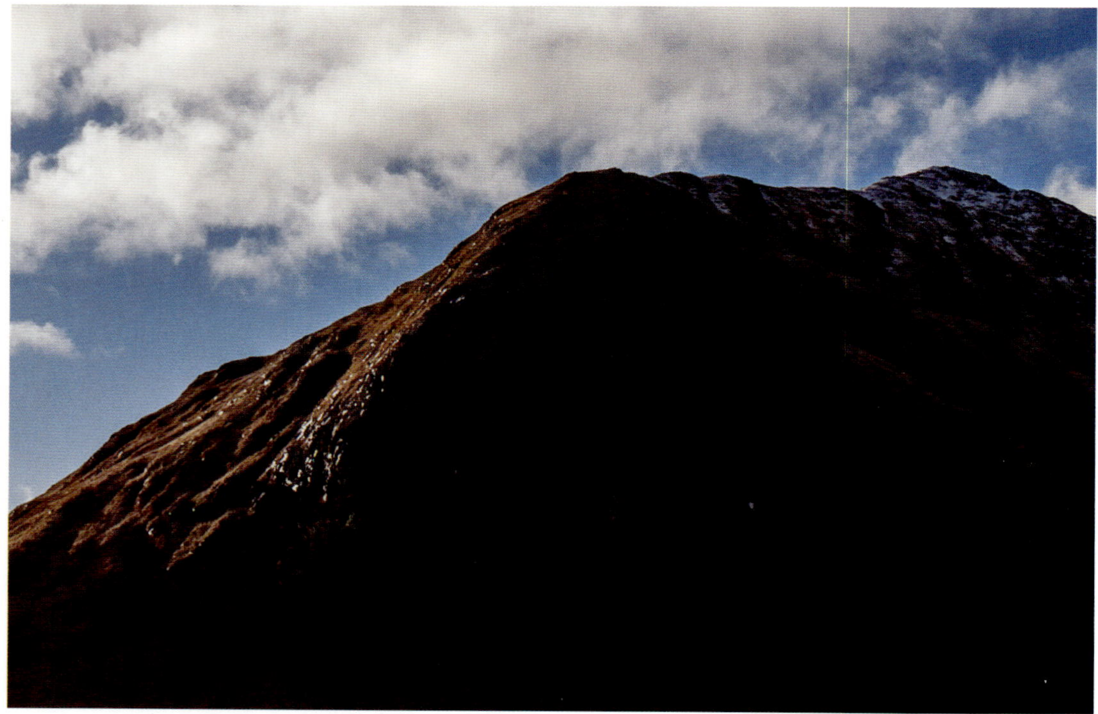

Shutter speed and aperture control the amount of light that reaches the sensor, but it is the ISO setting that controls how much light the sensor actually needs to make an image. The base ISO of a camera is usually the lowest available setting, when the sensor is at its least sensitive to light (although some cameras also offer extended "lo" settings; see Notes, right). Raising the ISO increases the sensitivity of the sensor, which means that less light is required to make a correctly exposed image. The advantage to this is that you can use a faster shutter speed and/or a smaller aperture. The disadvantage is that noise increases as ISO is raised.

All digital images display noise to one degree or another. Noise is seen as random spots of color or variations in brightness in the image. This has the effect of reducing fine detail. There are two types of digital noise: luminance and chroma. Of the two, luminance is the least objectionable, as it has a gritty quality that resembles film grain (although typically less random). Chroma noise is less welcome and is seen as ugly color blotching that's harder to remove in postproduction. One of the big improvements in digital sensors in recent years has been the reduction of noise at all but the highest ISO settings. Size is important, though, as larger sensors tend to control noise better than smaller sensors.

However, despite these improvements, base ISO is the setting to use if you want to maximize image quality and retain fine detail in your images. This may mean extended shutter speeds, which is why a tripod is such an important addition to your photographic equipment. Another advantage of using the base ISO is that there's greater latitude for adjusting the exposure in postproduction. Use a high ISO and that flexibility is reduced: exposure adjustments are more likely to result in an unacceptable drop in image quality.

On many cameras the ISO can be set to adjust automatically as light levels alter. While this is a useful option when handholding a camera, it is not recommended if you are shooting with the camera on a tripod or are using filters. Using light-sapping filters will cause the ISO to increase artificially, usually negating the effect that was required by fitting the filter.

Long Exposure Noise

As well as increasing at higher ISO settings, noise also becomes more apparent when extended shutter speeds are used. The longer a sensor is exposing, the hotter it gets, and heat corrupts image data, increasing the risk of noise. Cameras often have a long-exposure noise-reduction function to counter this, which is typically activated when the shutter speed exceeds 1 second. Unfortunately, the process takes as long again as the original shutter speed (so a 1-second exposure will take 2 seconds including noise reduction, a 2-second exposure takes 4 seconds, and so on). To spare your camera battery—and to make low-light photography less frustrating—it pays to switch long exposure noise reduction off. This means noise will need to be removed in postproduction, but it is generally a small price to pay in order to keep shooting without interruption.

Above: Noise is most easily seen in areas of even tone, such as the sky and in shadow areas. This is also true of long exposure noise, particularly when shooting at night when the sky is usually the darkest part of the image.

Exposure Values

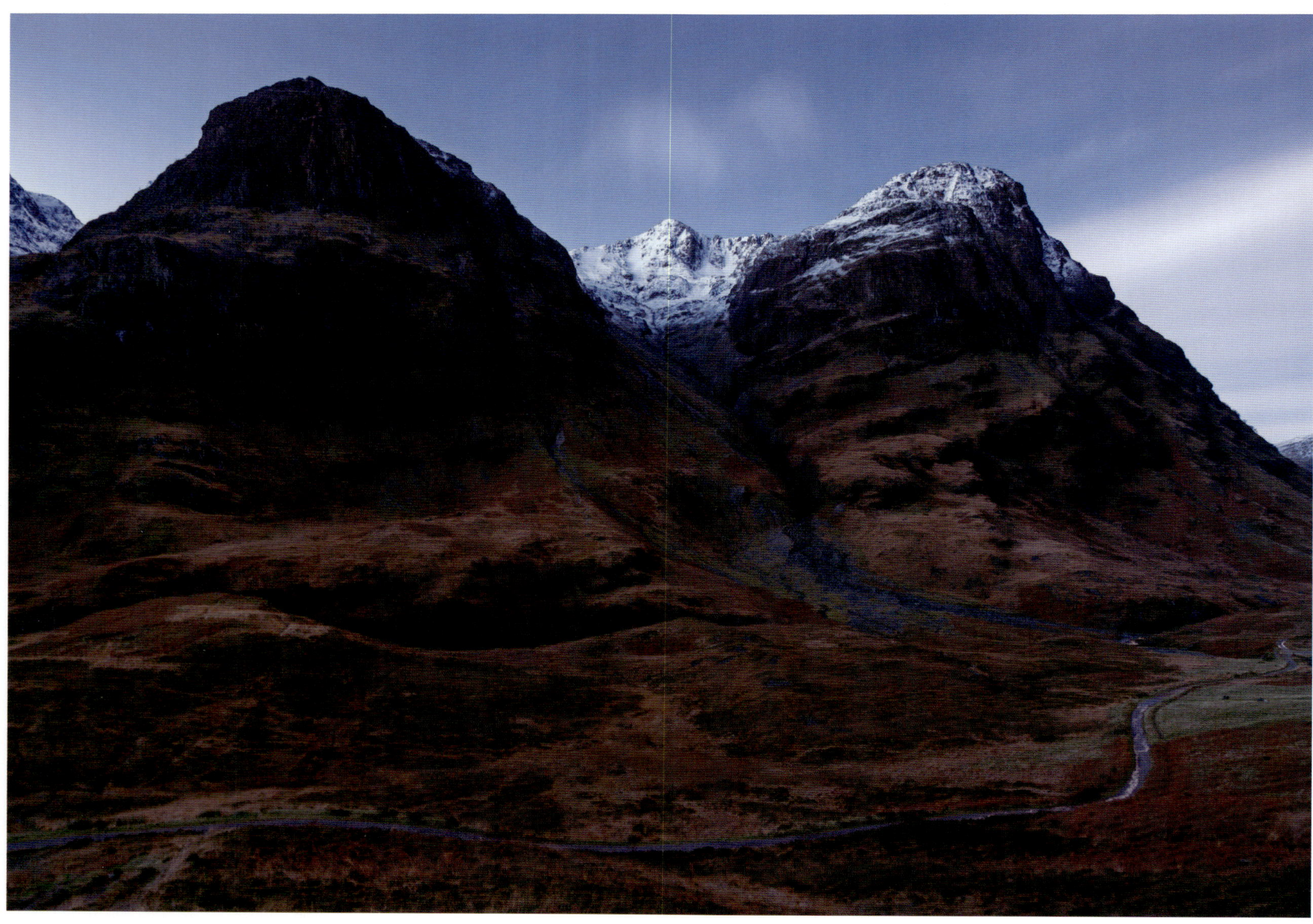

Exposure meters help to automate the image-making process. However, it's possible to achieve acceptable exposures without reference to a meter. This is because light levels will always be the same under certain conditions. The most common example of this is referred to as the "Sunny 16" rule. It refers to the fact that on a sunny day, when the aperture is set to f/16, the correct shutter speed will always be 1/100 sec. at ISO 100. From that basic premise it's possible to work out what the shutter speed would be if the aperture were made smaller or larger under the same conditions, or the ISO were changed.

This idea that light levels are always the same under certain conditions can also be applied to other shooting situations. To make things easier,

Above: I judged this moonlit scene to be approximately EV -2. This required an exposure of 4 minutes using an aperture of f/8 at ISO 100. However, by increasing the ISO to 200 I was able to reduce the time to 2 minutes.

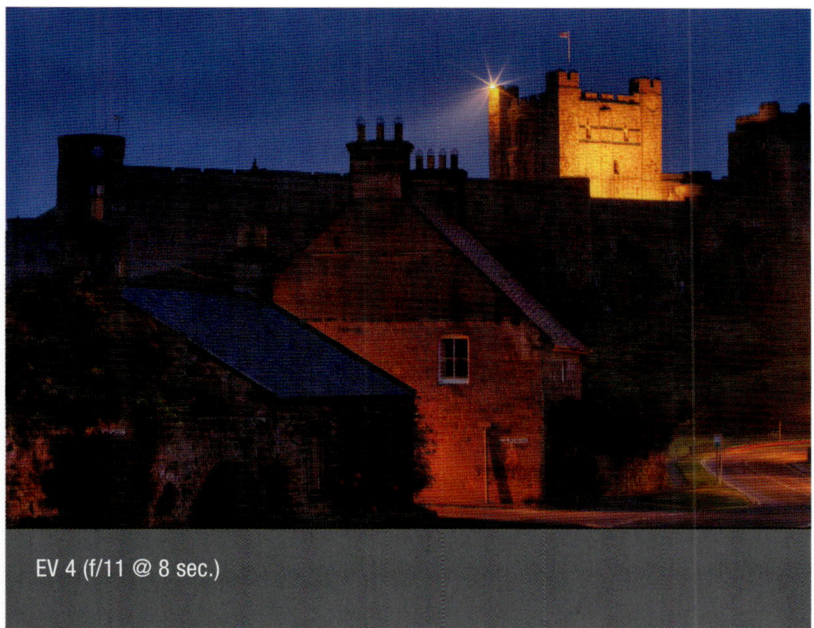

EV 4 (f/11 @ 8 sec.)

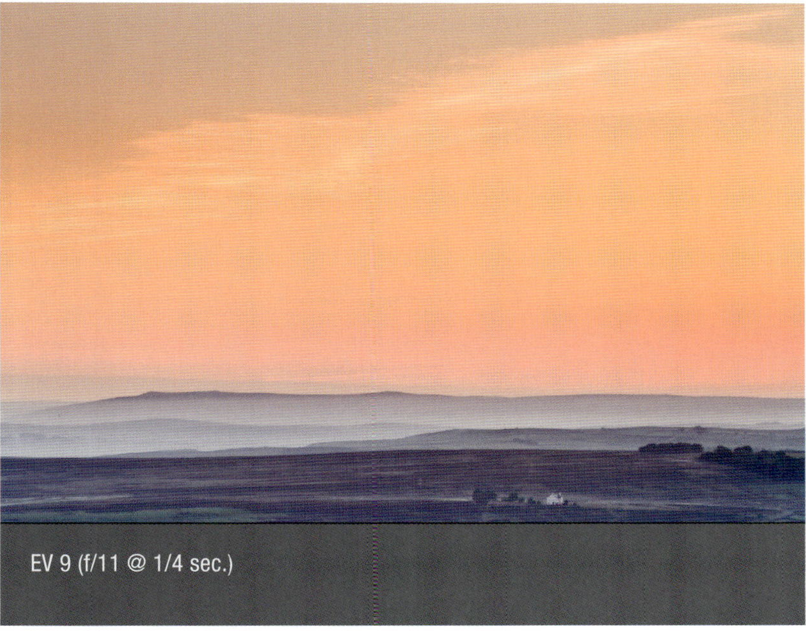

EV 9 (f/11 @ 1/4 sec.)

Above & Left: Deciding where a scene falls on the exposure value chart takes practice. This is initially easier to do after shooting. You can do this by looking at the exposure metadata of your images and comparing that information to the grid on the following page. Here are a few images with which you can do exactly that.

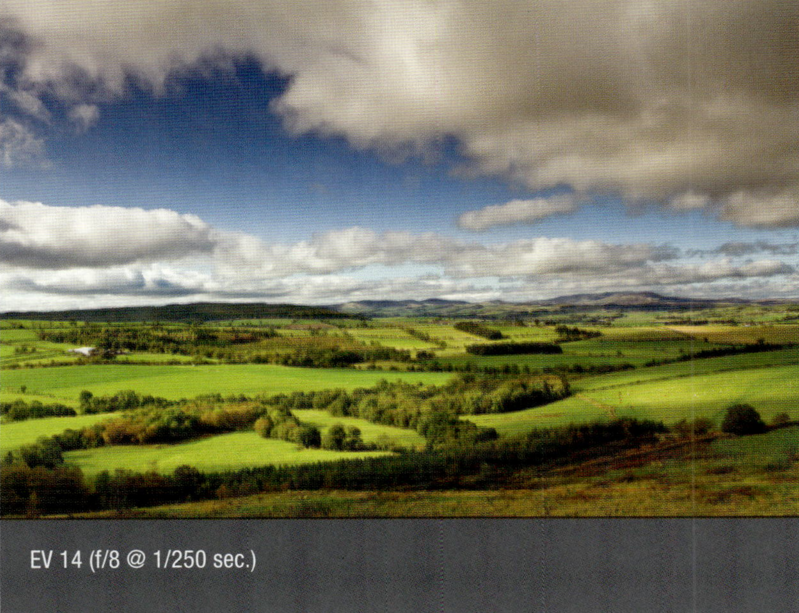

EV 14 (f/8 @ 1/250 sec.)

You'll need to take filter factors into account when setting the exposure using the EV chart. As an example, a polarizing filter absorbs 2 stops of light, so you would need to look at the EV for the relevant lighting situation and then deduct 2 from that value to find the correct exposure setting to use. For example, if you were photographing on a bright, overcast day (EV 13) with a polarizing filter, you would use the exposure settings for EV 11 instead.

different lighting conditions are assigned a number known as an exposure value or EV. Exposure values specify the range of shutter speeds and apertures that can be combined to produce a correct exposure under these specific conditions. The grid on the following page covers the range of exposure values from EV -5 through to EV 17. This takes in a vast number of shooting situations, from shooting aurora in near darkness to very intense artificial lighting. To use the chart you'll need to judge the conditions you're shooting under, manually match the relevant aperture and shutter speed on your camera, and set the ISO to 100 (or adjust the aperture or shutter speed accordingly).

Exposure Values at ISO 100

EV	f/2.8	f/4	f/5.6	f/8	f/11	f/16	
-5	4 min.	8 min.	16 min.	32 min.	64 min.	128 min.	Northern/Southern lights (medium bright). Moonlit scene (Moon quarter phase).
-4	2 min.	4 min.	8 min.	16 min.	32 min.	64 min.	Northern/Southern lights (bright). Moonlit scene (Moon gibbous phase).
-3	1 min.	2 min.	4 min.	8 min.	16 min.	32 min.	Moonlit scene—night (Moon full).
-2	30 sec.	1 min.	2 min.	4 min.	8 min.	16 min.	Moonlit scene (Moon full).
-1	15 sec.	30 sec.	1 min.	2 min.	4 min.	8 min.	Ambient light from dim artificial lighting.
0	8 sec.	15 sec.	30 sec.	1 min.	2 min.	4 min.	Ambient light from artificial lighting.
1	4 sec.	8 sec.	15 sec.	30 sec.	1 min.	2 min.	Cityscapes at night.
2	2 sec.	4 sec.	8 sec.	15 sec.	30 sec.	1 min.	Eclipsed moon. Lightning.
3	1 sec.	2 sec.	4 sec.	8 sec.	15 sec.	30 sec.	Fireworks. Traffic trails.
4	1/2 sec.	1 sec.	2 sec.	4 sec.	8 sec.	15 sec.	Candle light. Floodlit buildings.
5	1/4 sec.	1/2 sec.	1 sec.	2 sec.	4 sec.	8 sec.	Traffic at night.
6	1/8 sec.	1/4 sec.	1/2 sec.	1 sec.	2 sec.	4 sec.	–
7	1/15 sec.	1/8 sec.	1/4 sec.	1/2 sec.	1 sec.	2 sec.	Deep woodland cover.
8	1/30 sec.	1/15 sec.	1/8 sec.	1/4 sec.	1/2 sec.	1 sec.	Bright neon-lit urban areas. Bonfires.
9	1/60 sec.	1/30 sec.	1/15 sec.	1/8 sec.	1/4 sec.	1/2 sec.	Ten minutes before sunrise or after sunset.
10	1/125 sec.	1/60 sec.	1/30 sec.	1/15 sec.	1/8 sec.	1/4 sec.	Immediately before sunrise or after sunset.
11	1/250 sec.	1/125 sec.	1/60 sec.	1/30 sec.	1/15 sec.	1/8 sec.	Sunsets. Deep shade (no shadows).
12	1/500 sec.	1/250 sec.	1/125 sec.	1/60 sec.	1/30 sec.	1/15 sec.	Heavily overcast daylight. Open shade (no shadows).
13	1/1000 sec.	1/500 sec.	1/250 sec.	1/125 sec.	1/60 sec.	1/30 sec.	Bright overcast daylight (shadows just visible).
14	1/2000 sec.	1/1000 sec.	1/500 sec.	1/250 sec.	1/125 sec.	1/60 sec.	Weak sunlight. Full moon (very soft shadows).
15	1/4000 sec.	1/2000 sec.	1/1000 sec.	1/500 sec.	1/250 sec.	1/125 sec.	Bright or hazy sunny conditions (distinct shadows).
16	1/8000 sec.	1/4000 sec.	1/2000 sec.	1/1000 sec.	1/500 sec.	1/250 sec.	Brightly lit sand or snow (dark, hard-edged shadows).
17	1/16000 sec.	1/8000 sec.	1/4000 sec.	1/2000 sec.	1/1000 sec.	1/500 sec.	Very intense artificial lighting (very dark, hard-edged shadows).

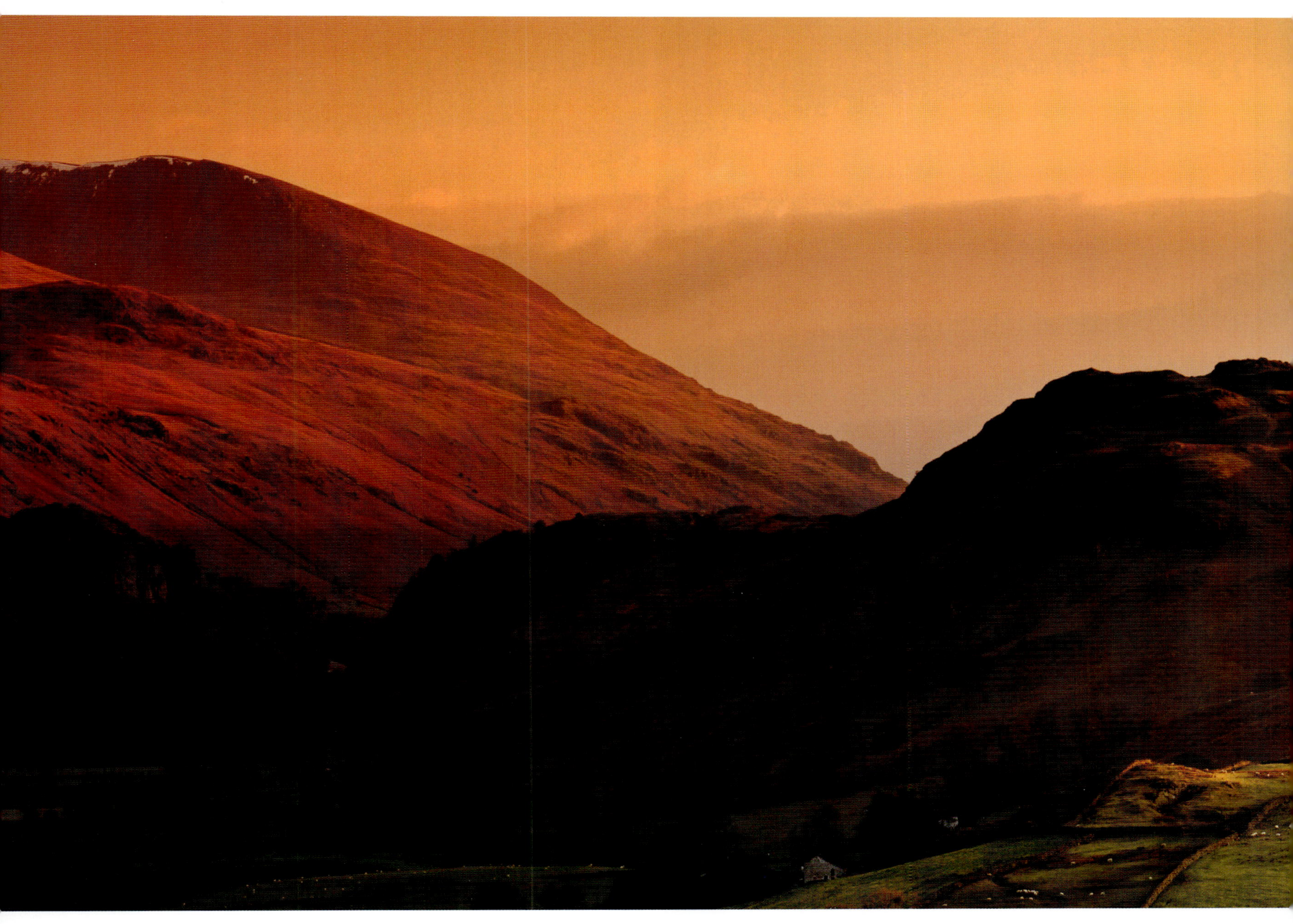

Above: Th s image was shot just before sunset in winter. The "correct" EV for the scene is 10, but as a polarizing filter was used, an EV of 8 was more appropriate. The final exposure selected was 1/2 sec. at f/11, using ISO 100.

Dynamic Range

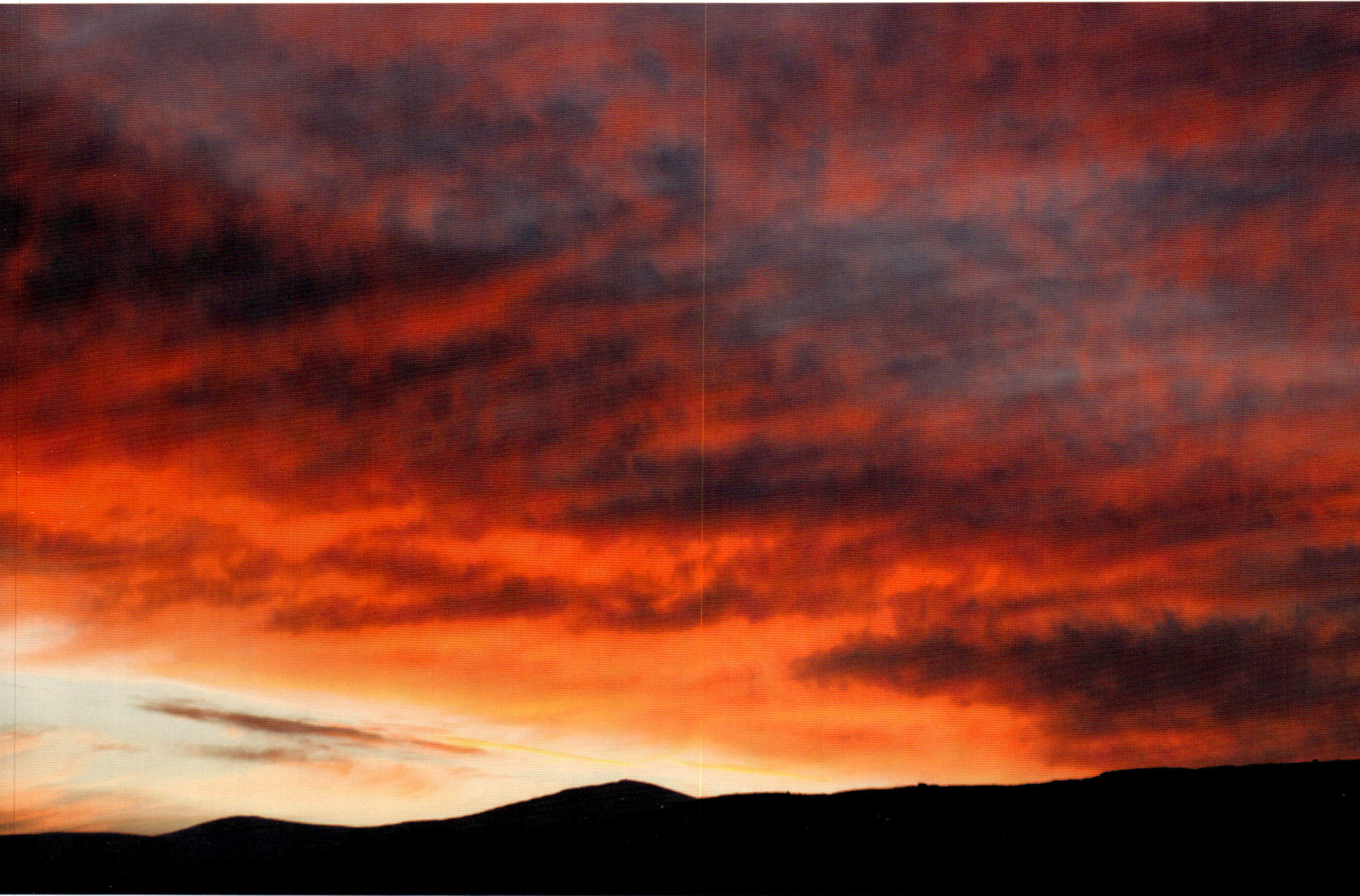

A camera cannot record the same range of brightness levels that we can see with our eyes. With high-contrast scenes this often means that if you set an exposure that will preserve the highlights you will lose detail in the shadows, and vice versa. The range of brightness levels a camera can record is known as its dynamic range. Sensor technology is improving year on year and expanding dynamic range is one of these improvements. However, currently it doesn't seem likely that a sensor will be developed that can match the human eye.

Dynamic range is generally affected by the size of the sensor used: the smaller the sensor, the

Above: Shooting into the light means dealing with high levels of contrast. With relatively simple subjects, one solution is to expose for the highlights to create a silhouette.

smaller the dynamic range. It is for this reason that full-frame cameras remain popular for landscape photography, despite the price premium in comparison to cameras with smaller sensors.

One of the skills that needs to be developed as a photographer is the ability to "see" like a camera and judge when contrast will prove problematic. It's then either a case of knowing how to reduce the contrast—either by using filters or reflectors—or whether trying again later, under different conditions is the best option.

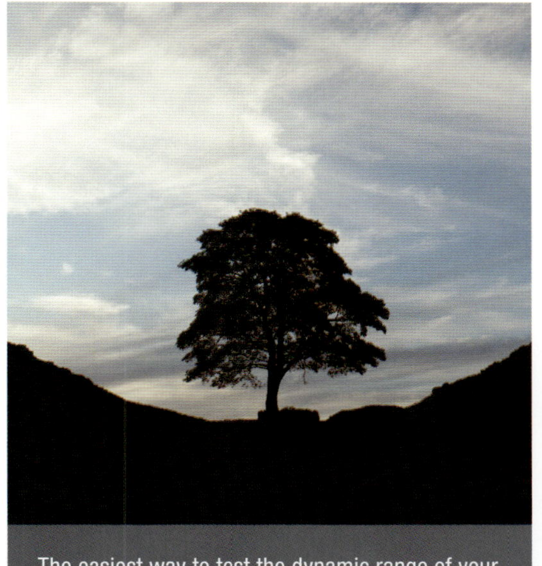

The easiest way to test the dynamic range of your camera is to shoot a silhouette image with your camera set to Raw. Set the exposure so that detail is retained in the highlights.

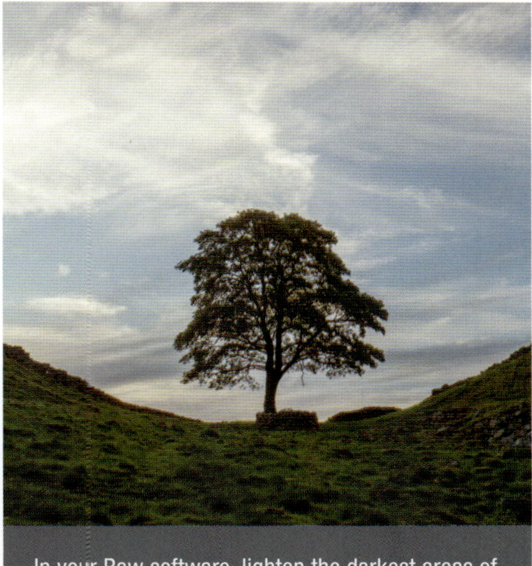

In your Raw software, lighten the darkest areas of the image without altering the highlights.

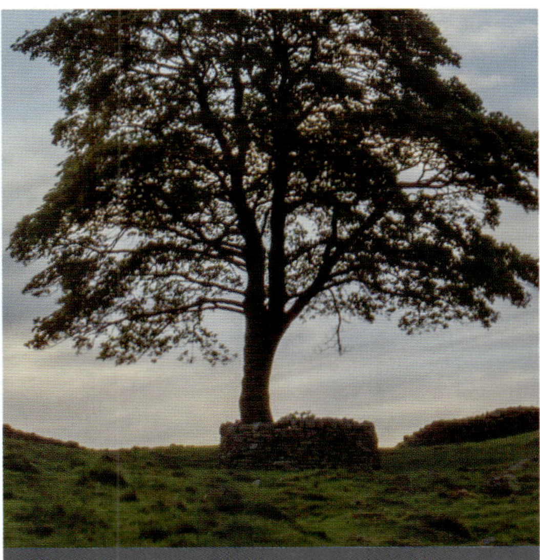

The greater the dynamic range of your camera, the more you can adjust the shadows without noise becoming unacceptable. With some full-frame cameras it's possible to recover a significant amount of shadow detail.

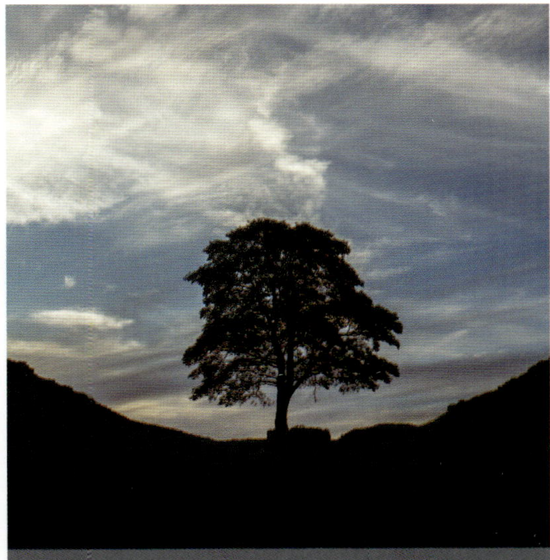

However, just because you can recover shadow detail doesn't mean that you have to. Doing so reduces contrast, and can lessen the impact of the image. In this instance I actually increased contrast in order to reduce detail in the shadow areas still further and to add more "punch" to the sky.

Histograms

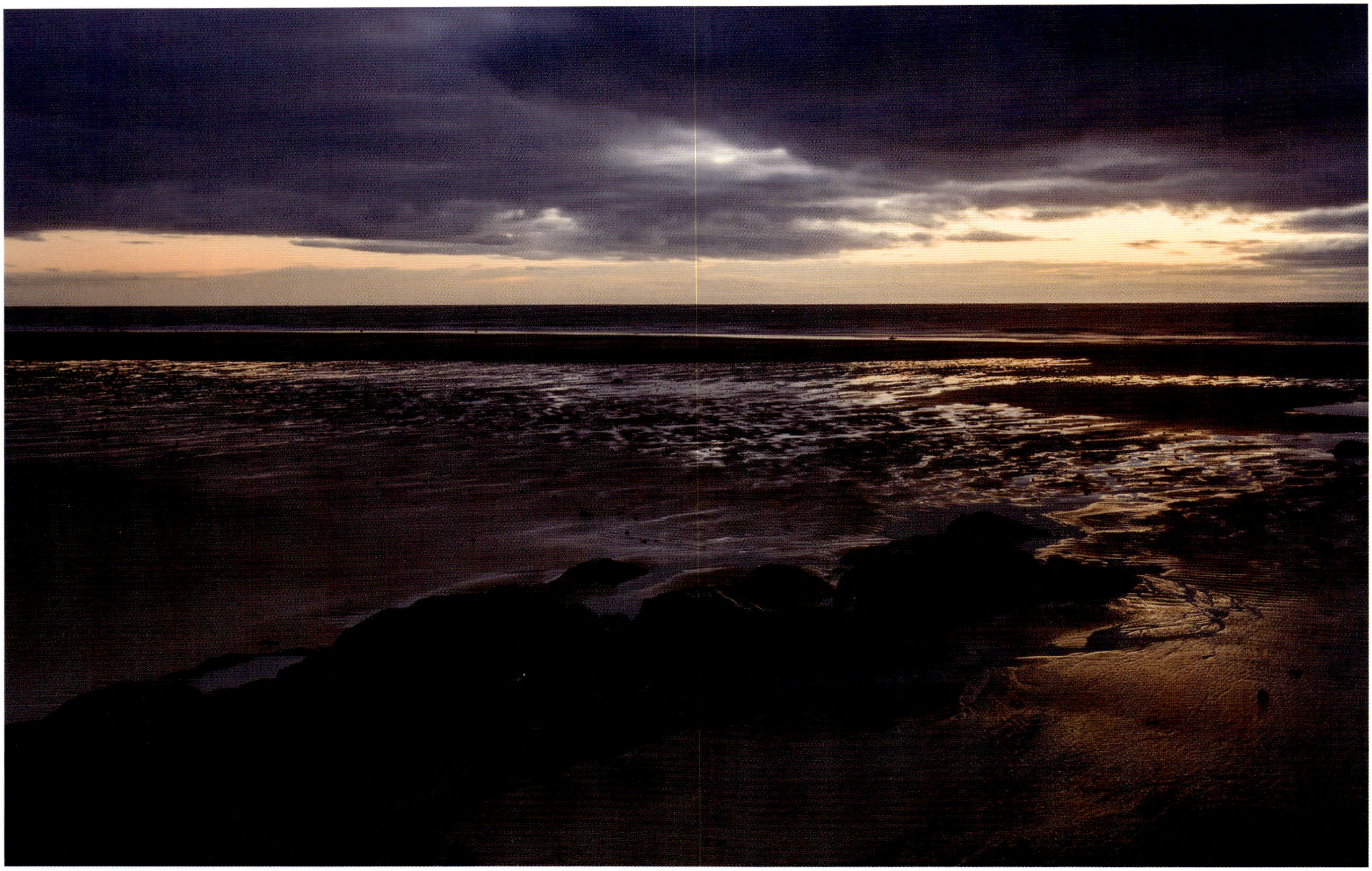

Apart from its built-in exposure meter, your camera has another way of displaying the exposure of an image: the histogram. A histogram is a graph that shows the tonal range of an image, from black (and the shadow areas of the image) at the left to white (and the highlights) at the right, with the midtones halfway across. If a correctly exposed midtone subject filled the frame entirely, the resulting histogram would peak in the middle. Vertically, the histogram shows how many pixels of a particular tone are in the image.

There's no ideal shape for a histogram—it is merely a guide to the distribution of the image's tonal range—but ideally you should avoid "clipping" the ends. This is when the histogram "leans" against either the left or right edge. When this happens it indicates there are pixels in the image that are pure black or pure white respectively: these pixels no longer contain usable image data.

If clipping occurs you may want to adjust the exposure, typically by using exposure compensation. However, if contrast is high it may

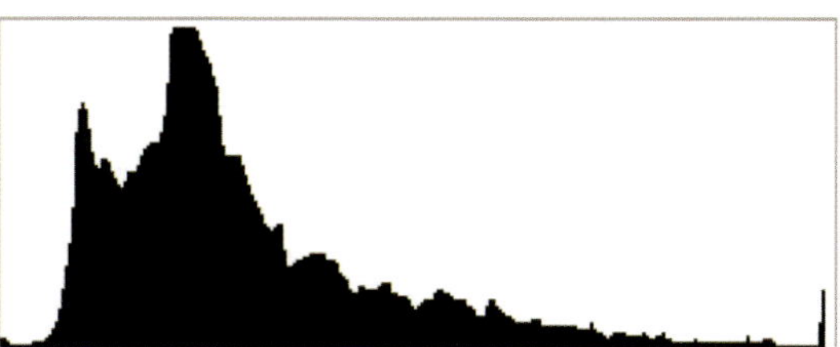

Above: The histogram for this image is heavily biased toward the left. However, the image is still exposed correctly—the histogram is simply showing that most of the tonal range is darker than a midtone.

be impossible to avoid clipping one edge of the histogram. If contrast can't be controlled—through the use of filters or additional lighting/reflectors—then you need to decide which part of the tonal range can be sacrificed. Generally, it looks more natural if the highlights are retained—we expect shadows to be dark, so it doesn't appear quite so odd to clip the shadow detail.

NOTES

Histograms can be displayed in image review after shooting, but some cameras can also display a histogram in Live View. This is particularly useful when assessing the effect of adding filters.

Bright light sources, such as the sun or streetlighting, will naturally clip a histogram.

Below: This image is also correctly exposed: the histogram may be shifted to the right, but it is simply indicating that the majority of the tones in the image are light.

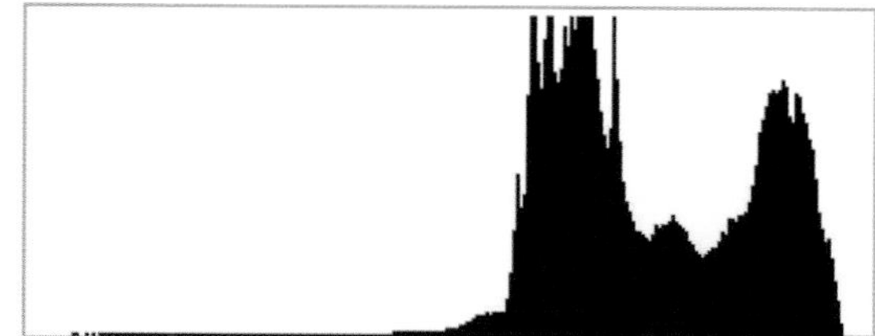

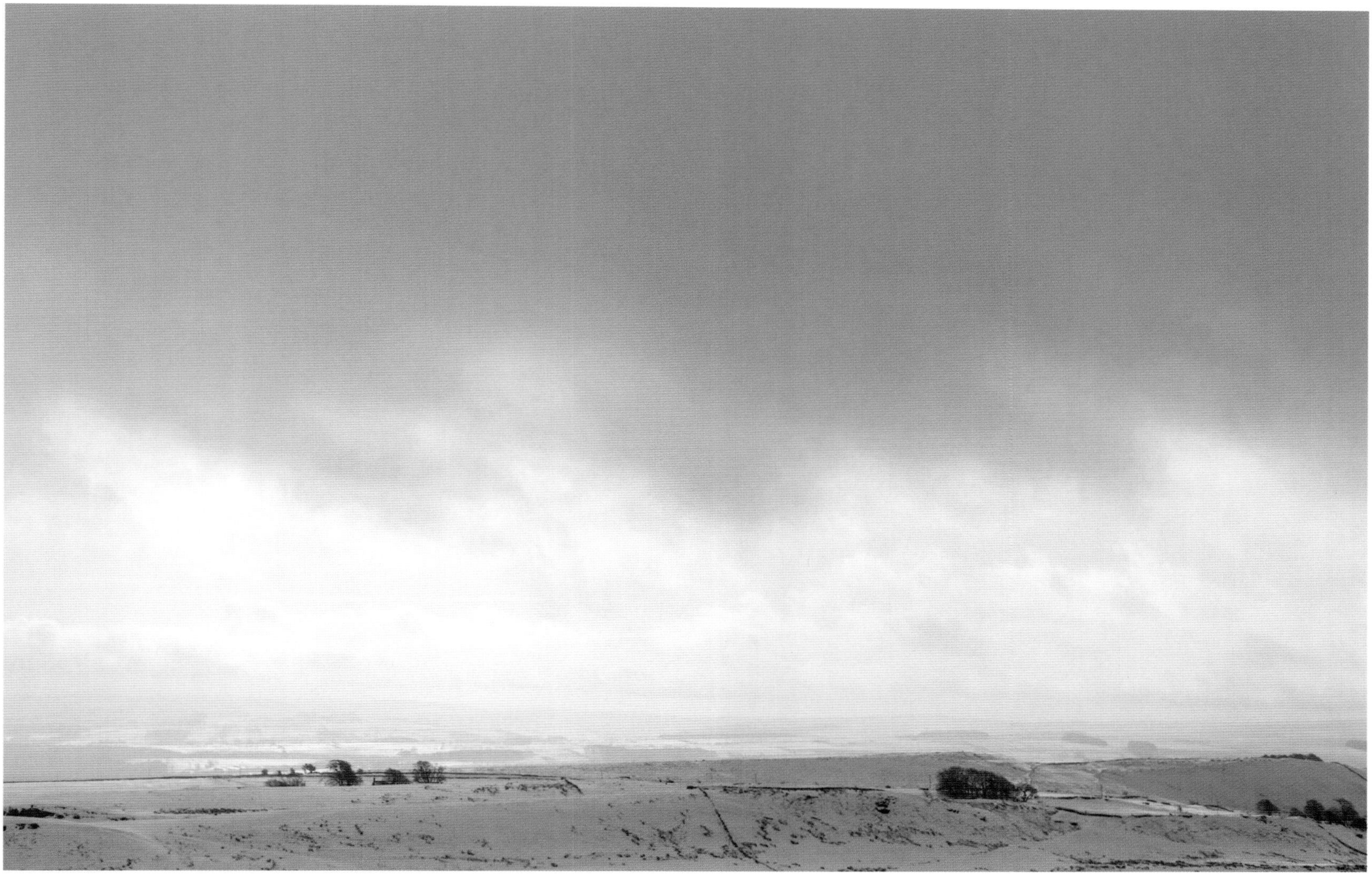

Exposing to the Right

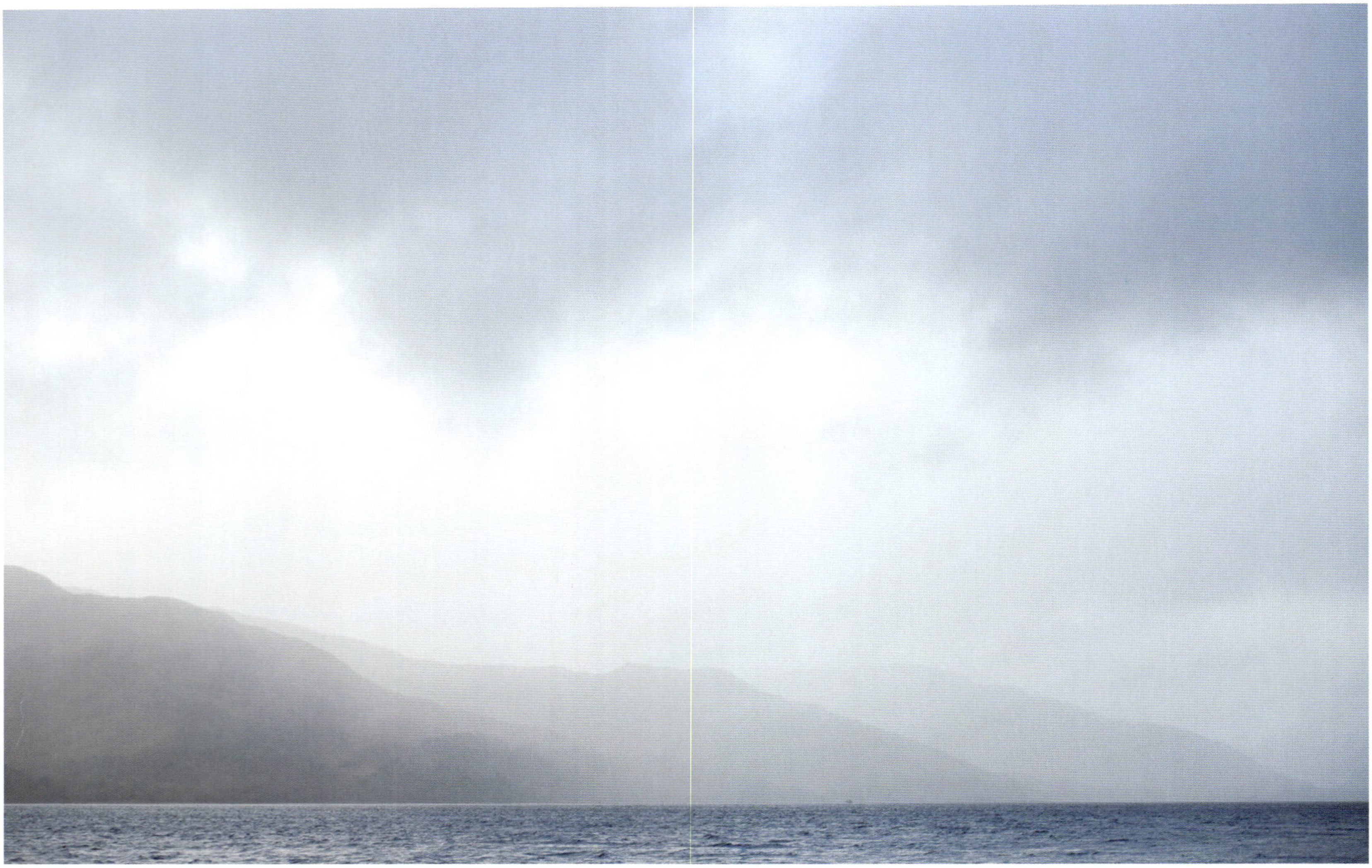

Digital sensors generally capture more image data in the highlight areas than in the shadows. Therefore, unless your camera has a particularly high dynamic range, lightening the shadows will result in an increase of visible noise.

One solution to this problem is to use a technique known as "exposing to the right," or ETTR. The name is derived from the fact that you expose a Raw image so that the resulting histogram is skewed as far to the right as is possible without clipping.

This means that you don't necessarily expose the image "correctly," but it will retain as much detail in the shadows as possible.

Shooting to expose to the right is limited by the contrast of a scene: it's more difficult when contrast is high and the danger of clipping the highlights is increased.

ETTR images often look pale and washed out when viewed on the camera's LCD, but this is perfectly normal. The idea is to correct this in postproduction when you convert the Raw file.

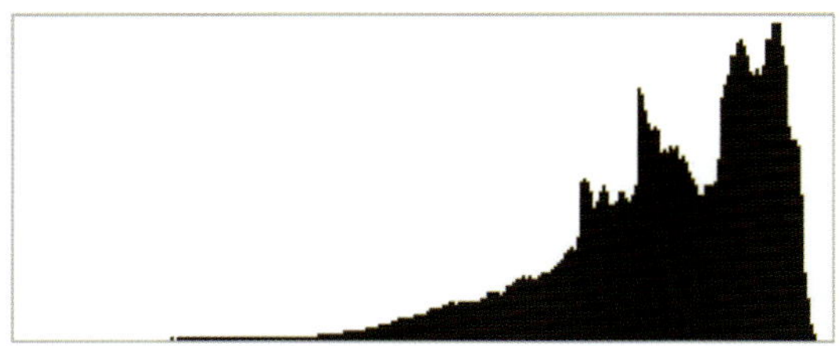

Above: This image was shot using ETTR principles. On the camera's screen, the results didn't look that inspiring, but this isn't the point. Note that the histogram for the image is skewed to the right but hasn't clipped the right edge.

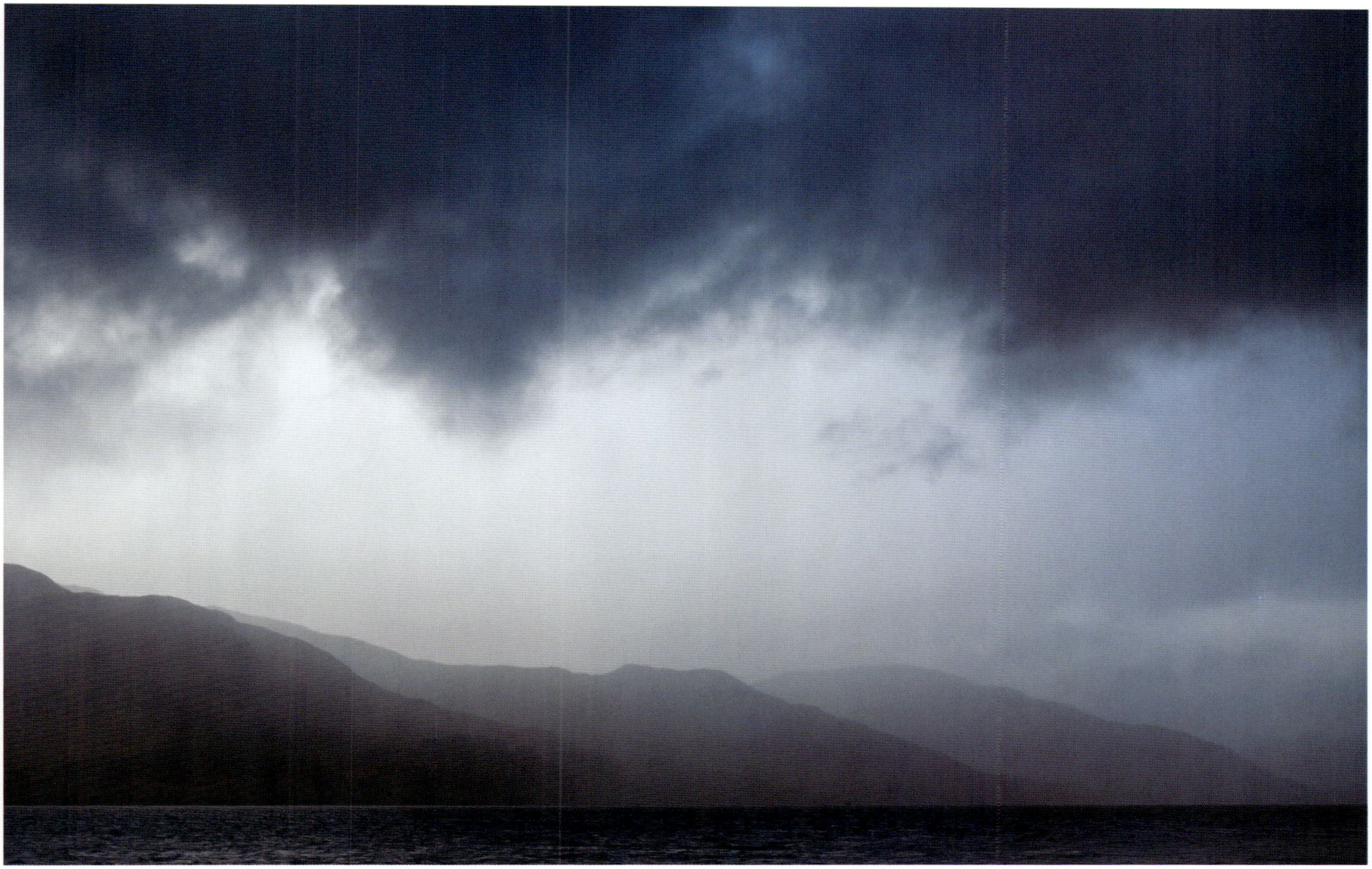

Currently there are no camera meters that allow you to expose to the right automatically. Therefore, to expose to the right you will need to either use Manual mode or apply positive exposure compensation. The technique is usually easier to get right when shooting in Live View with a live histogram to guide you.

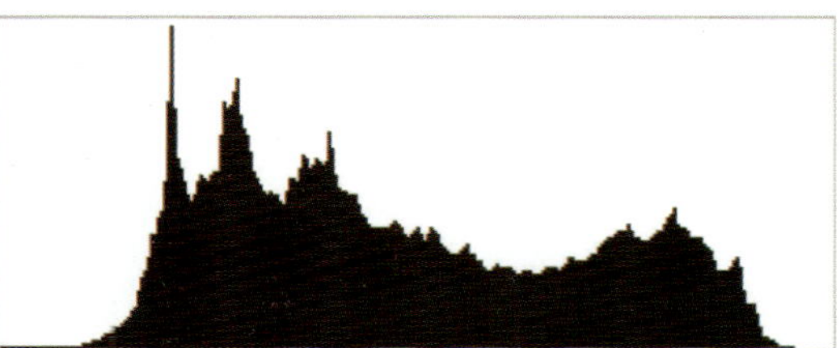

Above: The image's brightness and contrast can be adjusted to suit once it's been imported into suitable Raw software. Note how the shape of the histogram has changed compared to the original image.

Dealing with Contrast

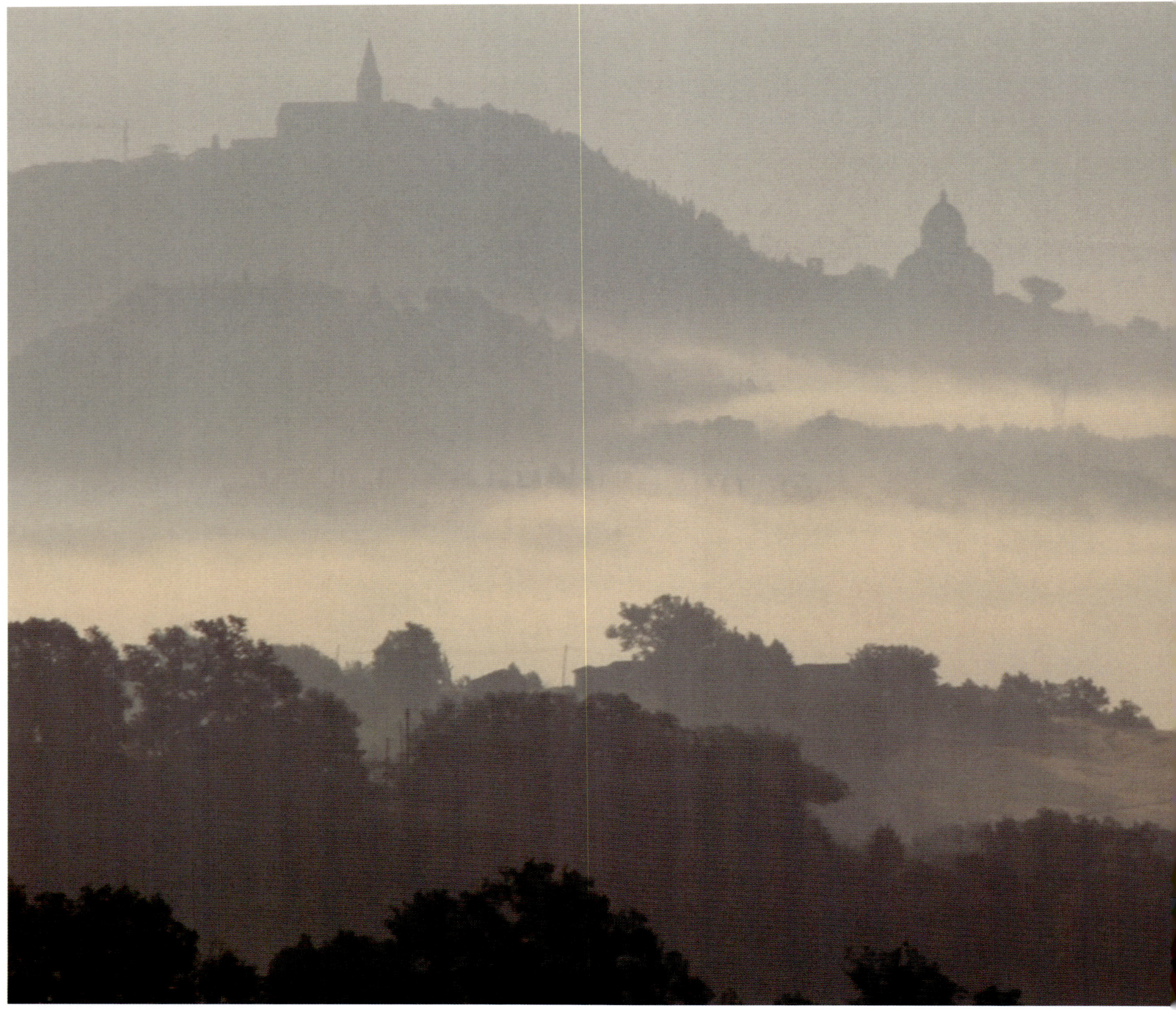

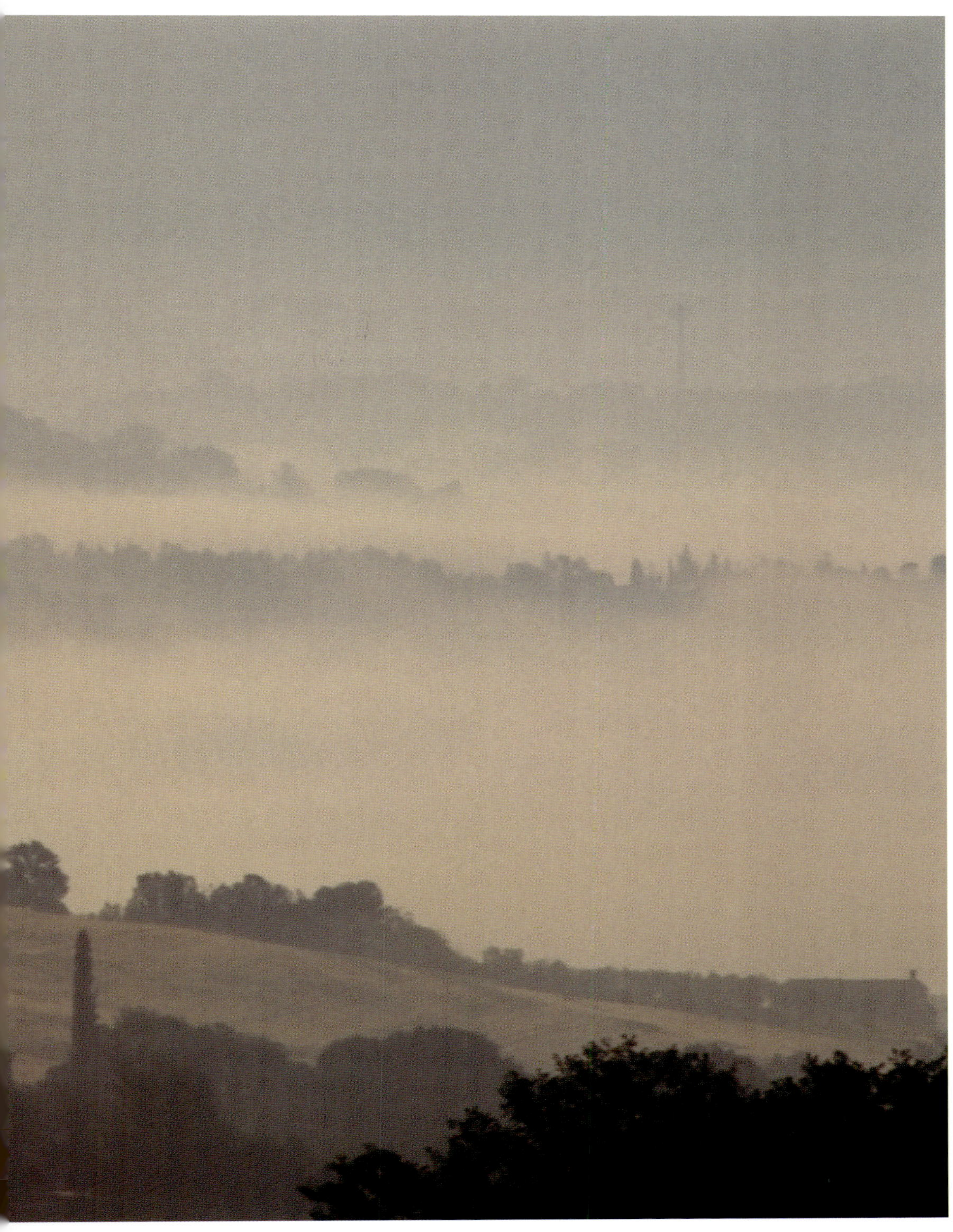

Contrast is determined by whether the light is hard or soft (see chapter 4). Low contrast means that there's very little tonal difference between the darkest part of the scene and the brightest. Misty days are low in contrast and often the difference between the shadows and highlights is minimal. Although mist can be very atmospheric, there's generally little in the way of drama.

A high-contrast scene sees the tonal difference between the shadows and highlights pushed to the extreme (the most extreme example of this would be a scene that was comprised of black and white with no other tones in between, although this is almost unheard of in landscape photography). High-contrast scenes tend to be dramatic and produce striking graphic images.

It's generally easier to add contrast to an image in postproduction than to remove it, so landscape photography often involves trying to reduce contrast at the time of shooting. When shooting details this is relatively straightforward: a reflector can be used to "bounce" light into the shadows to reduce contrast, for example. With a sufficiently large reflector the subject can also be shaded, which reduces contrast further (or you could use your body to cast a shadow onto the subject, although this is only easy to do if your camera is on a tripod).

For more expansive landscape subjects, reflectors aren't a practical proposition, so contrast is controlled largely by clouds modifying the sunlight. However, some types of contrast, such as the contrast between the sky and the ground, can be controlled through the use of filters (see chapter 7).

Left: Misty days are generally low in contrast. Low-contrast images tend to have a histogram with one peak, similar to a bell curve. Adding contrast in postproduction changes the shape of the histogram, increasing the difference between the brightest and darkest parts of the image. This image required a contrast boost after shooting to prevent it from appearing too flat.

Chapter 3
Light

To make an exposure you need light. However, light has many different qualities. It's these qualities that will be one of the key factors in how aesthetically pleasing your images are. There's a saying in photography that there's no such thing as bad light, just bad photography. This refers to the fact that the light that's right for one subject isn't necessarily right for another. As a landscape photographer it's up to you to decide whether the light is right for your chosen subject or, if not, whether it can be modified in some way to improve it. Ultimately you may be better off shooting a different subject and returning on a different day when the light is more suited to your original location.

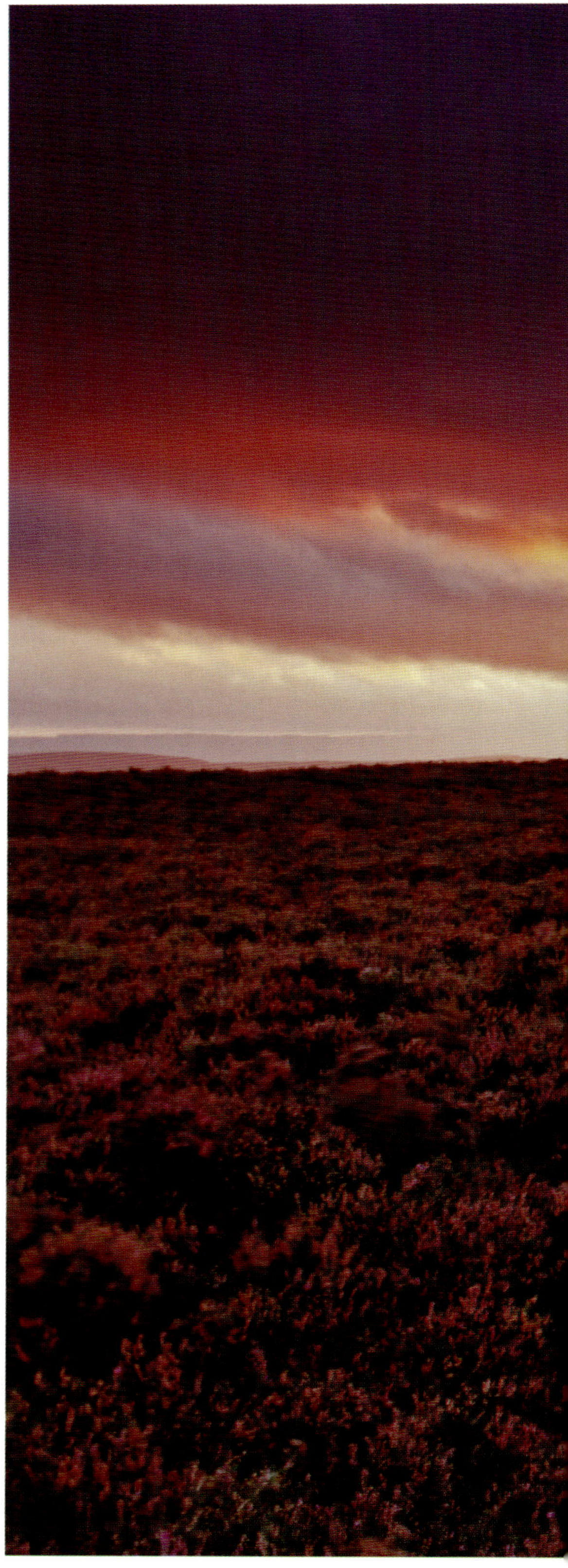

Right: The color of sunlight is affected by many factors. The amount of cloud cover at sunrise or sunset is one of those, and when there's just the right amount of cloud the results can be spectacular.

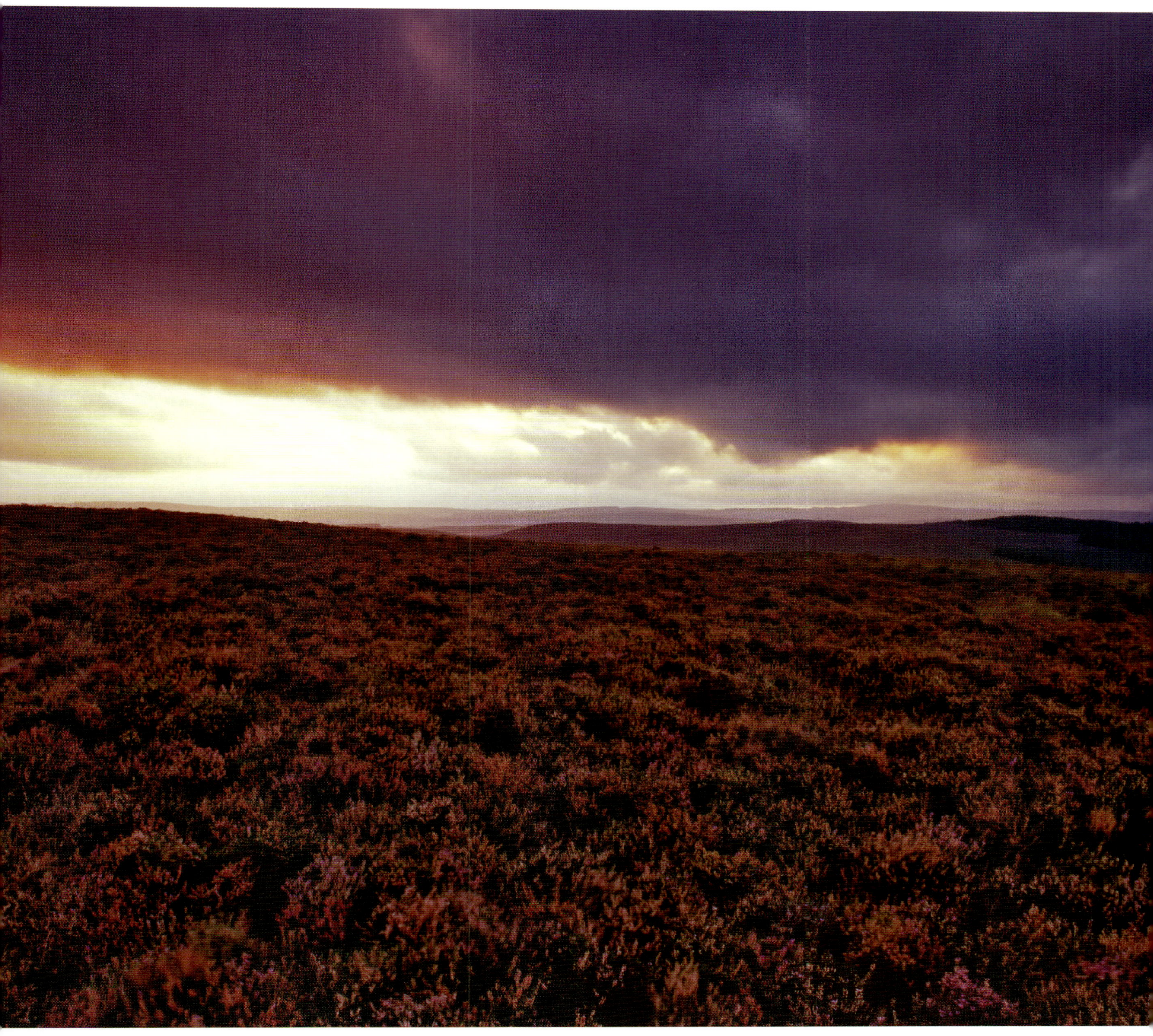

What is Light?

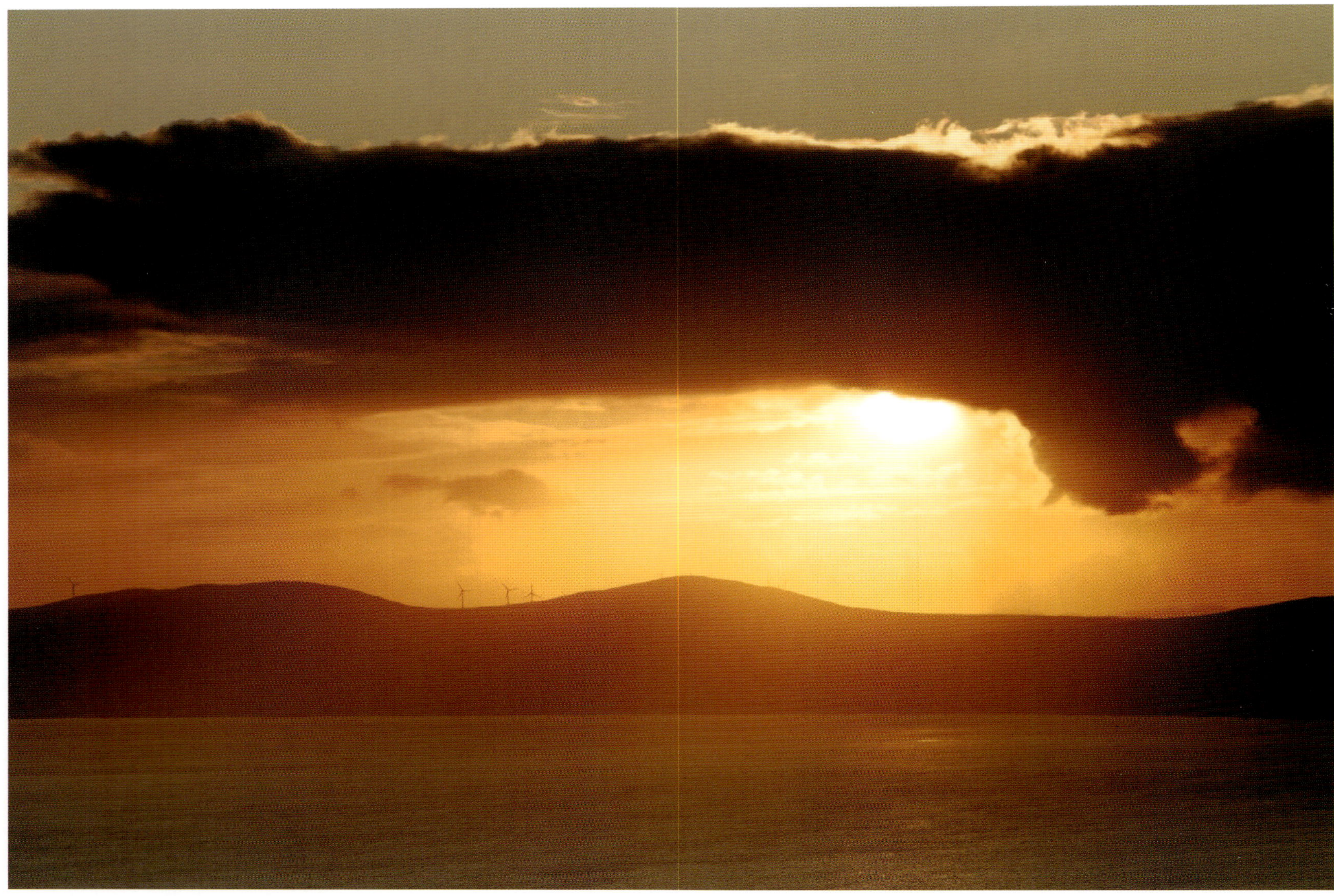

Light is a range of wavelengths in the electromagnetic spectrum that are visible to the human eye. The range starts at a wavelength of approximately 700 nanometers (nm) and ends at approximately 390nm (other animals, notably insects, can perceive wavelengths outside this range). When visible light is shone through a prism the various wavelengths are separated into the colors of the spectrum. The longest visible wavelength (at 700nm) corresponds to the color we perceive as red. The other colors—orange, yellow, green, blue, and indigo—have decreasingly shorter wavelengths until you reach the shortest wavelength of visible light, which corresponds to the color violet.

As the Earth's atmosphere isn't perfectly transparent, dust and other particles block or scatter shorter wavelengths. When the sun is low on the horizon at sunrise or sunset, this effect reaches its peak, so most of the bluer wavelengths are absorbed by the Earth's atmosphere. This results in the sun's light being heavily biased toward the red-orange end of the spectrum.

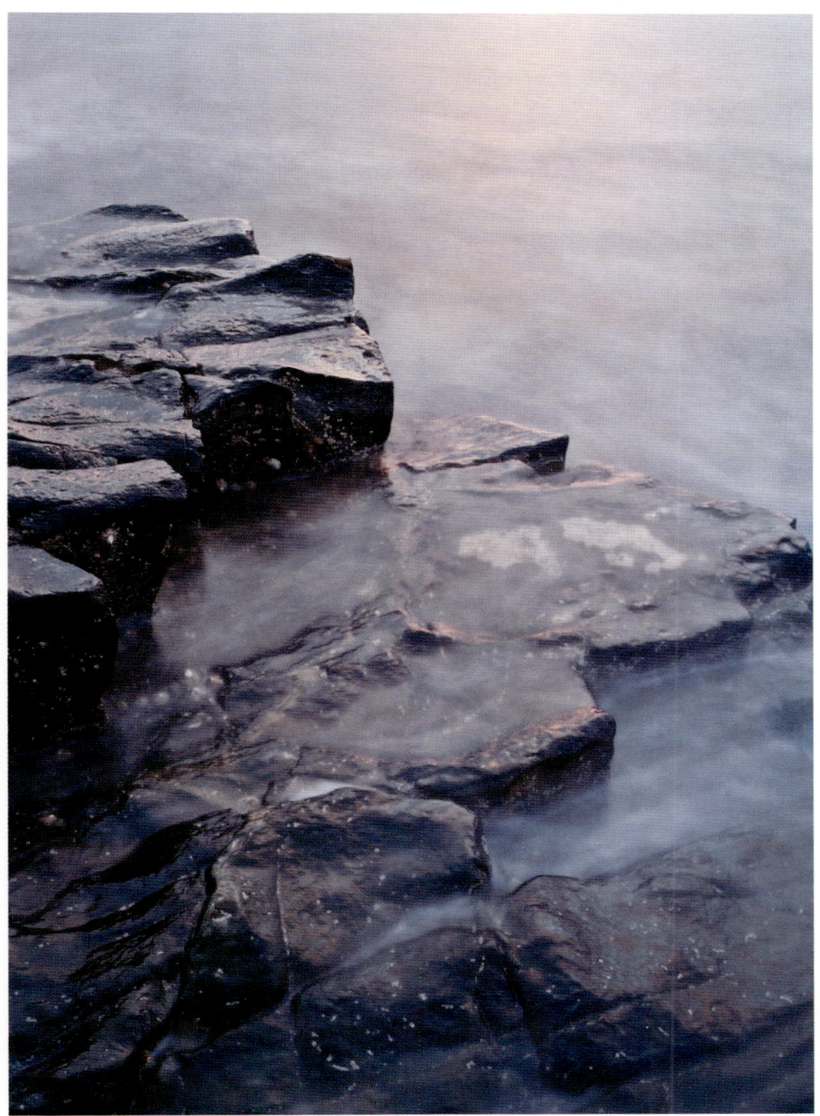

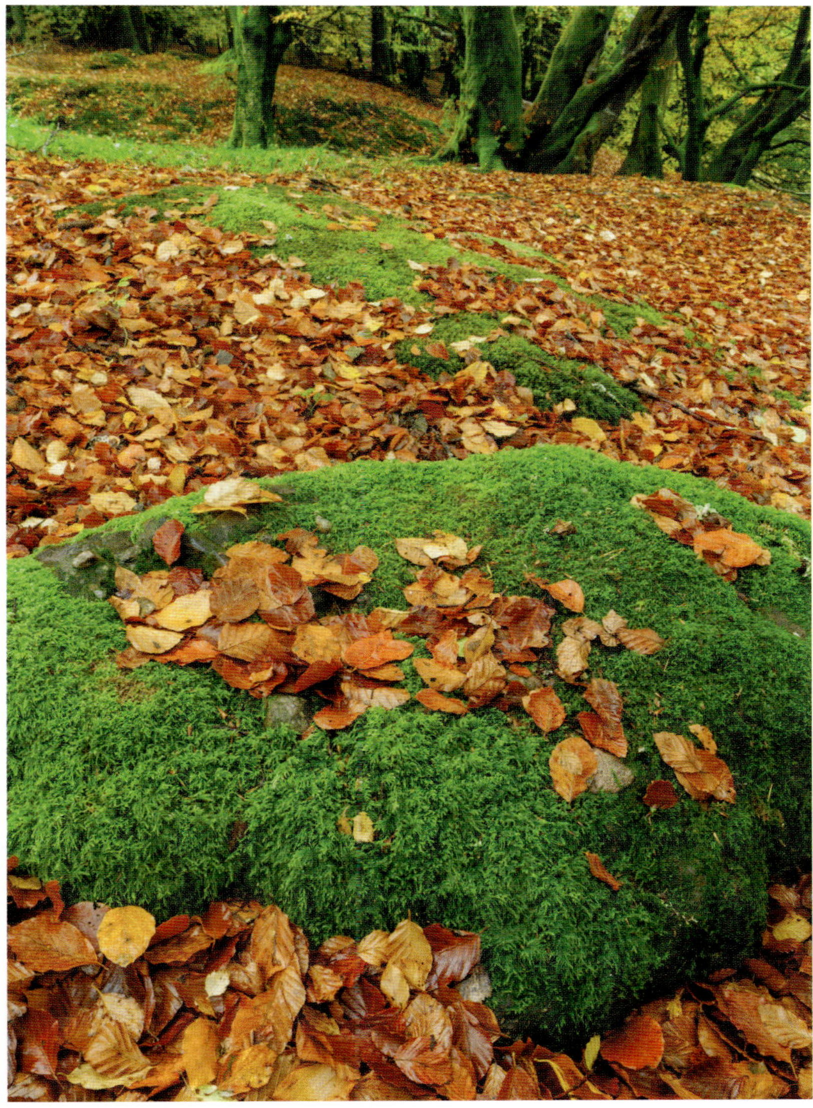

Above: When light strikes an object it is partially absorbed and partially reflected. The balance between the two is determined by the texture of the object's surface. The smoother and glossier the surface, the more reflective it is. Still water is highly reflective, for example, while wet rocks are less reflective, as they have a rough surface below the sheen of water. However, wet rocks still reflect the ambient color of light very effectively. This image shows wet rock reflecting the warm light of sunrise.

Left: The lower the sun, the more biased the light is toward red-orange. However, other factors, such as the amount of dust or pollution in the atmosphere, can intensify the effect.

Above: The color of an object is determined by which wavelengths of light it absorbs and which it reflects. For example, objects that are pure green will absorb all wavelengths of light except those that correspond to green. The reflected green wavelengths reach our eyes and our brain interprets the subject as green.

The Qualities of Light

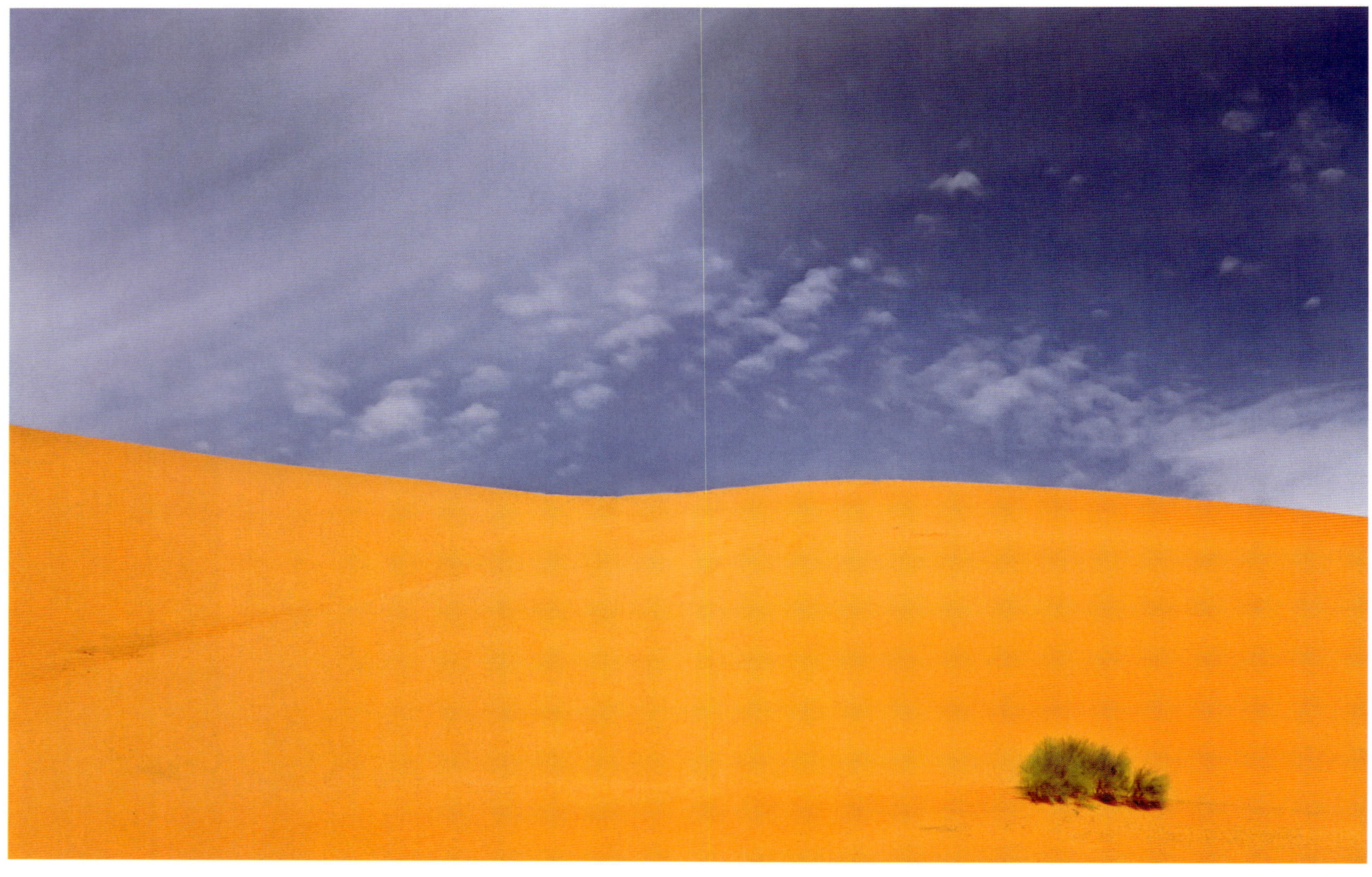

Light has various qualities, such as its direction and its hardness. When shooting in a studio these qualities can be controlled through the position of lights, the use of diffusers and reflectors, and so on.

The sun's light is less easily modified: the time of year and the time of day will determine the direction of sunlight, while the weather will affect the hardness or softness of the light. A key to successful landscapes is taking these factors into account when planning a photography session.

NOTE

Lens flare is light that's scattered around the glass elements in a lens. It's generally caused by strong point light sources (such as the sun) pointing directly into the lens. However, it can also be caused by light entering the lens from the side.

Above: Frontal light tends to flatten texture. This quality can be used to produce bold, but simple, graphic images.

Lighting Direction

There are four basic directions that light can fall onto a landscape relative to your camera: from the front, from the side, from above, and from the back.

Frontal lighting occurs when the light source is directly behind your camera, illuminating the scene in front of you. This immediately throws up one major problem: you and your camera's shadow will potentially project into the image space, especially if you're using a wide-angle lens. Another problem with frontal lighting is that your subject's shadows will be hidden. This is important, because shadows help to give shape to objects. Consequently, frontal lighting can produce flat-looking images with little sense of a subject's form or textural qualities. The one thing in frontal lighting's favor is that accurate exposure is relatively easy to determine.

Sidelighting is light that falls across a scene at roughly 90° to the camera position. The most common time to see sidelighting is at either end of the day, when the sun is low on the horizon. Of the four lighting directions, sidelighting is generally the preferred light for landscape photography. This is because it reveals texture and form, creating shadows than can make a landscape image appear three-dimensional (the lower the sun, the longer the shadows). The problem with sidelighting is that it can be high in contrast, so it can be difficult to work with on cloudless days.

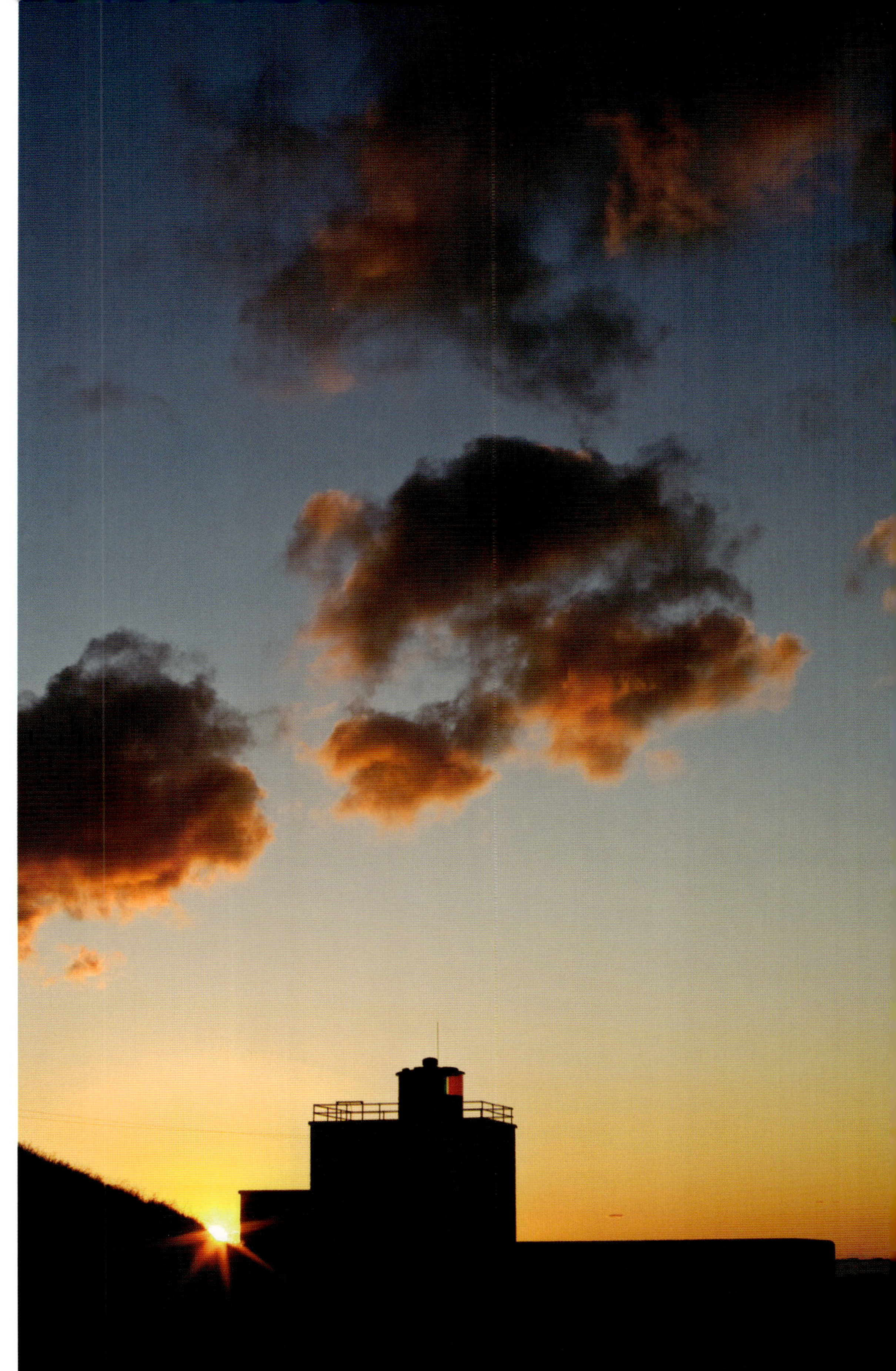

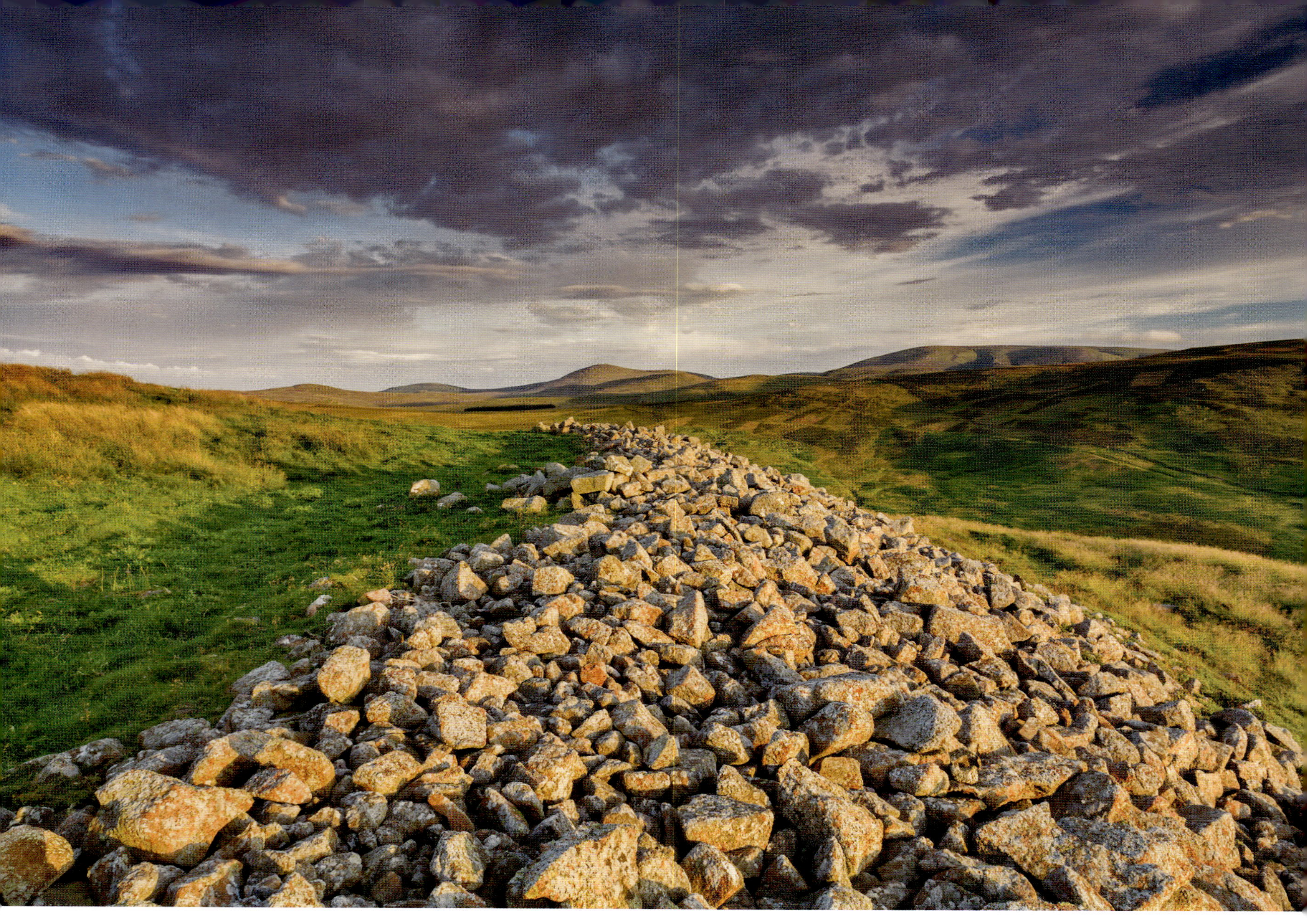

Light from above is arguably a variant of sidelighting. However, unlike sidelighting, light from above doesn't help to convey depth in an image, as shadows sit below the subject, rather than projecting away from it. Light from above is typically seen at midday in summer when the sun is at its highest in the sky. It is not a particularly attractive light to shoot under and should generally be avoided.

Backlighting occurs when light is behind your subject, shining toward the camera. This results in very high contrast, causing your subject to be rendered as a silhouette unless additional lighting is used (or an overexposed background should you set the exposure for the subject).

However, silhouettes can be very effective with the right subject. They work best with elements that are easily recognizable: a lone tree or a distinctive geological formation, for example. Complex or interlocking subjects are more difficult to "read" and can look messy visually.

Above: Sidelighting can be too contrasty without some softening of the light. In this image the last light of day was diffused by the clouds reflecting light into the shadows.

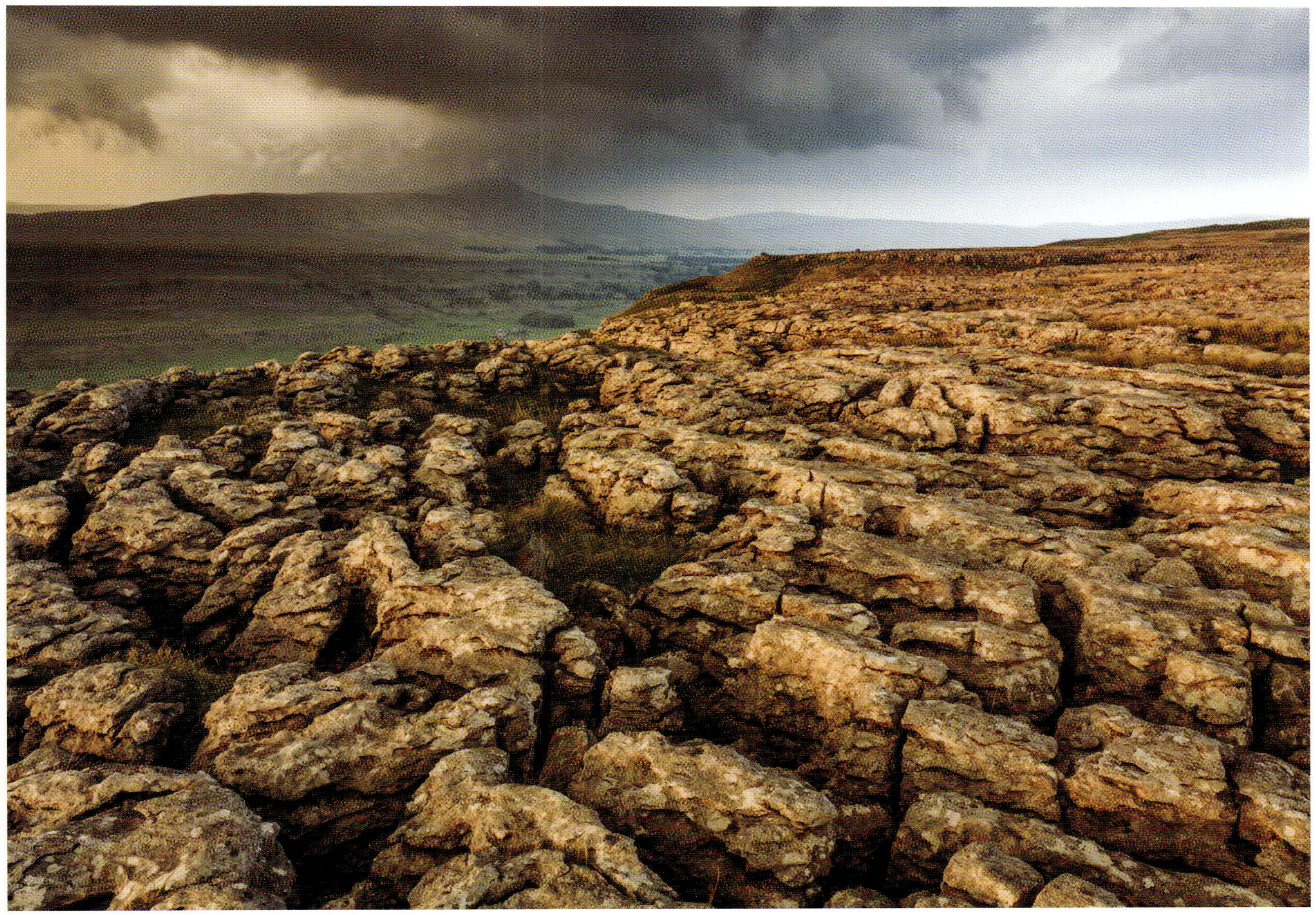

Hard & Soft Light

The second quality of light to be aware of is how hard or soft it is. Hard light emanates from a point light source and is strongly directional. A point light source is one that's smaller than the subject it illuminates. The sun on a cloudless day is a point light source. Although the sun is huge, because of its distance it is relatively small compared to most subjects you'll shoot in the landscape.

Hard lighting in high in contrast, producing deep, dark shadows with a sharp transition from light to shade. Glossy objects will also exhibit intense specular highlights, and although highly glossy objects are rare in nature, they do exist: leaves, particularly holly, often have distracting specular highlights in hard, direct lighting.

Very hard lighting is often undesirable for landscape photography as it suits geometric subjects better than softer, organic elements. However, rock formations and architecture within the landscape can benefit from hard light.

Above: Landscape photography often requires a "Goldilocks" light that's neither too hard nor too soft. Clouds soften sunlight by lightening shadows (rather like giant reflectors). However, too much cloud and the light will be undesirably soft; too little cloud and the light can be excessively hard. This is why locations sometimes need revisiting until the conditions are "just right."

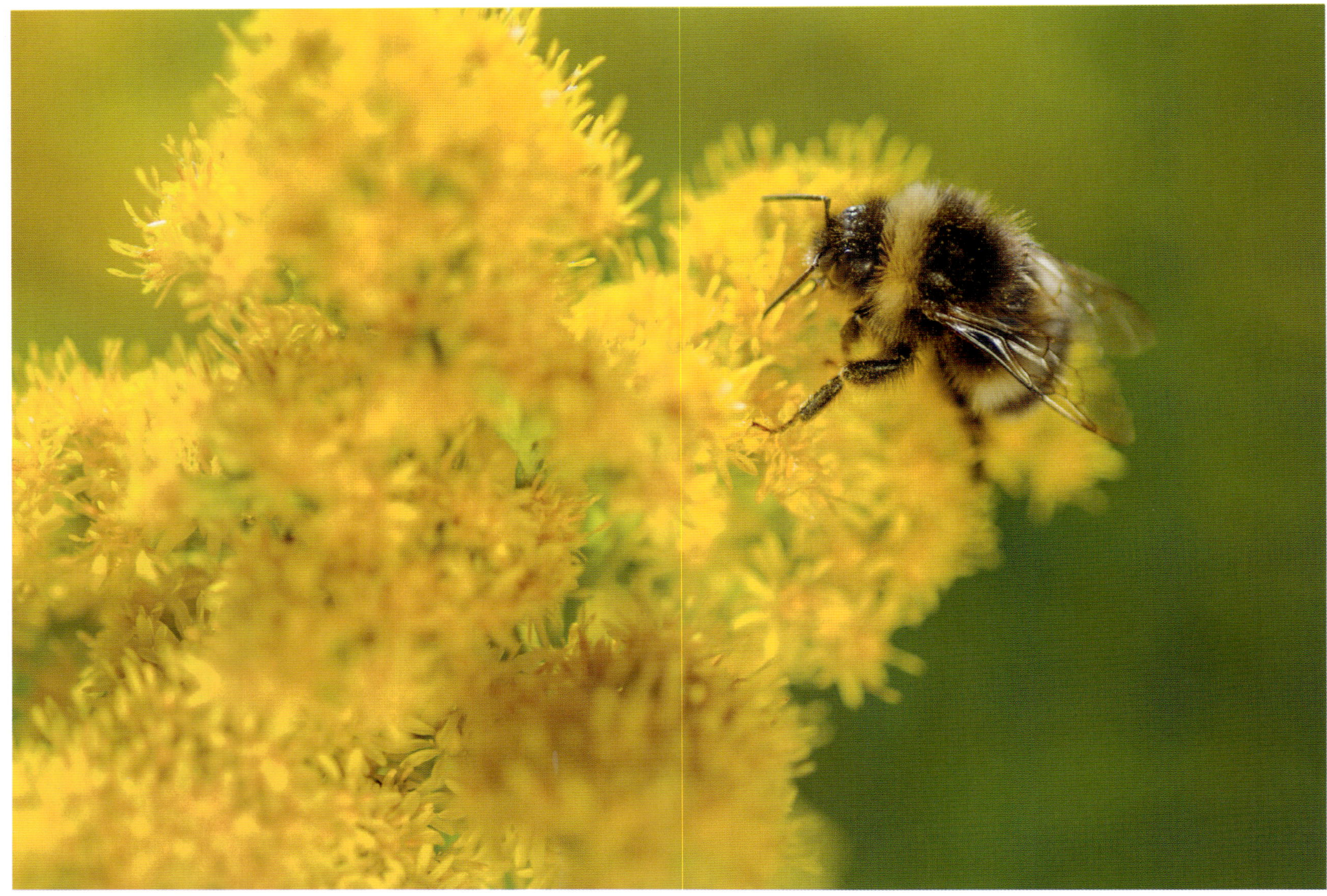

Soft light is created when the light source is larger than the subject being illuminated. Soft light is inherently low in contrast, so shadows are less deep and more attenuated than those created by hard lighting. Specular highlights are also less common, as any highlight created by soft lighting is less intense and spread out more.

In landscape photography, the light on an overcast day is the softest you will encounter. The light from the sun is spread out and diffused by the clouds, making it larger relative to the landscape. This is ideal for photographing details within the landscape, but very soft light is almost as undesirable as very hard light for broader landscape work. This is because shadows are a lot softer, so texture and form is less obvious. The exception to this is if you are working in woodland (see chapter 5).

Above: Soft lighting is ideal for soft, organic subjects. If the sunlight is too direct I will either use a reflector to fill in the shadows, or shade the subject to soften the light.

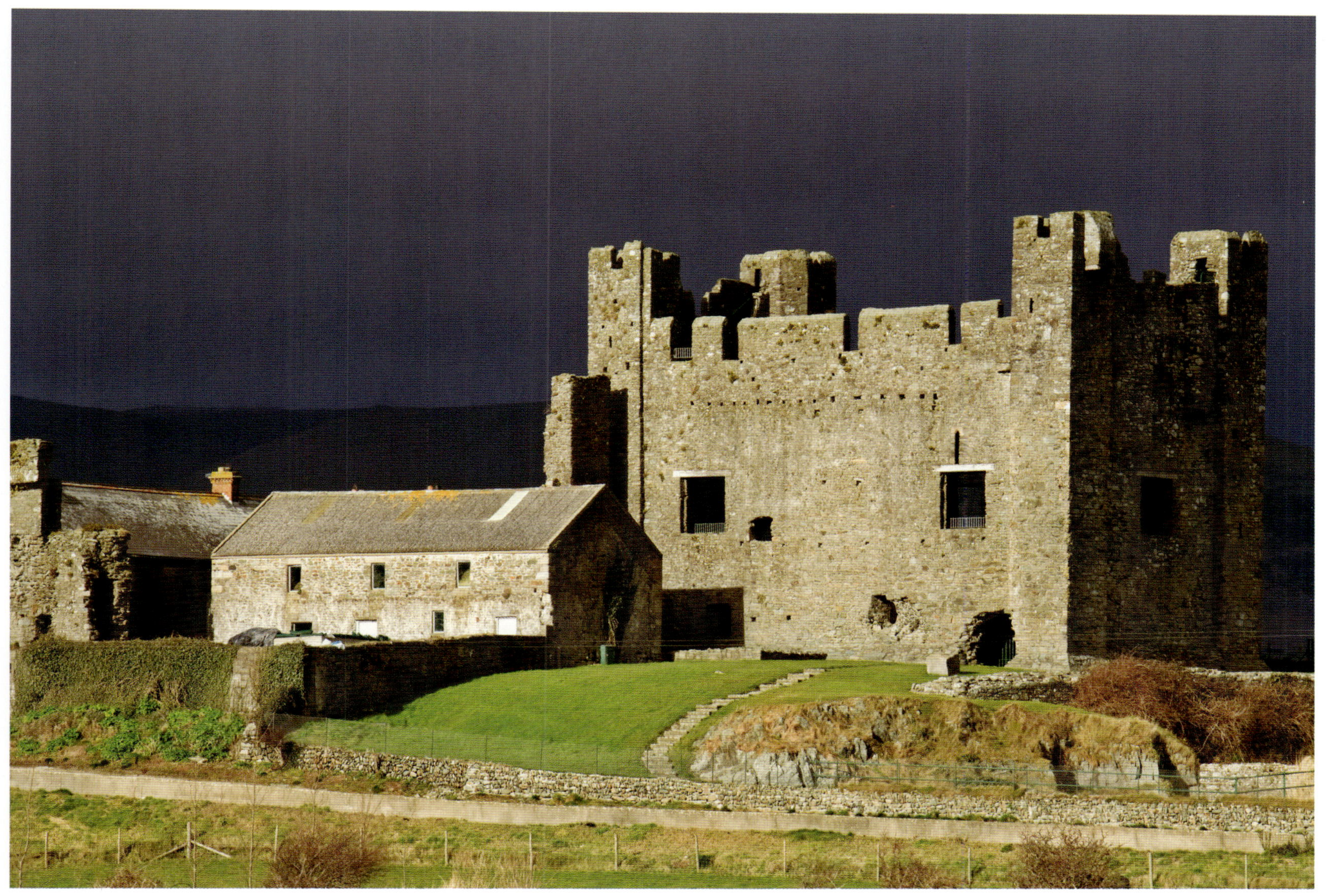

Tip

As soon as you shade a subject you'll need to alter the white balance, as the color temperature of the light will be higher.

Above: Hard light is best suited to more geometric subjects or those with strong textural qualities. Hard light is most often seen on cloudless days, although early morning or late afternoon sunlight breaking through low cloud will also produce a hard, spotlit effect.

Color Temperature

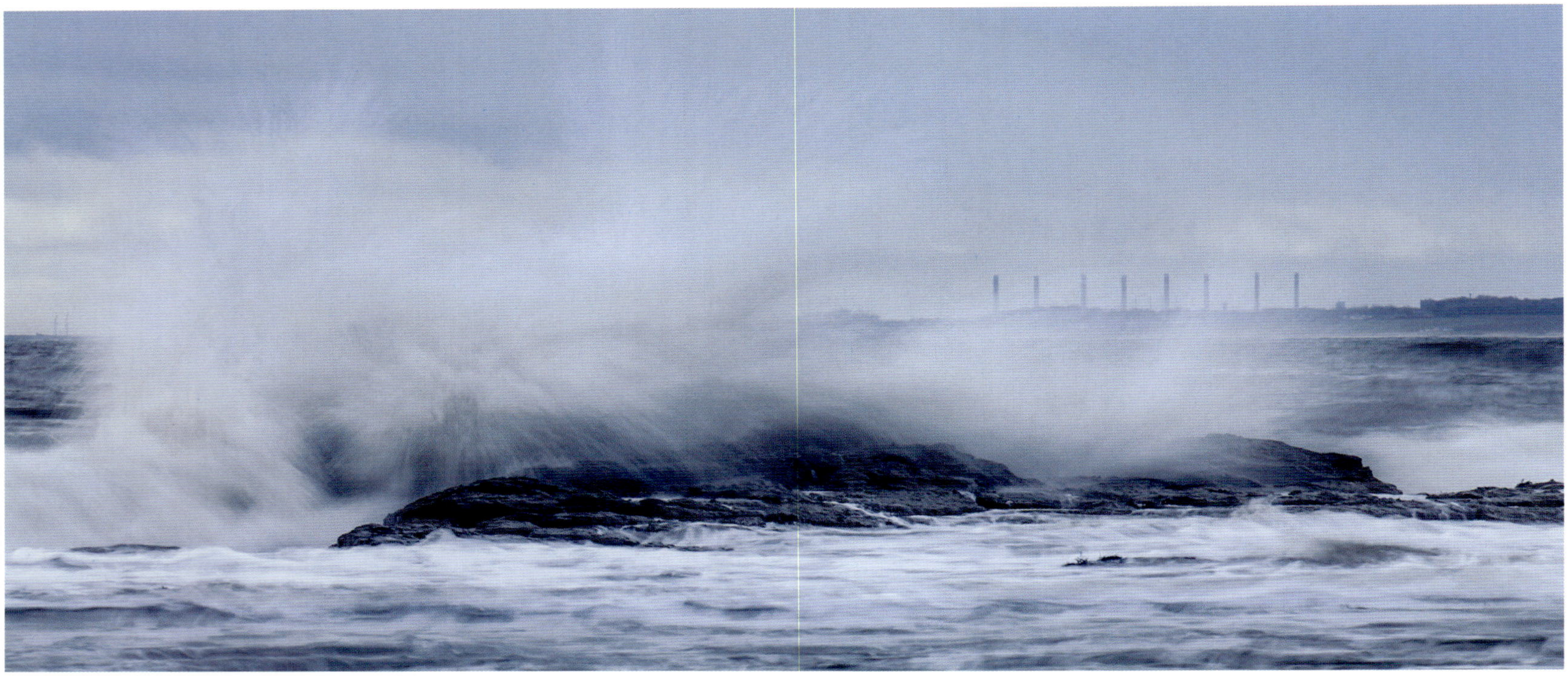

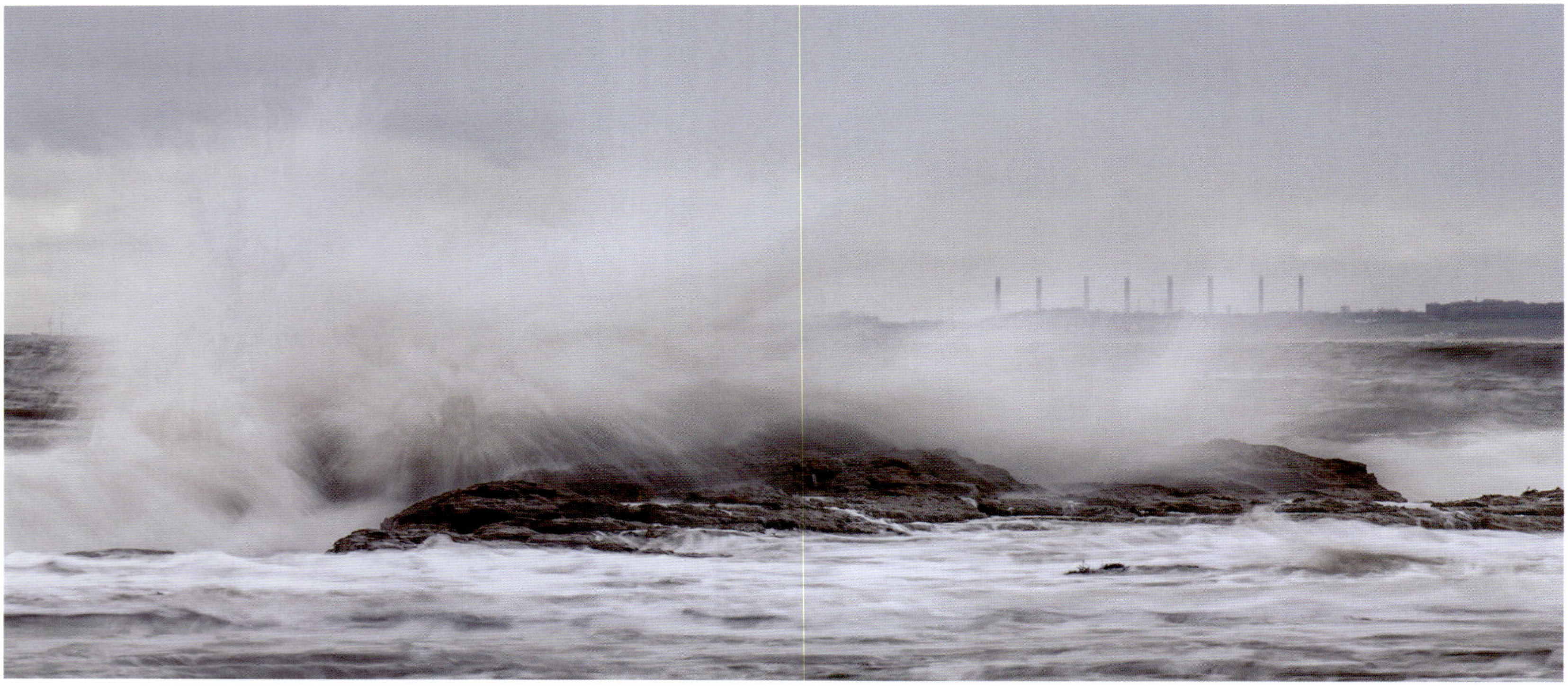

Light that has an equal mix of wavelengths is said to be neutral. However, if the light is biased toward a particular range of wavelengths it will change in color. Light that is biased toward red will be warm in color, whereas a blue bias will result in cooler light. This has nothing to do with heat, but psychologically red-orange light is felt to be "hotter" than blue light. This change in the bias of wavelengths affects what is referred to as the color temperature of the light, which is measured using the Kelvin scale (K).

Ordinary flames (from burning wood or candlelight) have a very low color temperature of 1800K, and is one of the warmest naturally occurring light sources. Light that is perfectly neutral is approximately 5200K (the color temperature of electronic flash and the light from the sun at midday). Light on an overcast day is far cooler, at approximately 6000–6500K, while the coolest light commonly encountered is the ambient light in deep shade (approximately 7000K). The grid to the right lists the color temperature of these and other light sources.

1800–2000K	Candlelight
2500K	Torchlight
2800K	Domestic lighting
3000K	Sunrise/sunset
3400K	Tungsten lighting
3500K	Morning/afternoon sunlight
5200K	Midday sunlight
5500K	Electronic flash
6000–6500K	Overcast conditions
7000–8000K	Shade

White Balance

The human brain is remarkably adept at adjusting for color temperature. It's only when the color temperature is extreme, or when two light sources with different color temperatures are juxtaposed, that we really take notice. A camera has a similar facility to correct for the color bias of light, which is known as "white balance."

This can be set to adjust automatically using a camera's auto white balance (AWB) function, or it can be set using a preset value or corrected manually (either by setting a specific Kelvin value or by creating a custom white balance).

White balance is achieved by adding more of a particular color into an image to counteract its absence from the light source. If a light source is cool blue in temperature, more red will be added to compensate, and vice versa.

Custom White Balance

Auto white balance automatically corrects an image to neutralize any color bias. However, it's not always entirely accurate. It can be easily fooled if there's a predominance of one color in a scene, for example: green woodland scenes are often falsely 'corrected" by the addition of magenta.

In many ways this isn't a problem when shooting Raw, as the white balance can be corrected during postproduction, but when shooting JPEGs it is more important to set the right white balance at the time of shooting.

The most accurate option is to set a custom white balance. The procedure varies between camera models, but the basic idea is that an image of a neutral gray surface (placed in the same light as your intended subject) is shot and assessed by the camera to produce a custom white balance.

There are certain types of light, such as the golden light of sunrise, that you wouldn't want to neutralize, but the light in woodland and on overcast days often benefits from the creation of a custom white balance.

White Balance Settings

Your camera's white balance control allows you to set your camera to match the color temperature of the prevalent lighting conditions. "Neutral" light has a color temperature of approximately 5200K, which is the color temperature of the sun at midday.

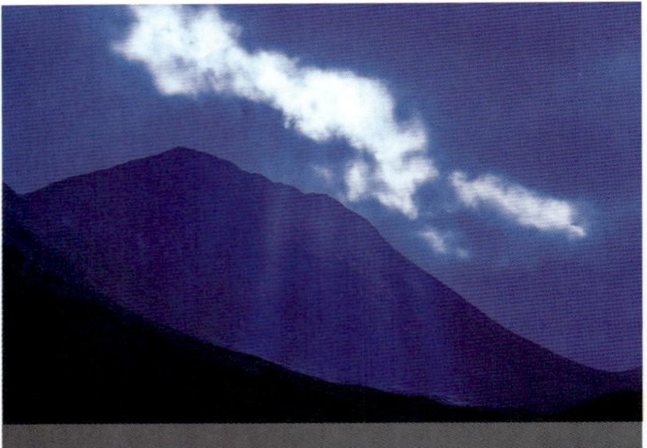

2000K
Often the lowest Kelvin setting available on a camera. Unless the light source is very red-orange, this setting will produce images that are a deep blue color.

TUNGSTEN
Designed to correct the orange tint of incandescent bulbs, produces more subtly blue images that can add atmosphere to a landscape image.

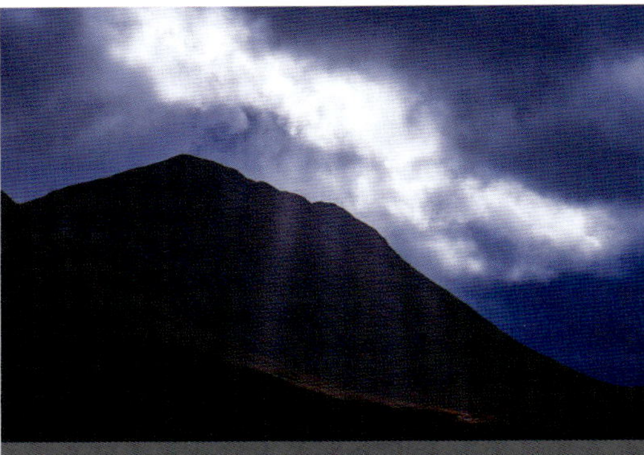

FLUORESCENT
Fluorescent lighting tends to be cooler than incandescent lighting, so requires less red-orange correction. adds magenta to correct for the green bias of fluorescent lighting.

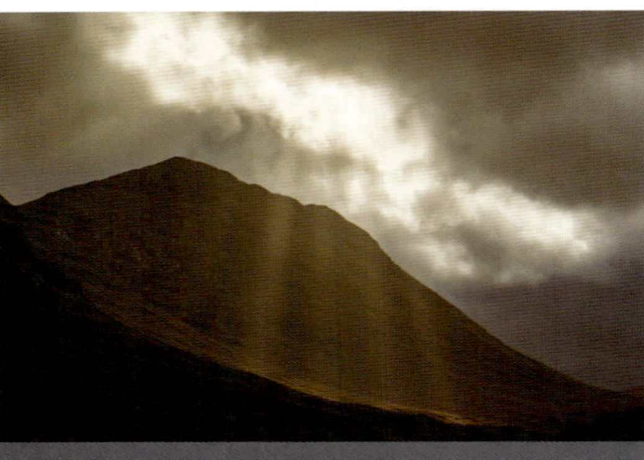

FLASH
Flash light is neutral (so that there's no color bias). It's reasonably close to , to the point that the two can often be used interchangeably.

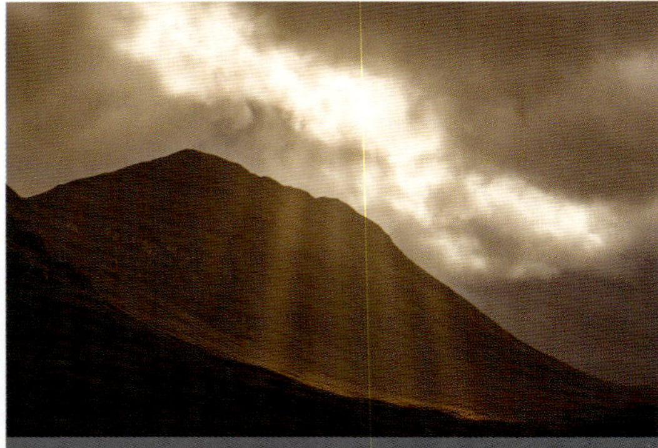

CLOUDY
The ambient light from total cloud cover is appreciably cooler in color than sunlight. To counteract this, adds red-orange to an image, warming it up.

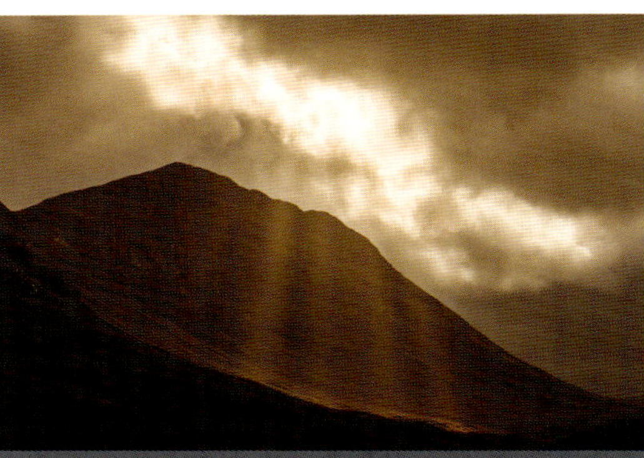

SHADE
The ambient light of open shade is considerably cooler than overcast light. To control this warms an image up still further. Used in normal daylight, produces over-rich images that look decidedly unnatural.

DAYLIGHT ☀

☀ is designed to be correct at midday on a cloudless day. As a default it's a good starting point if you're planning to adjust white balance in postproduction.

10,000K

Often the highest possible Kelvin setting on a camera. 10,000K is only suitable to correct very blue light, such as ambient light before sunrise or after sunset. However, uncorrected images would arguably have more atmosphere at these times.

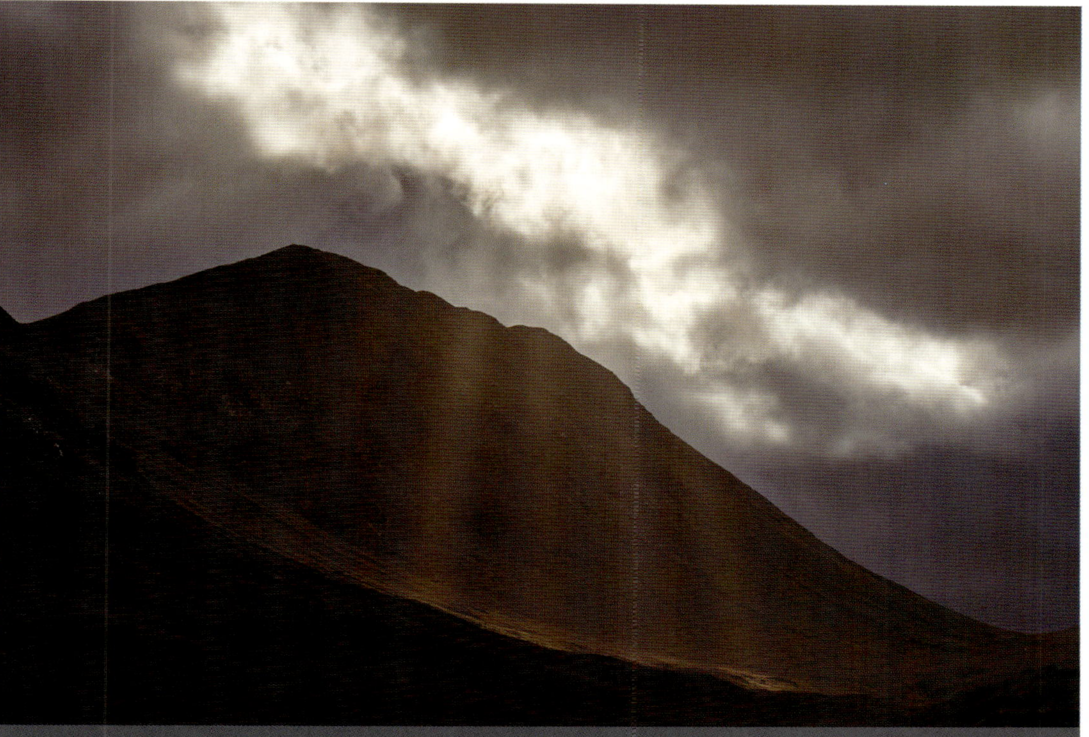

CUSTOM

The greatest control over white balance comes from your camera's custom setting. This allows you to set a white balance for the color temperature of a specific lighting condition. This was the setting used to create this image (5000K with no green/magenta adjustment).

Time of Day

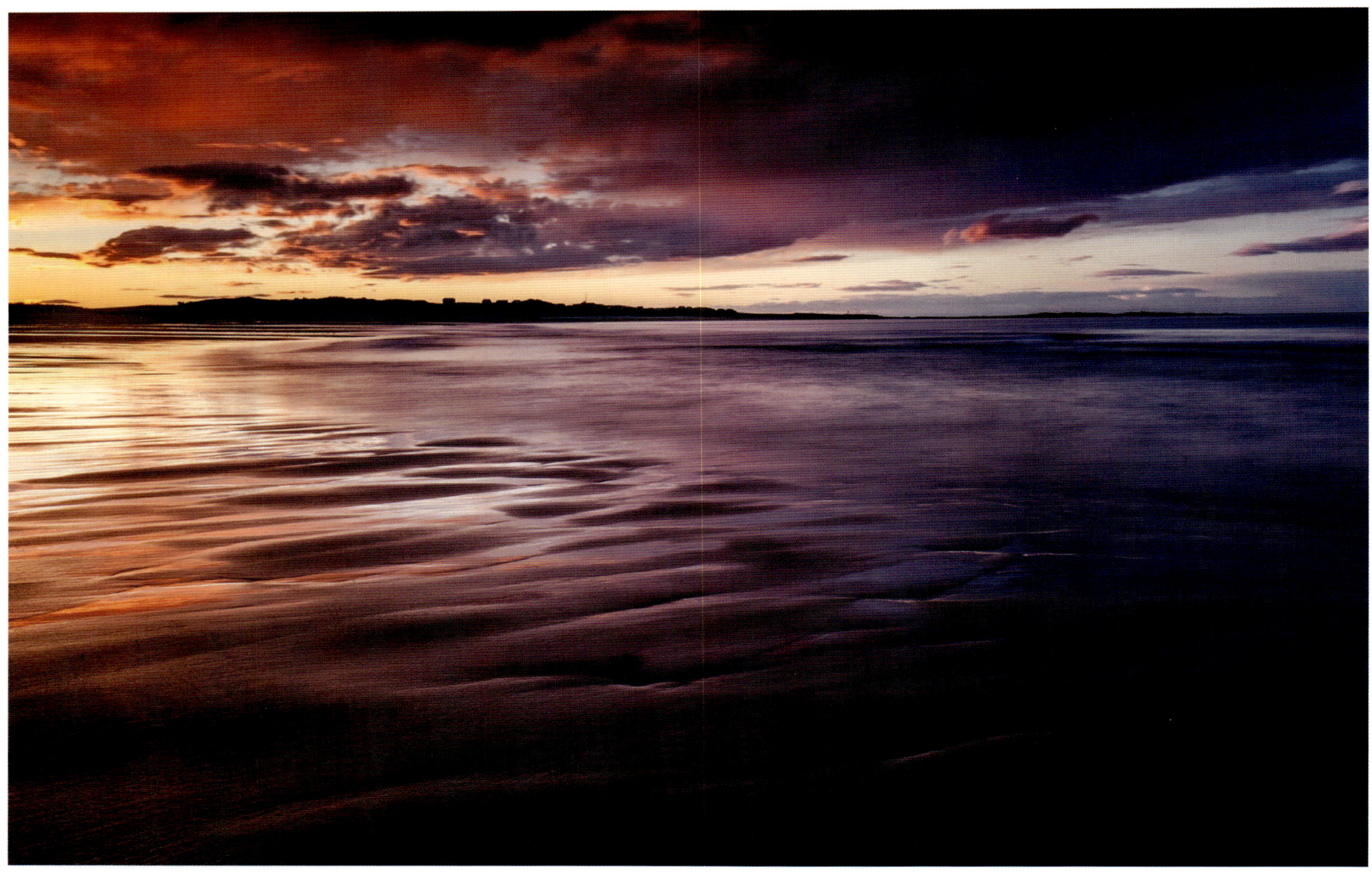

The light from the sun is biased toward red at sunrise and sunset (with a color temperature of around 3000K). This is because the blue wavelengths of light are scattered and absorbed by the atmosphere to a far greater degree than the red-orange wavelengths. The light also tends to be less intense and softer at this time of day.

As the sun rises, the color temperature of the light becomes more neutral, with a more balanced range of wavelengths. At midday, when the sun is at its highest, the light is at its most neutral (although during the local winter months the sun doesn't rise high above the horizon so the light can remain warm throughout the day). At this time the sun's light is also at its most intense, so in a cloudless sky the contrast can be high.

Once past midday the sun sinks in the sky and the color temperature becomes lower, with the light becoming gradually more red-orange again.

Above: Sunlight is at its warmest before sunrise or after sunset. However, this warmth doesn't illuminate the landscape directly. It can only be seen if there's sufficient cloud to reflect it back down onto the landscape.

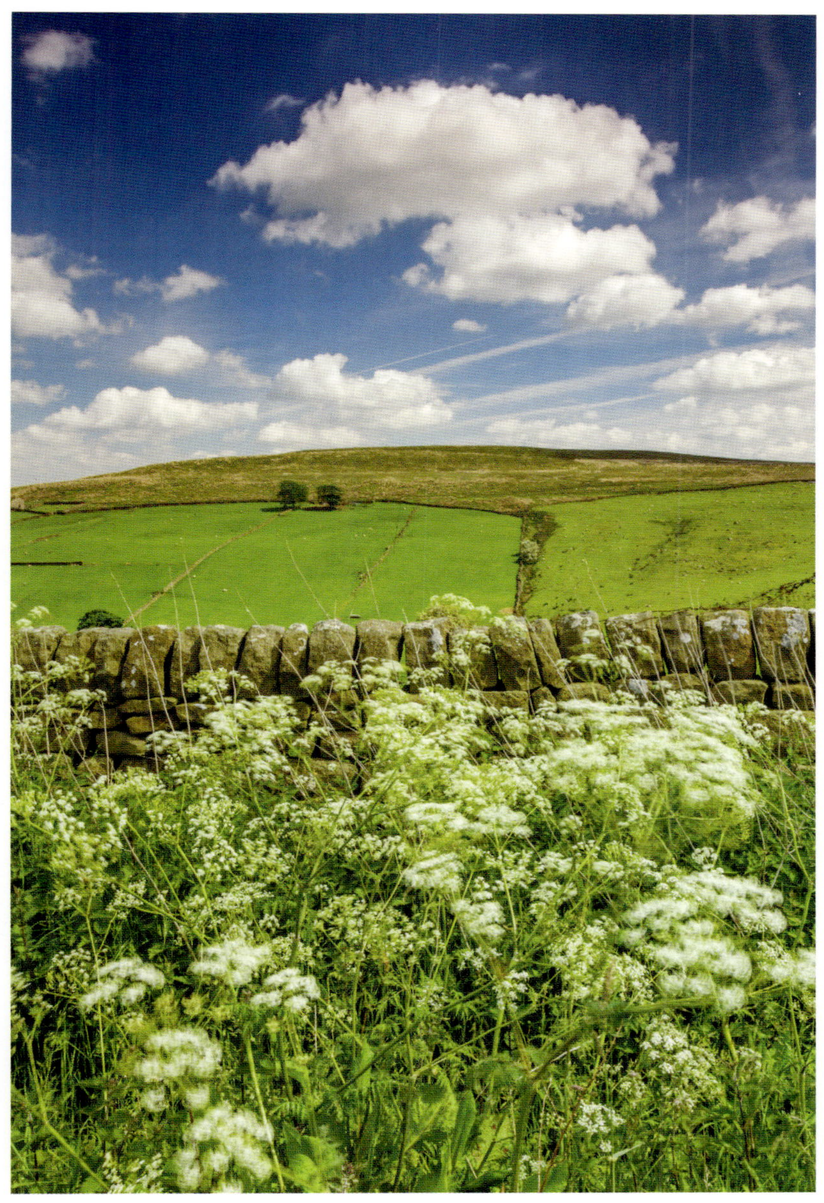

Above: Sunlight stays relatively neutral for most of the day during the summer months. This image was shot in the middle of the afternoon and—in terms of color—there's a neutral quality to the light.

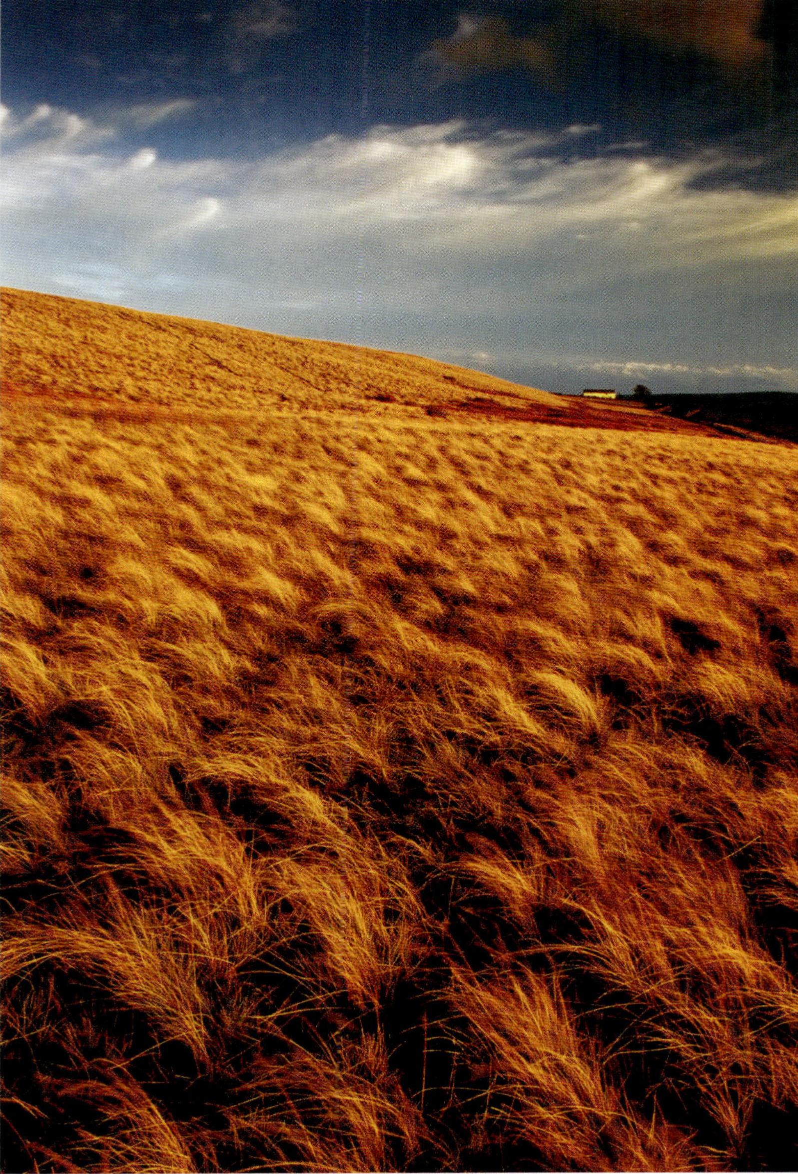

Above: Winter sees the color of sunlight stay relatively warm throughout the day (although ironically it's usually cool or even cold in terms of temperature). This image was shot about 30 minutes before sunset, when the intensity of the color was building toward its maximum.

NOTE

The "Golden Hour" is a period of roughly one hour after sunrise and one hour before sunset when sunlight is at its warmest. This period lasts a shorter length of time in summer than it does in winter.

Weather & Light

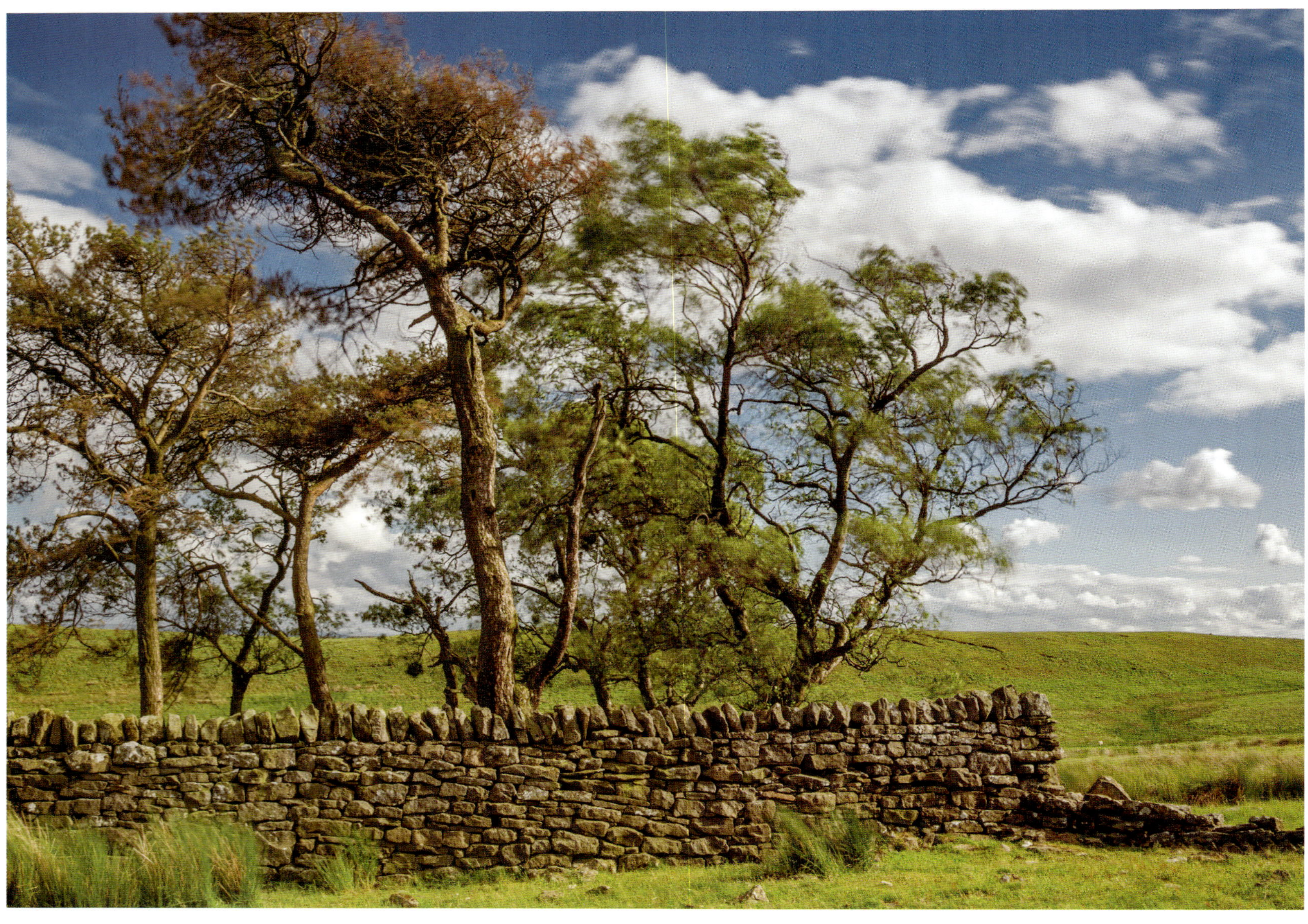

The weather has a strong effect on the quality of the light. Clouds soften sunlight, either by covering the sun entirely or by bouncing light into shadows, and hazy conditions can produce a similar effect. Periods of settled weather over several days can cause haze to gradually build, and this is particularly true in summer when dust and pollution can be trapped by high-pressure weather systems. After a few days this can produce a thick, unattractive haze that severely reduces visibility.

It's only when rain finally returns that the air is "washed" clean again and visibility is restored. Haze does have one redeeming feature, though: sunsets can often be spectacular, if the haze isn't so thick that the sun disappears prematurely into the murk.

Above: Unsettled weather often means high winds. This can make it difficult to keep your tripod and camera steady, so in these conditions you may find it beneficial to shoot with the camera lower to the ground.

In many ways, settled conditions—whether long periods of sunshine or rain—aren't that rewarding for landscape photography. Instead, the most interesting and rewarding times to be out shooting are when the weather is unsettled; when rain is either on its way or receding. This means that you have to be prepared to get wet, and to adjust and react to the situation as it develops.

However, this is often worth the inconvenience, as the light in these conditions can be fleeting, dappling the landscape then disappearing as rapidly as it arrived. This makes it hard to predict what you'll be able shoot, but that's half the fun.

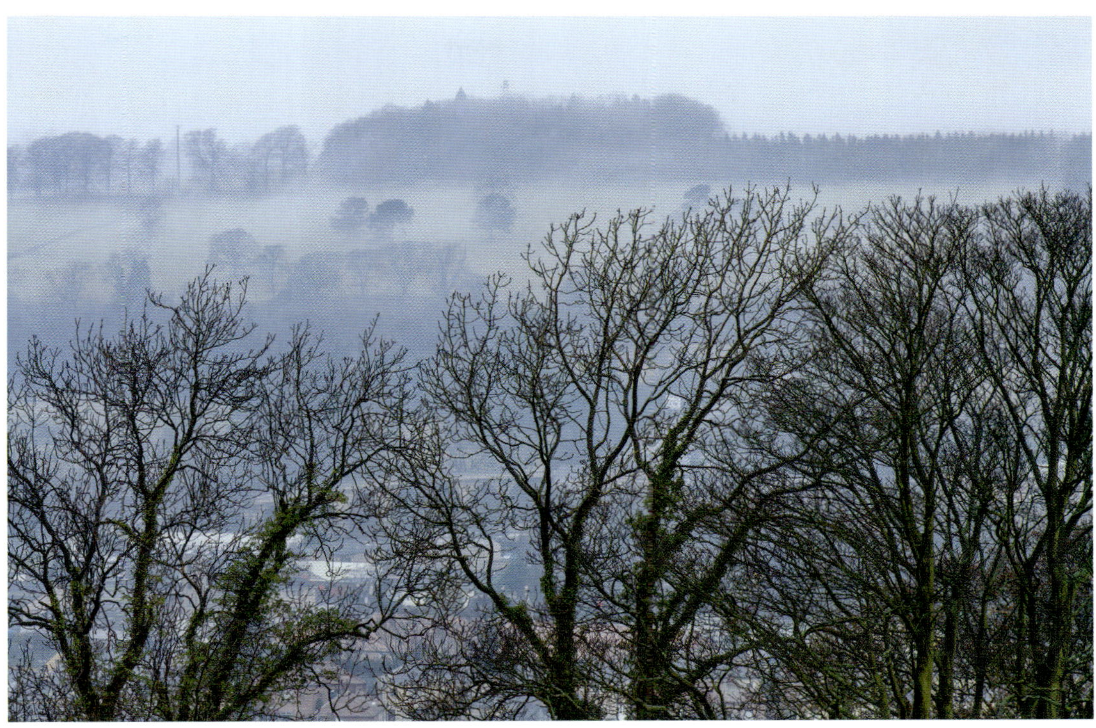

Right: Mist or low cloud softens and diffuses light. If the sun is obscured, the color temperature will be biased toward blue.

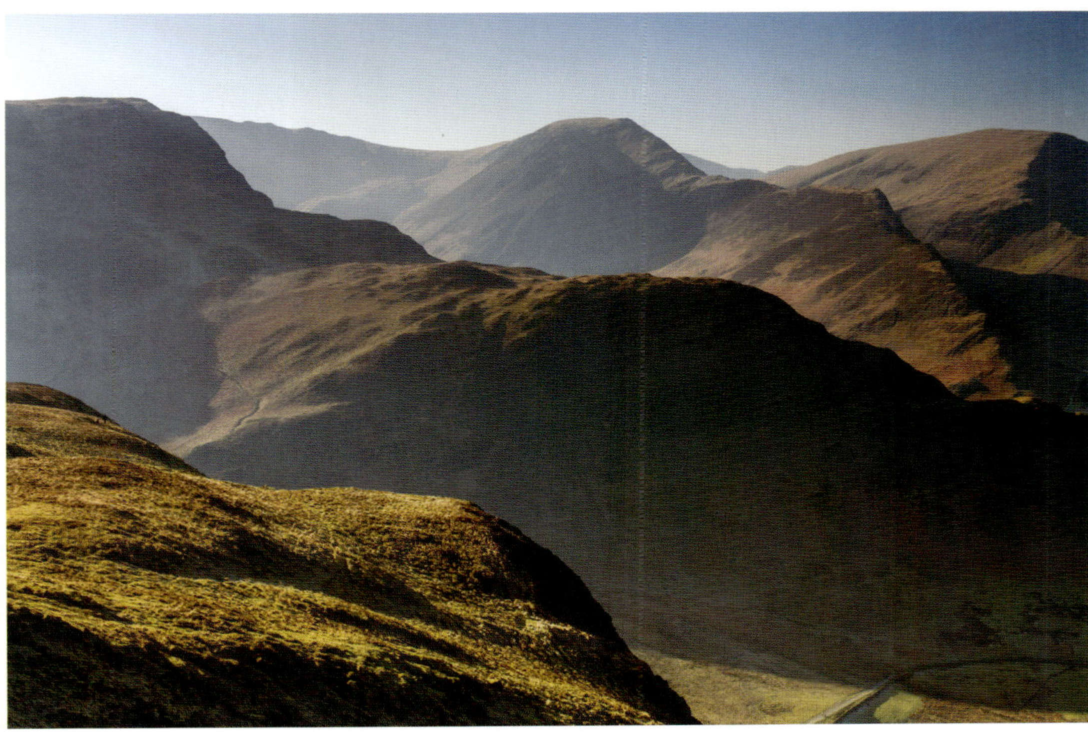

Right: Cloudless days result in high-contrast lighting, but for some subjects this can be advantageous. Although slightly softened by haze, the hard shadows on these hills help to define the shape and texture of the landscape.

Chapter 4
Preparation

To make the most of your landscape photography it's important to plan ahead. There's nothing more certain to disappoint than arriving at a location at the wrong time of day or even at the wrong time of year; planning a shoot will help you iron out any potential problems before you arrive at your chosen location. Fortunately, landscape photographers are spoilt for choice when it comes to web sites and apps that provide useful information, so it's possible to work out sunrise times, tides, and even moon phases far ahead of time. This isn't to take away the delight that an unexpected photographic event can bring, but the more information you have ahead of time, the greater your chances of success will be.

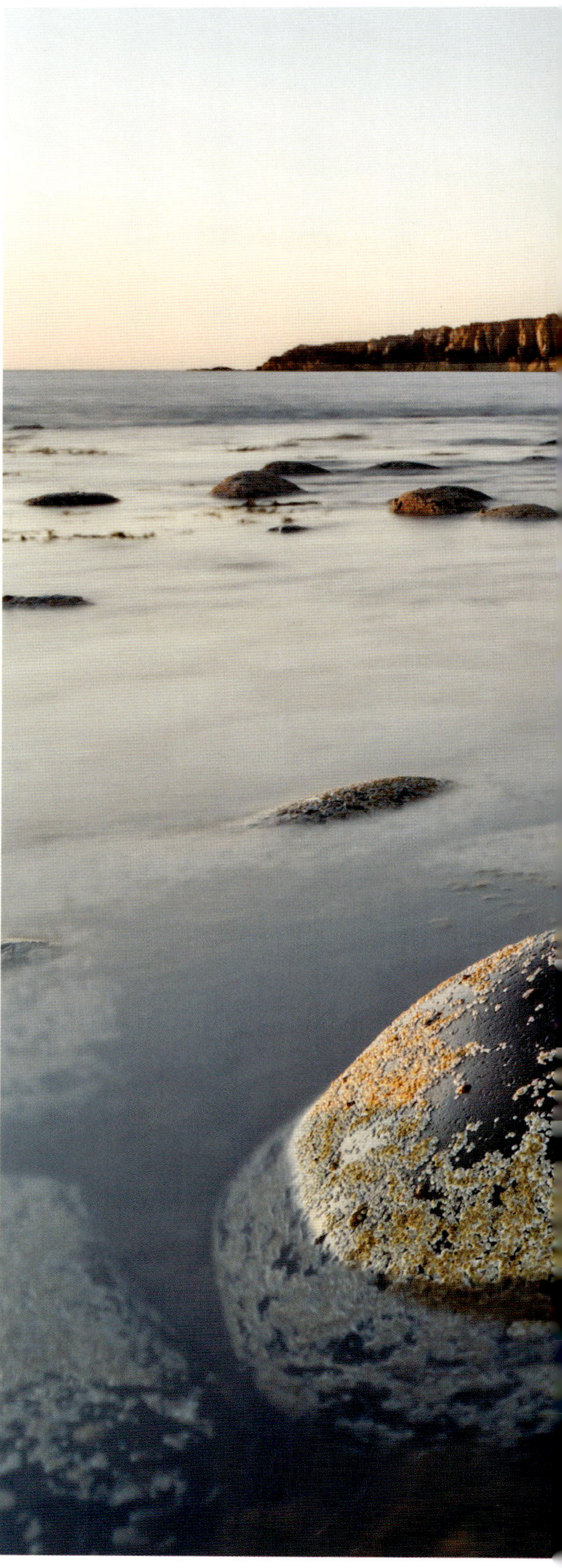

Right: Knowing where and when the sun will rise is important when planning a shoot. That information was vital here, as was knowing the times for high and low tide. This image was shot in summer when the sun rose in the north east, lighting this north-facing beach.

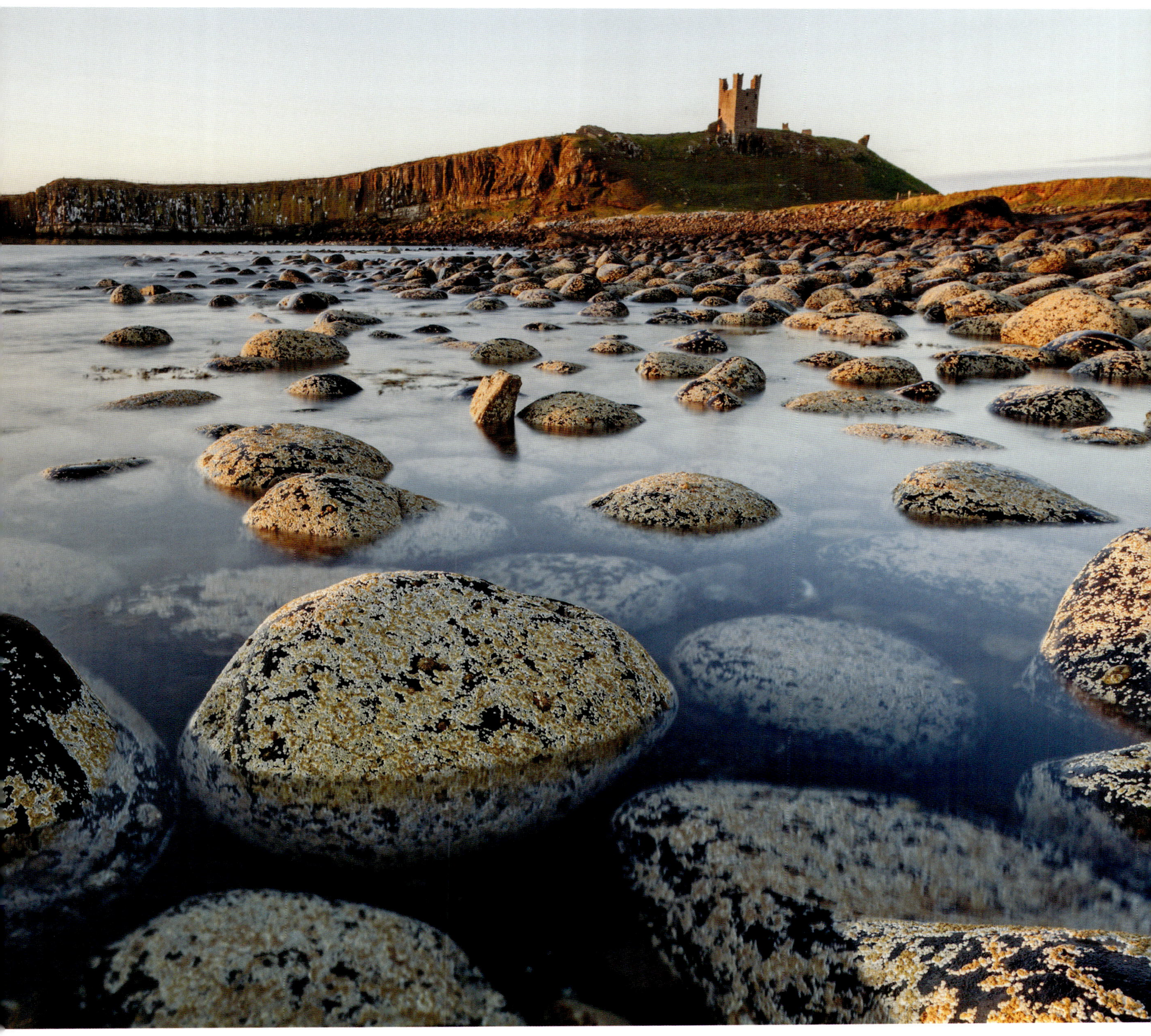

The Sun

Early morning or late afternoon is a good time to be out photographing the landscape. This is mainly due to the quality of light at these times of day, which are known as the "Golden Hours." This is when the sunlight is at its warmest in color, which only occurs when the sun has just risen or is close to setting. Knowing the local sunrise and sunset times should therefore be an important element of the planning process. However, that's not the entire story: knowing *where* the sun rises or sets will also help you calculate how your chosen subject will be lit at these times of day.

Seasonal Variability

The further north or south you go relative to the equator, the greater the sun's seasonal variation over the course of the year. Latitude affects the time that the sun rises and sets, the direction it rises, and the maximum height reached at midday (it also affects the weather, although other factors also play a part in how cold, warm, wet, or dry a particular place is over the course of a year).

March and September 20/21 mark the equinoxes, when the hours of day and night are roughly equal across the globe.

On June 20/21 the northern hemisphere sees its summer solstice, on which date the hours of daylight are at their longest (for a period around the summer solstice the Arctic Circle experiences 24 hours of daylight, with the sun never setting). On the same date, the southern hemisphere sees its winter solstice with daylight hours at their shortest (and for a period the Antarctic Circle experiences 24 hours of night, with the sun never rising).

This situation is reversed on December 20/21 when the northern hemisphere experiences its winter solstice and the southern hemisphere sees its summer solstice.

The change in where the sun rises is more subtle. At the equinoxes, the sun rises almost

SUNRISE/SUNSET DIRECTION

Latitude	Nearest city (northern/southern hemisphere)	Local summer solstice		Local winter solstice	
		Sunrise	Sunset	Sunrise	Sunset
70°	Tromsø/–	-	-	-	-
60°	Oslo/–	35°	325°	140°	220°
50°	London/Puntas Arenas	49°	311°	128°	228°
40°	New York/Valdivia	58°	302°	120°	240°
30°	Austin/Porto Alegre	62°	298°	117°	243°
20°	Querétaro/Iquique	65°	295°	115°	244°
10°	Limon/Palmas	66°	293°	114°	246°
0°	Singapore/Quito	67°	293°	113°	247°

MAXIMUM SUN ELEVATION

Latitude	Nearest city (northern/southern hemisphere)	June		December	
		Northern hemisphere	Southern hemisphere	Northern hemisphere	Southern hemisphere
70°	Tromsø/–	43°	–	–	43°
60°	Oslo/–	53°	7°	7°	53°
50°	London/Puntas Arenas	63°	16°	16°	63°
40°	New York/Valdivia	73°	27°	27°	73°
30°	Austin/Porto Alegre	83°	37°	36°	83°
20°	Querétaro/Iquique	86°	47°	47°	86°
10°	Limon/Palmas	77°	57°	57°	77°
0°	Singapore/Quito	67°	67°	67°	67°

NOTE

The equator sees very little seasonal variability. Daylight hours are broadly equal to night and the sun rises and sets roughly east and west over the course of a year.

directly due east and sets due west. From the March equinox through to June, the sun rises and sets at a gradually more northerly angle, reaching its northern peak on June 21. From that date onward the sun gradually starts rising and setting closer to direct east and west once more.

From the September equinox through to March, the sun rises and sets south of east and west respectively, with the most southerly extent occurring on December 21st. The extent of this variability is affected by latitude. The further north or south you travel relative to the equator, the greater the north/south variability over the course of the year.

Finally, the height (or elevation) of the sun at midday changes over the course of the year as well. At local summer solstice the sun reaches its highest possible elevation in the sky. However, come the local winter solstice, the elevation of the sun at midday is much lower. The closer to the poles you travel, the lower the elevation will be, with the sun not rising above the horizon at all in the Arctic and Antarctic circles.

As mentioned previously, the color of sunlight is warmer the closer the sun is to the horizon, which is why winter is such a good time to be out photographing the landscape. Because the sun doesn't climb as high in the sky the light stays warmer in color over the course of the day. In summer any warmth in the color temperature is lost relatively early in the morning and occurs relatively late in the afternoon.

Right: Ideally, you should be at your location at least 30 minutes before you need to begin shooting. This will give you time to work out what you want to photograph, and how. If you're aiming for a specific event (such as sunrise or sunset) you should work backward from the time of the event, taking into account your setting up time and the time it will take you to get to your chosen location. I underestimated the time it would take me to get to this location for sunrise; as a result I was more rushed and flustered than I should have been!

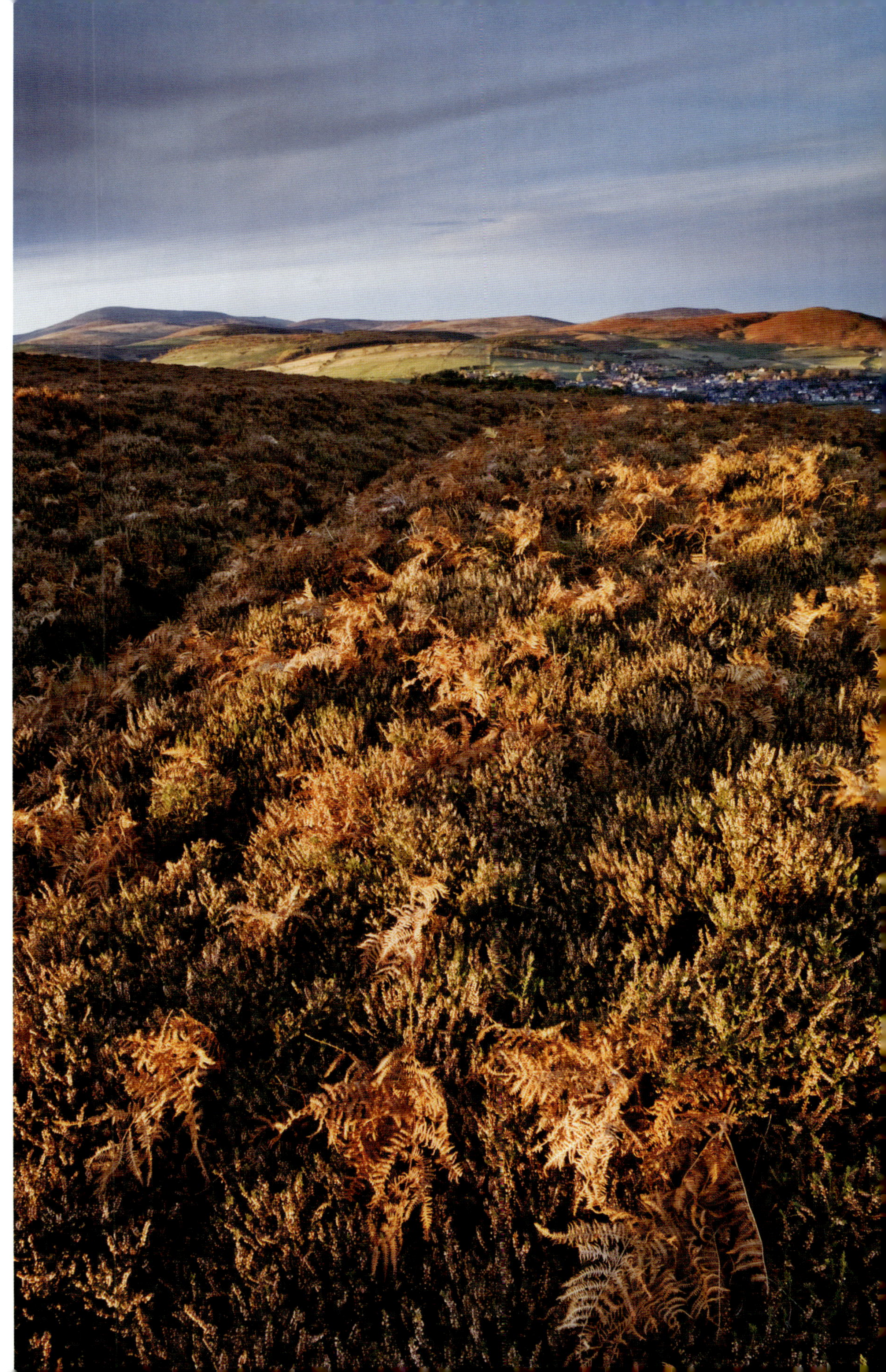

On Location

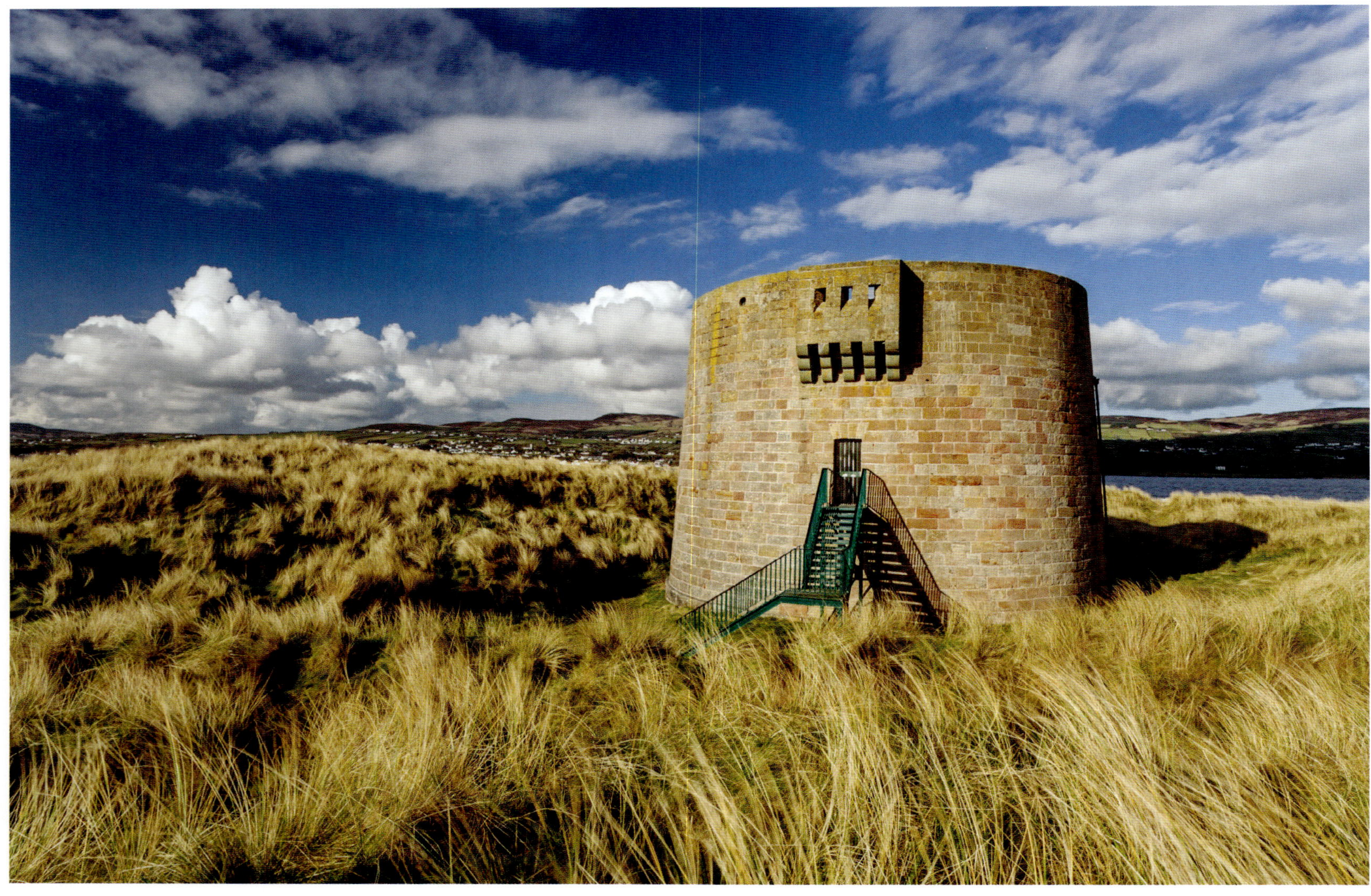

There are two types of location: locations that are close to home and locations that are further afield. Locations that are close to home are obviously easier to visit on the spur of the moment, and while you might think that familiarity would breed contempt, there's something to be said for locations you can revisit over and over. Seasonal changes and different weather conditions mean that a location will look different in some way each time you visit. Getting to know a location over several years is a good way to see how the landscape changes over time. The trap to avoid is shooting the same image repeatedly: looking for something new in a familiar location is a good exercise for developing your compositional eye.

You'll be able to use your local knowledge when planning a trip to a nearby location, which isn't possible with a location that's further away. Research beforehand is the only way to make the best of more distant locations, and thanks to the Internet it's far

Above: This image was shot on a two-week photography trip to Northern Ireland. To prepare for the trip I bought maps and downloaded relevant brochures from local tourist information web sites. I then spent time before traveling drawing up a "wish list" of interesting locations and the times of day that would best suit them.

easier now to research potential destinations. You shouldn't forget traditional sources of information, though. Paper maps (particularly those with contour

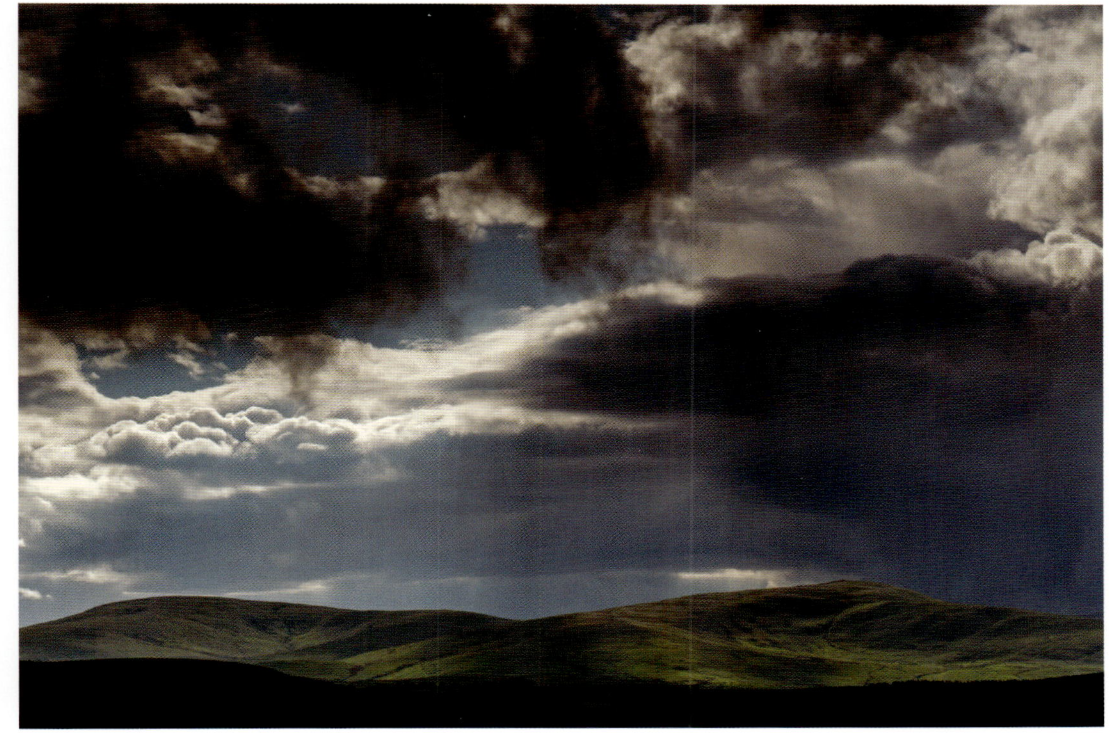

> **Tip**
>
> Sometimes there's a need to be away from home overnight to be at a location at the right time. This obviously requires further planning: either booking accommodation or finding somewhere to camp (depending on your comfort needs). If you stay in accommodation make sure you can get out easily first thing in the morning if you're planning a dawn shoot. There's nothing more frustrating than not being able to get out of a place until everyone else is awake.

lines) will help you get a sense of the shape and form of a landscape, which is important if you plan to be at a location for sunrise or sunset. You don't want to arrive at a chosen spot to discover an inconvenient hill blocks the sun at the wrong moment!

Taking Care of Yourself

Although landscape photography isn't inherently dangerous, there are still risks and discomforts that come with any physical activity in the outdoors. However, these can be minimized by thinking ahead.

Cold Weather

The first consideration should be wearing suitable clothing. Even in summer the weather can change quickly in hilly areas, so carrying layers of warm clothing that is both windproof and waterproof is essential. There can often be long periods of waiting around for light when shooting landscape images, so while you may be warm when you arrive at a location your temperature can drop rapidly once you stop. This is why multiple layers are often better than one or two thick items of clothing—you can add or remove layers to control your temperature. Consider investing in comfortable boots that support your ankles, although for working at the coast, rubber boots are preferable (they're less affected by salt water as well as being more waterproof).

The one part of the body that it's difficult to effectively protect in cold weather is your hands. Thick gloves make using your camera's controls difficult, while taking the gloves off to press buttons or turn dials rather defeats the purpose. Thinner, more tactile gloves aren't as effective at keeping your hands warm either. The solution is to combine the two so that you have a thick pair of outer gloves and less heavy inner gloves. You can then take the outer gloves off to use your camera, but still have some protection for your hands.

Hot Weather

Dehydration and sunburn are the biggest problems when working in hot conditions. Avoiding the midday sun is the easiest solution, and this will also mean avoiding the flattest, least aesthetically pleasing light of the day. It's generally cooler at either end of the day and the light is often more pleasing. If you've no choice but to be out in the blazing sun, try to find shade for you and your camera whenever you can. Wear light, loose clothing that covers both your arms and legs. A broad-brimmed hat will prevent your forehead and face from becoming burnt, but any

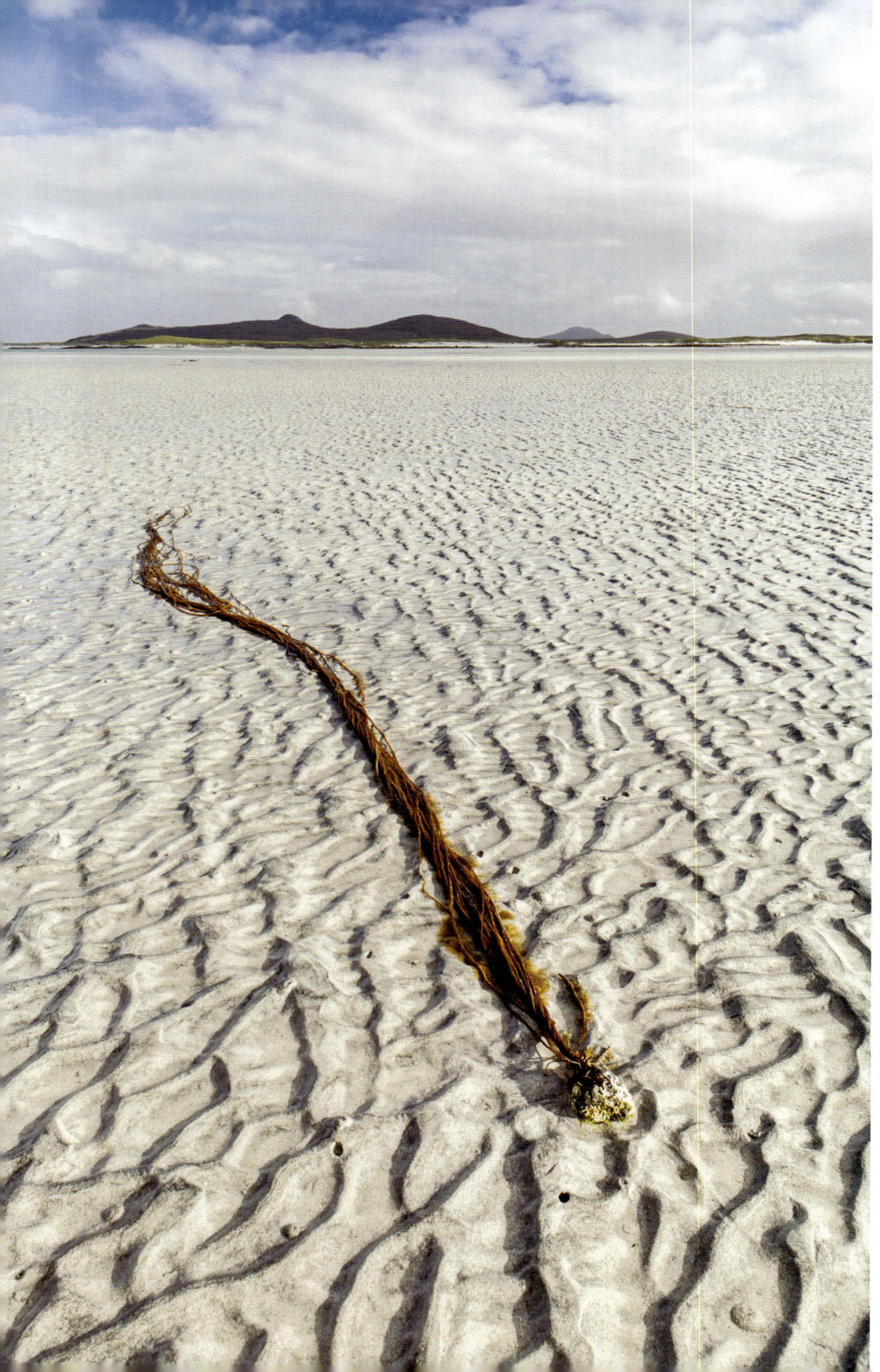

areas of skin that aren't covered should be coated in high factor sunscreen. Take plenty of water with you and be sure to drink regularly, not just when you start feeling thirsty.

General Safety

If you need to walk some distance to reach your chosen location you should decide on the route beforehand and let someone know the route. If possible, let that person know your approximate time of return as well. Cell phones are useful for emergencies, but they shouldn't be relied upon—in hilly areas it's often difficult to get a signal. For this reason, carrying a whistle is also recommended. The signal for distress in Britain is six short blasts followed by a period of silence; this is repeated until help arrives.

Pack an up-to-date map of your intended location in your camera bag, along with a compass (and learn how to use both effectively). GPS systems are useful as well, but like cell phones they shouldn't be relied upon—batteries can die at awkward moments and make the device useless.

Packing a head torch is also recommended, especially if you intend to be out before dawn or after sunset. Wearing a head torch frees your hands to hold a map or keep balance when clambering over rocks.

Right top: This image was shot relatively late in the afternoon in Morocco. I benefited from the lower temperatures at that time of day and aesthetically the longer shadows were more pleasing.

Right bottom: The most satisfying time to be shooting at the coast is when the tide is close to high, there are waves crashing on the shore, and the weather is interesting. Planning to be out on these occasions involves careful coordination of several information streams.

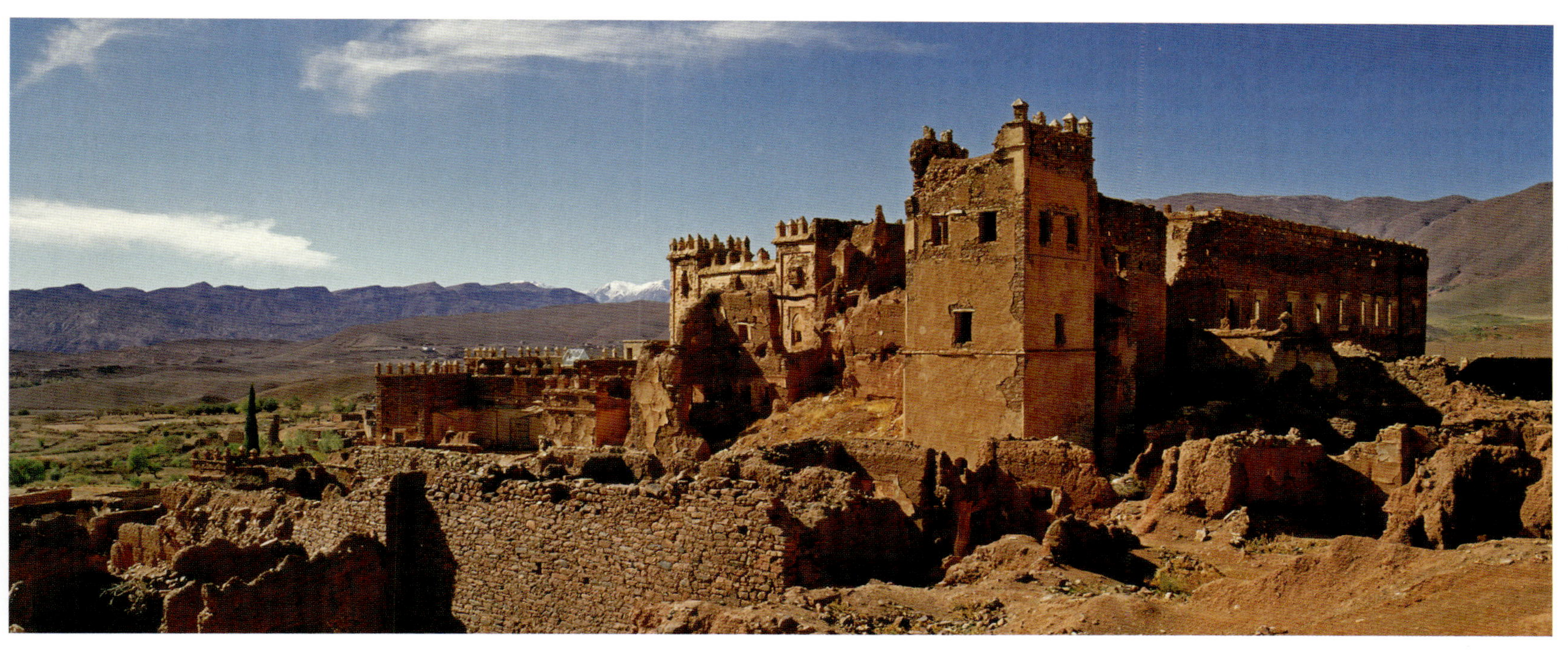

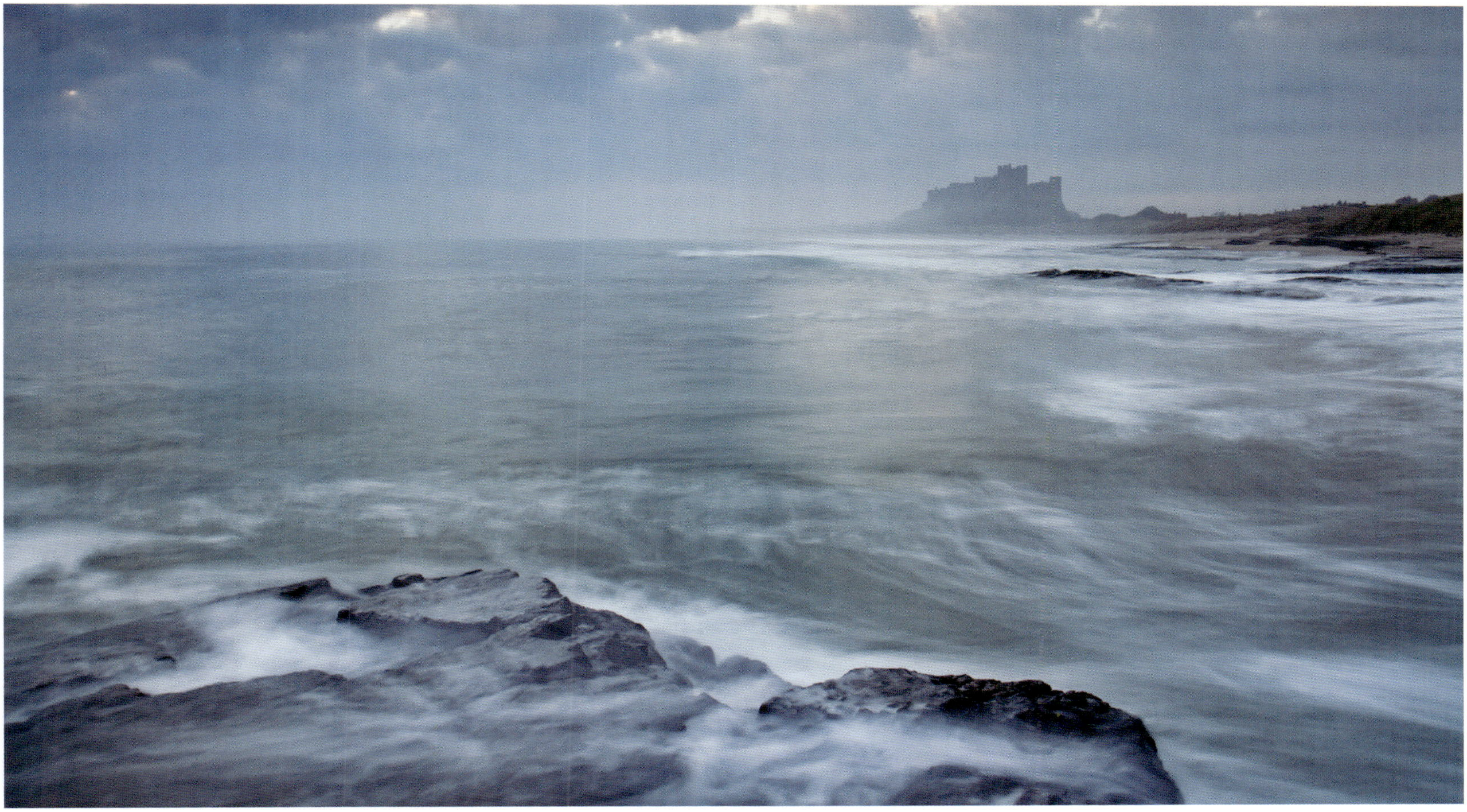

What to Pack

It's tempting to keep your camera bag stuffed with every piece of photographic equipment you own. However, it's worth thinking more carefully about your needs for a shoot and swapping equipment in or out as necessary: there's little point in risking damage or loss to equipment that isn't needed that day.

Your personal comfort is a factor that should be considered too. If you need to walk some distance to your chosen location, you should be as discerning about your equipment needs as possible. You may also need to consider carrying food, water, and a tent if you'll be away from civilization for a reasonable period of time.

Day trip	Two days +
Camera body	Camera battery charger
Required lenses	Cell phone charger
Tripod	Laptop (or other storage device)
Filters (graduated ND/polarizer)	Plastic water bottle
Filter holder	Alarm clock
Lens cloths	Tent/sleeping bag (if camping)
Remote release	Spare clothing
Spare batteries	
Spare memory card(s)	
Notebook and pen	
Map and compass/GPS	
Head torch	
First aid kit	
Cell phone	
Reflector	

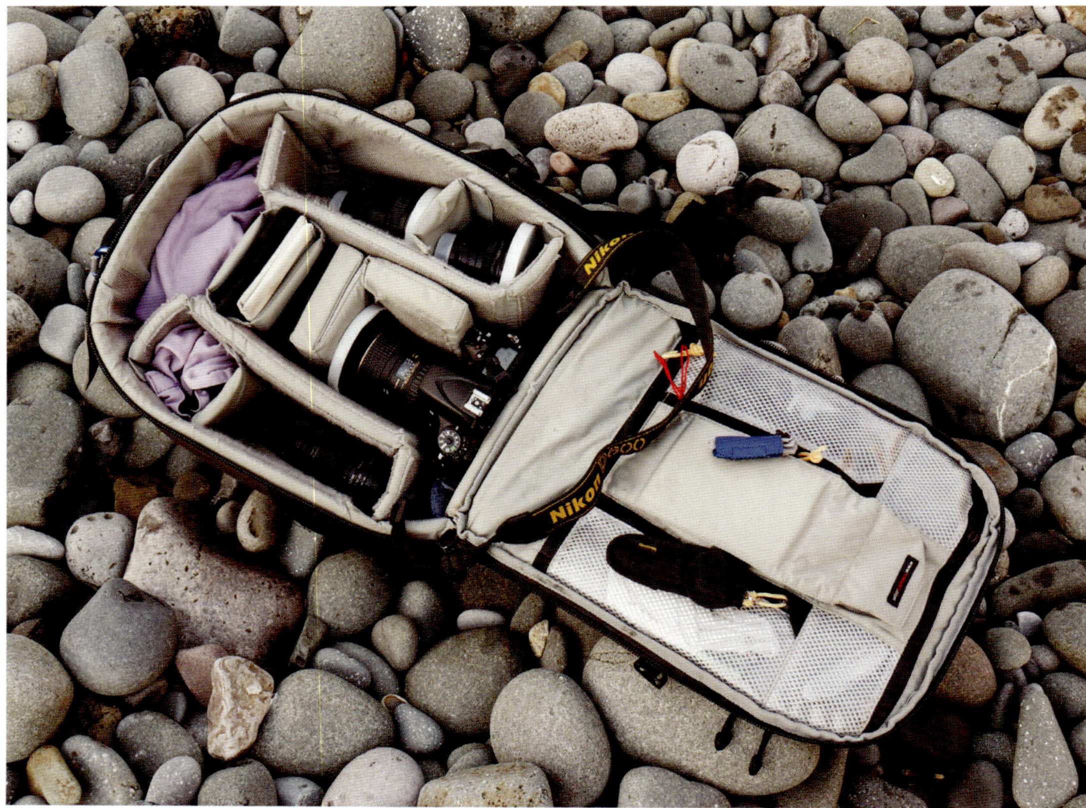

Right: A camera bag is the equivalent of a toolbox to a craftsperson. Arranging the contents in a logical (and consistent) way will allow you to find a certain piece of equipment quickly and easily.

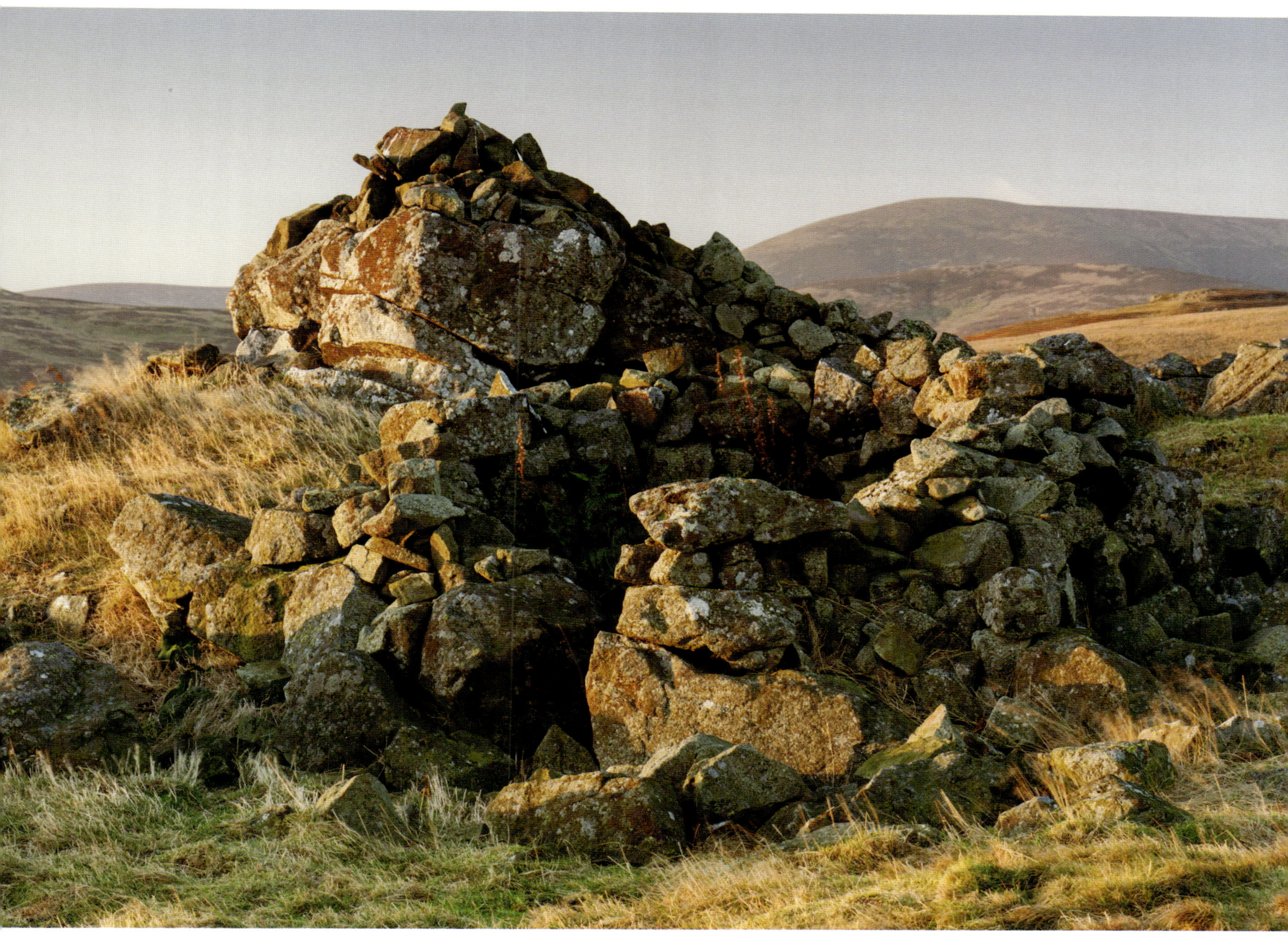

Above: If I'm hiking to reach a location I tend to leave my telephoto lens behind. It's heavy and is used less than my other lenses. Instead, the longest lens I take is 100mm, which is a relatively small lens, but it still delivers a semi-telephoto perspective.

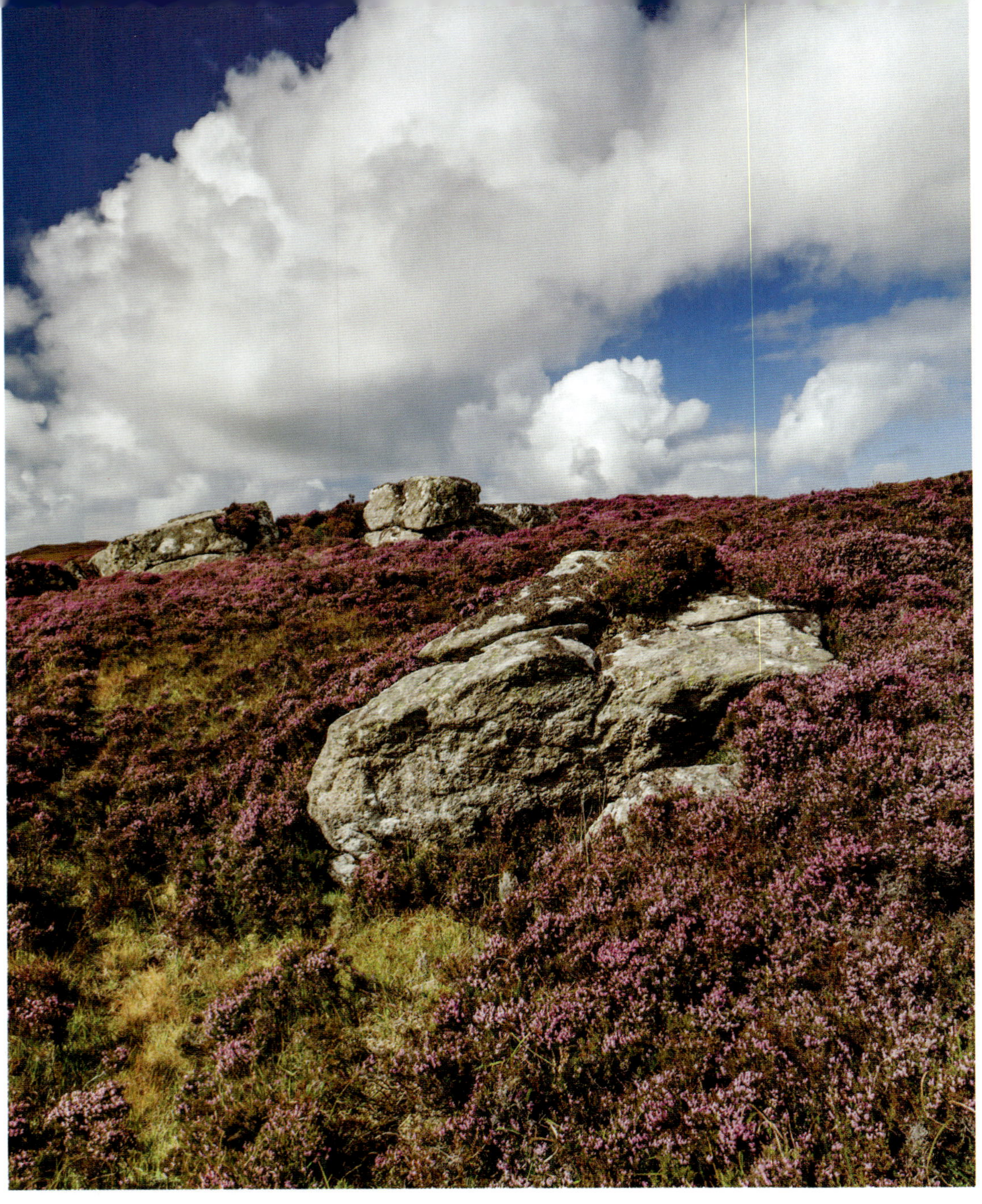

Good Tripod Technique

There are certain skills that it's useful to practice and refine, and good tripod technique is one of these: it's disappointing to shoot an unsharp image when handholding a camera, but it's doubly disappointing when you're using a tripod! Used correctly, a tripod should be stable and keep your camera steady. However, it's all too easy to set a tripod up so that it's easily knocked or even tips over.

The first thing to check is that the legs of the tripod are extended evenly (and pushed out to their maximum extent). The center column of the tripod should be perfectly vertical. Adjust the leg length if necessary to achieve this on uneven ground, and on soft ground push your tripod down to settle it as much as possible.

The center column should only be raised as a last resort if additional height is required. This is because raising the center column raises the center of gravity of your tripod, making it more unstable. Extend the tripod's legs to their maximum height before contemplating using the center column.

If you're shooting with a DSLR, switch on mirror-lock (if your camera has it). The movement of the mirror prior to the shutter firing can actually cause a slight vibration in the camera. This is particularly true of full-frame cameras with their larger mirrors. Mirrorless cameras and DSLRs in Live View mode don't suffer from this problem.

Another potential cause of movement is you. It's all too easy to knock a tripod accidentally when pressing the shutter-release button, so use either the camera's self-timer facility or a remote release instead. On sand or ground with give avoid moving around the tripod during an exposure to prevent the legs from sinking accidentally.

Handholding a Camera

Landscape photography and tripods were made for each other. The need to use small apertures to increase the depth of field often means using a slower shutter speed, so handholding a camera often isn't really an option. However, there are

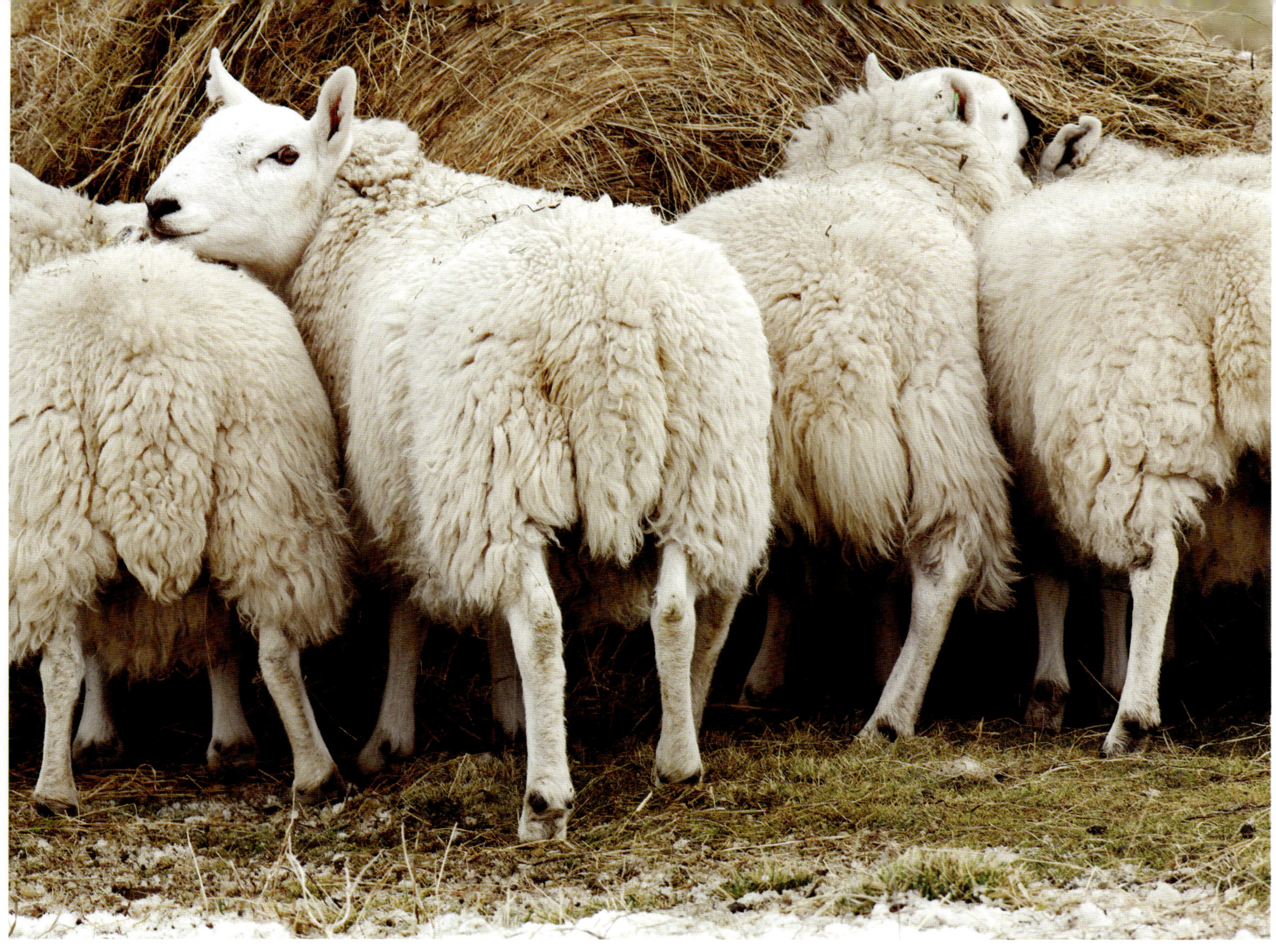

times when using a tripod isn't physically practical, so even landscape photographers sometimes need to handhold their camera.

The major problem with handholding a camera is that the risk of camera shake is increased. Assessing how steady you are at handholding a camera is relatively straightforward. Start by strapping a small flashlight to your camera. Then, in a darkened room, switch on the flashlight and point the beam of light toward a wall. Hold your camera as you would normally—if you can see the circle of light wobbling noticeably then you're not handholding your camera steadily.

The key to handholding a camera successfully is assuming the correct posture. Stand as upright as possible, keep your feet shoulder-width apart, and tuck your elbows lightly against your body for support. Grip the camera firmly with your right hand and use your left hand to support the lens from below. Breathe in and then slowly out. Before you breath in again gently squeeze the shutter-release button to take the shot. When shooting from a kneeling position, steady your upper body by resting your elbow on one knee.

Above: Animals in the landscape tend to move too quickly for a tripod to be effective. It's also when you'd be most likely to use a telephoto lens, making camera shake more of a possibility. This is one of the few times that I switch to Auto ISO. My camera allows me to specify a minimum shutter speed that Auto ISO will use, which allows me to shoot handheld, confident that the camera will adapt to changing conditions.

File Formats

Unless you're shooting with a cell phone or low-specification compact camera, you'll usually have the choice of two different file formats: JPEG and Raw. Both formats have advantages and disadvantages, but if you're serious about making the most of your landscape images you'll need to shoot Raw (or at the very least shoot Raw+JPEG for the best of both worlds).

JPEG

The big advantage that JPEG has over Raw is that it's a "finished" file. Once a JPEG has been shot it can be downloaded and used in any application that supports the format. This includes word processors, design packages, and the Internet. However, the fact that a JPEG is "finished" is also a disadvantage. Settings such as white balance, sharpness, and contrast are all "baked" into the image data at the time of exposure. Although your camera will allow you to modify these settings before shooting, it means that you have to make decisions about the image immediately. If you decide later that these settings were inappropriate there's no going back. Although you can modify a file later to some degree, image quality is likely to suffer and some settings, such as black and white, really are irreversible.

A second issue is that the data in a JPEG image is compressed, which allows you to fit more images onto a memory card than when shooting Raw. However, this compression works by reducing the level of fine detail. Therefore, if you decide to shoot JPEGs it pays to use the lowest level of compression (the highest quality) available, as this will best preserve fine detail.

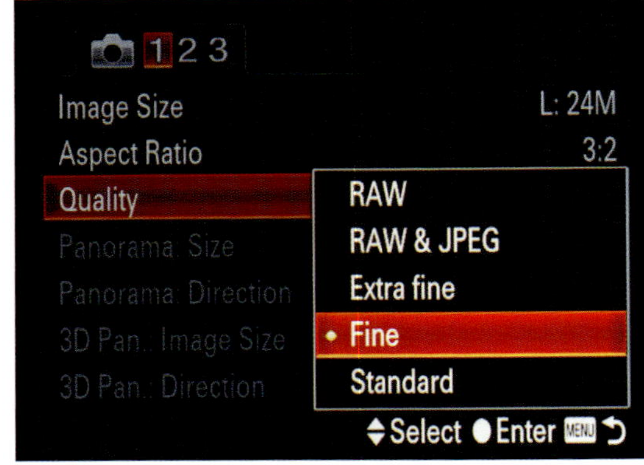

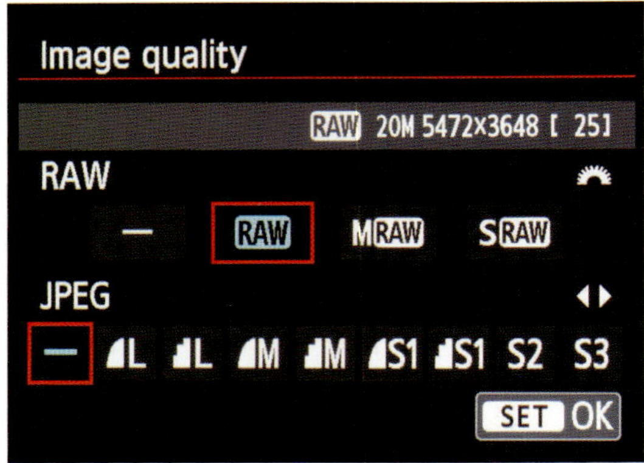

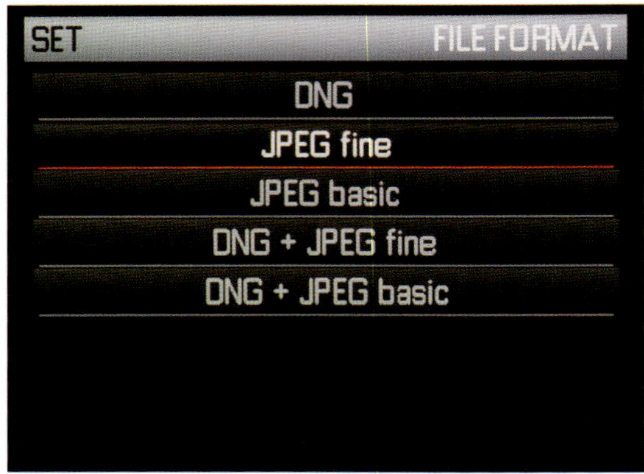

Above: There's no standard naming convention for the different levels of compression on cameras. The closest is the use of Fine to denote the lowest compression level (and therefore the highest image quality). Standard or Normal is generally used for the highest compression level (smallest file size), although Basic is occasionally used too.

Raw

There's no standard Raw file format, so each camera manufacturer uses its own proprietary format (NEF for Nikon, CR2 for Canon, and so on). The closest to a standard is the Adobe DNG format, which was designed as a "universal" Raw format that would make life simpler for everyone. Unfortunately, although DNG is supported by a few camera manufacturers, such as Leica and Pentax, it hasn't been embraced by all of them, so multiple Raw formats remain.

Regardless of the specific format used, a Raw file is a package of all the image data gathered by the camera's sensor at the moment of exposure. There is no processing applied to Raw data (as there is with a JPEG), so when a Raw file is opened in compatible Raw software you have complete freedom to modify the image as you wish. You also never overwrite the data in a Raw file, as the changes you make are either stored in a separate file (known as a "sidecar file"), or in your Raw software's database. This means you can revisit a Raw file and change it over and over again without any loss of image quality.

The downside is that processing a Raw file takes time—you often need to spend as long sorting out images from a session as you did shooting them. However, this is usually time well spent if it means that the final image is as good as it can be. Once you're happy with your work on a Raw file it can be exported to a more generally useful file type such as TIFF or JPEG.

Raw files are often compressed to save space on the memory card, but unlike JPEG compression there is no loss of detail. However, Raw files will take up far more room on a memory card than an equivalent JPEG (generally at least twice as much space). Shooting Raw therefore means investing in higher-capacity memory cards (and faster memory cards, as Raw data takes longer to write).

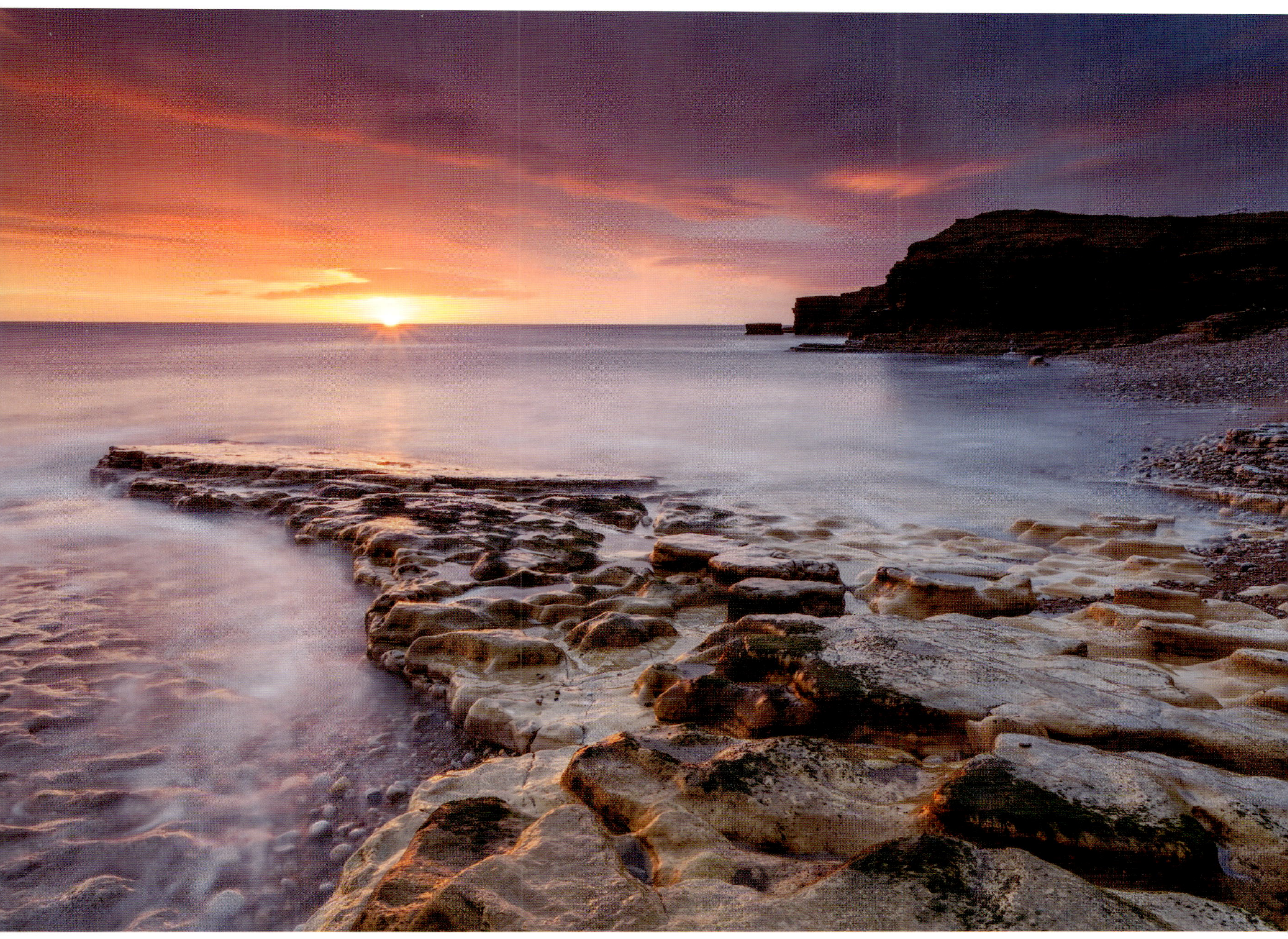

Above: There's virtually no latitude to recover blown highlights when shooting JPEG: once they've gone, they've gone. Shooting Raw gives you a safety net, though. As long as the highlights aren't too badly overexposed it's often possible to recover them in postproduction. That was the case with this shot—the detail around the rising sun was recovered using Adobe Lightroom's Highlight tool.

Picture Controls

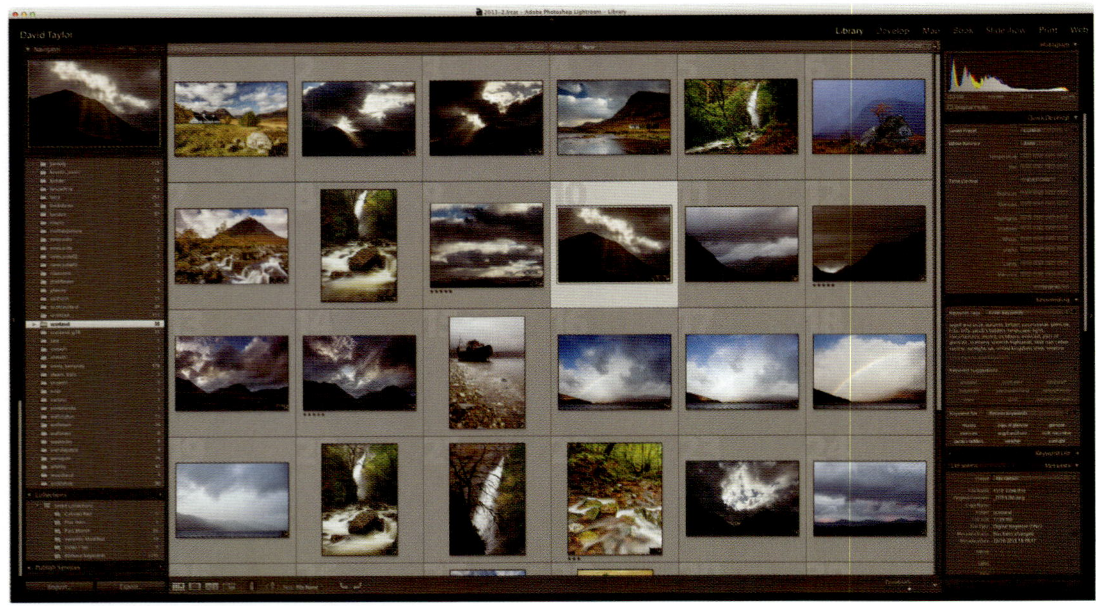

Above: Cameras are usually bundled with proprietary Raw software. However, there are better third-party alternatives, such as Capture One, Aperture, or Lightroom (pictured).

The image you review after shooting uses the picture controls set on the camera at the time of exposure. This is true regardless of whether you shot Raw or JPEG. Picture controls are settings that allow you to adjust the look of an image, such as its contrast, sharpness, and color saturation, and whether it has been converted to monochrome. Other picture controls include lens corrections (which compensate for the known defects of a particular lens) and the color space tagged to the image.

Setting the various picture controls is relatively unimportant when shooting Raw, as they can all be undone when the Raw files are converted. However, they will make a big difference to the look of your JPEGs, so it's worth experimenting with your camera's picture controls to see which settings you prefer in different shooting conditions.

COMMON PICTURE CONTROLS		
Description	*Common options*	Suggested setting
Color space	*sRGB; Adobe RGB*	*Use sRGB if you intend to upload your images to the Internet or print directly after shooting. Otherwise select Adobe RGB.*
Lens correction	*Vignetting; Chromatic aberration correction*	*Only important when shooting JPEG. Generally unnecessary unless you are shooting close to a lens' maximum aperture. Third-party lenses are not commonly supported.*
Dynamic range control	*Off; Low; Medium; Strong*	*Only important when shooting JPEG. Adjusts highlights and shadows to balance tonal range. Avoid using the strongest setting if you want more naturalistic results.*
Picture parameter presets	*Standard; Portrait; Landscape; Neutral; Vivid; Monochrome*	*Set according to taste if you don't plan on adjusting images later. Set to low contrast/low sharpening/low color saturation if you intend to modify images in postproduction (JPEG only).*

Tip

Image sharpening is particularly difficult to remove in postproduction, as is contrast.

Right: Cameras generally have a series of presets that allow you to select a particular look for your images. These vary in the degree that they adjust color, contrast, and sharpening. Although the Landscape preset would seem to be the best option, this is often overly saturated and more difficult to undo if you are shooting JPEG.

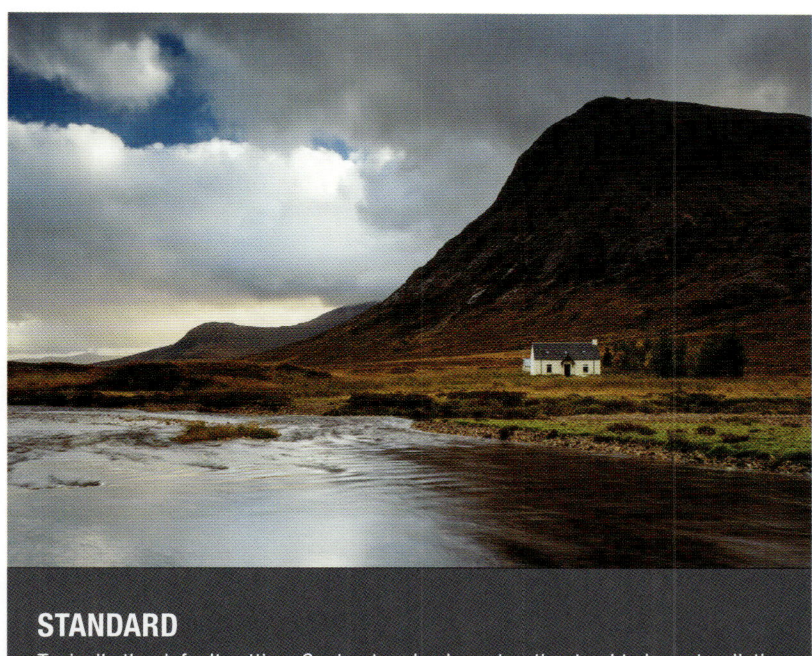

STANDARD

Typically the default setting. Contrast and color saturation tend to be naturalistic.

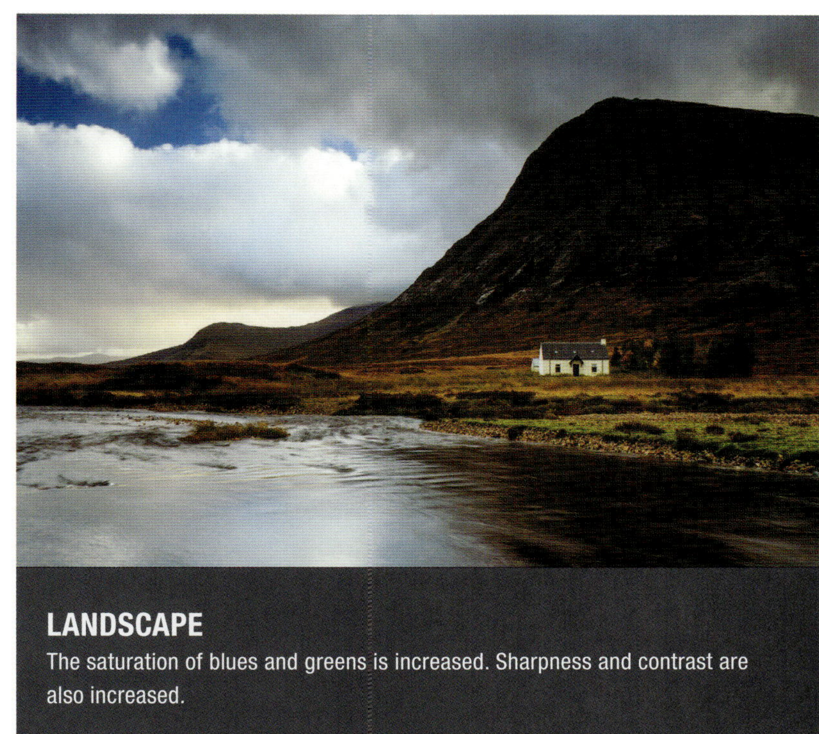

LANDSCAPE

The saturation of blues and greens is increased. Sharpness and contrast are also increased.

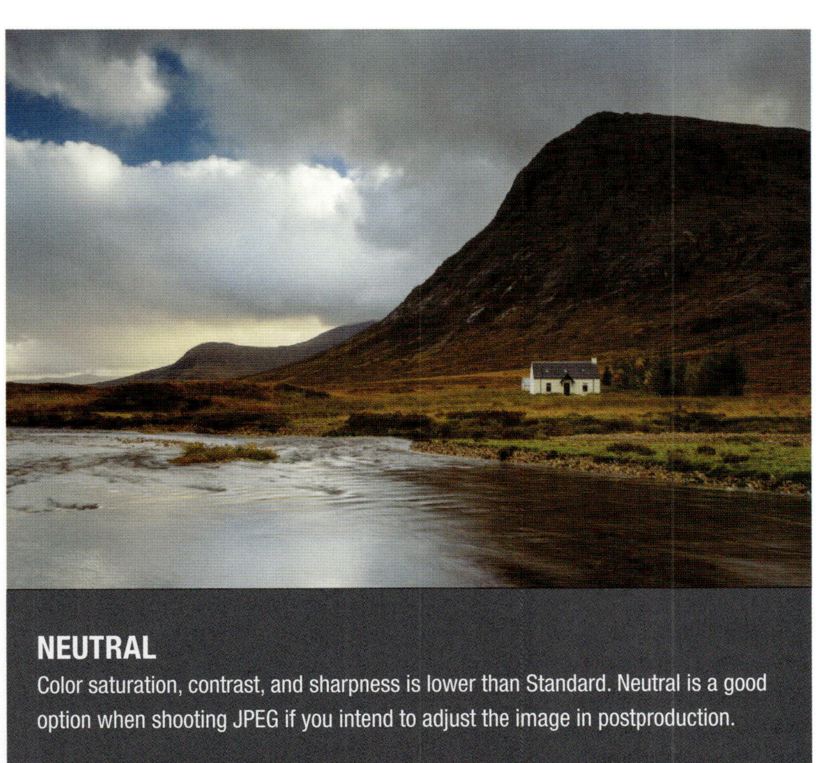

NEUTRAL

Color saturation, contrast, and sharpness is lower than Standard. Neutral is a good option when shooting JPEG if you intend to adjust the image in postproduction.

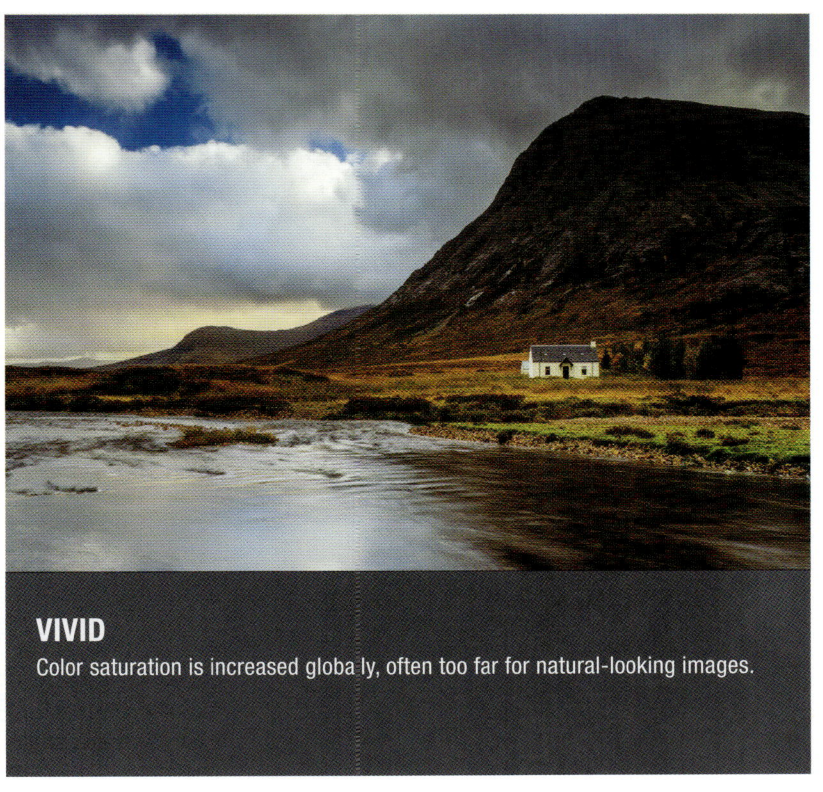

VIVID

Color saturation is increased globa ly, often too far for natural-looking images.

Chapter 5
Subjects

The term "landscape photography" can be applied to a wide range of subjects—even some macro shots could be described as landscape, albeit in miniature. Personal preference and your geographical location will largely determine the landscape subjects that you shoot; this chapter describes the options that you could consider.

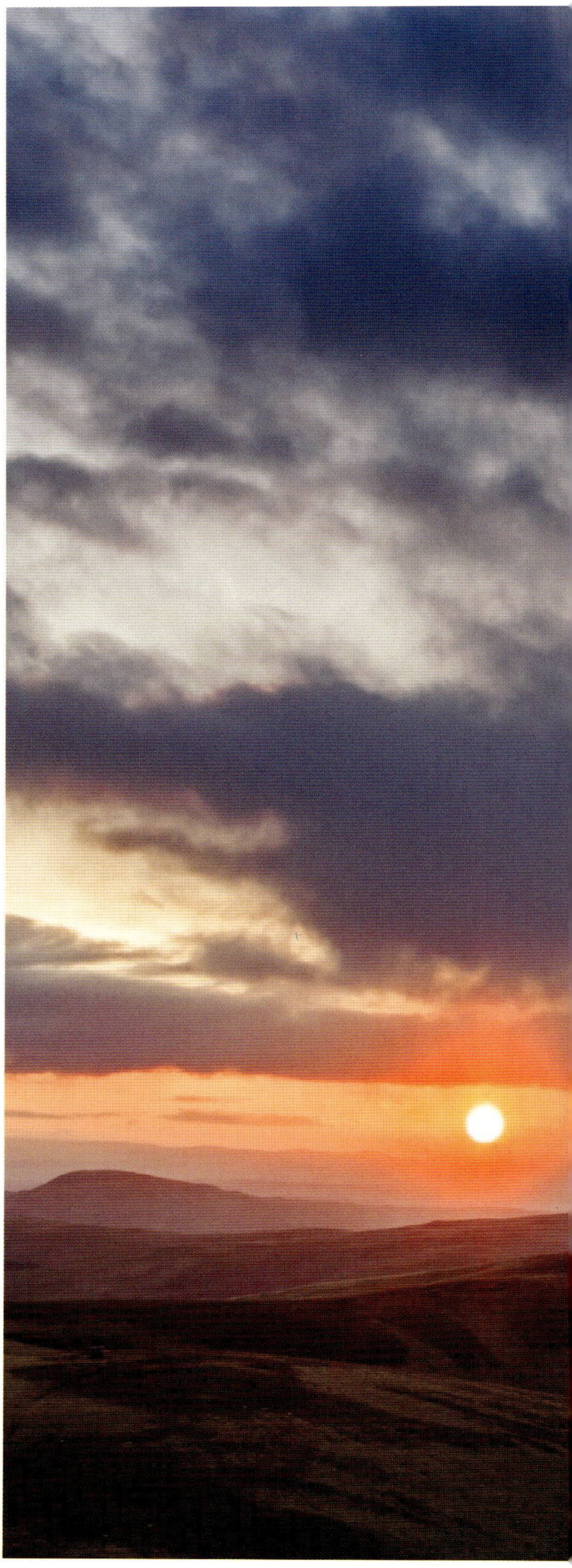

Right: I live in Northumberland, in the northeast corner of England. The country is at its narrowest here, which makes the coast easily accessible both east and west. However, it's the hilly spine that runs south through the middle of the county that attracts me most. Although the hills are relatively low by world standards, I find them endlessly fascinating and challenging to photograph.

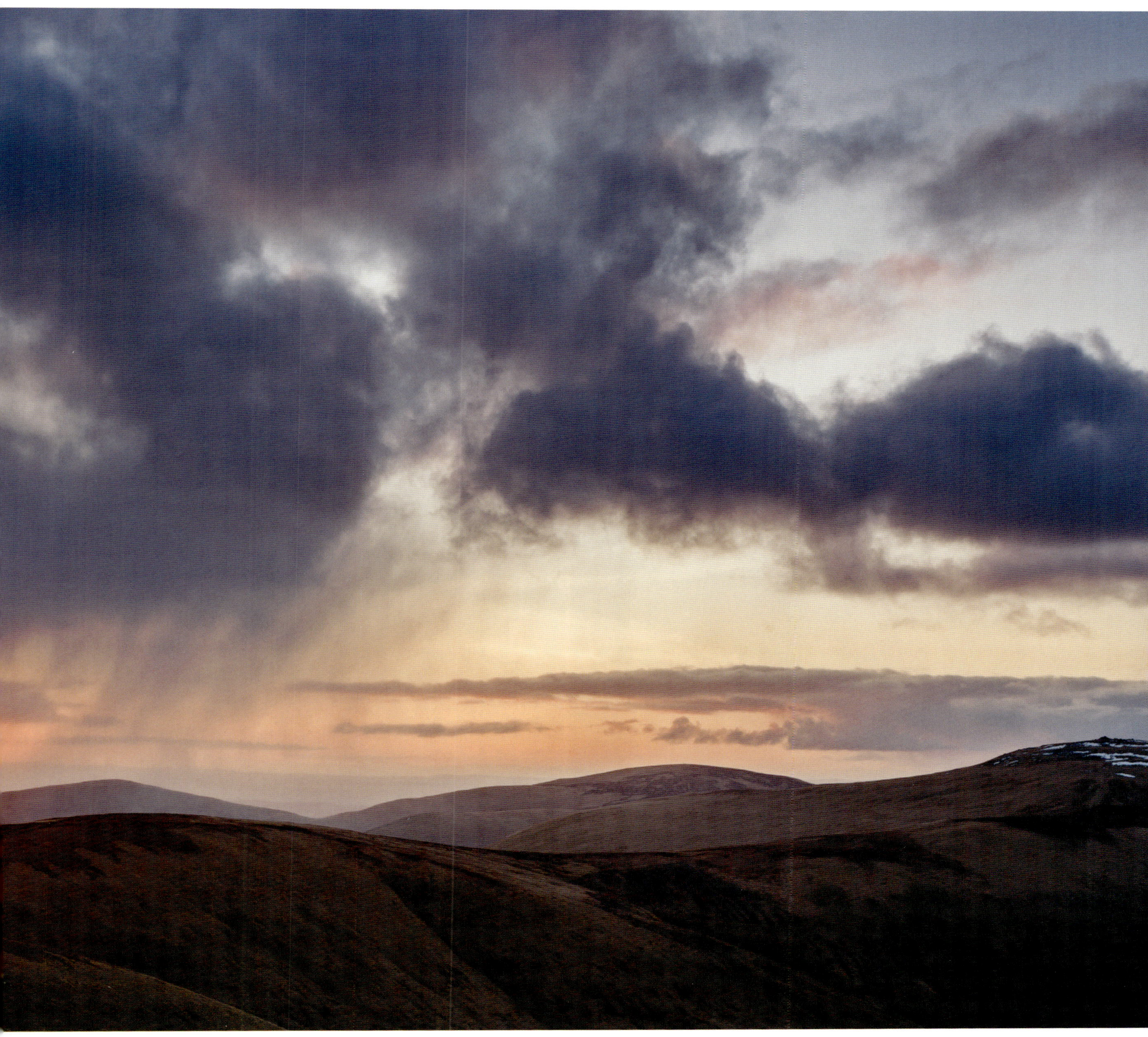

Coastal

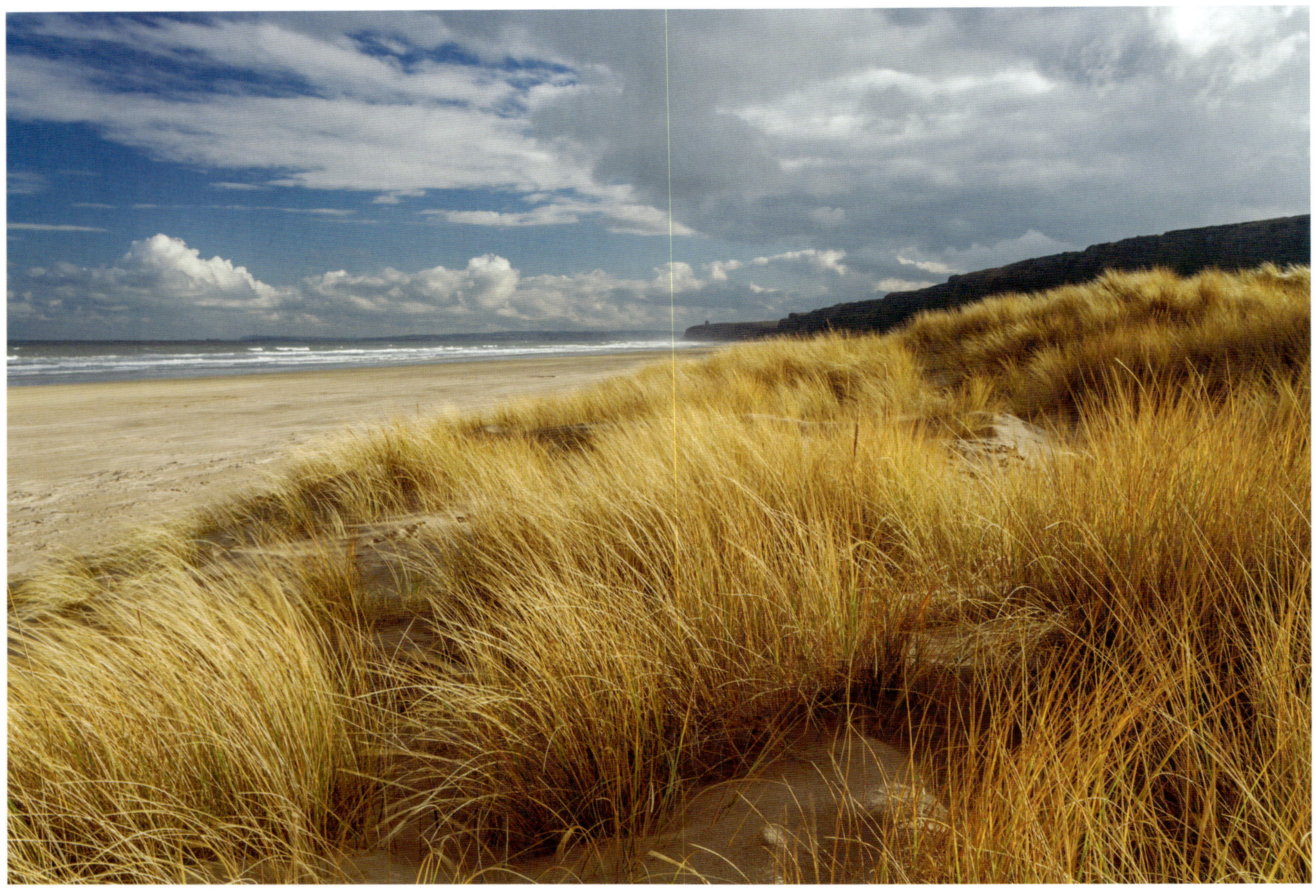

An appealing aspect of coastal regions is the constant change. Tides sweep beaches clear twice a day, removing or depositing new details. The tides also vary depending on the phase of the moon or because of weather conditions out to sea, so you could visit the same beach daily and always find something new or different to photograph. For these reasons it's arguably more important to plan ahead when contemplating a trip to the coast.

"Coastal region" is also a very broad term for a wide range of different geographical features. A coast could be sandy or rocky, bounded by cliffs or by dunes, or feature a series of intimate bays or wide-open spaces that seem to stretch to infinity. It's not surprising that photographing the coast can be such a rewarding prospect.

Above: It's difficult to get a sense of scale when viewing wide-angle shots of empty sandy beaches. Incorporating foreground details, such as grass-covered dunes, can help to effectively convey the size of a beach.

Planning

Often the best time to visit the coast is early in the morning after a high tide. This is particularly true of sandy beaches, as they are more likely to be free of distracting footprints. Of course, what you shouldn't do is then accidentally add your own—if you need to walk around to find a composition, try to walk either in the water or around the edge of the beach. Although footprints can be cloned out in postproduction, it's time-consuming and can be easily avoided by being careful.

Later in the day there's more chance that beaches will be busier with people. This presents different opportunities photographically, but there's a fine line between a landscape image with people in it and a photograph of people in a landscape. People are visually heavy and can dominate a scene unless they're relatively small in the frame.

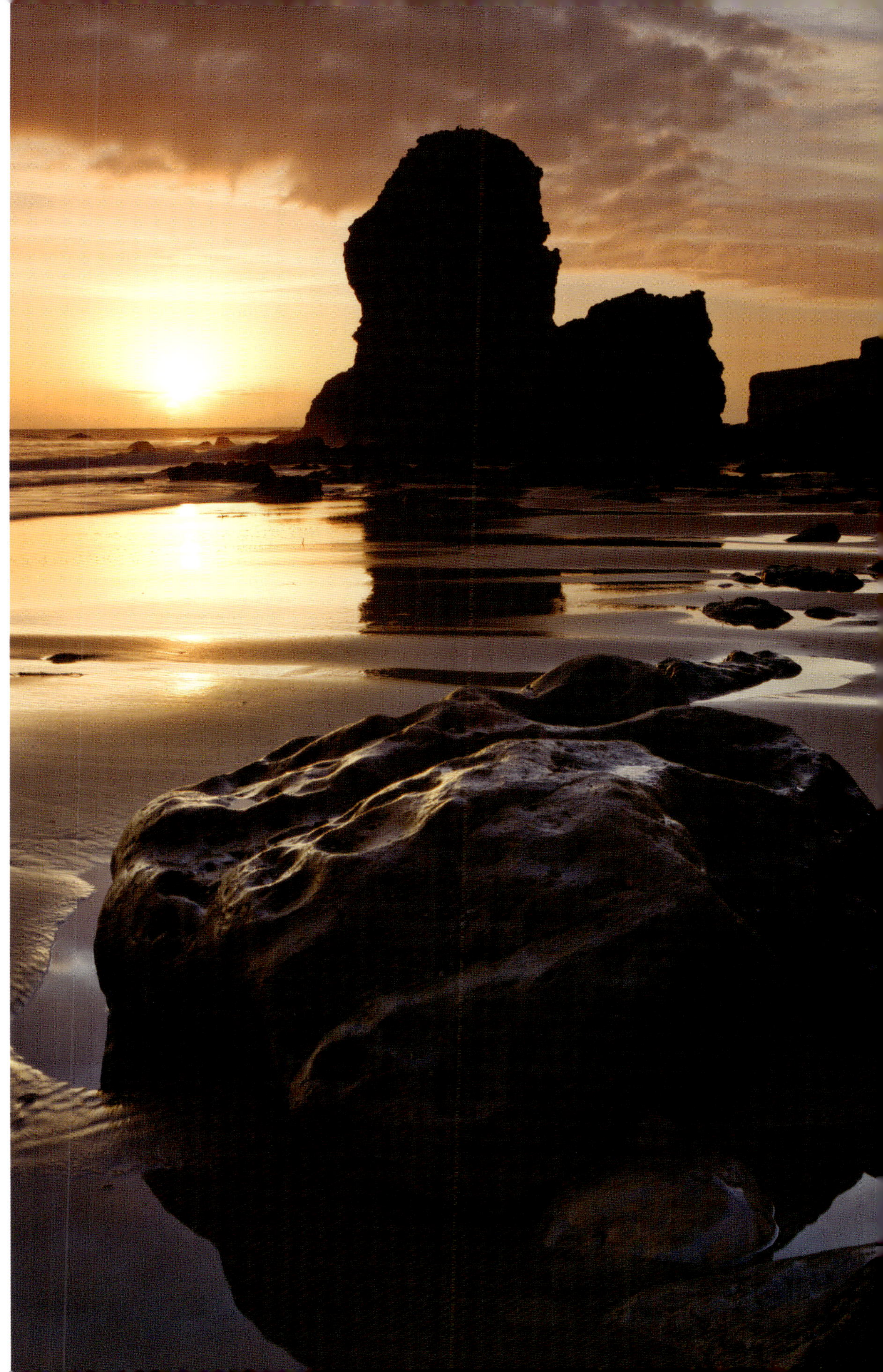

Right: I made the classic mistake of walking directly across this beach instead of sticking to the margins. When I found a composition I liked it frustratingly also included my footprints across the sand in the middle ground. This meant work in postproduction that should have been unnecessary.

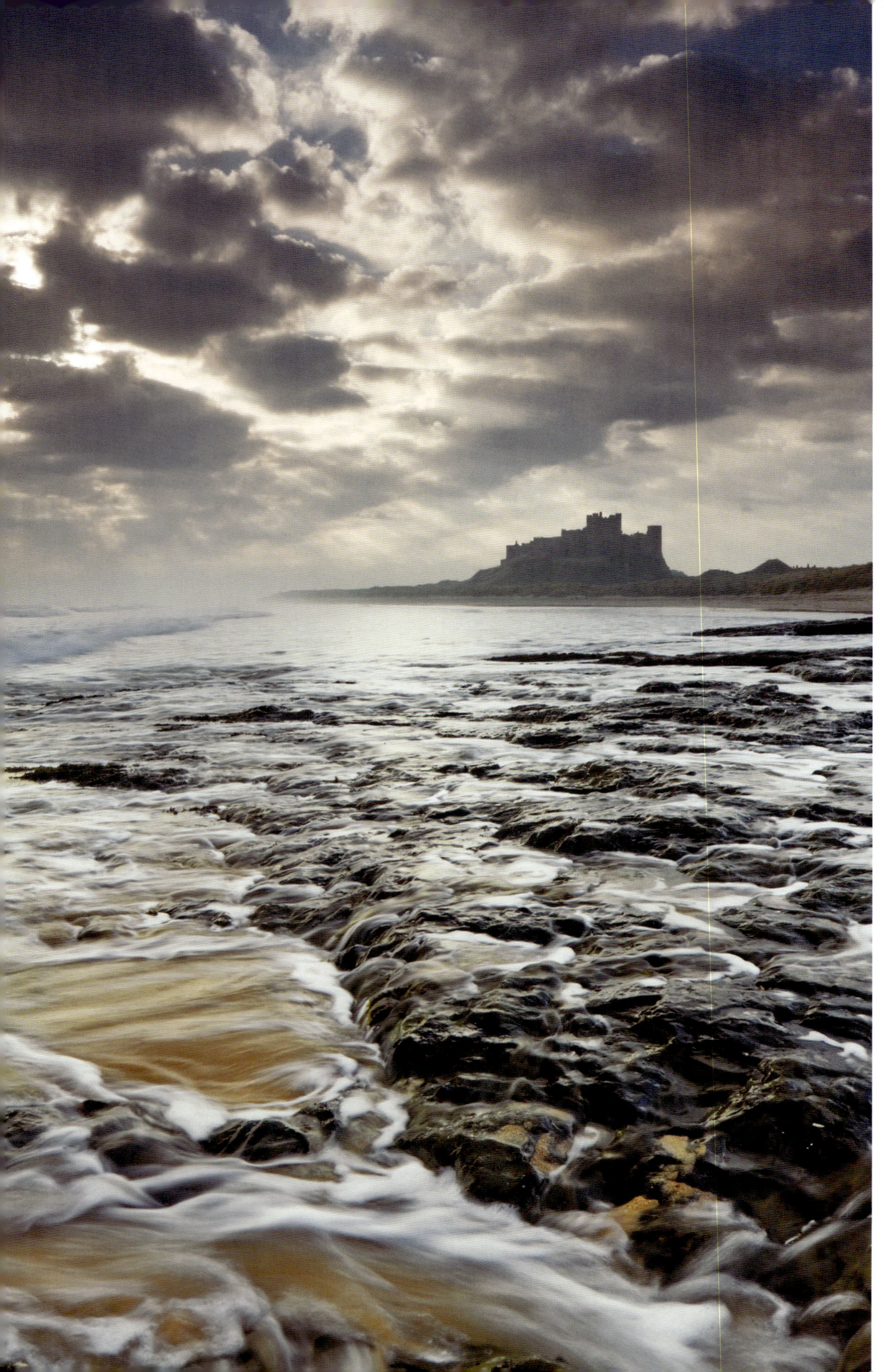

Movement

One aesthetic choice that you'll need to make at the coast is how the movement of the sea is recorded. A faster shutter will "freeze" the movement of waves, but this is often difficult in low light without resorting to large apertures or high ISO settings. Conversely, a slower shutter speed will smooth out the movement of water—the slower the shutter speed, the more pronounced the effect. In bright conditions you may need to use your camera's base ISO setting and an ND filter if you want to use a long shutter speed.

One type of movement that you don't want to experience, though, is your camera sinking into sand during an exposure. This can happen if you move your feet around as the camera is exposing, but it happens more commonly when waves wash around the feet of your tripod. To reduce this risk push down firmly on your tripod when you set it up, to compact the sand around the tripod's feet.

Tips

Use a polarizing filter to reduce the glare from wet sand. Polarizing filters can also be used as 2-stop ND filters.

Regularly check your lenses and filters for sea spray and clean it off with a dry, lint-free cloth.

Left: A shutter speed of 1/3 sec. has created a sense of movement, blurring the waves washing over the foreground rocks. However, there's still a sense of texture to the water—it looks relatively naturalistic, but with a sense of energy to the movement.

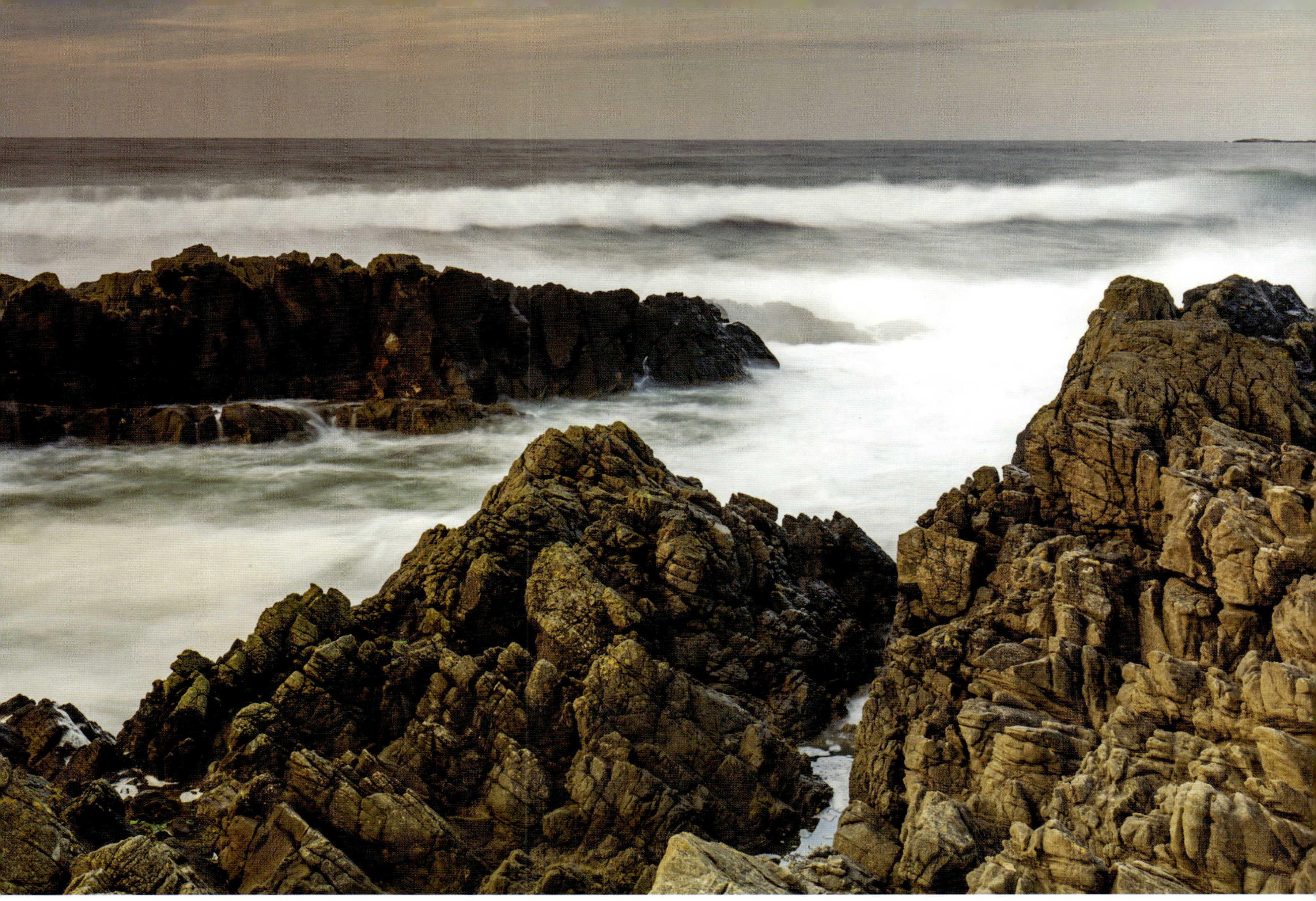

SUGGESTED SHUTTER SPEEDS WHEN SHOOTING WAVES	
Shutter speed	*Result*
1/125 sec. or faster	Detail frozen
1/4 sec.	Blur with texture
1 sec.	Blur with less obvious texture
15 sec.	Milky effect
1–2 min.	Wave form lost entirely

Above: Keeping your camera straight is critically important when shooting at the coast—water doesn't slope and it looks very odd when it appears to do so in a photograph. It's worth investing in a hotshoe spirit level to help align your camera (although some tripod heads feature a spirit level they tend to only work when the tripod head is horizontal). Some cameras feature an electronic level, although this may not be entirely accurate unless calibrated regularly.

Woodland

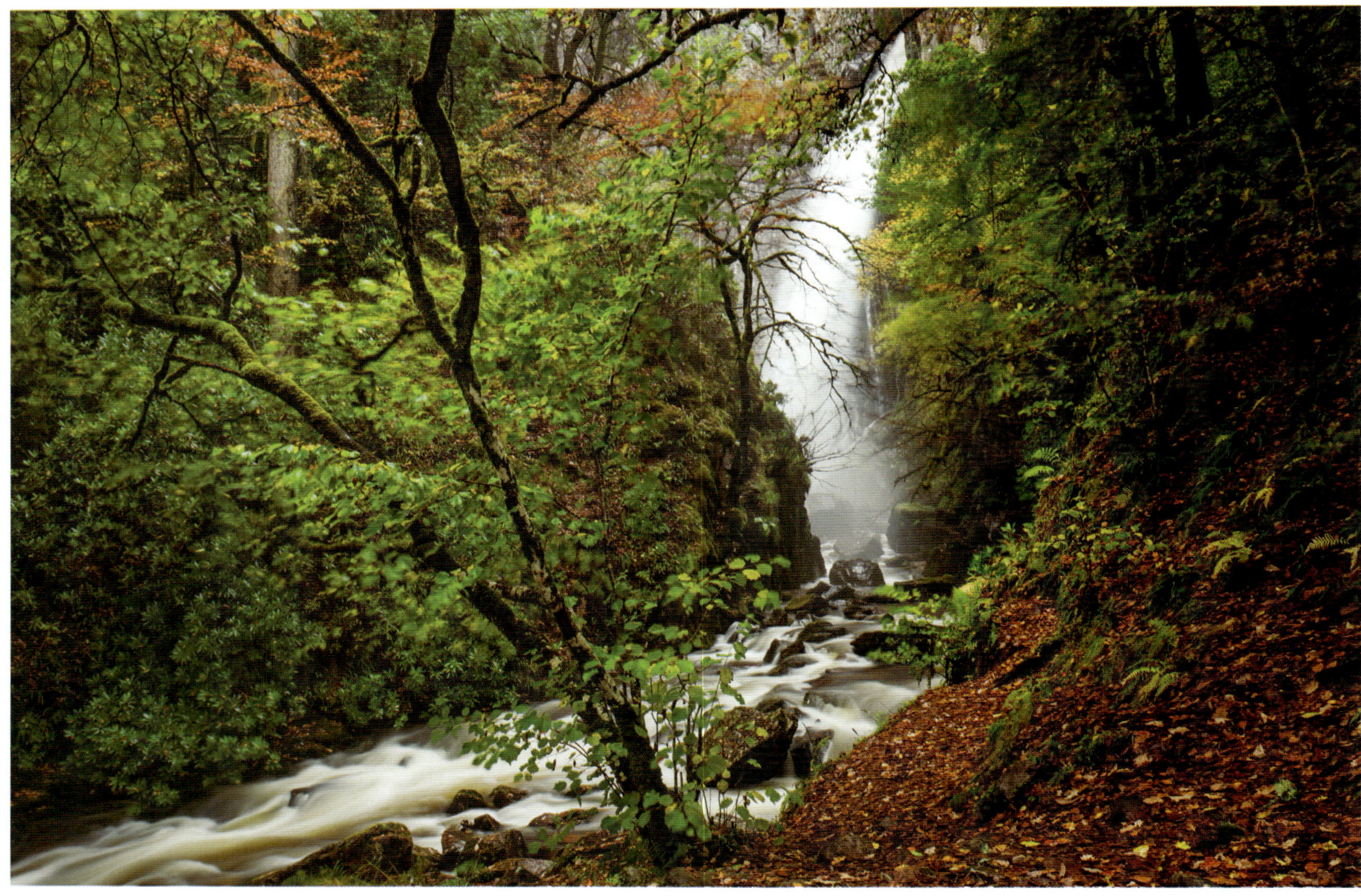

Shooting in woodland can be a challenging experience. With the exception of commercial plantations, woodland tends to be chaotic in nature. This can make finding a pleasing composition difficult. Fortunately, shooting in woodland is often less time critical than other types of landscape. Although early morning or late afternoon offers the possibility of raking light, creating interesting shadow shapes, woodland is often more rewarding in the soft light of an overcast day. This means that it's possible to spend time finding compositions that are aesthetically interesting without feeling that you're working to a looming deadline.

Woodland is generally rich in interesting detail, such as fallen trees, fungi, and root systems. Using a wide-angle lens and filling the foreground with these details is a good way to simplify your compositions. Telephoto lenses also have their uses, as they will allow you to crop in and exclude unwanted detail, and allow you to photograph details that you may not otherwise be able to reach, such as backlit leaves.

Deciduous woodland is very seasonal. The most popular time of year to photograph woodland tends to be fall, as the reds and yellows at this time of year are very attractive. However, the other seasons can be equally rewarding: bare winter trees have a very graphic, stark quality, while spring brings fresh foliage and woodland flowers.

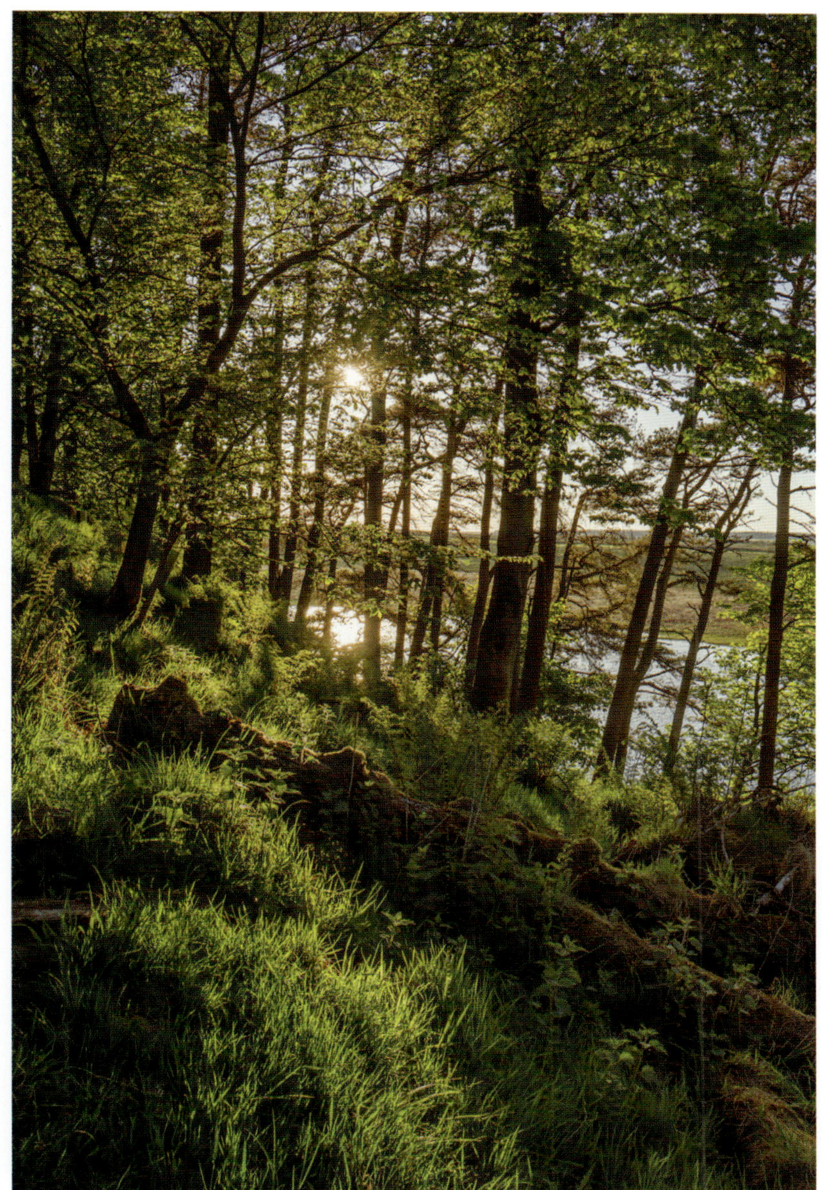

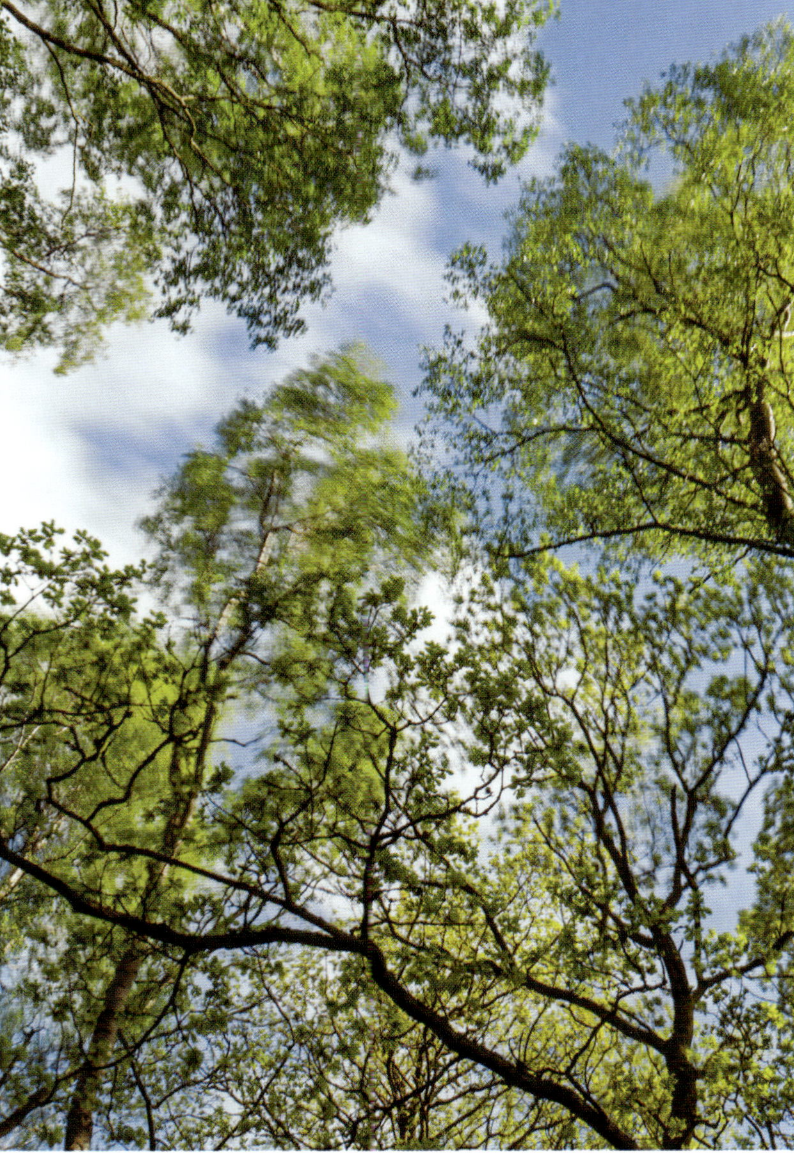

Above: Low raking light is ideal for shooting backlit woodland scenes. To avoid flare hide the sun behind leaves or branches.

Above: As with water, long exposures can be used to convey a sense of movement. This is most apparent when there are leaves on the trees from spring through to fall.

Left: Woodland is a subject that benefits from overcast conditions, as soft light helps to avoid the contrast problems of extreme light and shade. Despite the lack of direct light, polarizing filters are useful when you want to reduce the distracting sheen of wet leaves.

Hills & Mountains

Photographing in hills and mountains can be challenging. The first challenge is to get to your chosen location. If you intend to shoot at dawn it's often easier (and less stressful) to wild camp close to your intended location. However, this isn't an option if you're unsure of your outdoor skills, particularly if there's a risk of bad weather. Climber's huts and bothies offer an easier alternative, although you'll still need to think carefully about supplies such as food and water, as well as extra clothing and sleeping bags.

Shooting at sunset causes a similar dilemma. Coming down a hill or mountain in the dark requires navigating by flashlight, which is something you should only do if you're confident of your navigational skills.

There's a grandeur to hills and mountains that's often lost in a photograph. This is usually because there's little sense of scale (rocks come in all sorts of shapes and it's not immediately obvious how large one is in a photo). Including elements such as trees or people as a size comparison will instantly help to convey scale.

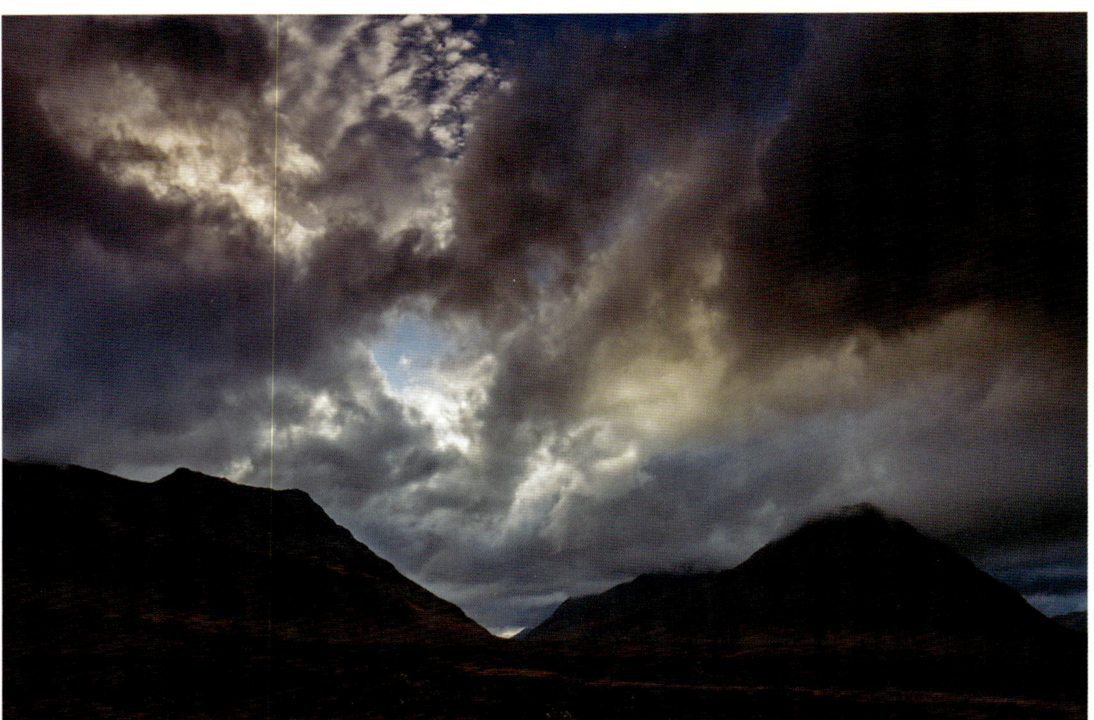

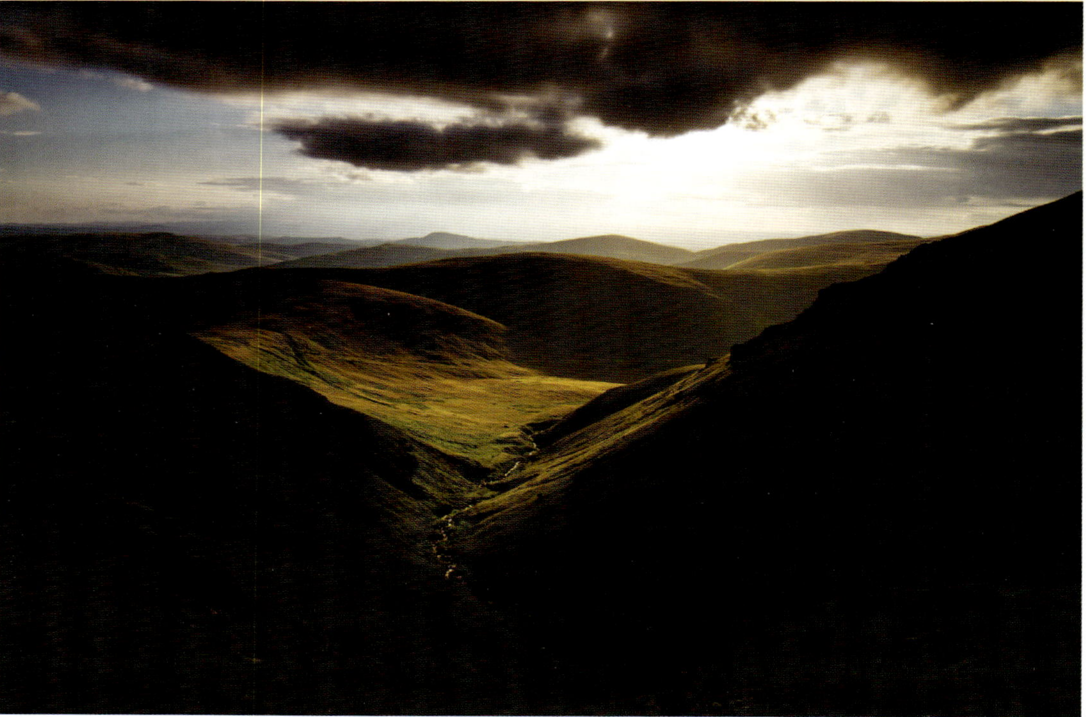

Top right: Mountainous regions often have "micro-climates," so the weather differs markedly from nearby low-lying areas. For a landscape photographer this is both a disadvantage and an advantage. Although it can be frustrating when planning a shoot, when the conditions are in your favor the weather can be spectacular.

Right: Photographing hills and mountains invariably means climbing them. Leave yourself plenty of time for the assent if you're aiming for a specific time of day. It is also a good idea to take the minimum amount of photography equipment necessary, to save on weight.

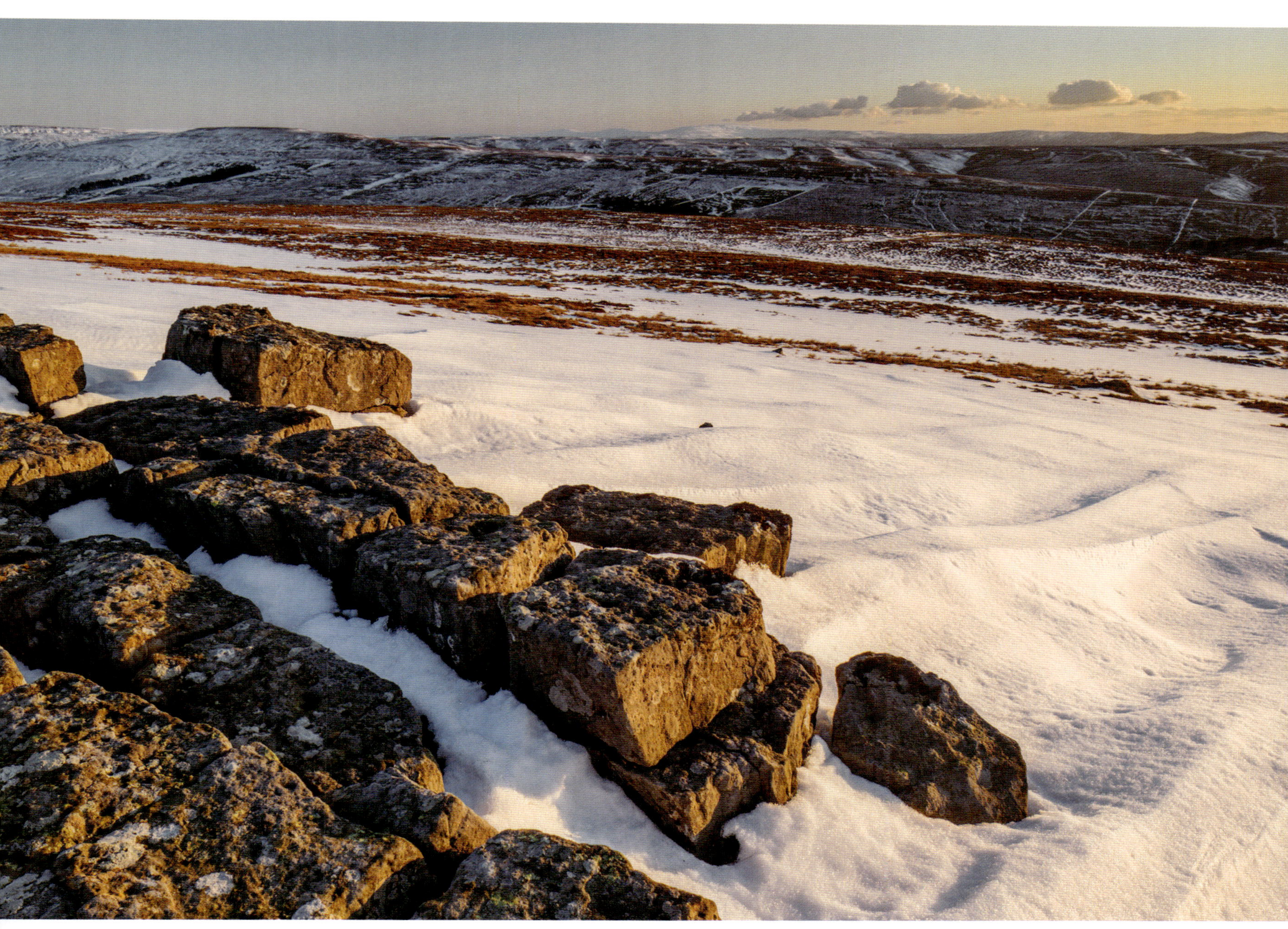

Photographing hills and mountains is rewarding at any time of year, but they're arguably at their most dramatic in winter when they have a snow and ice covering. As with sandy beaches, be careful where you walk to avoid adding footprints to an area that you might later want to include in a composition. This also means that you'll need to be out early, before anyone else decides that the conditions are ideal for walking in.

Above: Snow may cause problems with exposure metering, but it is very useful for setting a custom white balance. This is particularly important if you want to avoid a blue color cast when shooting snow or ice details in shade.

Lakes, Rivers & Waterfalls

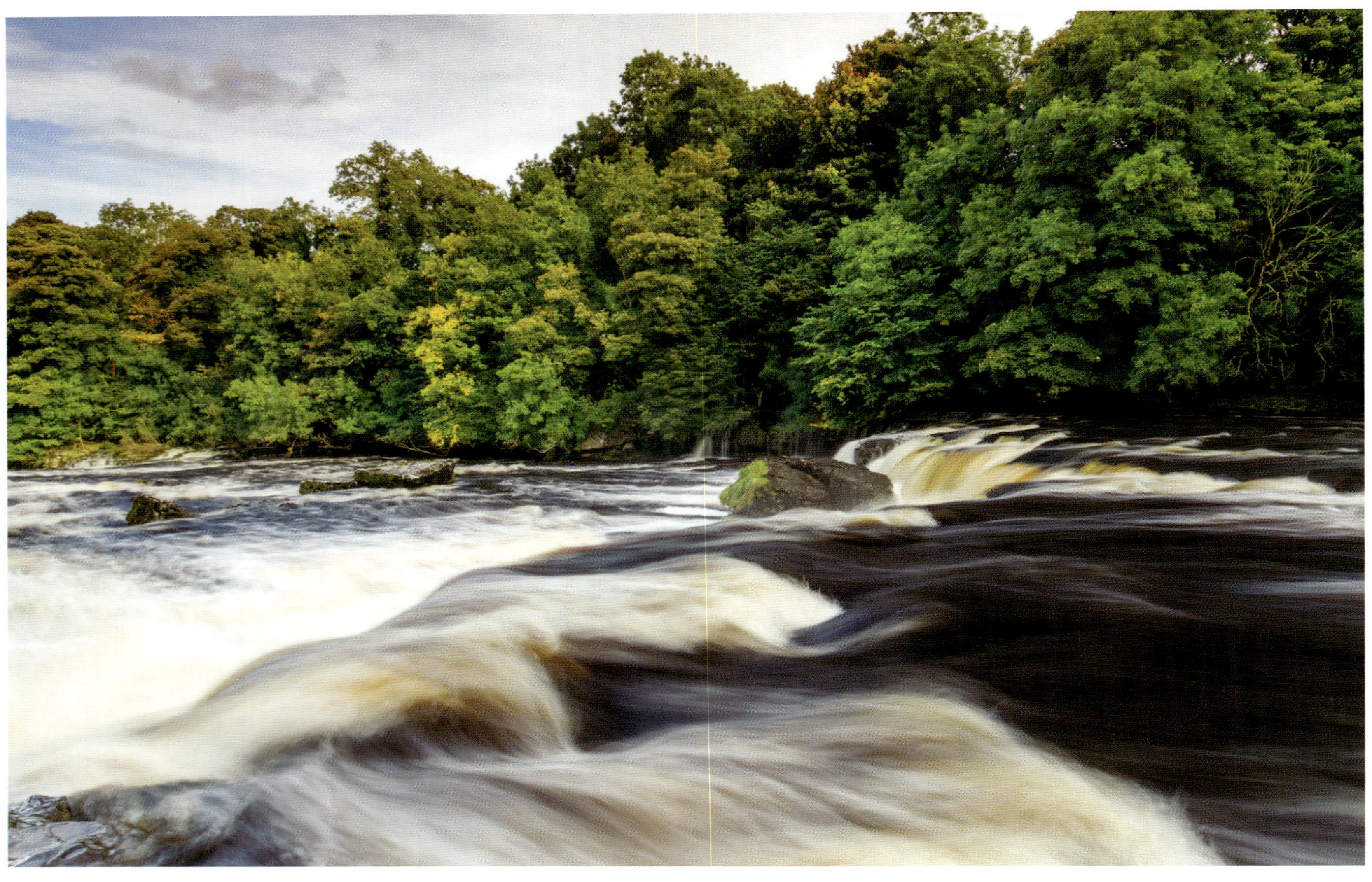

Shooting rivers and waterfalls involves the same decision as shooting at the coast: how should the moving water be rendered in the final image? It's a very personal decision and one that will determine the shutter speed you use.

However, your chosen shutter speed will also depend on how fast flowing a river or waterfall is: after heavy rain both can be more swollen and faster-flowing than normal. In these conditions you don't need as slow a shutter speed to create blur. In many respects it's often better to avoid rivers

and waterfalls after heavy rain, though, particularly if there's been flooding. Tree branches and other detritus are often deposited on river banks, making the environment visually messy. If there is a large amount of water you may also find that interesting rocks in the river that could be used compositionally are submerged.

Lakes are at their most attractive when the surface is still and has a mirror-like reflective quality. This is ideal for producing symmetrical images, but even a slight breeze can disturb the

surface, making it choppy and visually distracting. The use of longer shutter speeds will help to smooth out some of this choppiness, but it won't restore the desired reflective quality.

Generally, still conditions are more likely first thing in the morning around sunrise. After a still, clear night there's also a greater chance of mist, which can add an ethereal quality to an image. Bold colors work well when reflected—another good reason to be out shooting first thing in the morning if there's a chance of a colorful sunrise.

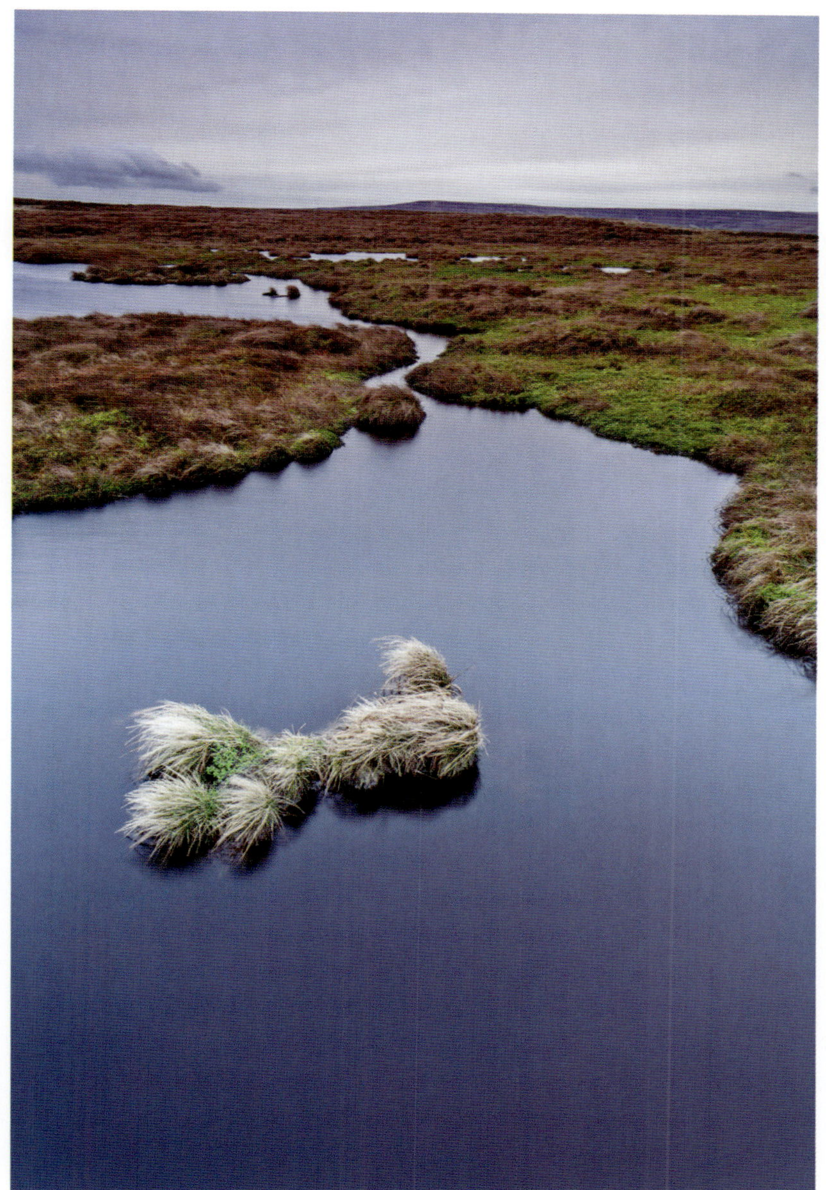

Above: Water picks up the colors of the ambient light. In this case it was the cool blue of an overcast, post-sunset sky. Strong wind whipping across the moor caused strong, visually-distracting ripples on the water's surface, but a shutter speed of 6 seconds was enough to smooth these out.

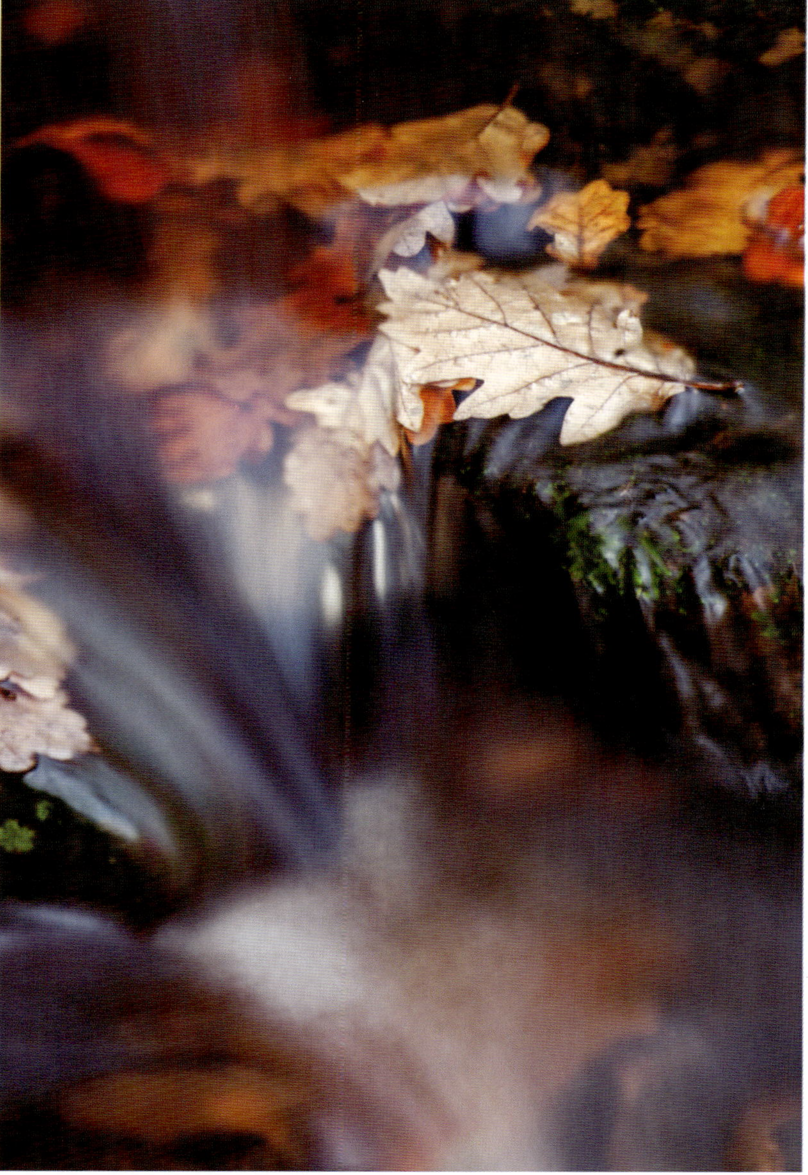

Above: Fall leaves often collect around the small waterfalls in woodland streams. These can help to add color and interest to your compositions.

Left: Long shutter speeds will blur waterfalls, but patches of white foam can easily burn out in direct sunlight. Shooting waterfalls in softer light reduces this risk.

People & Animals

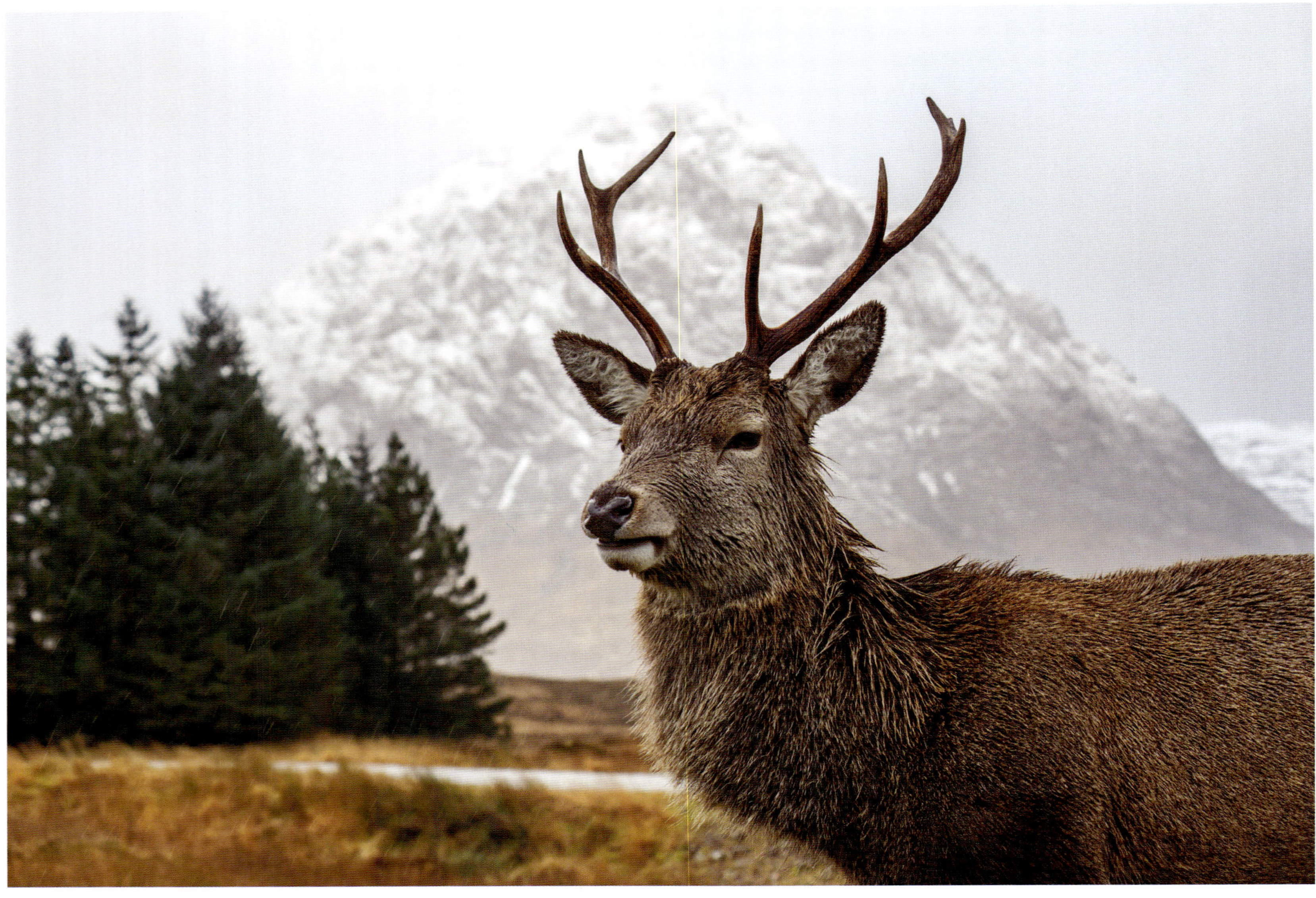

People or animals are useful for conveying a sense of scale in a landscape image: the smaller the subject is (relative to its surroundings), the greater the sense of space. People or animals also add narrative to an image and can be used to direct the viewer around the frame, as we are likely to follow the gaze of a person or animal in a photograph.

A person's body language will also influence how we feel about the image. A figure standing upright, with hands on hips, looking out across a landscape has a more positive feel than a crouched figure that is seemingly overwhelmed by his or her surroundings.

However, posed shots can stray into the realm of portraiture. It's often better to shoot candid images (agreed to beforehand), when your subject is unaware that you're shooting and is therefore acting more naturally.

Above: Animals can be useful for suggesting the location of an image. In Britain, red deer are closely associated with the Scottish Highlands. By framing the deer against a mountainous background the sense of place is reinforced.

Sunrise & Sunset

It's probably fair to say that sunrise and sunset are the two times of day most closely associated with landscape photography. There's a good reason for this: because the sun is low to the horizon, the light is warmer, and often softer, than at other times of day. However, landscapes can be equally attractive when lit by the ambient light of pre-dawn and post-sunset. For this reason arriving early (or staying late) will enable you to make the most of opportunities created by sunrise and sunset.

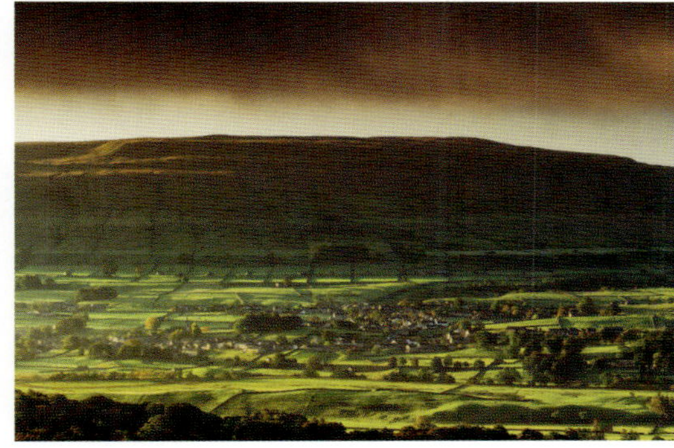

Above: The raking light of early morning or late afternoon is often best appreciated from above. Valleys with roads leading up and out often have viewpoints in scenic spots along the route. Maps generally show parking places. They'll also allow you to calculate whether the sun will shine down or across the valley on your chosen day.

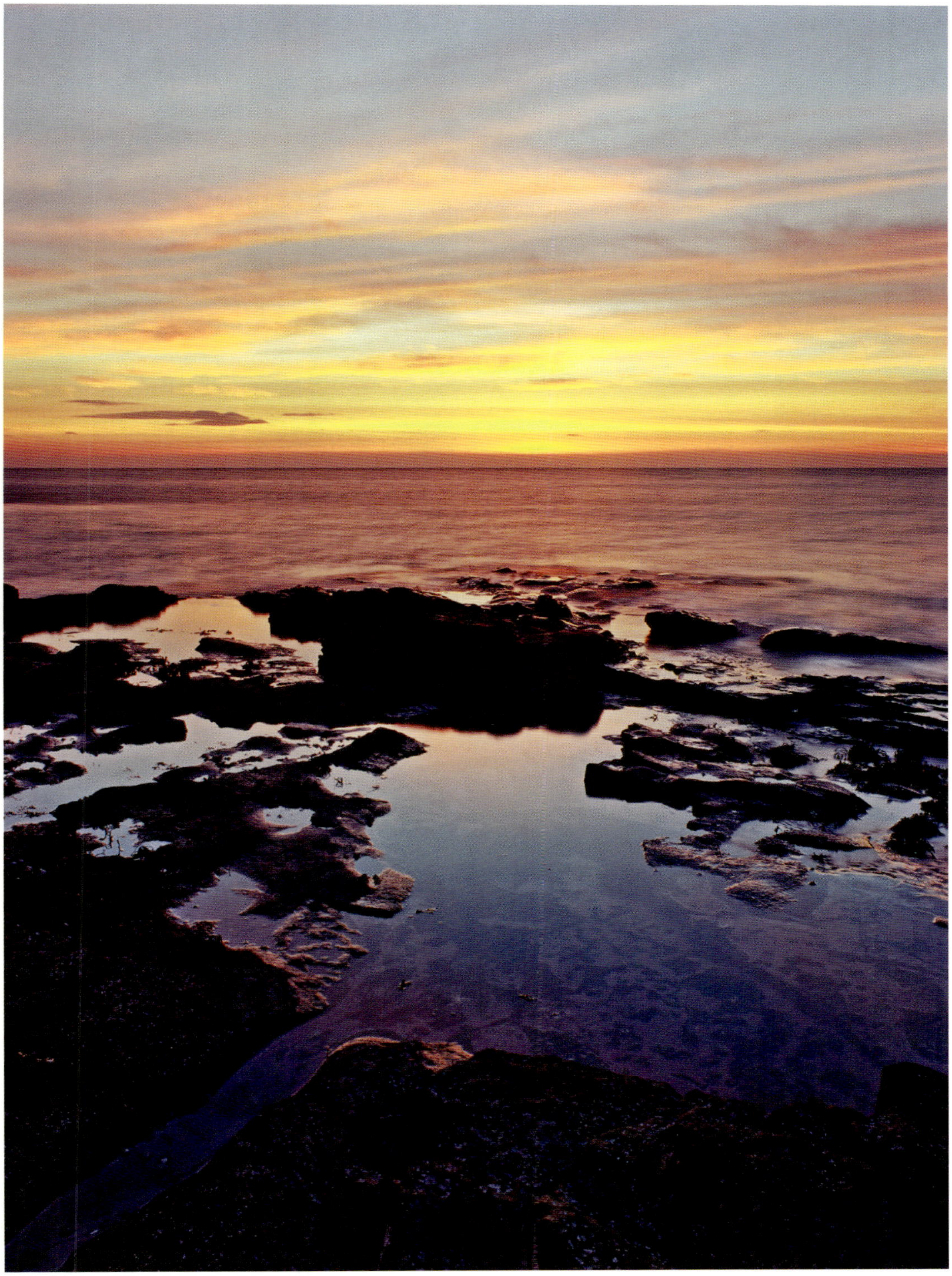

Right: Shooting into the light at sunrise or sunset means dealing with high levels of contrast. One solution is to use water: being reflective it brings color into a foreground.

The Seasons

The different seasons bring their own rewards and challenges. The biggest changes over the course of the year (away from the equatorial regions) are the length of the day, the direction that the sun rises, and the height the sun reaches in the sky at midday. However, there's more to the changing seasons than that.

The most obvious indicator of the changing seasons is plant life. As mentioned previously, deciduous woodland dramatically changes character over the course of the year. However, smaller plants such as grass and flowers make a big difference to a landscape as well.

Late spring and early summer (typically April through to June) sees the greatest abundance of wild flowers in rural fields. These add a splash of fresh color to a landscape that's very photogenic. If a field is covered with flowers use either a telephoto focal length to isolate one or two from the crowd or get down low with a wide-angle lens to really fill the foreground with flowers.

By midsummer the landscape is less fresh looking and often monochromatically green. It's not until late summer that the landscape starts to become more photogenic again as grassland starts to brown. Late summer also sees plants such as heather flower on moorland.

Fall means woodland color, but it also brings a greater chance of misty conditions. Fall is also the best time of year to find fungi.

By winter, plant life retreats as snow and ice cover the landscape. However, some plants manage to find their way through the snow—in some regions snowdrops cover woodland floors in winter, for example. These flowers are also a welcome reminder that spring isn't too far away and that the cycle is about to begin again.

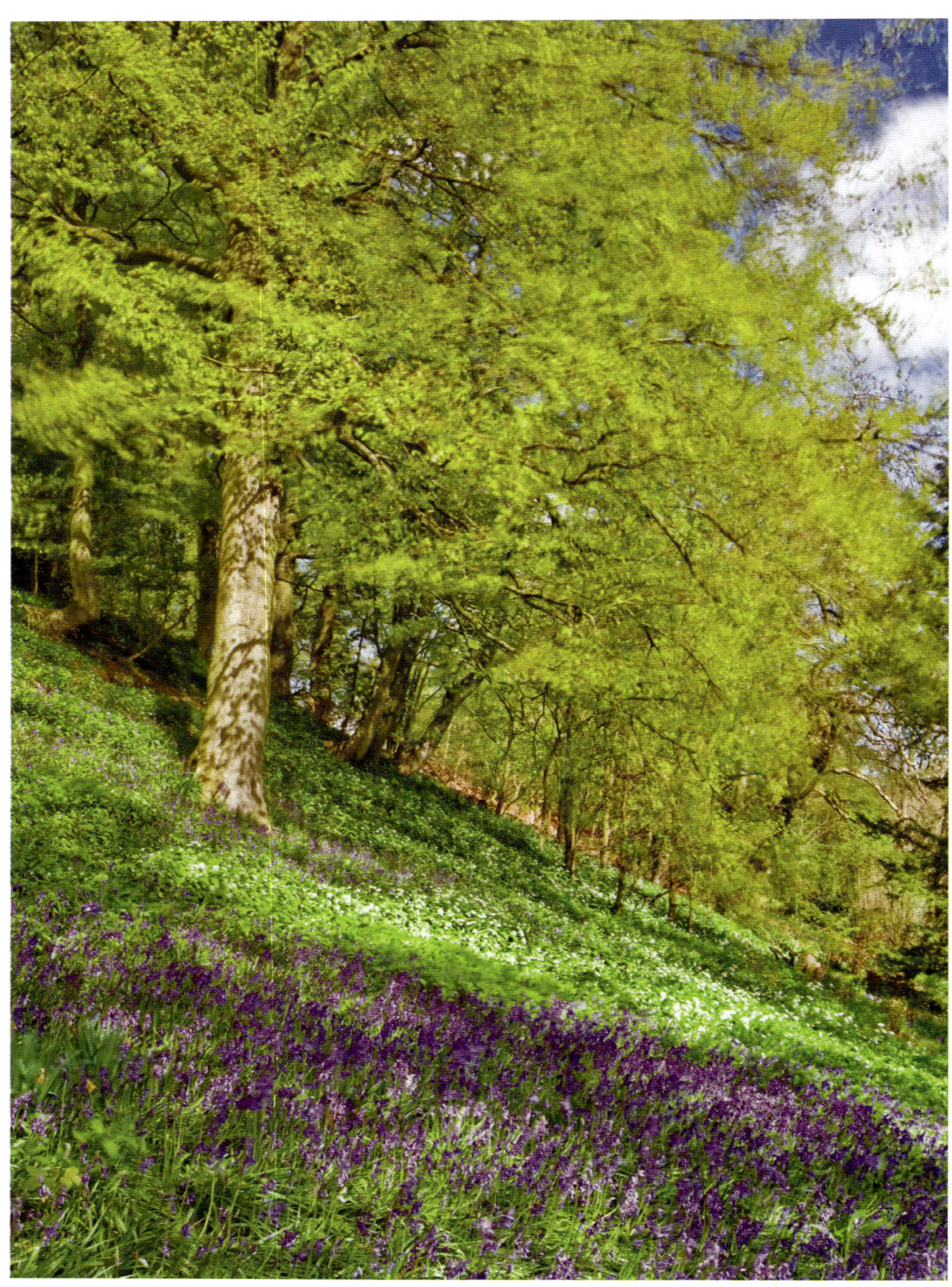

Right: Spring color has a freshness that almost borders on the luminous. Use a polarizer to help saturate these colors for maximum impact.

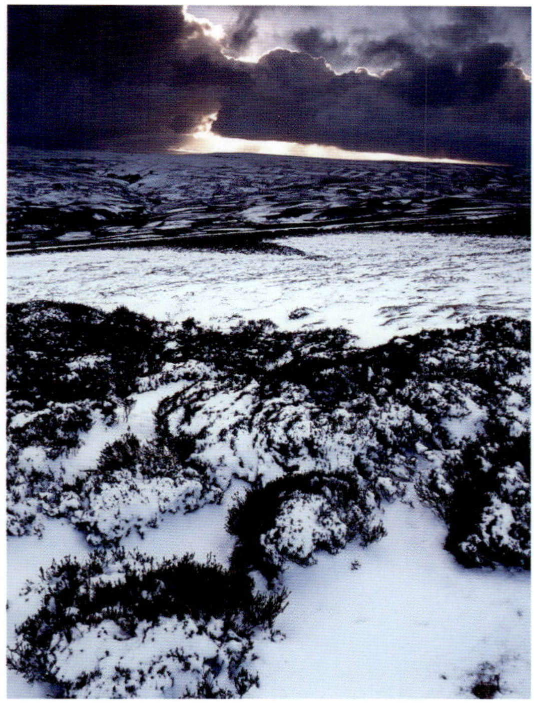

Winter

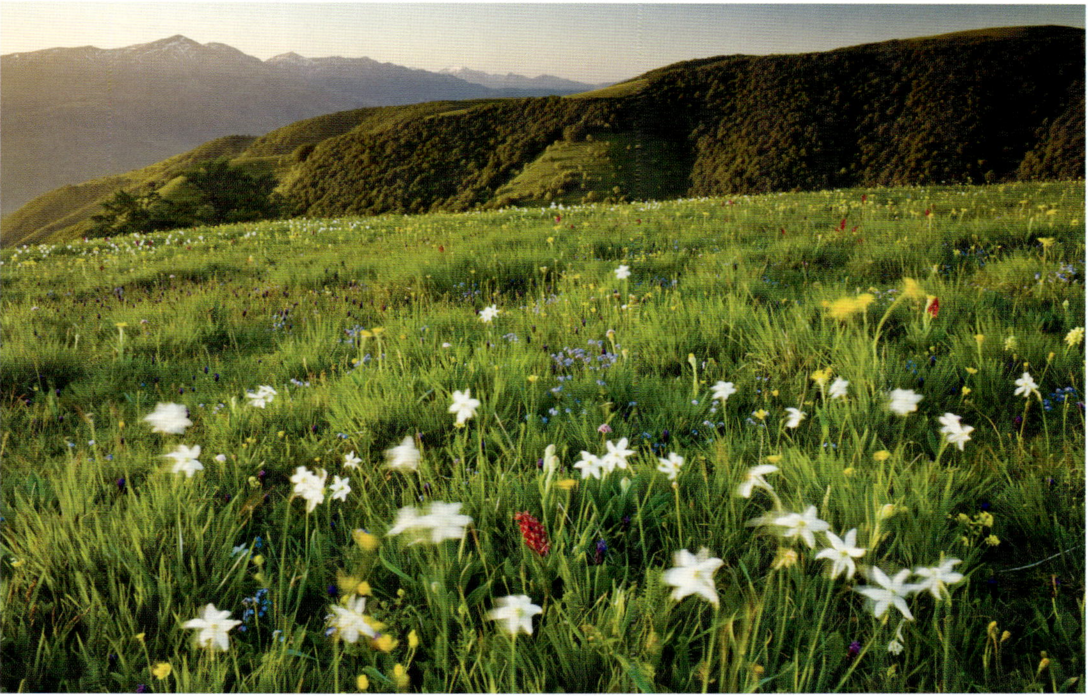

Spring

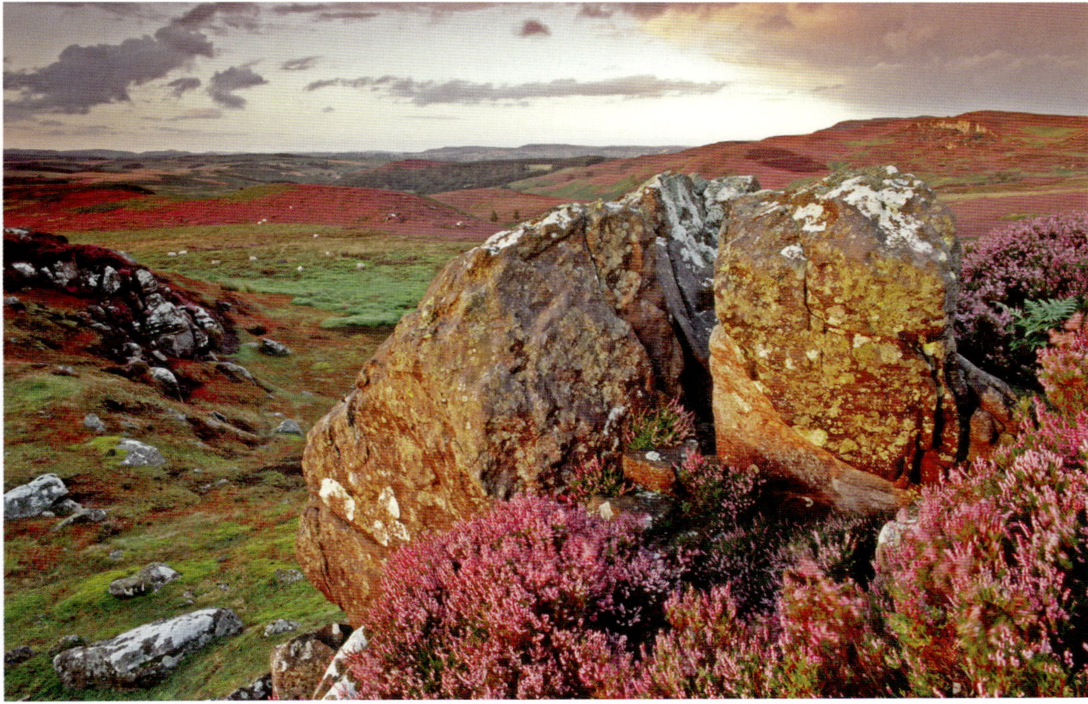

Summer

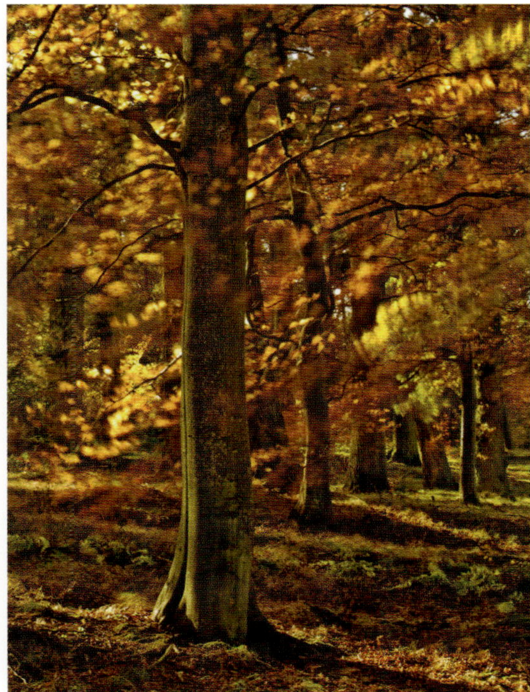

Fall

Above: One of the delights of seasonal change is the range of colors that can be seen throughout the year.

Buildings in the Landscape

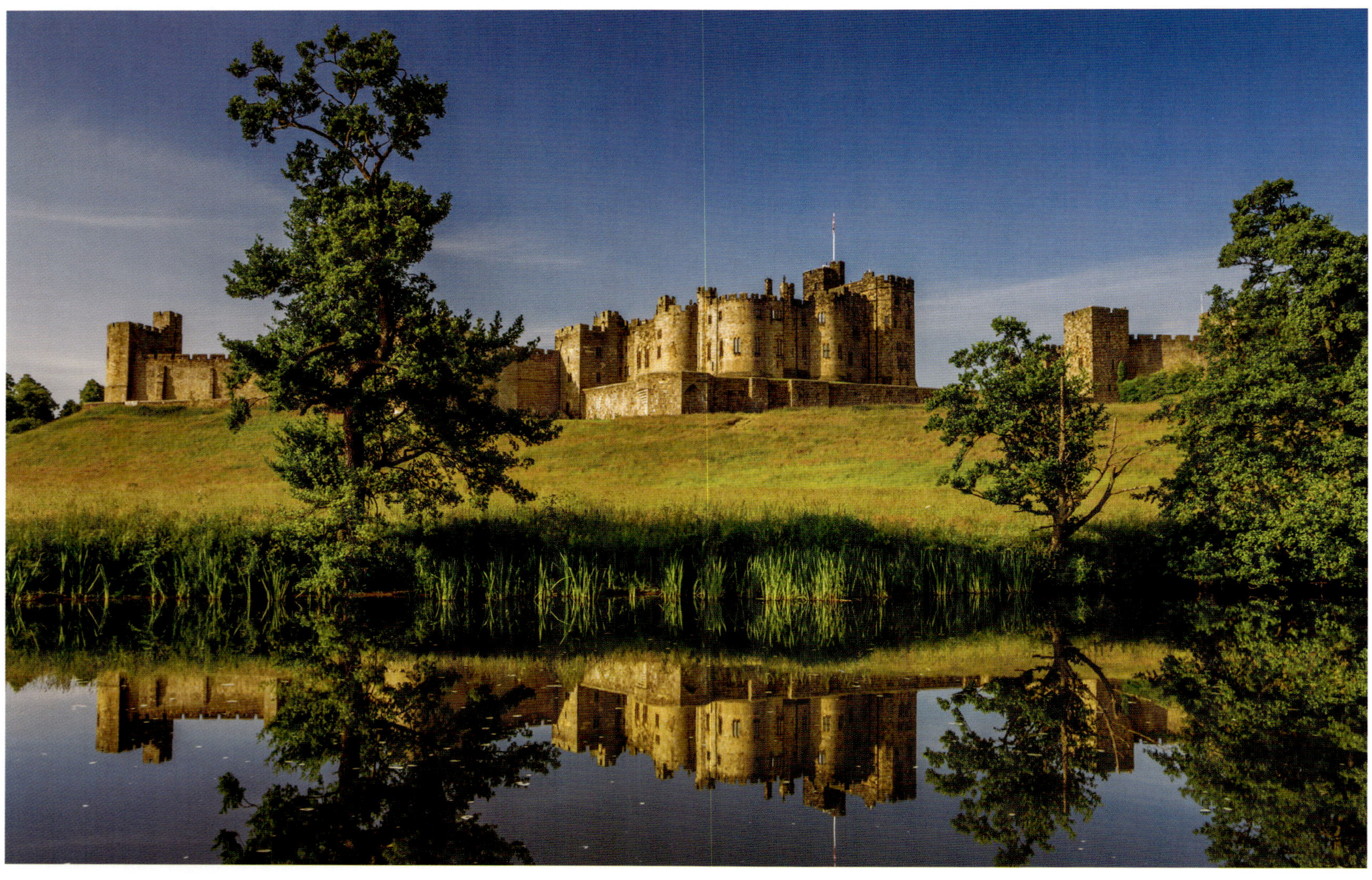

Above: This is Alnwick Castle in Northumberland, England. This is the classic view of the castle, reflected in the waters of the River Aln. As it's so photogenic it's popular with photographers. At some point I'd like to try something different from the same viewpoint—I've just not worked out what yet!

As with people, buildings in a landscape help to provide a sense of scale or a focal point, but there's also a decision to be made as to how prominent a building is within the image space. If the building fills the frame it will arguably cease to be a landscape shot and become an architectural study instead.

The problem with interesting buildings in the landscape is that they often become over-photographed (or, to put it a little more politely, they become "iconic"). This makes it difficult to find an original composition without copying someone else, even if it's unintentional. The Internet has arguably made this problem worse because it is possible to see numerous variations on a similar theme when researching your subject.

However, just because a subject is popular doesn't mean that it's impossible to find a new slant on it—you will have to try harder, but with effort it can be done. One aspect that's often overlooked is light and weather. Compositionally there may only be one or two views of a building that work, but shooting at unusual times of day—even at night—may be enough to make your photo stand out from all the rest.

Bad Weather Days

Just because the weather's bad doesn't mean there aren't photographic opportunities to be found. On overcast and wet days the light is softer, making it an ideal time to shoot details (including raindrops on wet leaves—after all, when would you see raindrops except during bad weather?). Puddles after rain has fallen are good for shooting reflections, particularly in woodland when there's an interesting tree canopy overhead.

Bad weather days are generally fairly monochromatic, so suit shooting in black and white. As the light is generally fairly constant they also work well with extreme ND filters, particularly if there's texture to the cloud formation and the formation is scudding along relatively quickly.

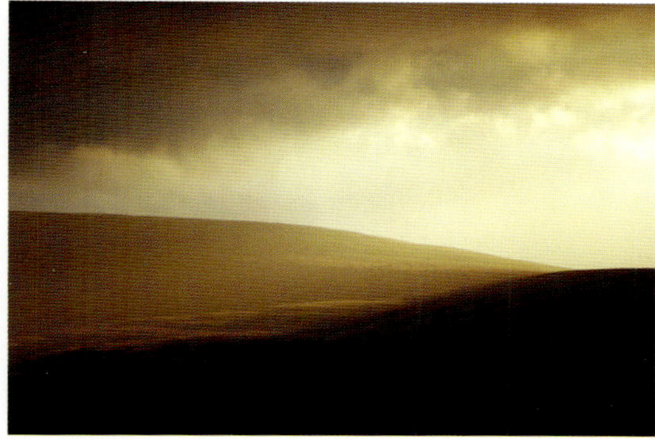

Above: Shafts of light through breaks in cloud cover can be fleeting, making it one of the few occasions when it's easier to handhold your camera, rather than setting it on a tripod.

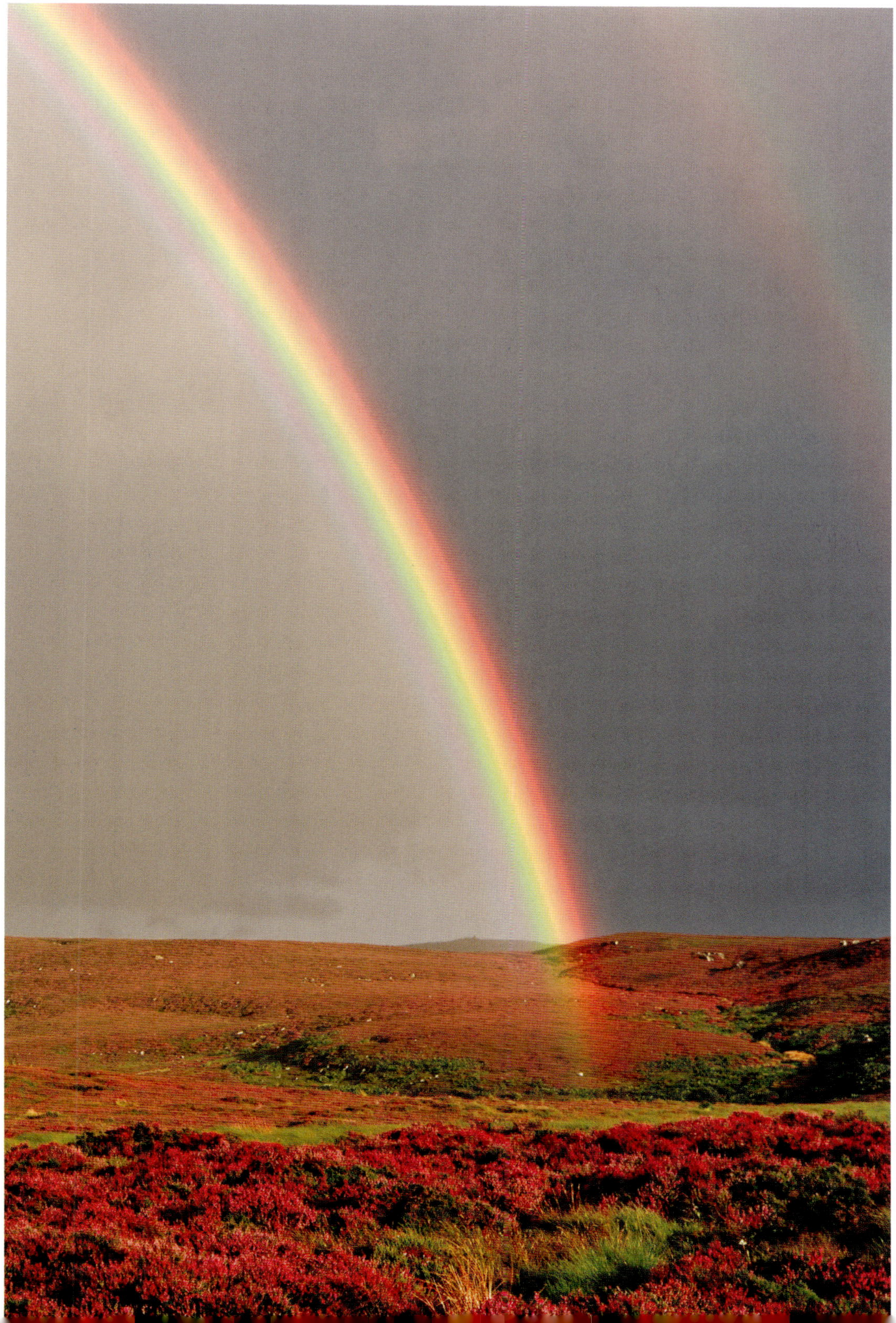

Right: Rainbows only occur when the sun is less than 42º above the horizon: the lower the sun, the more semi-circular the rainbow. For this reason, the most spectacular rainbows are seen just after sunrise or just before sunset. Rainbows are also more easily seen in winter than in summer as the sun never rises as high in winter.

Night Photography

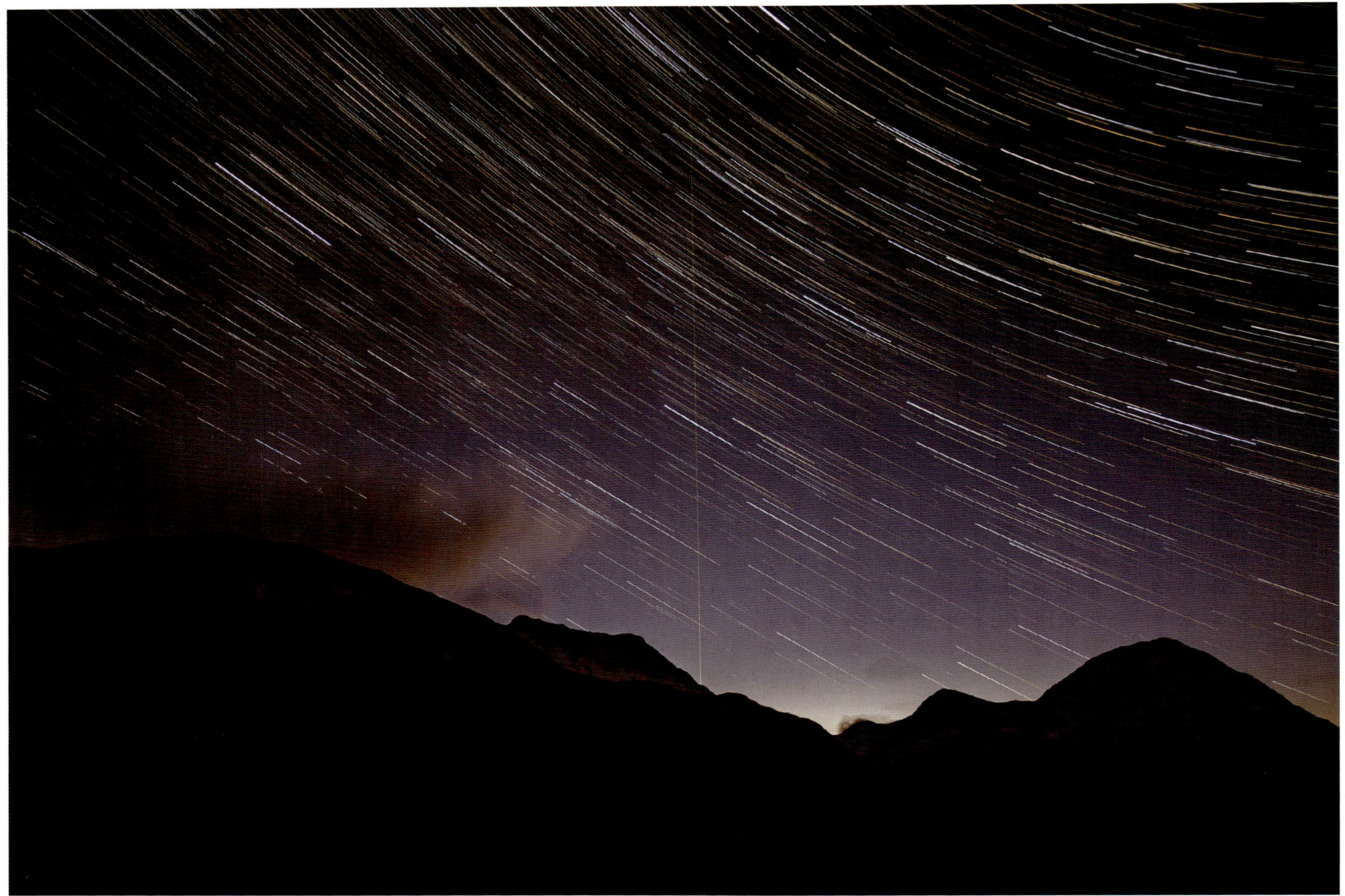

There's no escaping the fact that shooting the landscape at night means dealing with very low light levels. Even when there's a full moon the ambient light level is far lower than it is on a heavily overcast day. The obvious solution is to use a tripod. Shutter speeds will almost certainly be long unless you use a high ISO (which isn't recommended because of the resulting drop in image quality), and it's also possible that exposure times will exceed 30 seconds, so you may need to use Bulb and a remote release to hold the shutter open. To improve the light-gathering capability of your camera a fast lens is invaluable, which usually means using a prime lens.

There are two approaches to shooting stars in the night sky. You can either shoot to retain the stars as pin points in the sky, or expose your shot so the stars trail across the image space in an arc.

Above: Stars appear to move across the night sky due to the rotation of the Earth. By using a sufficiently long exposure this movement can be captured in the form of star trails. The exposure for this image was 20 minutes, which was long enough to convey a feeling of movement.

Shooting stars as pin points means using short shutter speeds, with the lens at maximum aperture and a relatively high ISO setting. It's worth experimenting to see which ISO gives you the best compromise between image quality and light sensitivity: modern full-frame cameras are often acceptable up to ISO 3200, whereas cameras with smaller sensors will be better if they're set no higher than ISO 1600 or even ISO 800.

Using a wide-angle lens will allow you to extend the shutter speed without stars appearing to streak, and make it easier to include foreground elements as well. The longer the lens, the more quickly any apparent movement will be noticeable.

Shooting star trails requires you to lock the shutter open for an extended period of time, and the longer the shutter is open, the longer the star trails will be (10 minutes is about the minimum time for a noticeable star trail). However, be sure to switch off your camera's long-exposure noise-reduction feature, as this will take as long again as the original exposure. Even without noise reduction activated, long exposures are draining, so start with a fully charged camera battery.

An alternative to shooting a single long exposure is to shoot a continuous stream of 30-second exposures over a period of time. You will need a remote release or camera with an intervalometer to time the exposures, which you can then blend in postproduction to produce the same effect as a single exposure. *Startrails. exe* and *StarStax* are two good hobbyist image-blending packages for Windows and Mac OS respectively. The advantage of choosing this method is that it doesn't matter if the camera battery dies after a period of time—you'll still have all the images shot up to that point to make a star trail image from.

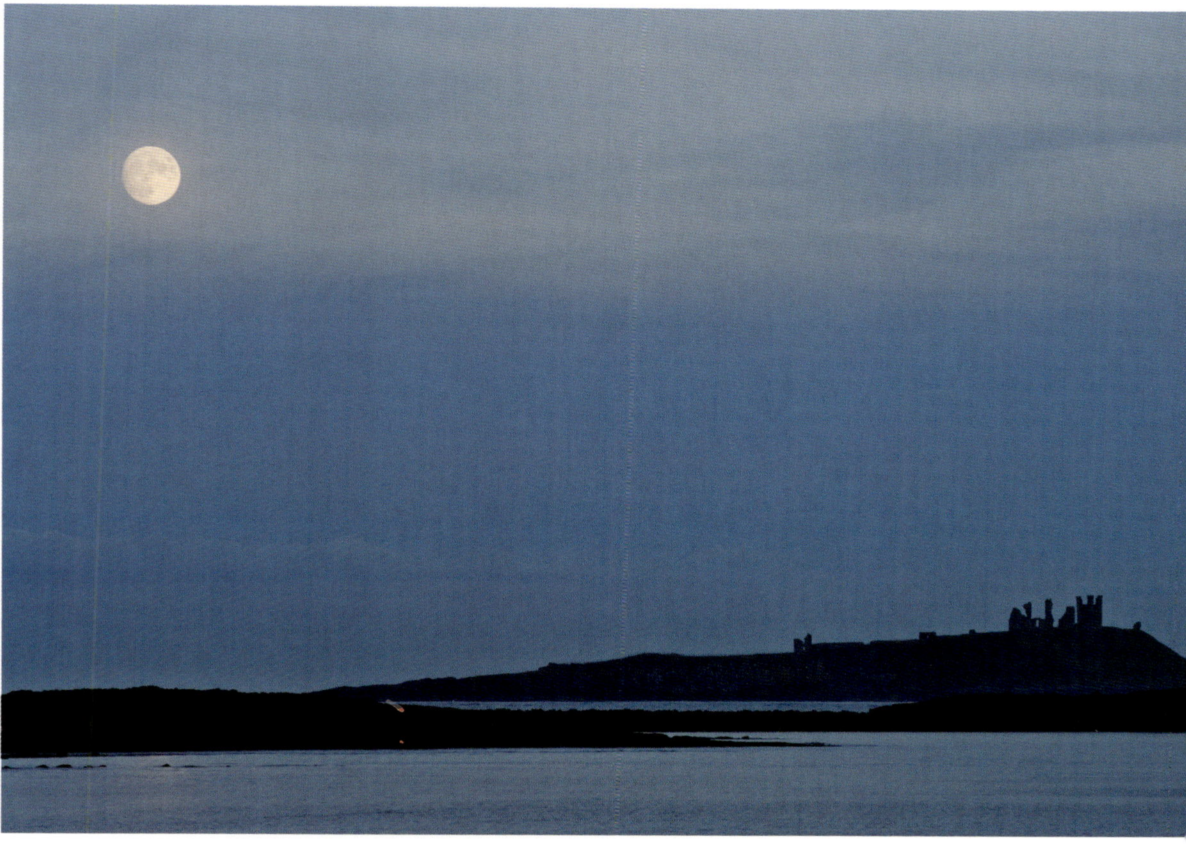

Above: The full moon rises as the sun sets. To photograph the moon and a detailed landscape it's better to shoot the evening before the moon is full.

Tip

A relatively easy way to calculate a shutter speed longer than 30 seconds is to increase your camera's ISO until the shutter speed is 30 seconds and shoot a test image. If this looks fine, calculate how many times you have to halve the ISO setting to reach your desired ISO. You can then calculate the required shutter speed by doubling the shutter speed (starting from 30 seconds) the same number of times. For example, if a 30-second exposure requires an ISO setting of 6400, the correct exposure at ISO 3200 will be 1 minute; at ISO 1600 it will be 2 minutes; at ISO 800 it will be 4 minutes, and so on.

Details

Details are the landscape in miniature. A standard or telephoto lens with a reasonably close focus is generally all that's required (wide-angle lenses aren't usually ideal), although a macro lens will allow you to really crop in on fine detail.

Simplicity is often the key to successful detail shots, but even close-to the natural world can be chaotic. There's nothing wrong with tidying up dead material from your chosen composition, but uprooting live plants or killing insects is frowned upon (and may even be illegal in the country or area that you're photographing in). Shooting in soft light will also remove distracting shadows and highlights.

Shooting details often means working close to the ground, which creates a number of physical challenges that need to be overcome. The first is getting your camera low and steady enough to shoot successfully. Lying down on your stomach and resting your elbows on the ground is one way to achieve this, but a less messy solution (if possible) is to take the center column out of your tripod and refit it upside down. Once the camera is attached—albeit upside down—it's simply a matter of raising the center column up and down until it's at the right height. Live View is very useful when using this technique, particularly if the LCD can be swivelled and angled so that it's easier to see.

Alternatively, if your tripod can go down to ground level without inverting the center column, using an angle viewer fitted to the viewfinder will help you compose your shots without the need to put your head too close to the ground.

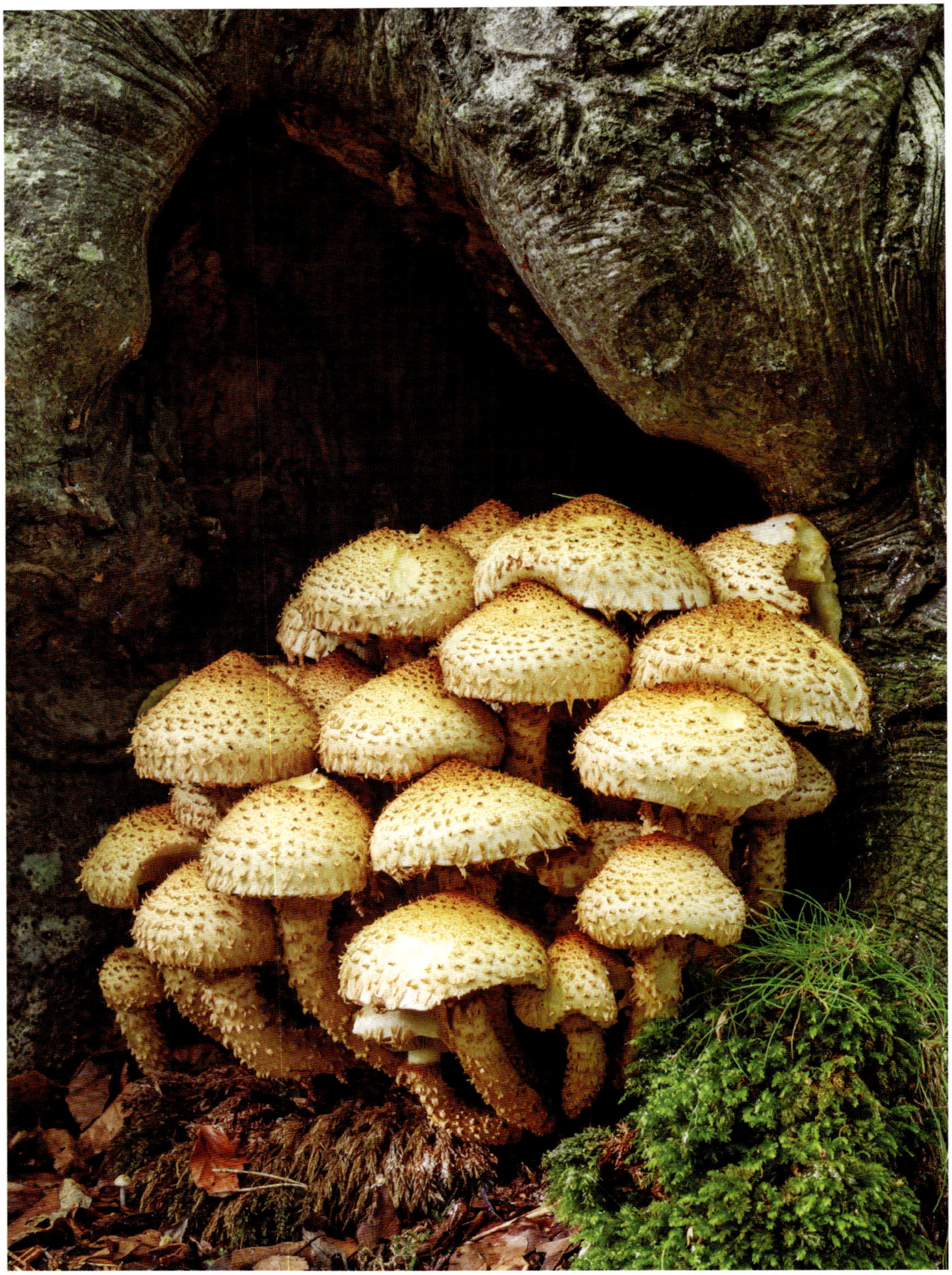

Right: Keeping a soft pad for kneeling on in your camera bag makes life less painful when shooting details. Foam kneeling pads are waterproof and can also be used as a shade to block out direct light.

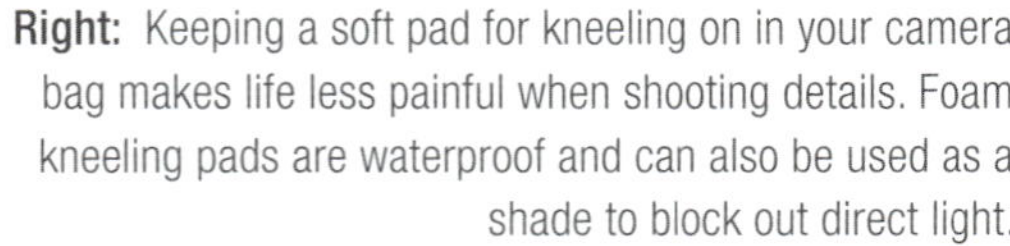

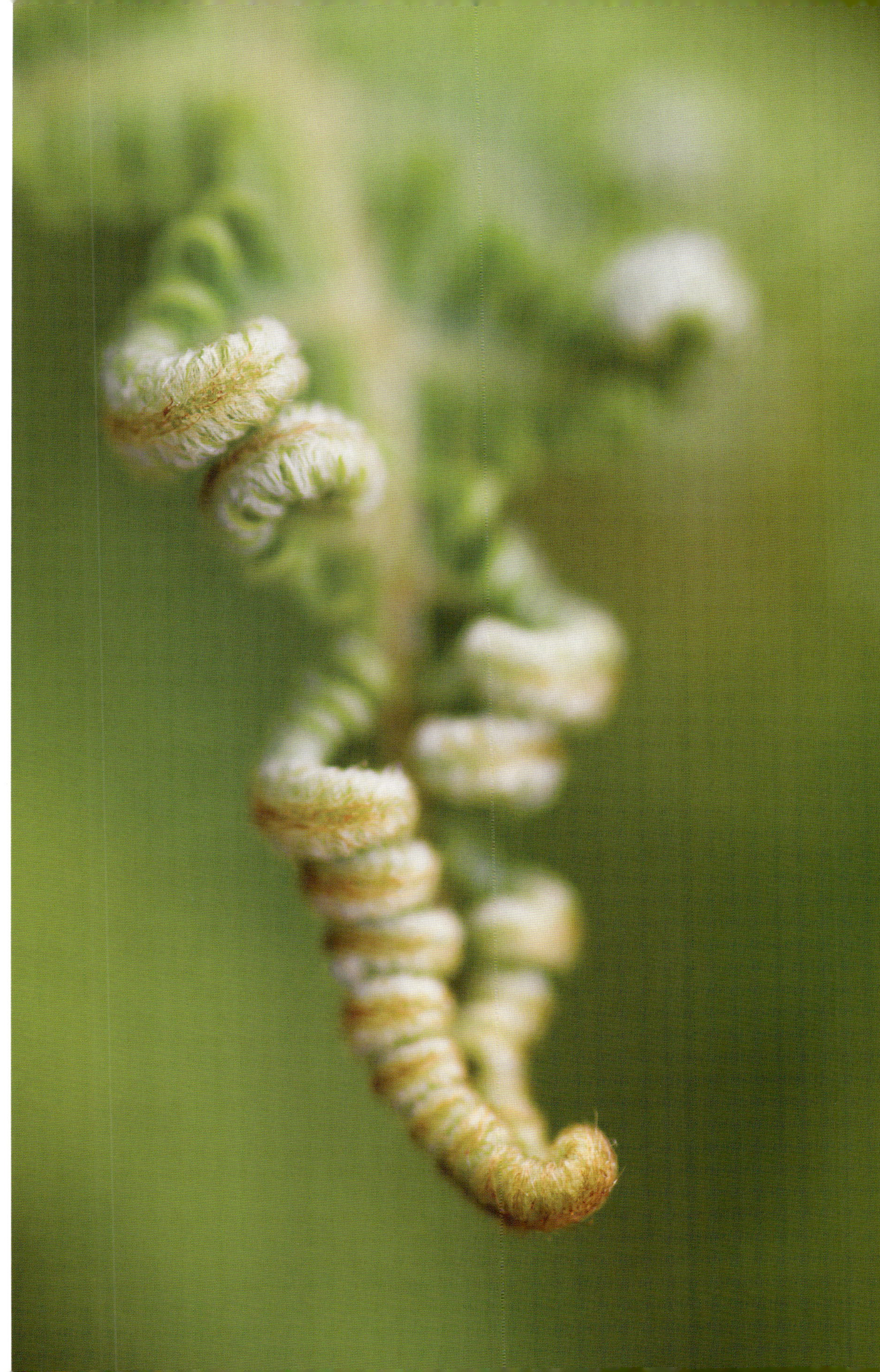

Right: The shorter the camera-to-subject distance, the
less depth of field there will be, even when using small
apertures. This makes choosing the correct focus point
more critical than when shooting standard landscapes. Live
View makes this process easier, particularly if your camera
allows you to zoom into the Live View image. When I was
setting up this shot I focused on the tip of the fern, as I felt
that was the most important part of the plant to have sharp.

Panoramic Images

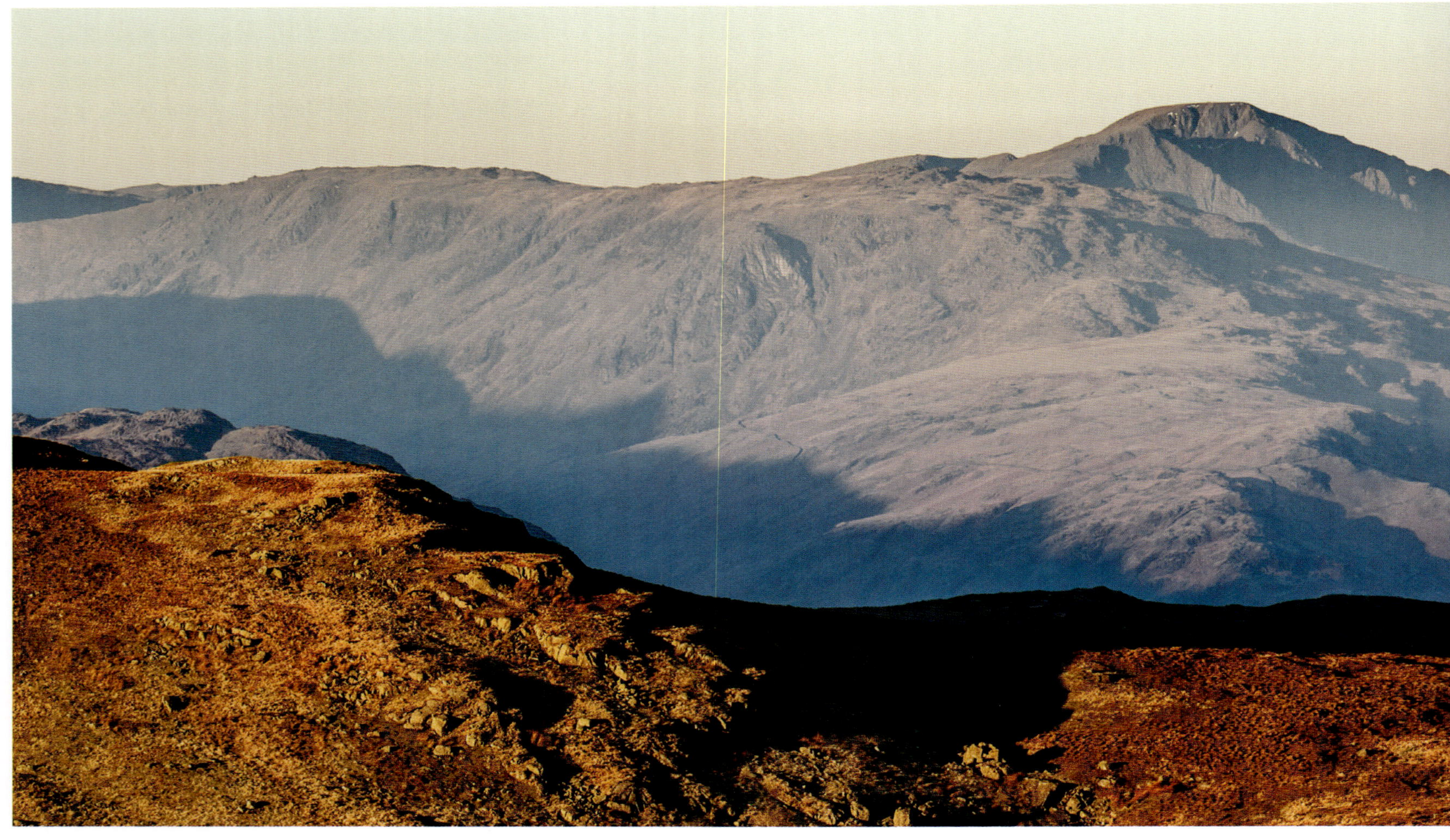

Panoramic landscape images have never been so popular. Digital photography has made it easy to create panoramic images, which were once only possible with specialized film cameras. The simplest way to create a panorama is to crop a regular photograph, but if you do this, the resulting image may have a relatively low resolution. Therefore, a more satisfying solution is to shoot a sequence of separate images horizontally (or vertically) and join—or "stitch"—them together during postproduction.

The key to creating a sequence that can be easily stitched is preparation. To make postproduction easier, all the images in the sequences should use the same exposure, ISO, focus, and white balance settings. The easiest way to achieve this is to switch exposure and focus to manual, set a fixed ISO, and use either a white balance preset or create a custom white balance.

The first decision you need to make when composing a panorama is to decide where the start and end points in your scene are. Don't be ambitious when first trying a panorama—the further apart the start and end points, the harder it will be to get everything right first time. However, it pays to be conservative and shoot slightly more, both horizontally and vertically, than you need. It's far easier to crop unwanted detail out than to add necessary (but missing) detail later.

Although it sounds counterintuitive, it's also best to shoot images for a horizontal panorama with the camera in a vertical orientation and vice versa. Although this means you'll need to shoot more images, it will give you greater scope for cropping later. As you shoot your sequence, overlap each image by roughly one third. This is because stitching software needs common points of reference between each image in a sequence in order to work effectively.

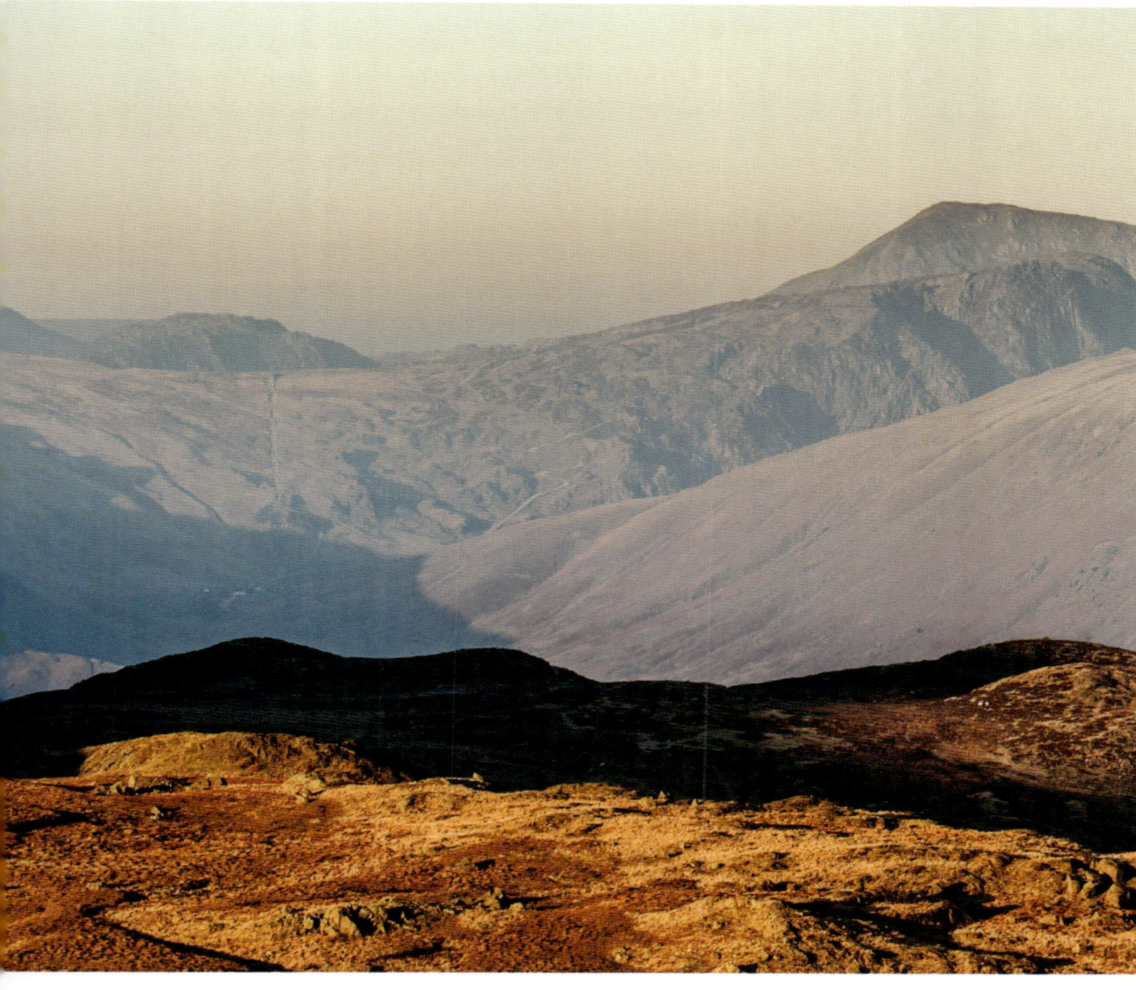

> **NOTE**
>
> Some cameras have a "sweep" panorama mode that allows you to create panoramic images in-camera by smoothly moving your camera in one fluid movement. The drawback with this method is that it's usually only possible to shoot JPEGs and the resolution is often limited.

Stitching

There are numerous software options that will allow you to stitch a panoramic sequence together and some camera manufacturers supply stitching software for free with their cameras.

Adobe Photoshop has a Photomerge option that offers a number of different ways to stitch sequences together, although the Auto setting usually works effectively. Alternative software options include *Panoweaver* and *PTGui*.

Regardless of the software you use, once the sequence has been stitched you'll need to crop your image to a rectangular shape, as the "raw" panorama will have ragged edges. The aspect ratio you choose will largely depend on the size of the rectangle that can be fitted into the stitched image. However, a 2:1 or 3:1 aspect ratio is often more pleasing than a longer, thinner panorama.

Another slightly counterintuitive aspect of shooting panoramic image sequences is that wide-angle lenses tend to work less well than standard lenses or even short telephotos. This is because wide-angle focal lengths introduce distortion, particularly at the edges, that stitching software sometimes struggles to overcome successfully.

Work smoothly, but quickly, as you shoot your panoramic sequence and try to keep your camera level. A hotshoe spirit level or an on-screen electronic level is very useful.

Although your camera will move during the shooting of the sequence, it's better if the elements in the scene do not, as this can create problems when it comes to stitching your individual images together. One subject that's particularly difficult to photograph in this way is moving water. Fast-flowing rivers and shorelines change constantly (and often dramatically), even within a short space of time.

Once a water sequence has been stitched it's worth viewing the resulting panorama at 100% and checking that all the joins are seamless. Clone and patch where necessary to repair imperfect blends.

Chapter 6

Composition

Composition is the art of creating an aesthetically pleasing image. Although many aspects of photography can be automated, composition is very much a personal choice that (for the moment) can't be left to your camera. Although there are compositional "rules" that you can follow or disregard, the final decision on how the various elements in a scene will be arranged within an image is entirely up to you.

Right: Composition is a puzzle that needs to be worked out. Sometimes you have time to think and experiment, but often nature doesn't cooperate and more intuitive decisions need to be made quickly. That was the case here, when rain threatened to sweep in just as I arrived at the location. I only had time to set up and shoot one frame before the rain arrived and the distant hills vanished into the gloom.

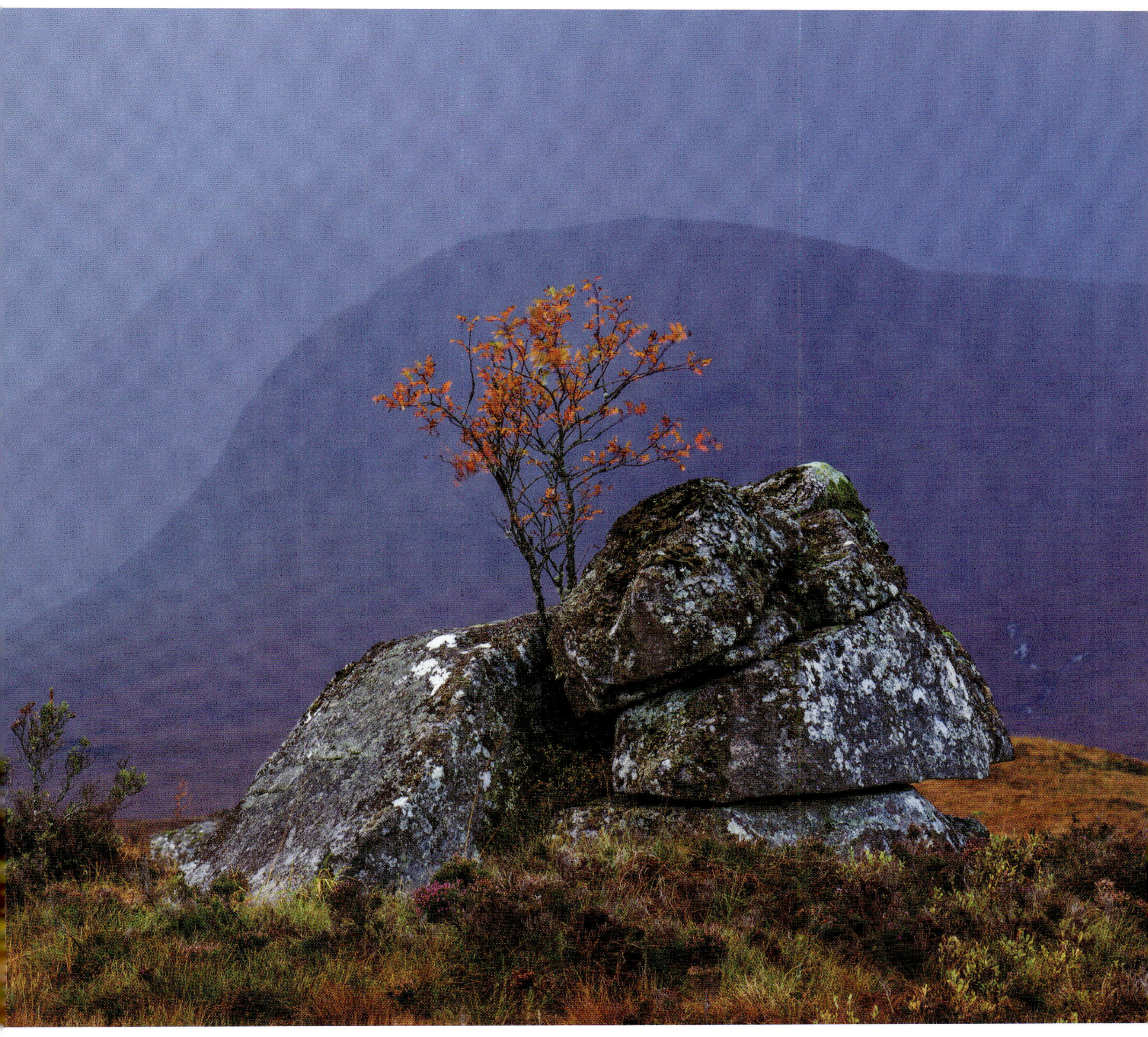

Compositional Rules

A rule is a command that really should be obeyed, but this implies a slavish adherence that is the opposite of creativity. So while there are established "rules" of composition, they should be seen as useful guidelines rather than ways of constraining how you compose an image. Perhaps the only rule to stick to is that a composition should be a pleasing whole: anything that doesn't add to an image or that detracts from it should be excluded.

The Rule of Thirds

If there's one compositional rule that almost everyone has heard of, it's the "Rule of Thirds." It's a very simple rule that helps you compose a pleasingly balanced image.

The Rule of Thirds requires you to divide the image space using two vertical and two horizontal lines spaced equally apart (if your camera can display a grid over a Live View image it may well divide the screen in this way). The basic principle is that horizontal or vertical elements in the scene are aligned with one (or more) of these imaginary lines or that the focal point of the image is placed at the point where two lines intersect.

A good example of when to consider using the Rule of Thirds is in the placement of the horizon in landscape images. Placing it centrally can appear contrived, as it artificially divides the image into an equal amount of foreground and sky, and images lack energy as a result. Placing the horizon on a third, however, immediately adds interest, and forces you to decide which is more important to the composition—the foreground or the sky.

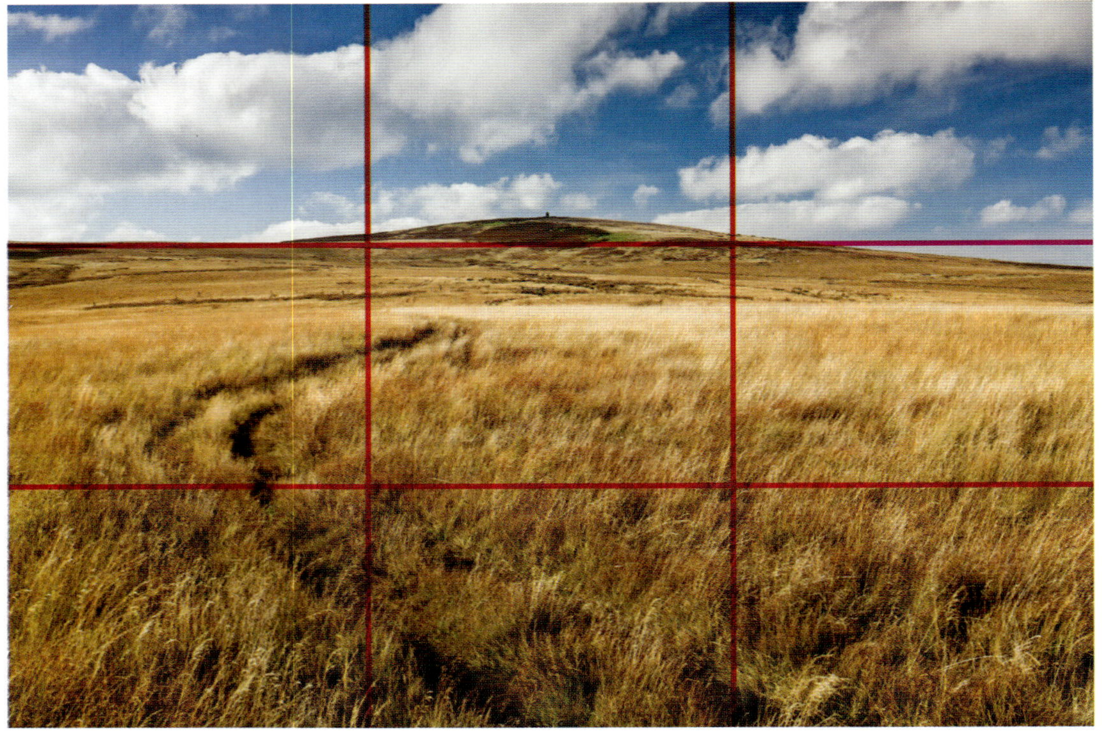

Above: In this image it was the foreground that I felt was most important. A ratio of two-thirds ground to one-third sky felt right, which corresponds to the Rule of Thirds.

The Rule of Odds

The Rule of Odds has it that an odd number of elements in a scene is generally preferable to an even number. With odd numbers of elements there is always one element framed by the others (whether that's one element on either side, or two, or four, and so on). By comparison, an even number of elements in an image doesn't feel as resolved compositionally. The rule of odds is less important when there are more elements in an image than can be immediately counted: a few odd-numbered trees is more effective than an odd number of trees in a forest.

NOTE

A focal point is an important element in the image (usually your chosen subject). It's where someone viewing your image would be most likely to look first, or would reach eventually by following visual clues through the image. Generally, the fewer focal points there are, the more striking the image—multiple focal points can be confusing and make the image harder to "read."

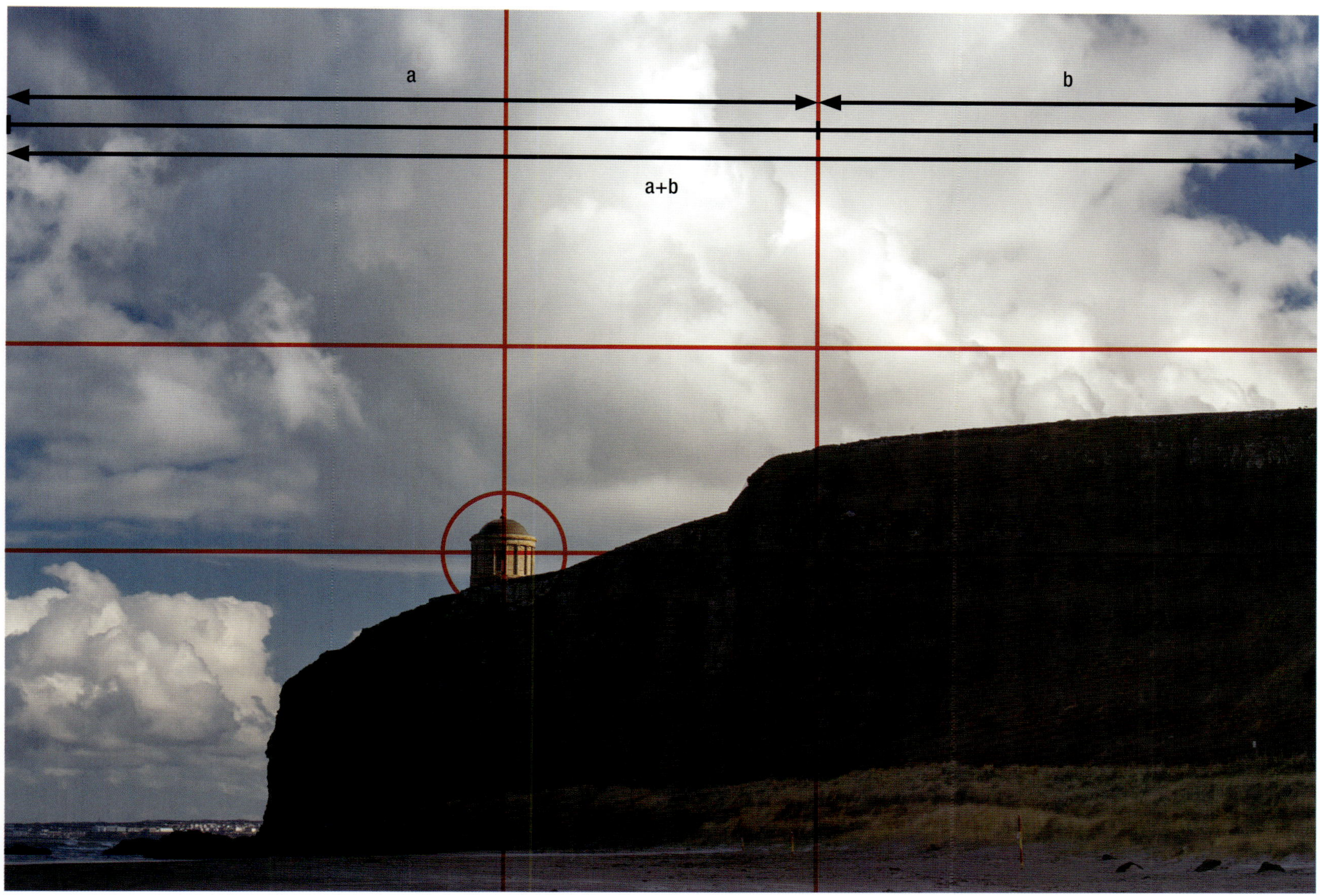

The Golden Ratio

The Golden Ratio refers to an incredibly interesting number: 1.618 (often shown using the Greek letter Phi/φ). Although it may appear arbitrary, it's the number you get when a line is cut in such a way that the longest part (a), when divided by the shorter (b), is also equal to the original line divided by (a). This is expressed mathematically as:

$$a/b = a+b/a = 1.618.$$

To apply the idea to a photograph you divide the image into two rectangles so that the smaller rectangle has the same ratio to the larger one that the larger one has to the original image shape. If you repeat this (by subdividing the sections still further) you end up with a grid that's not too dissimilar to that of the Rule of Thirds.

As with the Rule of Thirds, placing important elements of the composition on intersections creates a pleasing balance.

Above: The focal point of this image is the building on the clifftop. This has been placed on an intersection in the frame, divided using the Golden Ratio.

NOTE

The Golden Ratio pre-dates the Rule of Thirds by millennia. However, it's more difficult to visualize—and to explain—which is largely why it's less popular than the Rule of Thirds (which is essentially a simplified form of the Golden Ratio).

The Golden Triangle

The Golden Triangle divides an image space into
at least three triangles of different sizes, but which
have exactly the same shape. Two triangles are
made initially by slicing an image diagonally from
one corner to the other. A further two triangles are
made by slicing one of the initial triangles so that
the shape of the new triangles matches the larger,
main triangle.

Visually important elements are then placed
within the boundaries of the different triangles,
or following the lines of the boundaries. Placing
your focal point at an intersection point of
the triangles also (arguably) produces a more
dynamic composition than using a Rule of Thirds
intersection point.

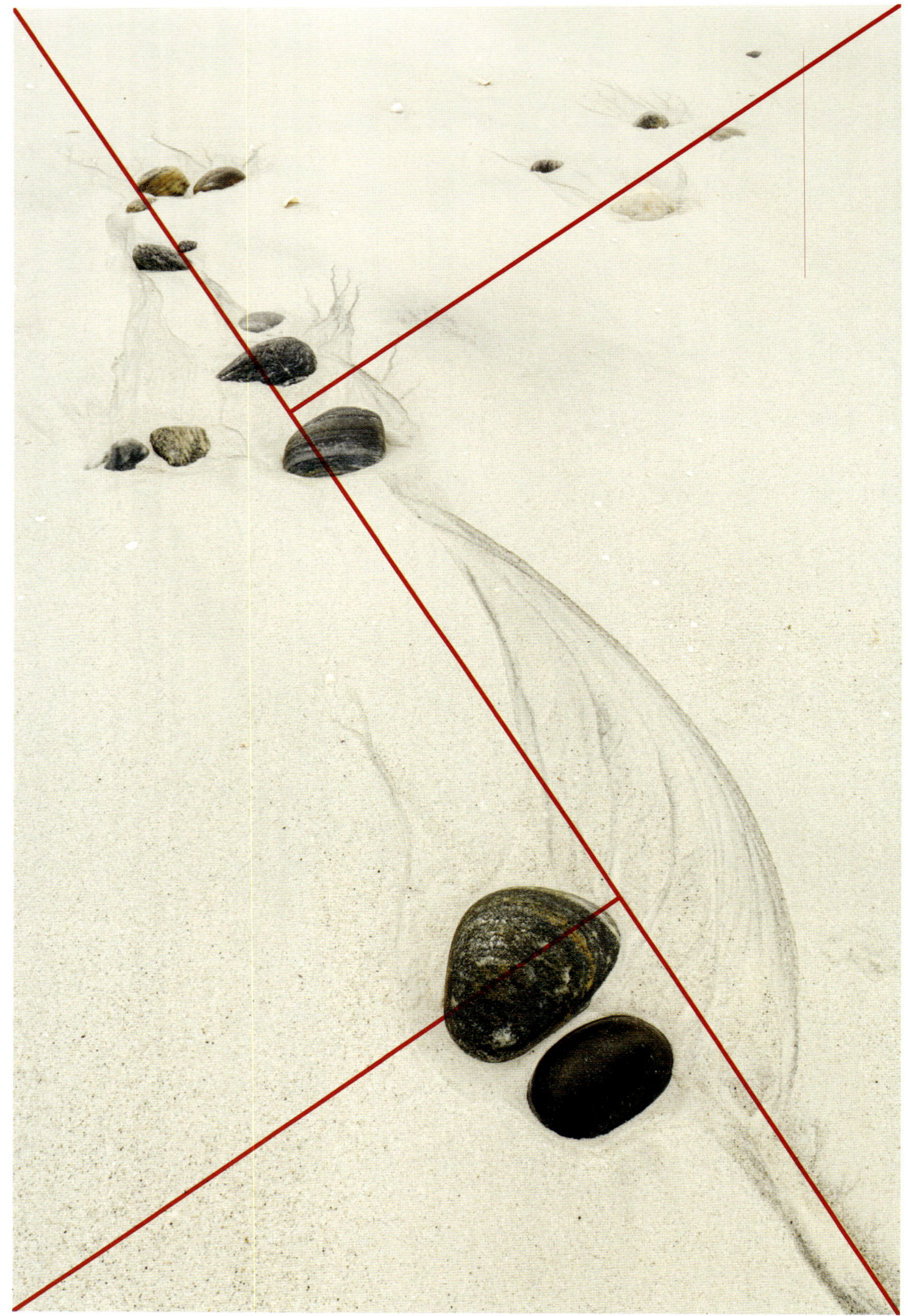

Right: As with all of the rules described here, the
Golden Triangle can be used on any shape of image
and in any orientation.

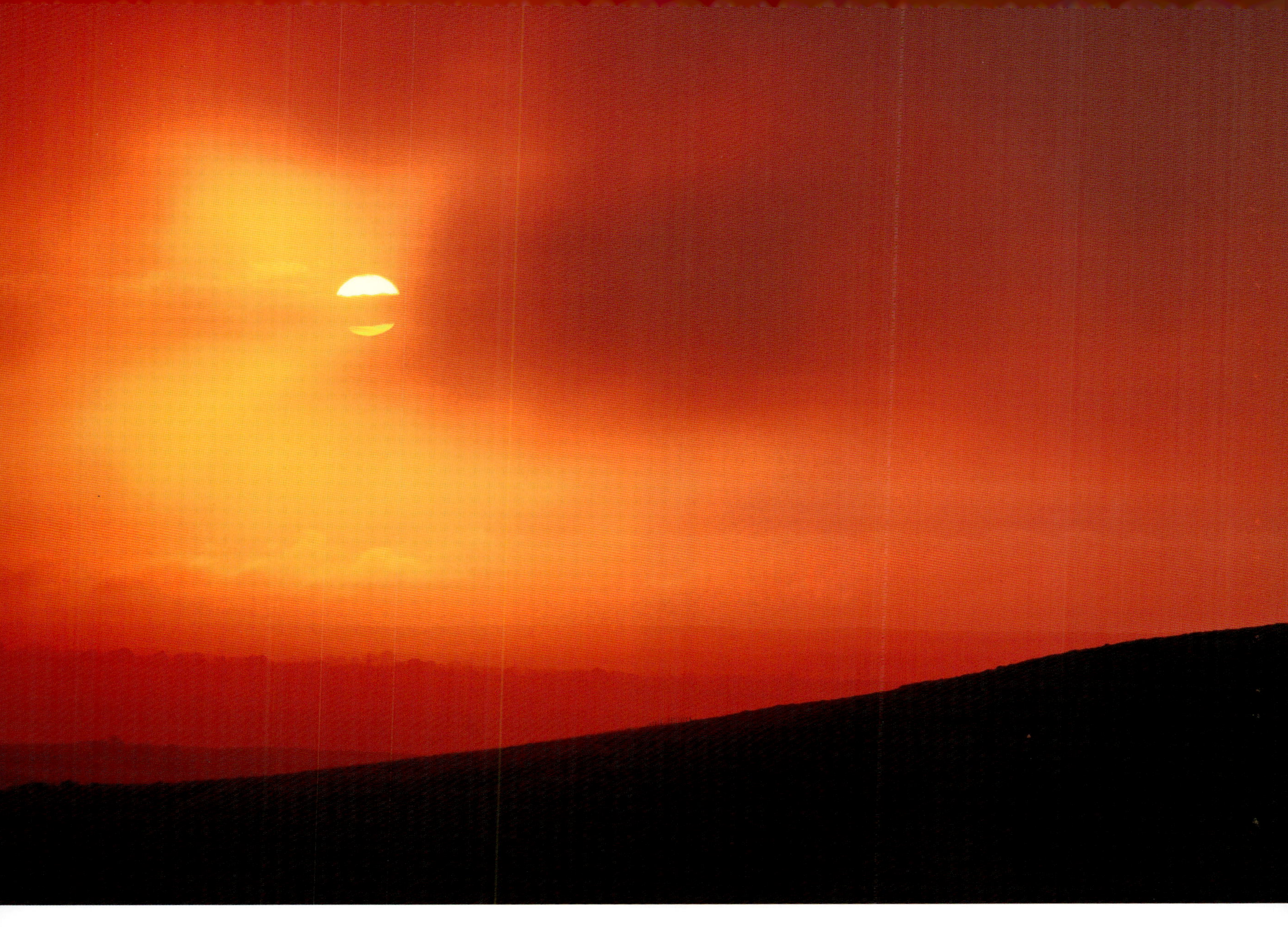

Above: Developing an intuitive sense for composition pays dividends when you need to work quickly. Fleeting weather conditions may only give you a few seconds to compose and shoot. In this minimal composition the position of the focal point—the sun—was critical.

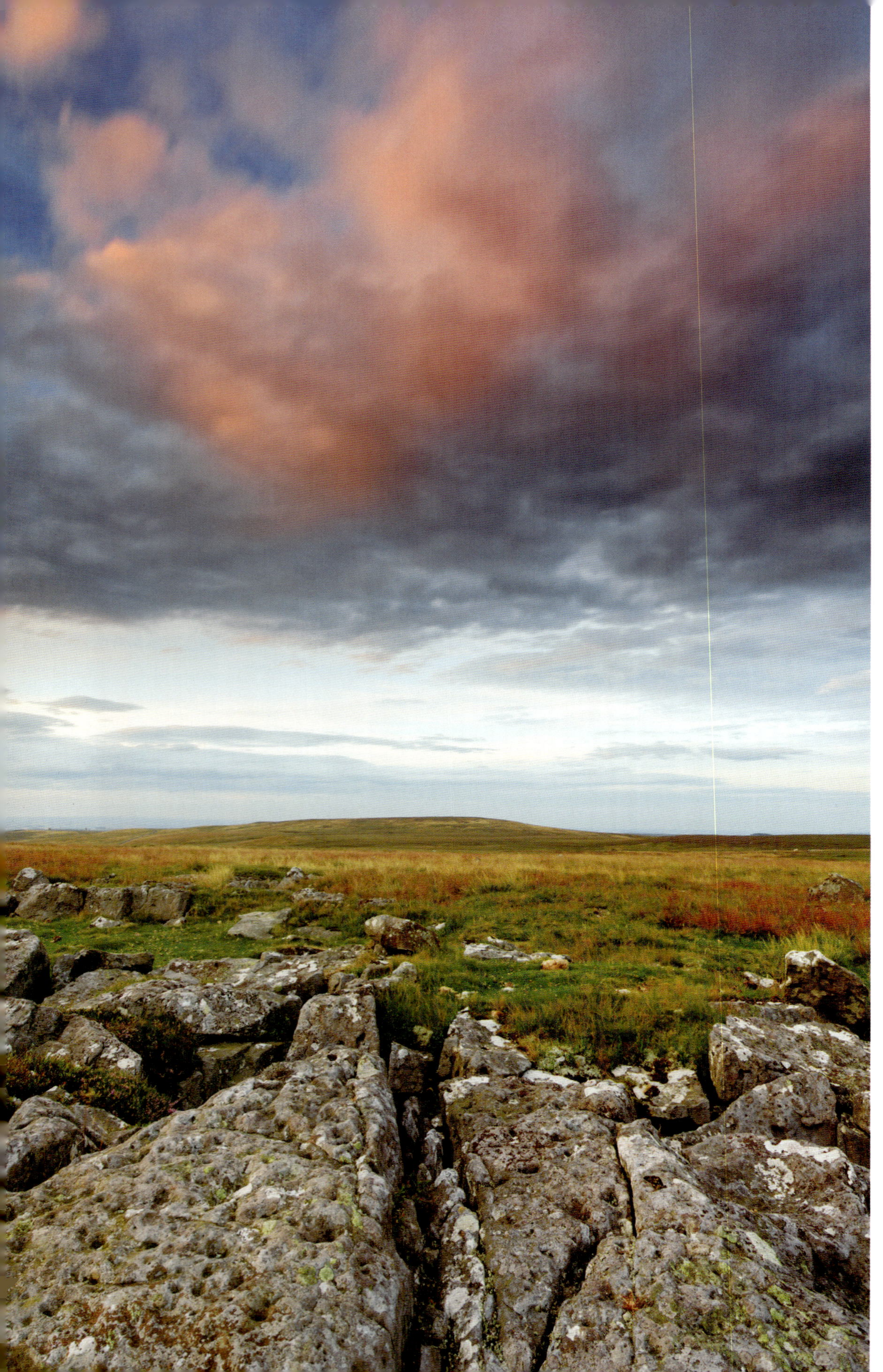

Breaking the Rules

You shouldn't be afraid to break the rules occasionally. Although the Rule of Thirds can help you compose aesthetically pleasing images, overuse will make your pictures appear formulaic.

With landscape photography, the Rule of Thirds implies that the horizon has to be one-third or two-thirds of the way up from the bottom of the image. Although this works for a lot of photographs it isn't necessarily right for every shot you take.

Indeed, placing the horizon centrally is important when composing symmetrical images or those that have a more tranquil feel, for example. Similarly, placing the horizon closer to the bottom or the top of the image can also make more of a statement than following the Rule of Thirds.

Another way to make a statement is to place your focal point somewhere on the vertical center line of the image. Again, this "breaks the rules," but there's nothing wrong with doing that if the composition works.

Left: This image breaks all of the rules described previously. However, I like it because it wasn't composed using any set formula.

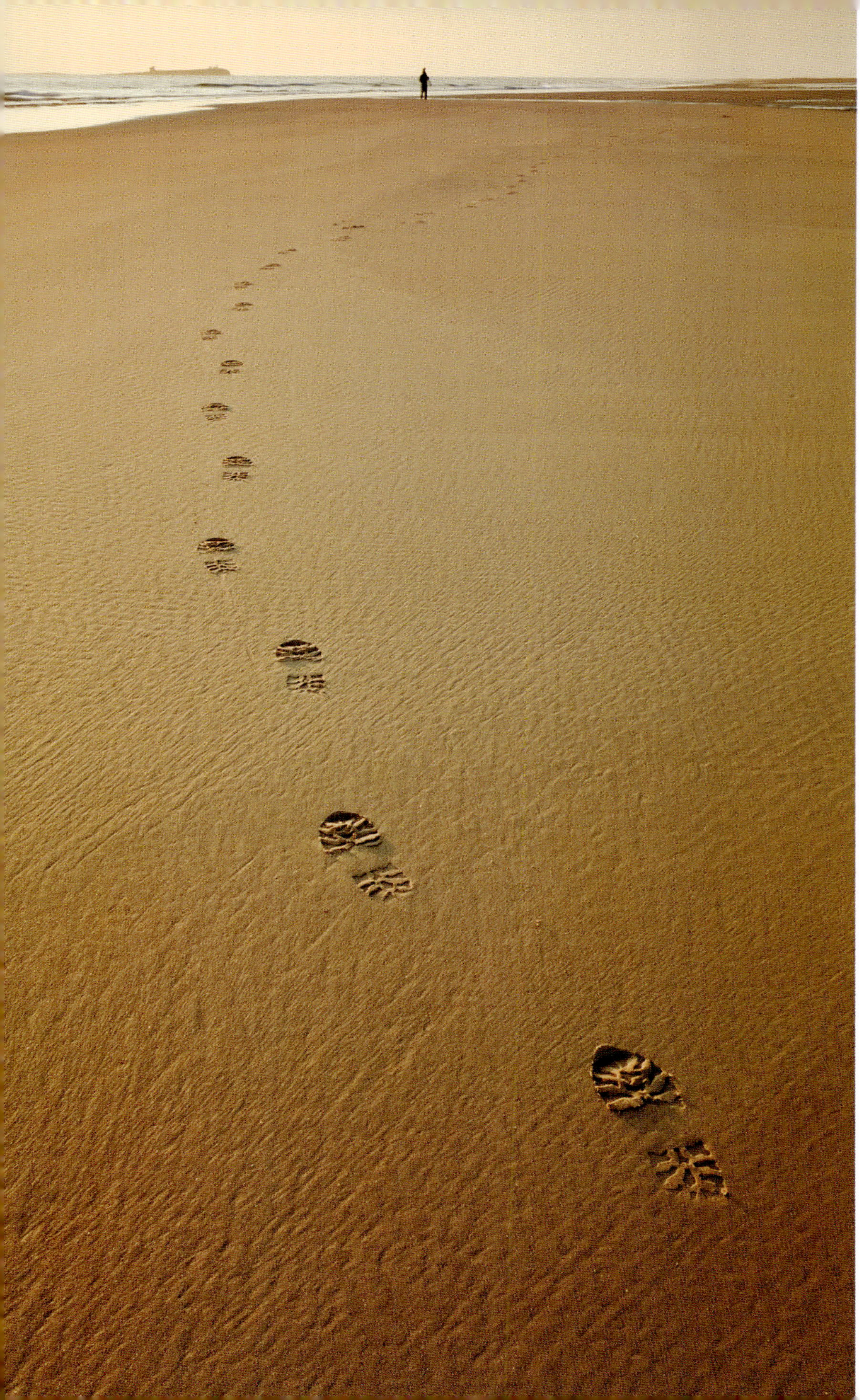

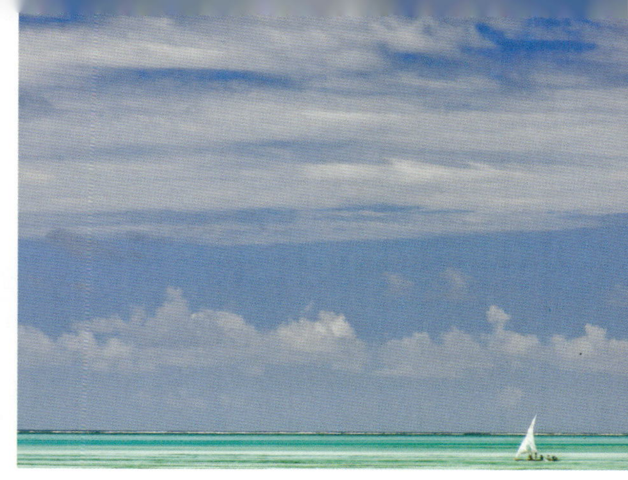

Above & Left: The horizon doesn't have to be placed directly across the center of an image, nor does it have to be placed one-third or two-thirds up the frame. A small sliver of land (or sea) in a composition will emphasize the vastness of the sky. Conversely, if the sky is relatively uninteresting (if it's clear or completely overcast) there's no reason not to reduce the sky to a small strip at the top of the picture.

Aspect Ratio

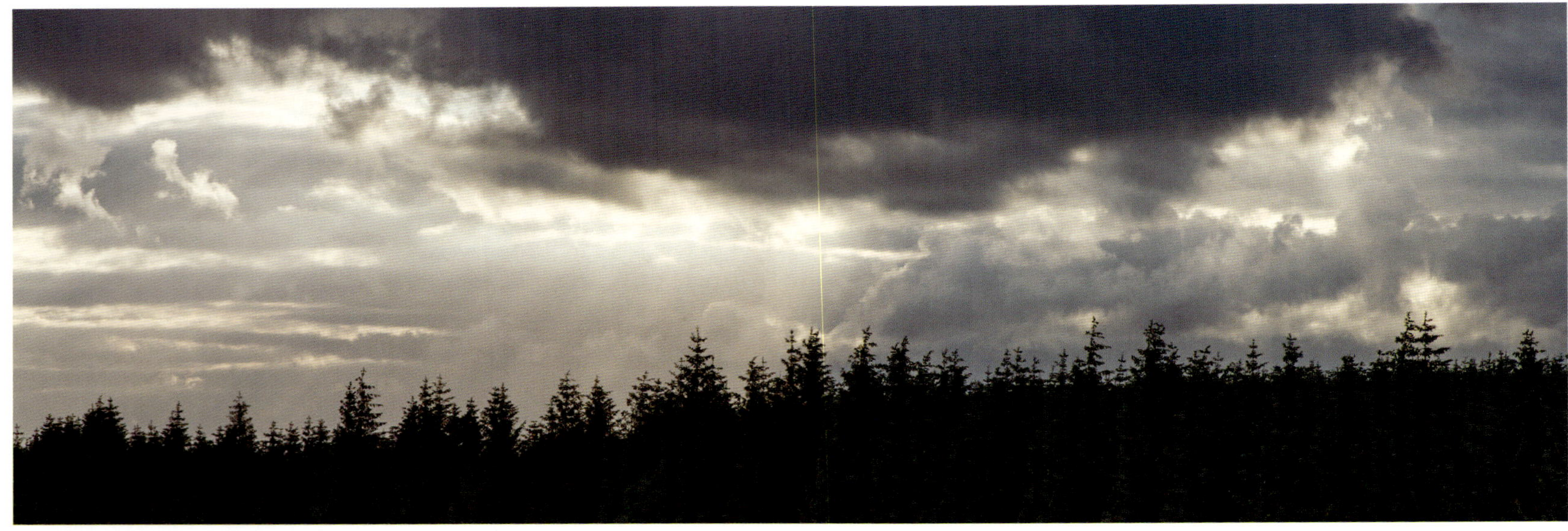

The aspect ratio of an image shows the relationship of its width to its height. This is commonly shown as x:y (where x is the width and y is the height). DSLR and APS-C cameras typically shoot at an aspect ratio of 3:2 by default (although when shooting JPEGs other aspect ratios can often be chosen instead). The 3:2 aspect ratio is a relatively long rectangle, which often feels too tall and thin when shooting landscapes vertically. It is well suited to landscape imagery when composing horizontally though, as a horizontal 3:2 image allows room for the eye to sweep from side to side in much the same way that we look at a view.

Micro Four Thirds and compact cameras use a slightly squarer aspect ratio of 4:3, which is the aspect ratio that was once the standard shape for analog televisions. In many ways this is an easier shape to compose with, and it suits vertical compositions more readily than 3:2.

Square images (with an aspect ratio of 1:1) were once the preserve of medium-format cameras, but now it's a shape more commonly associated with images shot using a cell phone. As the sides are all equal in length, square images are best suited to balanced compositions. The eye tends to sweep around a square image in a circular movement, which suits a more subtle, less dynamic composition than 3:2.

There's no standard aspect ratio for panoramic images. The closest to a standard is 16:9, which is the aspect ratio of HDTVs, but this isn't that different to 3:2. More pleasing panoramic images are those with aspect ratios of 2:1 and 3:1, which are shapes that suit wide open vistas that the eye can explore.

When shooting Raw, your camera will produce an image at the native aspect ratio of the sensor. However, if your camera can display grid lines (either in the viewfinder or on the LCD in Live View) these can be used to compose in the desired aspect ratio with the intention of cropping later in postproduction.

Above: An aspect ratio of 3:1 feels very "panoramic," but you need to compose with care so that visual interest is maintained across the image space.

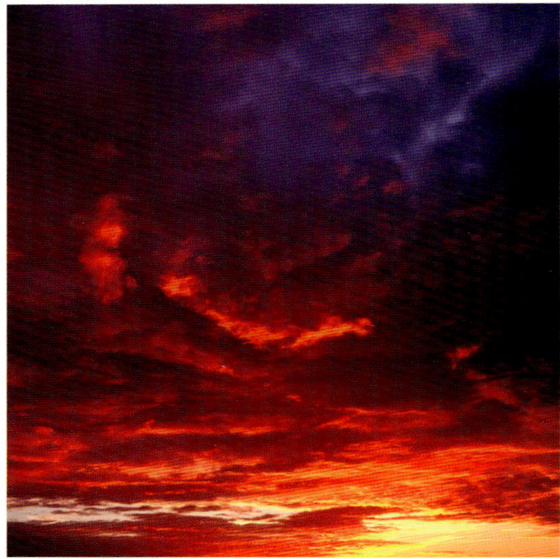

Above: Square images are commonly associated with cell-phone images, but it is a hard format to compose with.

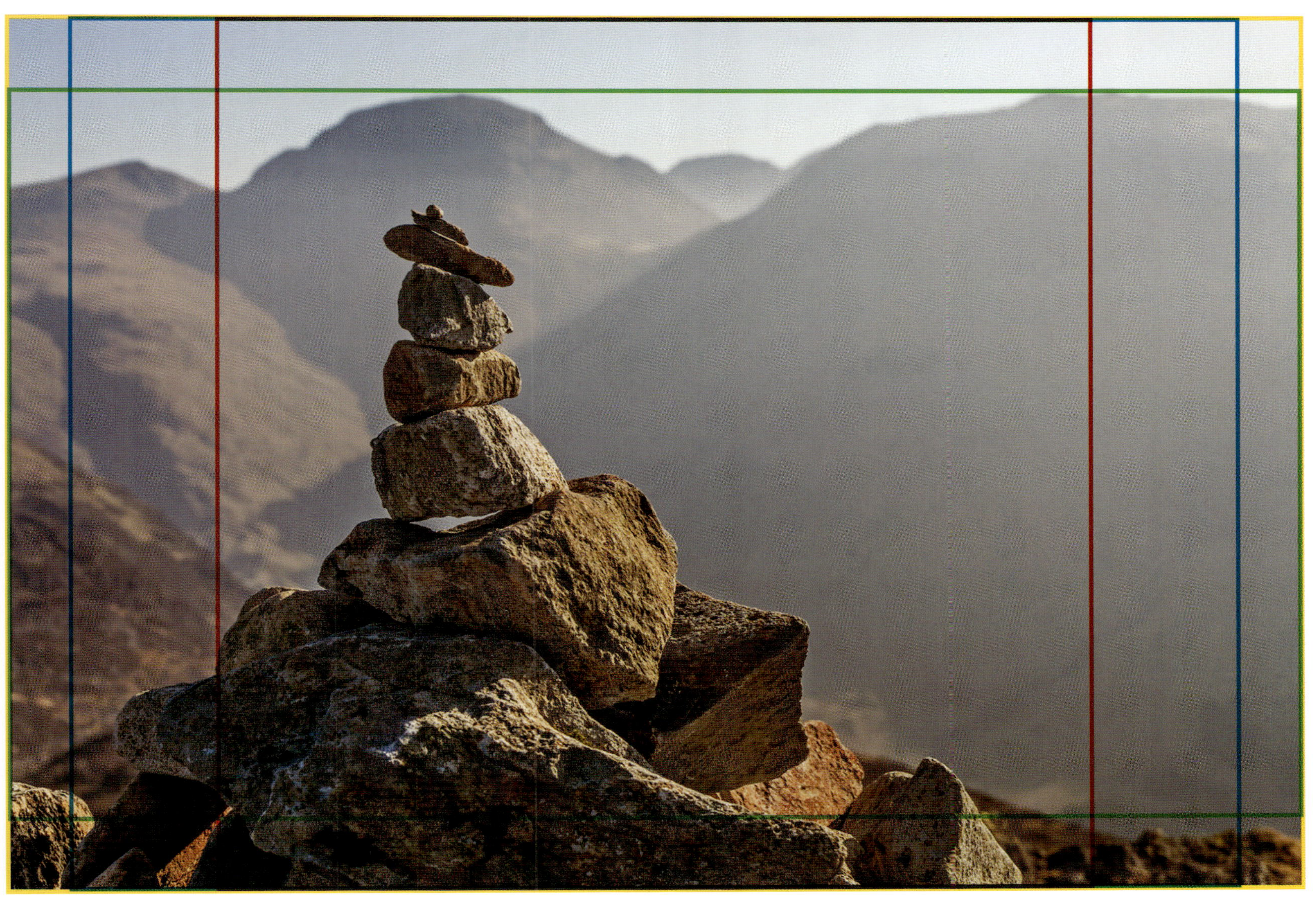

Ratios:

☐ **3:2** Camera types: Full-frame/APS-C DSLRs and mirrorless cameras.

☐ **1:1** Camera types: Cell phone/some medium-format cameras.

☐ **16:9** Standard aspect ratio for HDTV.

☐ **4:3** Camera types: Four Thirds/Micro Four Thirds/compact cameras. Standard aspect ratio for analog TV.

Orientation

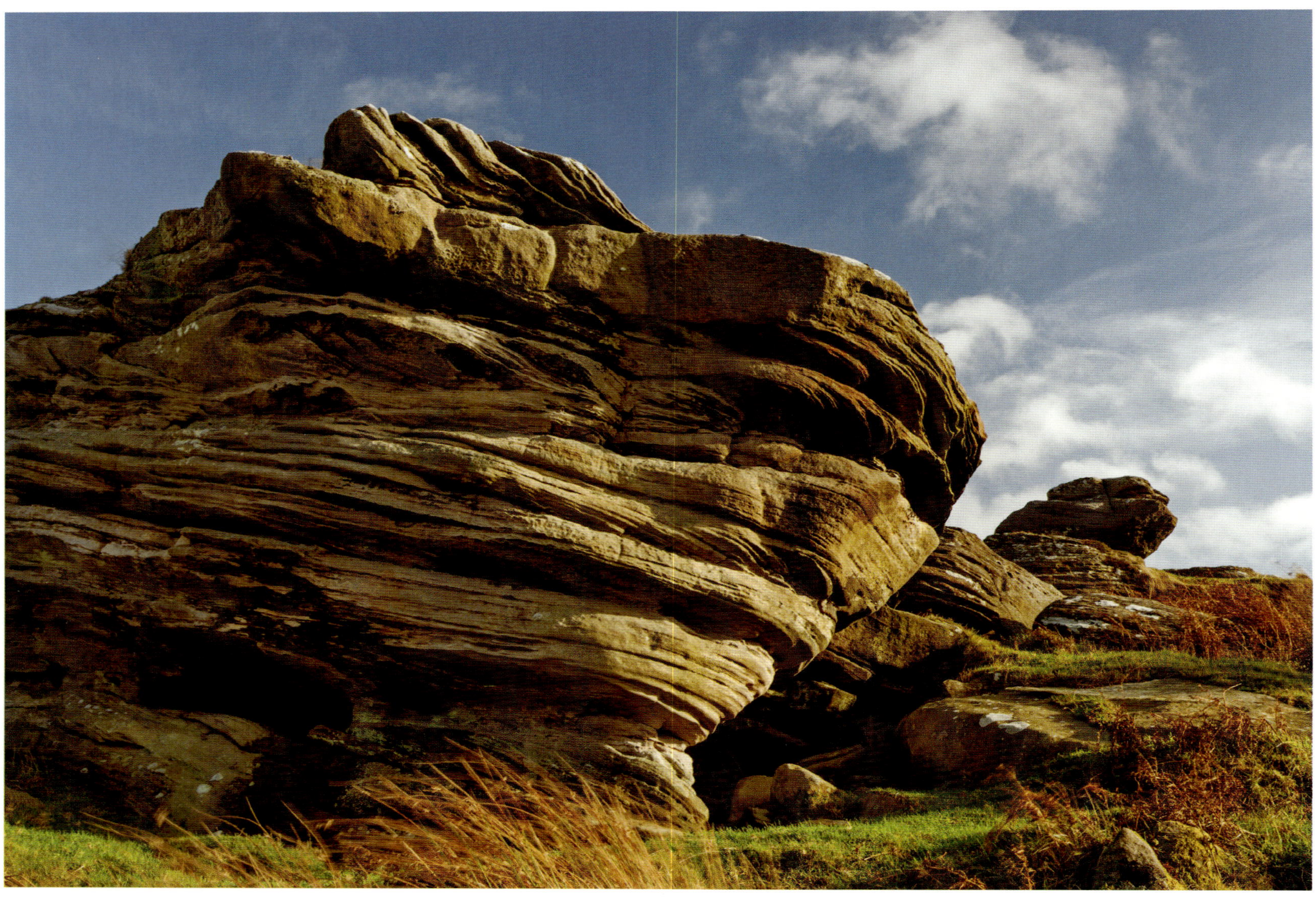

An important decision to make when composing an image is its orientation. Landscape images are most closely associated with a horizontal orientation; indeed, this is often referred to as "landscape format." In many ways this is understandable, as we tend to sweep our gaze across a view rather than up and down it (although cityscapes reverse that tendency). Because of their broader base relative to their height, horizontal images appear more stable than vertical ones. This can make them feel less dynamic, but this solidity is arguably a virtue for a permanent feature in a landscape.

However, there's no right or wrong answer as to whether an image should be framed horizontally or vertically. The deciding factor should be whether it suits your subject. Some subjects immediately suggest a horizontal approach (particularly if you want to convey a sense of space), while others will fit more readily into a vertical space.

Framing a shot vertically emphasizes height and depth over breadth. A lone tree is a good example of a subject that would probably benefit from being shot vertically, whereas a broad sweep of forest may be better framed horizontally.

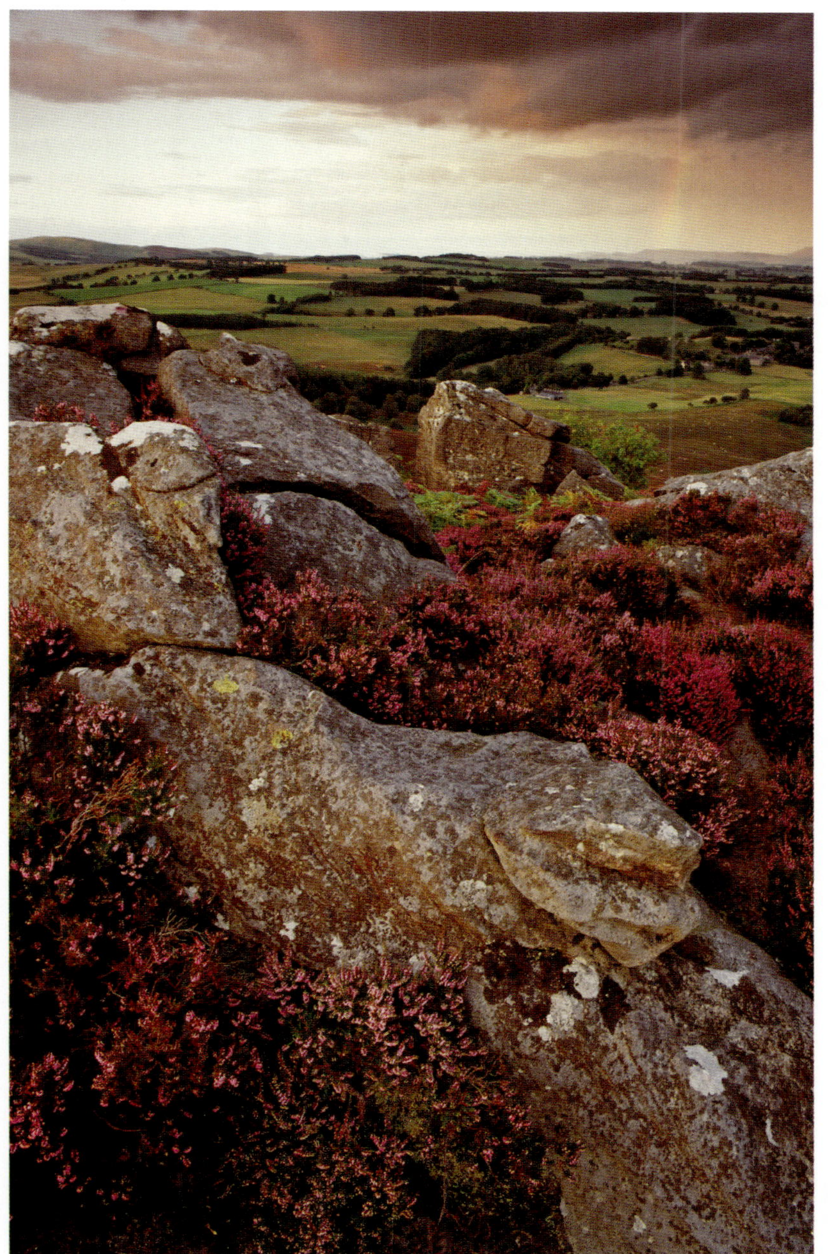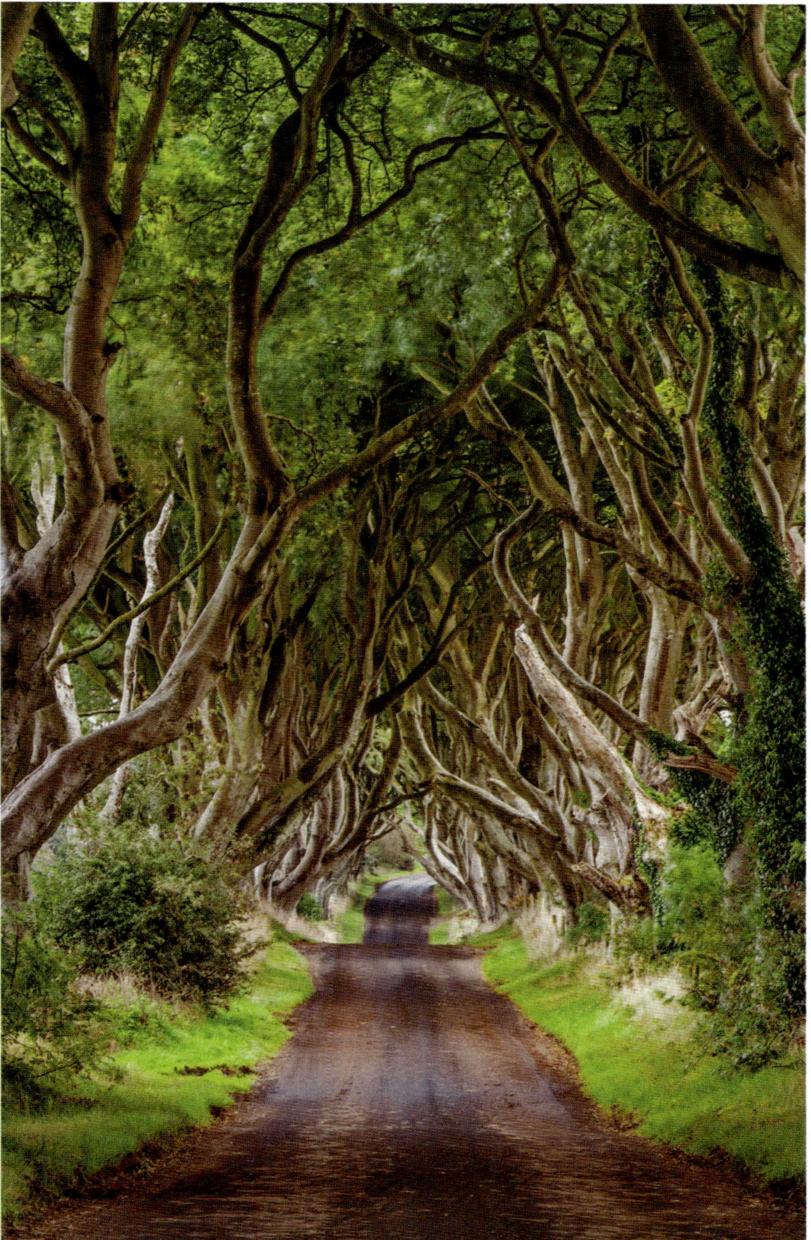

Left & Above: Two rock formations, two different image orientations. The orientation of the horizontal image (left) was determined by the very strong horizontal lines running across the rock. The composition felt forced and unnatural when I initially tried the shot vertically. The thought process, when deciding on the composition of the vertical shot, was similar: in this case the lines of the rock suggested a flow upward through the image.

Above: Shooting vertically in this location emphasized the height of this line of beech trees. A horizontal orientation was in tially tried, but wasn't as aesthetically pleasing. It also brought in distracting details at the sides that were very effectively excluded by composing the image vertically.

Visual Weight

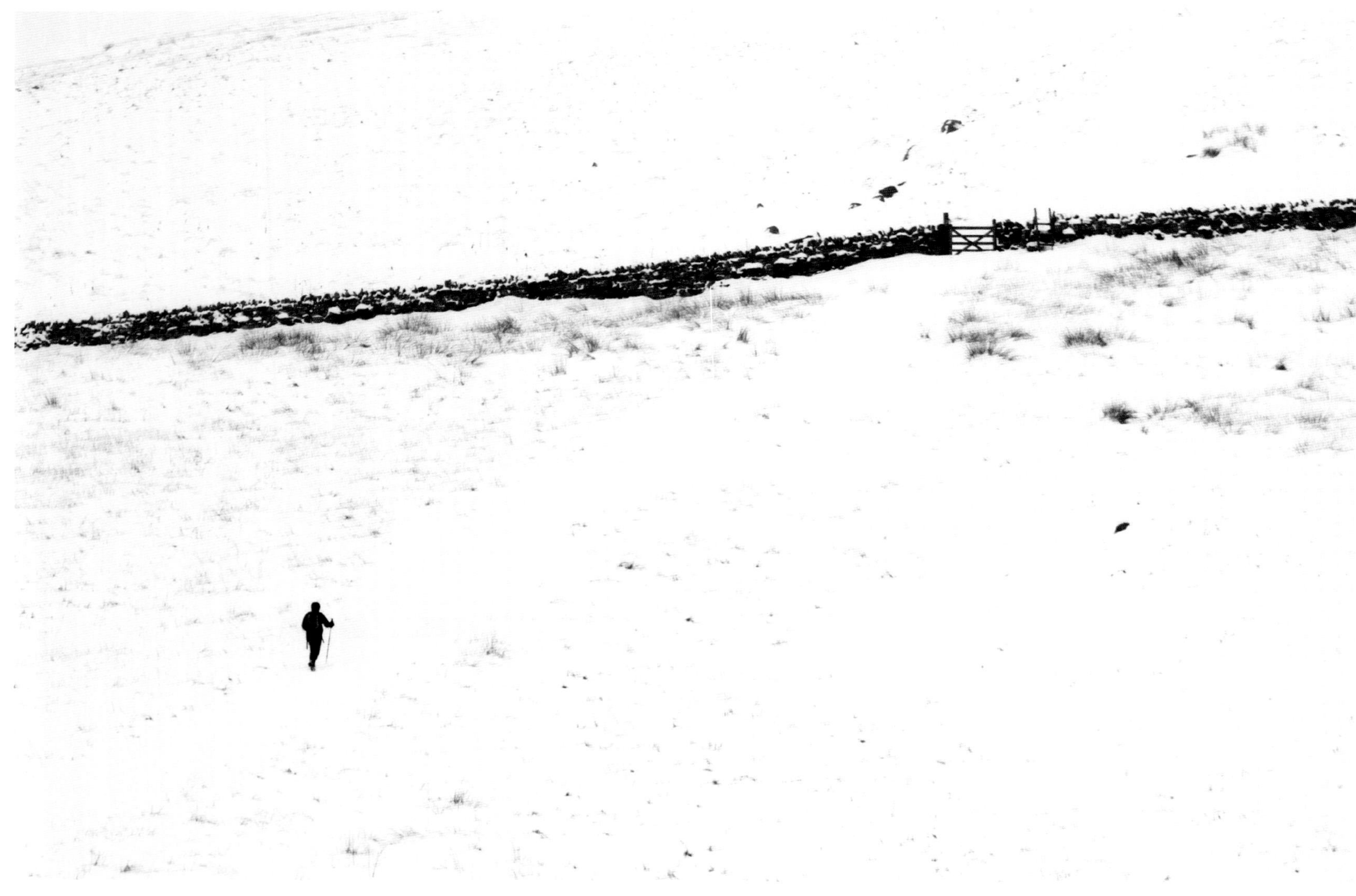

Not all parts of an image are equal. When we first look at a photograph our eyes naturally wander to certain areas of the image first. These are the elements that interest us visually more than others. Something that compels us to look in this way is said to have "visual weight."

Humans (landscape photographers included) are sociable creatures, so it's not surprising that people are visually heavy, with a person's facial features being visually more heavy than other parts of the body. This means that if you place a person in a landscape image, then he or she will be the center of attention, no matter how stunning the landscape is. This is worth remembering, as although people can be used to show scale, it may be better to avoid including them if you want the landscape to be the subject of your image.

It's not just people that have visual weight; some colors grab our attention more than others as well. Red is visually more heavy than blue or green, for example, while darker, more saturated colors have greater visual weight than lighter, less saturated colors. By extension, white is visually far heavier than black.

Visual weight is an important consideration when composing an image. Your focal point should always be heavier than something that is relatively unimportant in the scene. If it isn't, your subject may well be disregarded by anyone who looks at your image.

Right: There are certain subjects that have a
disproportionately "heavy" visual weight. We tend to look at
people in an image first above all other subjects. Writing is
also visually heavy, as are colors such as yellow.

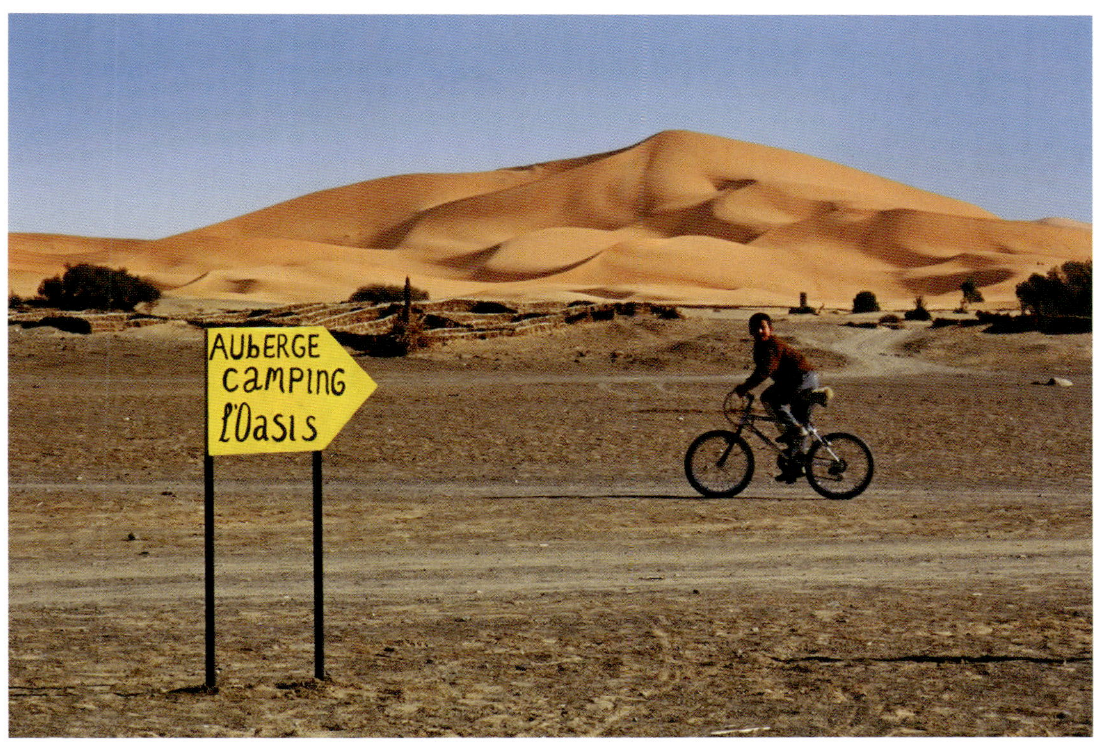
AUBERGE
CAMPING
l'Oasis

Right: White is visually heavy. Consequently, we usually
notice the brightest part of an image more quickly than
the darker areas.

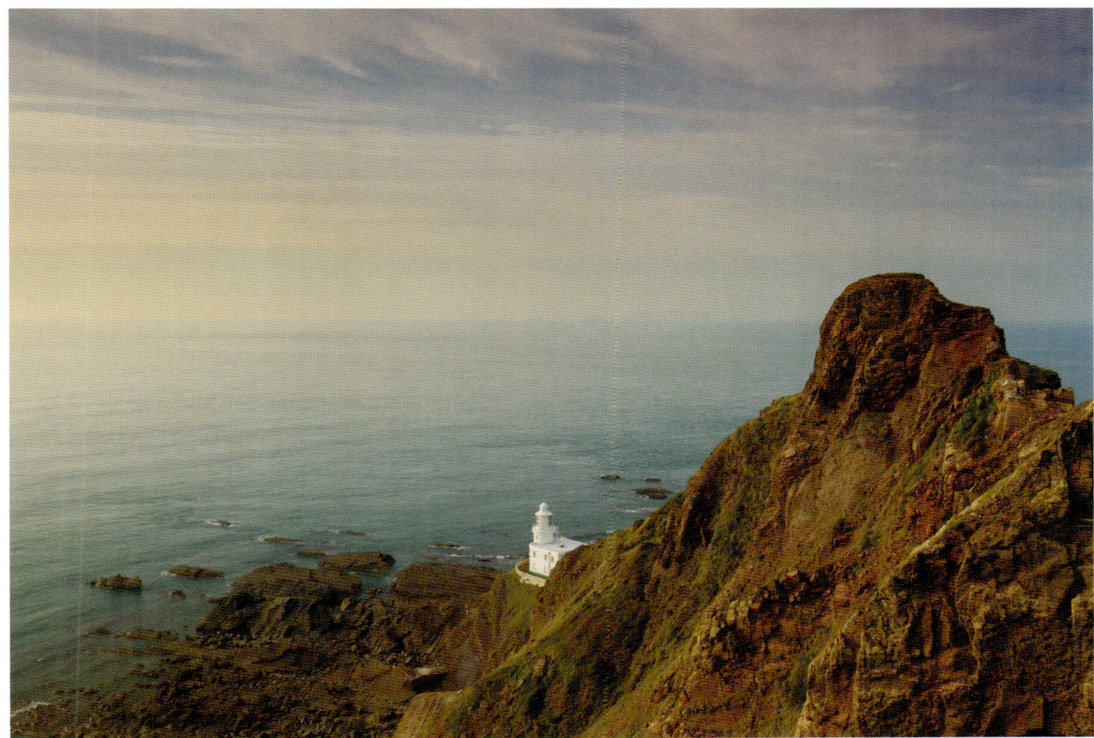

Left: Where did you look when you first saw this image?
Cover up the figure with a finger to see the difference it
makes to the composition.

Balance

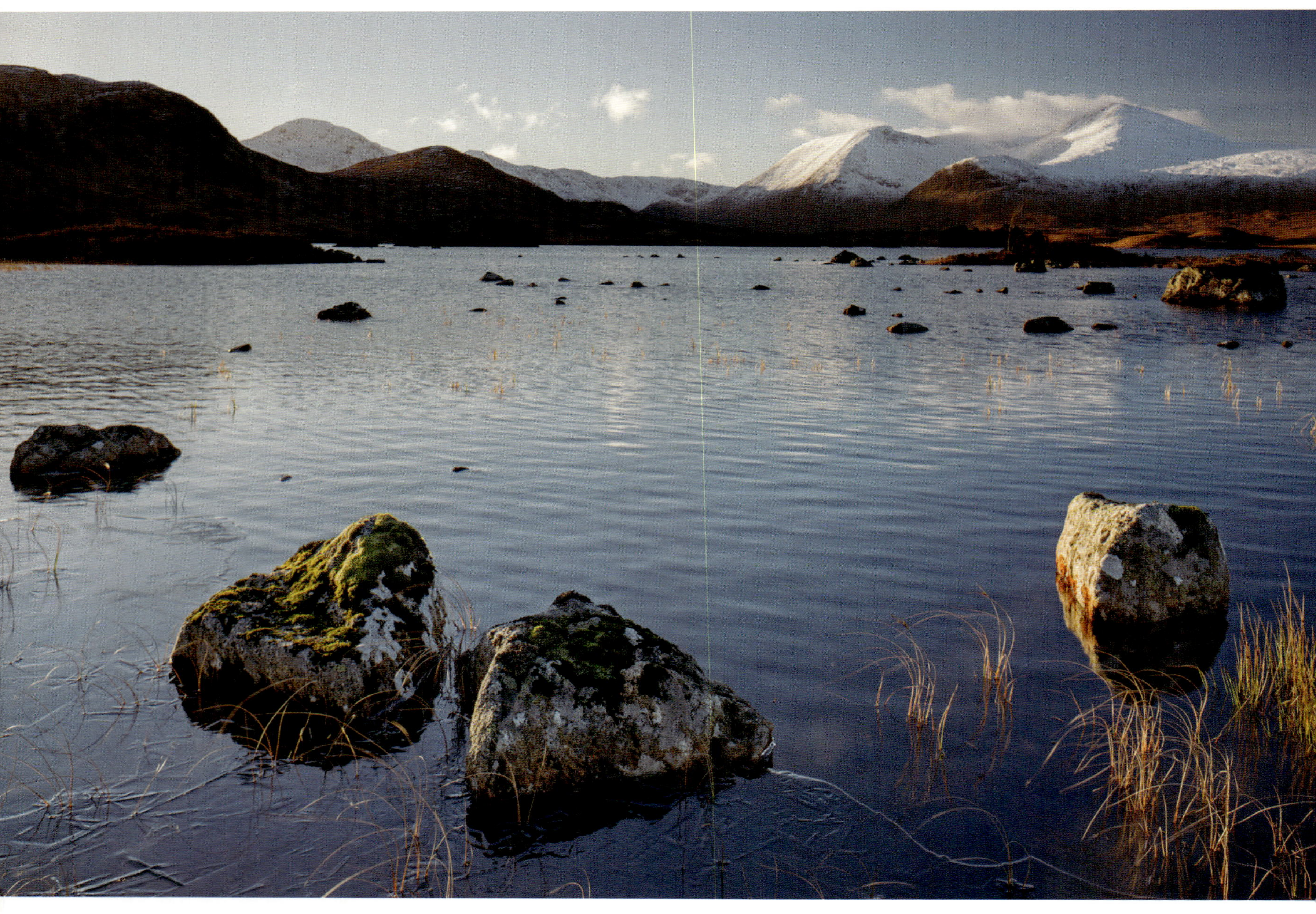

Imagine that a horizontal image is placed centrally on a pivot. Which way would it tip? Although there's no actual physical weight to an image, elements that are heavy in a visual sense can make it feel unbalanced. However, it's not just left/right balance that's important—images can also feel unbalanced vertically. An image that has visually heavy elements at the top can feel top-heavy. Fortunately, this is generally avoided in landscape photography as the foreground will tend to be in the lower half of an image.

Above: The balance in this image has been achieved through the position of the rocks in the foreground. The lighter rock at the right visually balances the darker rocks at the left.

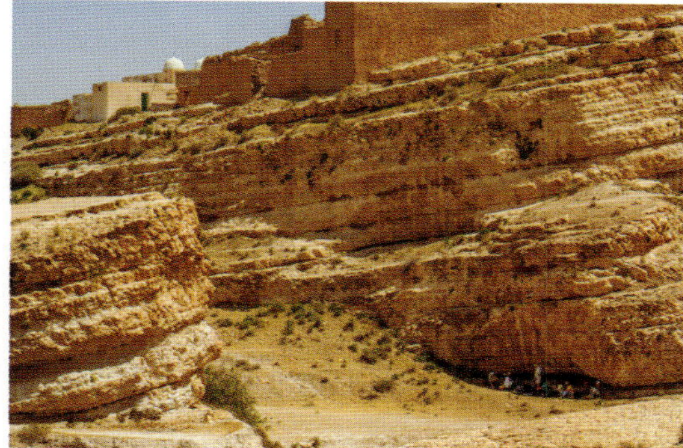

Above: This image has a slightly different balance point to the one on the page opposite. The people at the bottom right corner are balanced by the light architectural structures at the top right.

Right: A symmetrical balance has been achieved in this image. Note how the shape of the cloud and the wall are similar in shape and position in the image: spin the image around by 180º and they swap positions almost exactly.

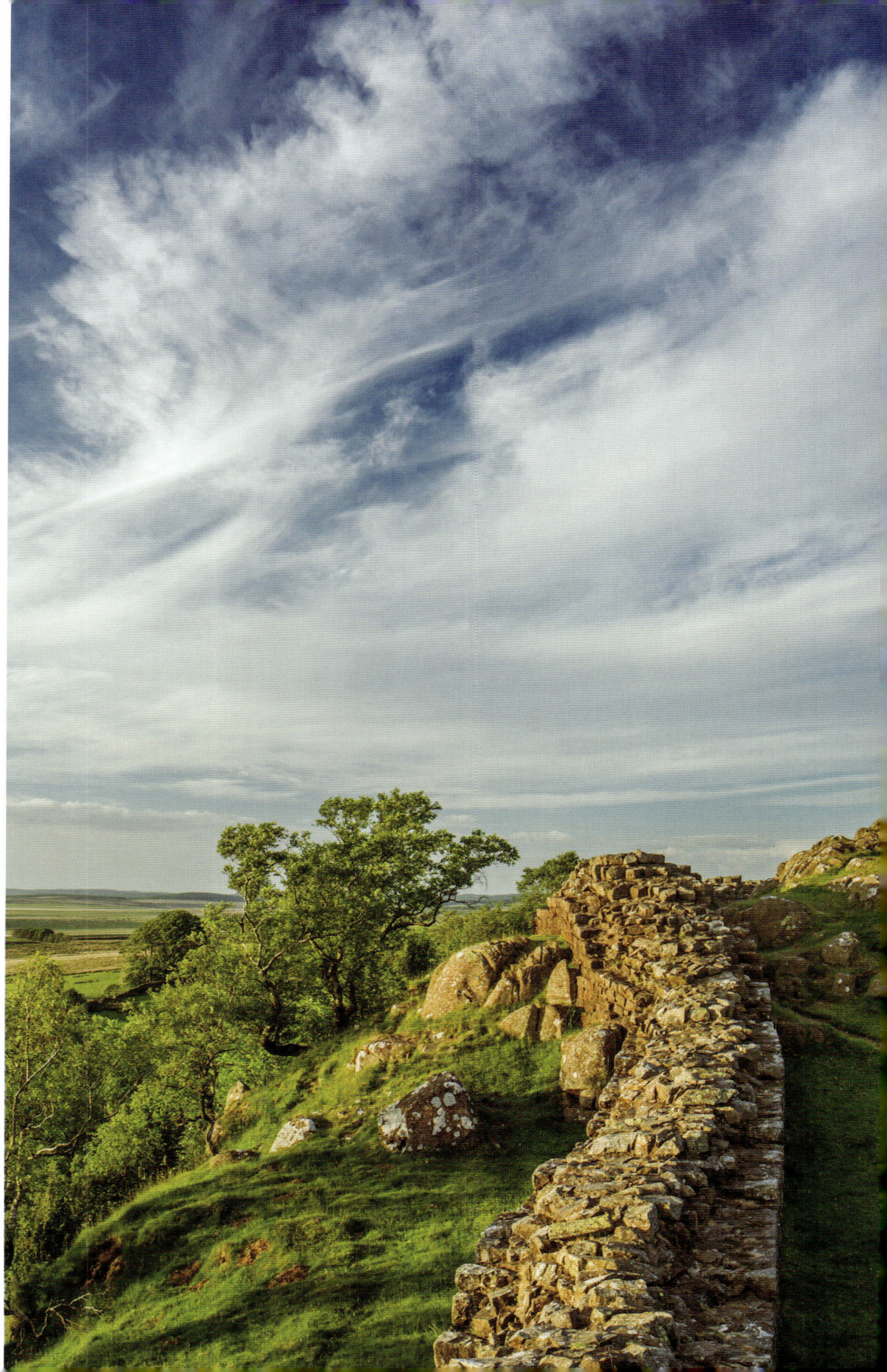

Color

We react emotionally to color in both negative and positive ways. How color is used in an image will therefore have an impact on how the photograph is perceived. The overall color bias of an image can be controlled by the camera's white balance, but you can also look for color in the landscape and emphasize or diminish it within your compositions.

When placed next to each other, colors can either harmonize or contrast. Colors that harmonize well sit adjacent to each other on a color wheel; this is known as an analogous harmony. A more visually interesting effect is achieved when colors opposite each other on a color wheel are combined; these are known as complementary colors.

When juxtaposed, complementary colors reinforce each other, with neither color dominating. Warm and cool complementary colors work well together, such as orange and blue. These two colors are often seen together in the landscape at sunrise or sunset when red-orange sunlight illuminates one side of an object, casting a cool blue shadow on the opposite side.

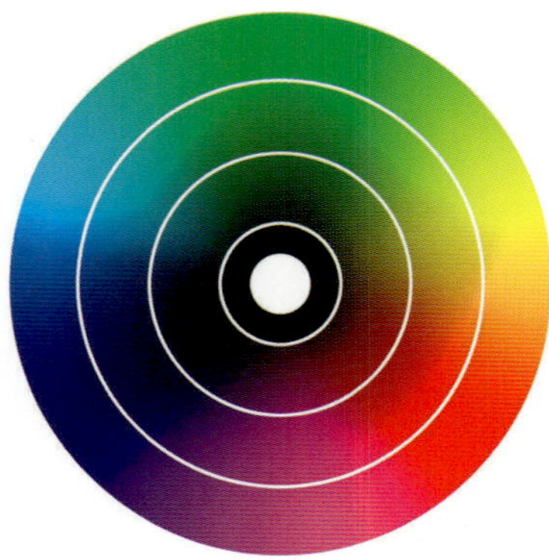

Above: The color wheel is a useful way to learn which colors are harmonious and which are complementary. It's also useful for black-and-white photography when judging which filter to select to create a particular monochrome effect (see chapter 8).

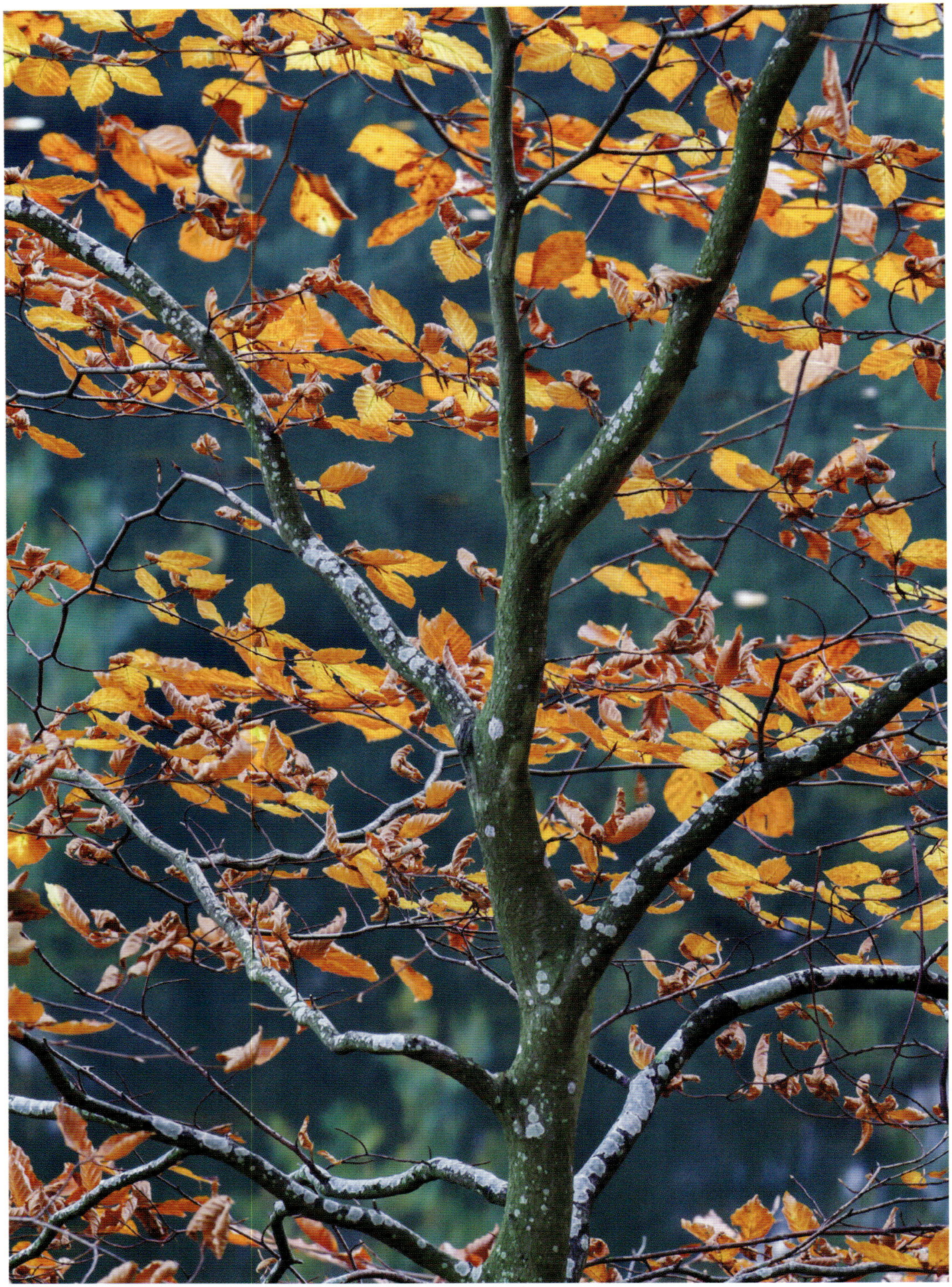

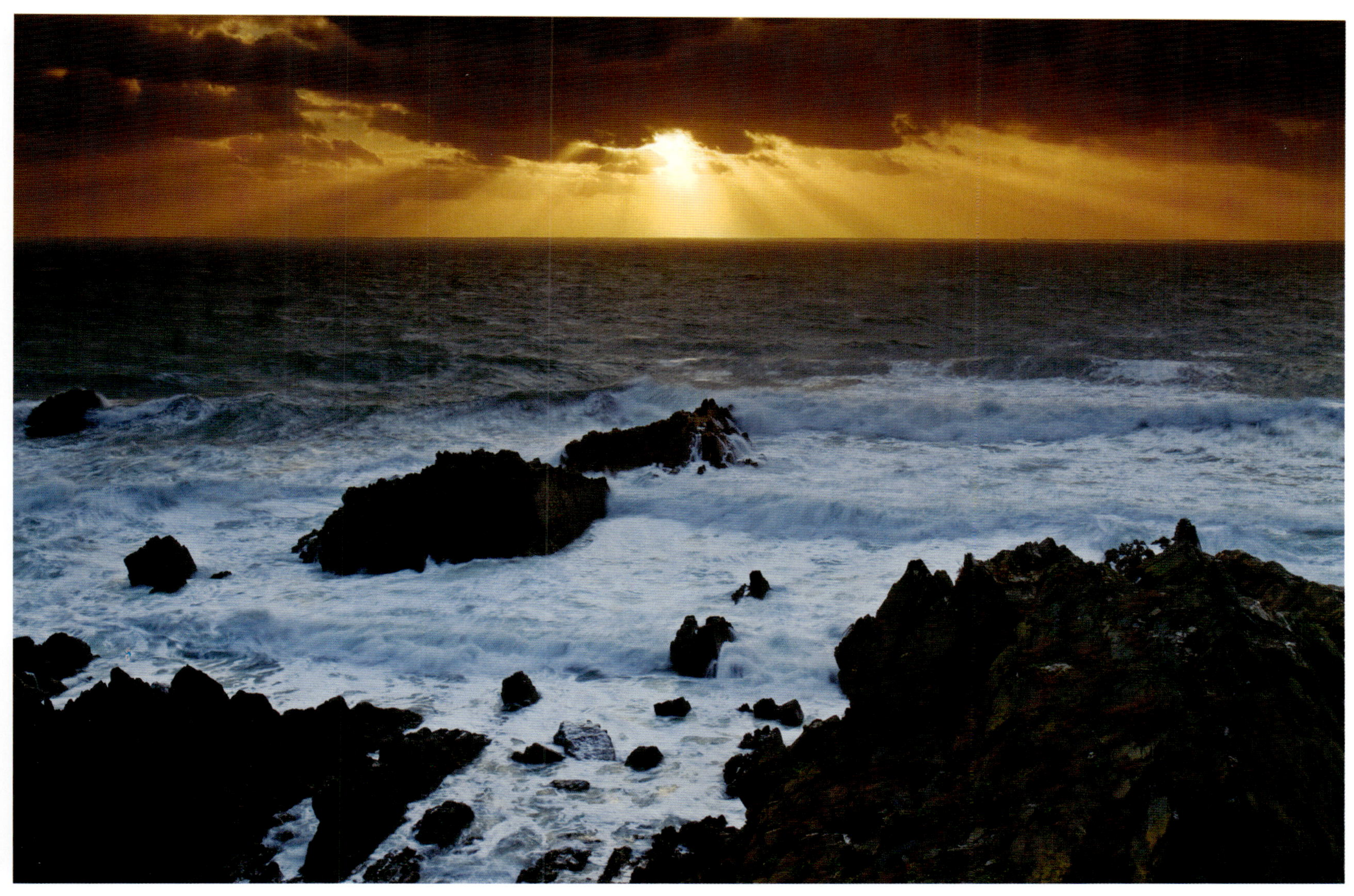

Left & Above: Orange and blue, being complementary colors, work well together in an image. However, less orange and more blue is generally more effective than the other way around. This is because cooler colors, such as blue and green, tend to recede in an image (they're known as recessive colors for this reason), while warmer colors tend to come forward (making them progressive colors). Warmer colors have more visual weight than cooler colors, so a little often goes a long way.

Color	Analogous harmonies	Complementary color
Red	Red–violet/red–orange	Green
Orange	Red–orange/yellow–orange	Blue
Yellow	Yellow–orange/yellow–green	Violet
Green	Yellow–green/blue–green	Red
Blue	Blue–green/blue–violet	Orange
Violet	Blue–violet/red–violet	Yellow

Symmetry

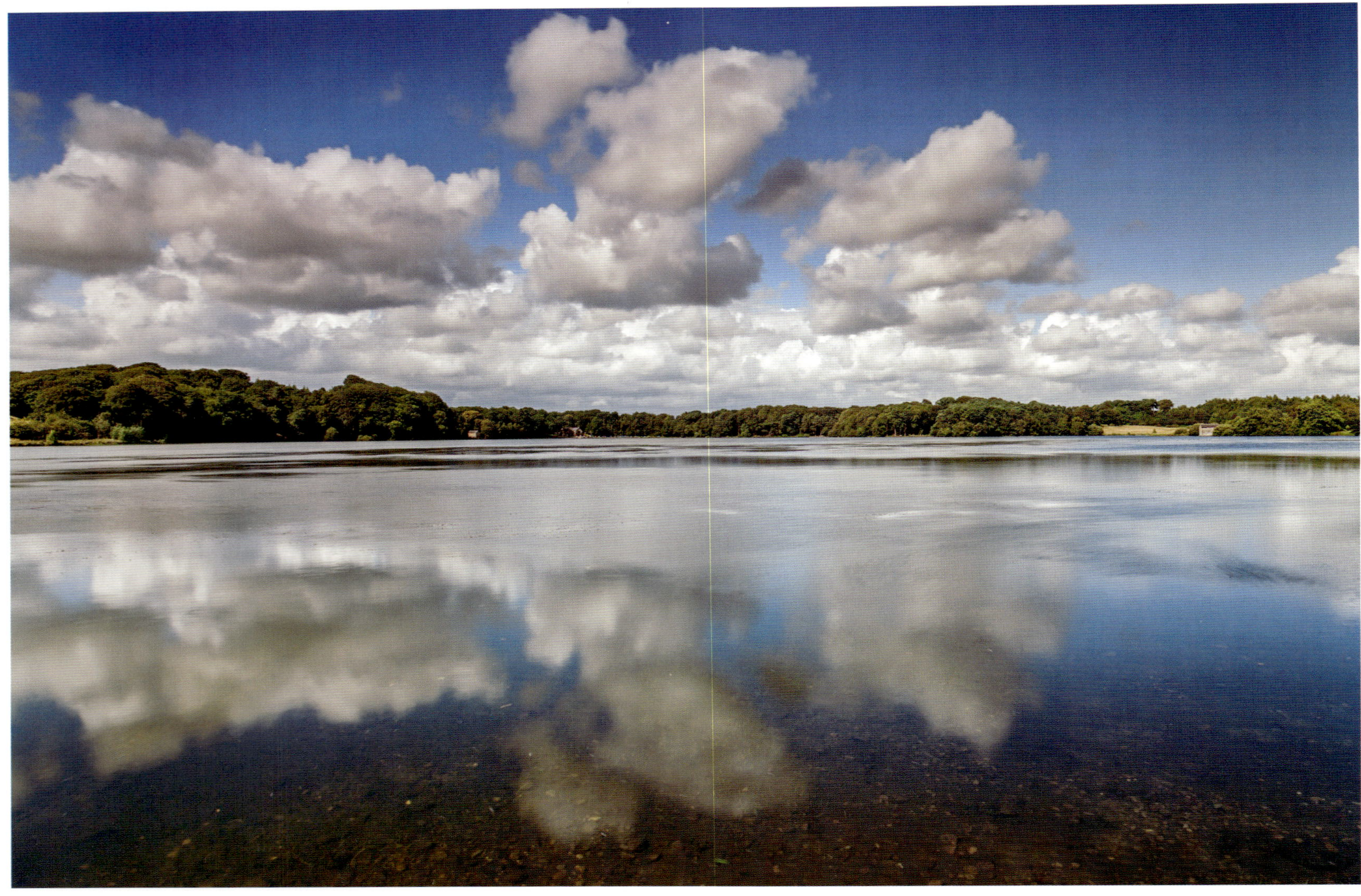

There are several types of symmetry that can be used in photographic composition. The easiest to use is bilateral symmetry in which one half of the image mirrors the other half in some way. The most common cause of bilateral symmetry is a body of still water that reflects the landscape and sky above it. However, bilateral symmetries don't have to be so literal. They can also be created by looking for elements in the landscape that match each other in shape or color.

Other types of symmetry include radial symmetry, which rotates around a central point. A common example of a landscape subject that displays radial symmetry is certain types of flower heads, such as daisies.

There's also strip pattern symmetry, which requires a regularly repeating pattern across the image space. Some plants, such as trees, display striking strip pattern symmetry as well as some types of animal, such as snakes.

The main characteristic of a symmetrical composition is that it is inherently static and restful. This makes symmetrical images pleasing to look at, but it also means that there's little tension or drama. One way to add interest to a symmetrical image is to include a focal point that breaks the pattern of the symmetry.

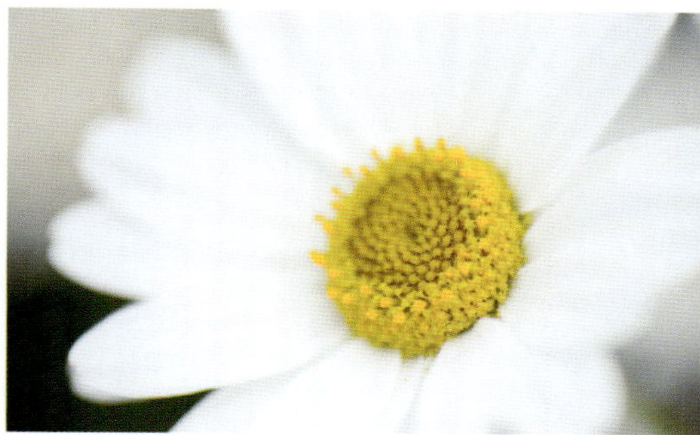

Above: Daisy heads display radial symmetry around the central point of the flower head.

Left: Bilateral symmetry is most commonly seen in reflections on still bodies of water. By its very nature this sort of symmetry works best when the image is split equally across the image.

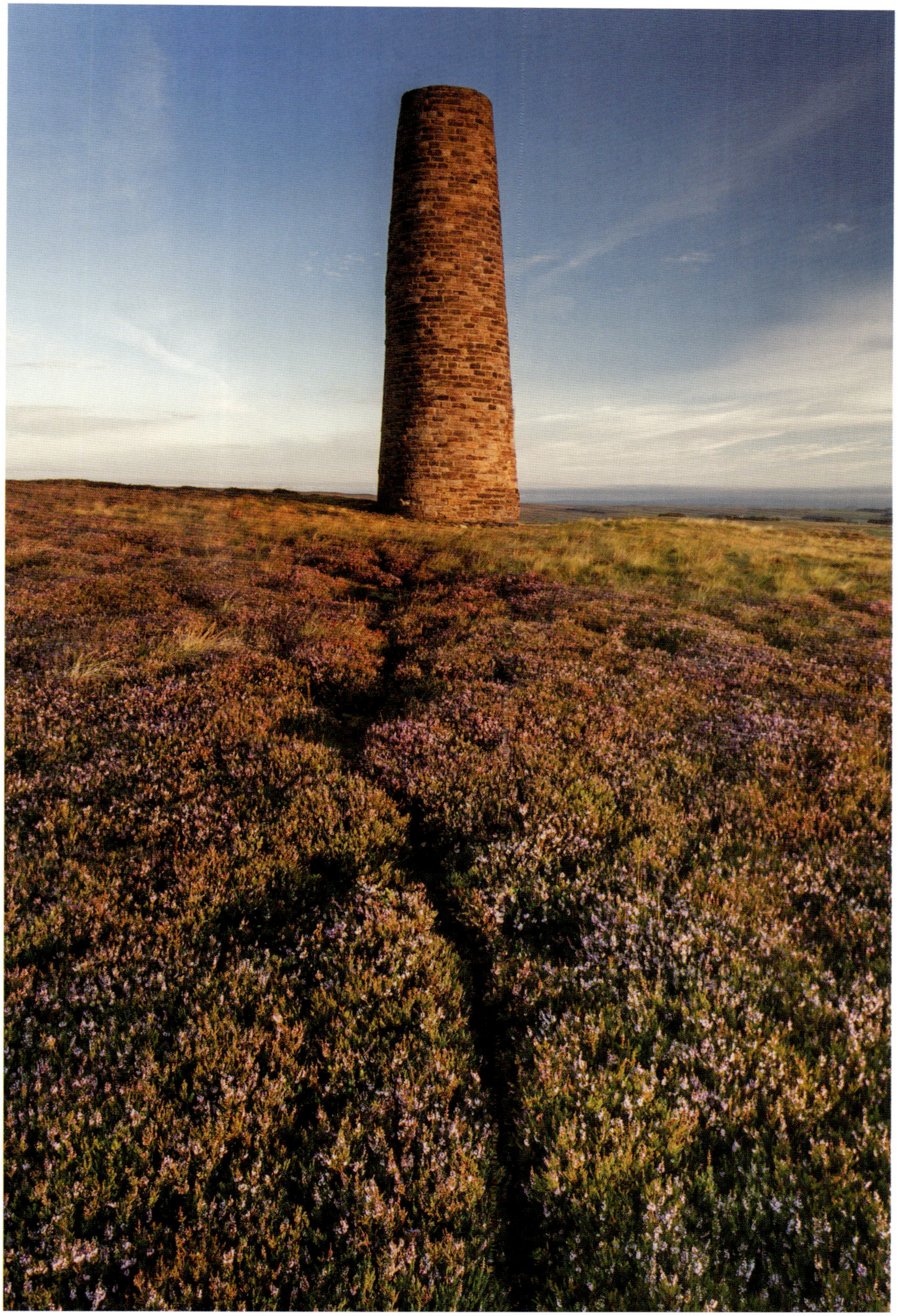

Right: Bilateral symmetries don't need to split an image horizontally—with the right subject they can work vertically.

Lines

Lines in an image are an incredibly powerful way to lead the eye through the picture space. A lead-in line is a line that leads the eye to the focal point of the image. Lead-in lines generally start in the bottom half of an image and guide the eye upward through the picture.

However, this is another "rule" that should really only be seen as a guideline. The problem with lines in an image is that they are so powerful that care must be taken to exclude any that lead the eye away from the main subject or even out of the image space altogether. In both instances, lines don't have to physically exist, they can also be implied through the alignment of different elements in a composition.

In landscape images, examples of lines include stone walls, rock strata and paths. Of a more temporary nature is the edge of the sea as it washes up on the shore. Because lines lead the eye through a scene they're a good way to imply depth. This is particularly true with lines created by subjects such as a wall or a road that will gradually diminish in size as they recede toward a vanishing point.

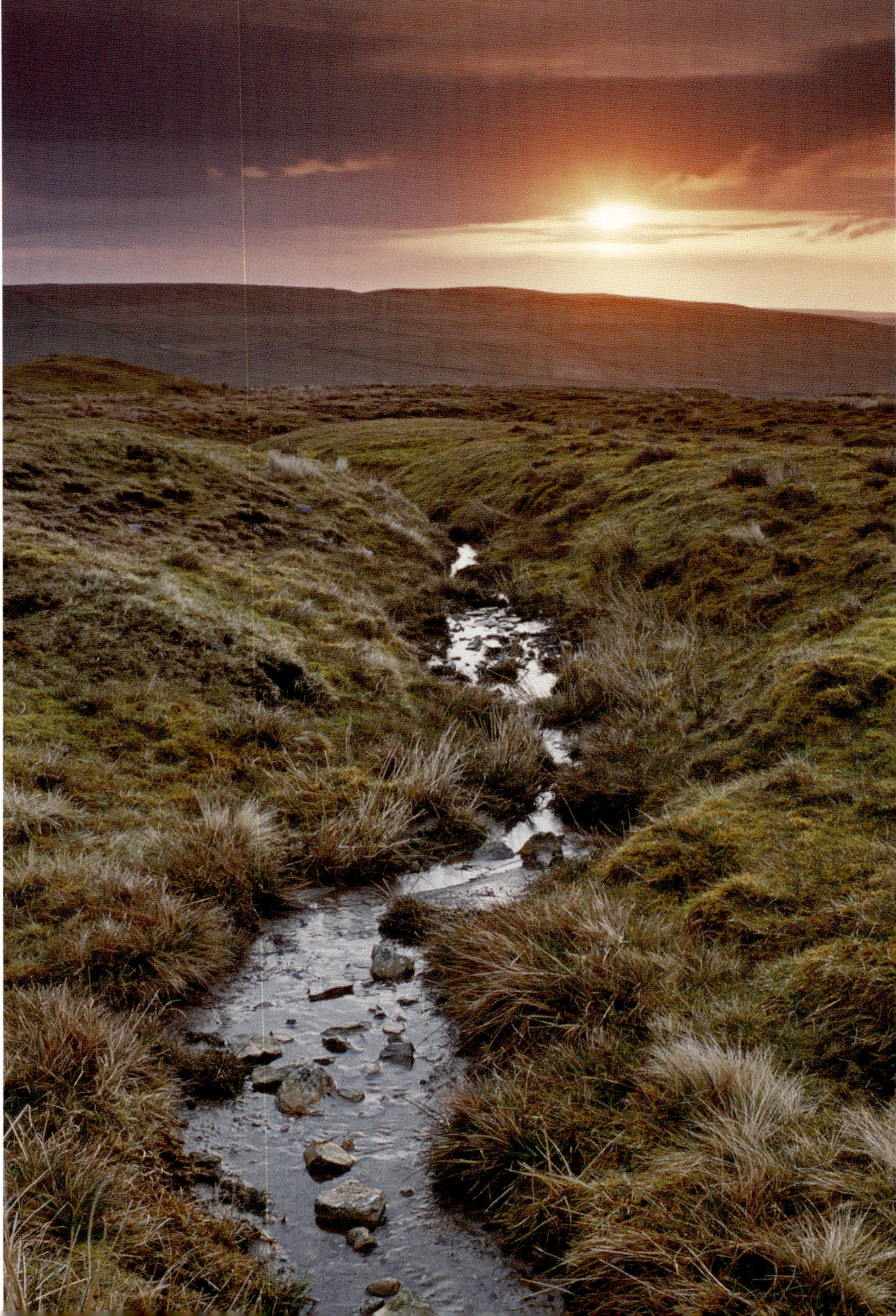

Right: A line through an image without a destination can often feel unresolved. The line of the river in this image leads the eye up through the landscape to the rising sun, which provides a satisfying end point.

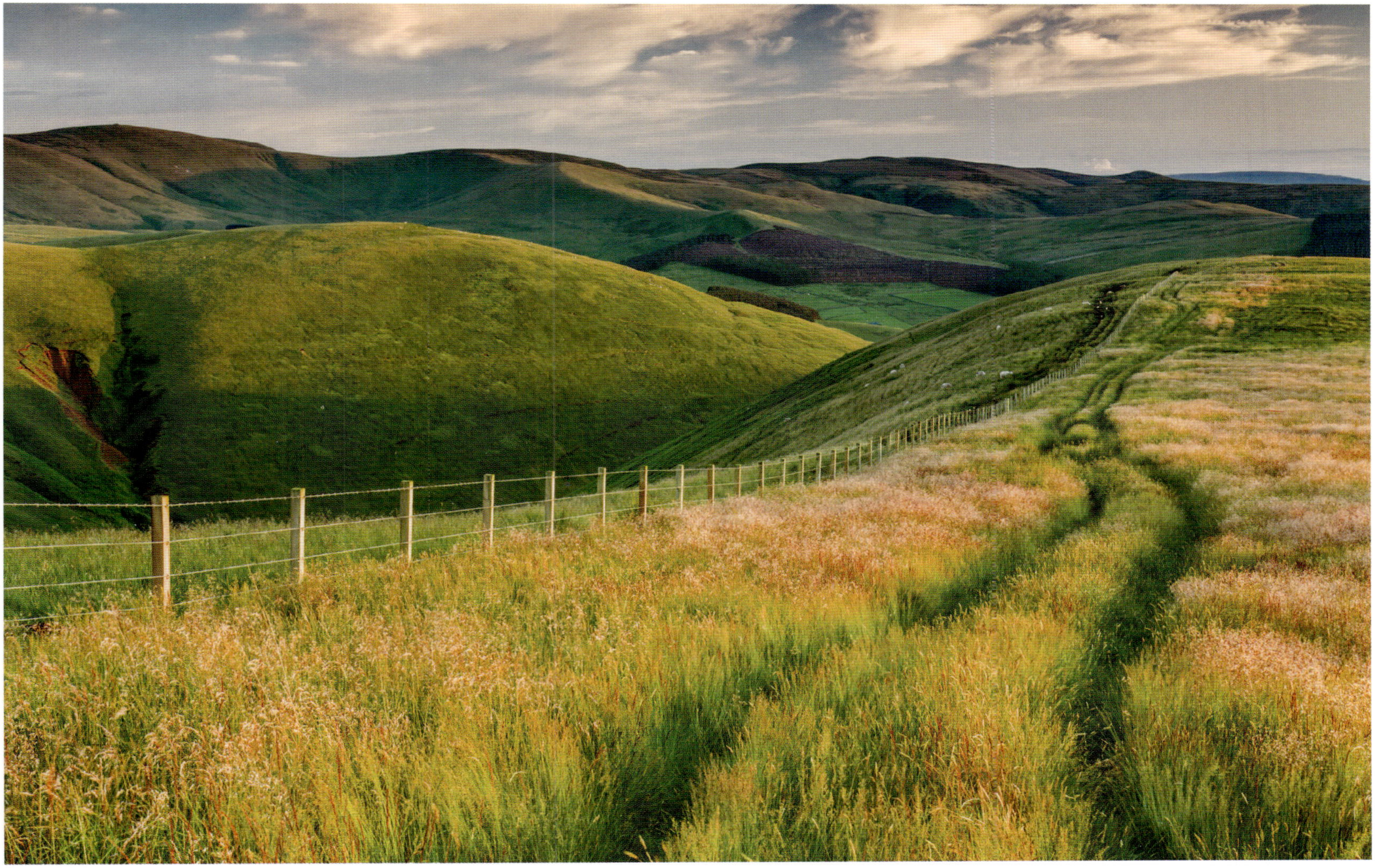

Above: A path in a landscape makes a powerful statement, as it implies a journey. We can't help but wonder where the path leads to and what can be found at the end.

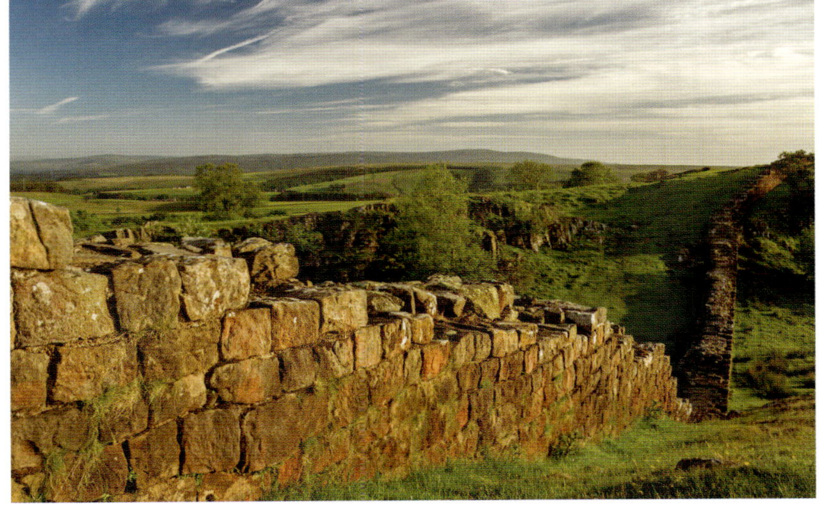

Right: Architectural subjects, particularly walls or paths, can be used to create compelling lines through an image. In this photograph the eye naturally follows the shape of the wall through the scene.

Creating Depth

A photographic image is two-dimensional. What makes an image appear three-dimensional is depth cues. There are various types of depth cue that can be used in a photo, the most common of which is perspective: objects appear smaller in size the further back they are in a scene. Wide-angle lenses exaggerate this effect in an image, while telephoto lenses tend to diminish it, arguably making them less effective at conveying depth.

However, there's more to creating depth than using a wide-angle lens. Landscape images often have a foreground, a middle-ground, and a background. The relationship between them is important in how depth is perceived, and this relationship is determined by the height of the camera. If the camera is set too low, the foreground will dominate, potentially obscuring the middle-ground and possibly even the background. Conversely, set the camera too high and the foreground is diminished, with the middle-ground and background dominating. As with so many aspects of photography, finding the right balance makes for a successful shot.

NOTE

As warm colors come forward and cool colors recede, using warmer colors in the foreground can help to convey depth.

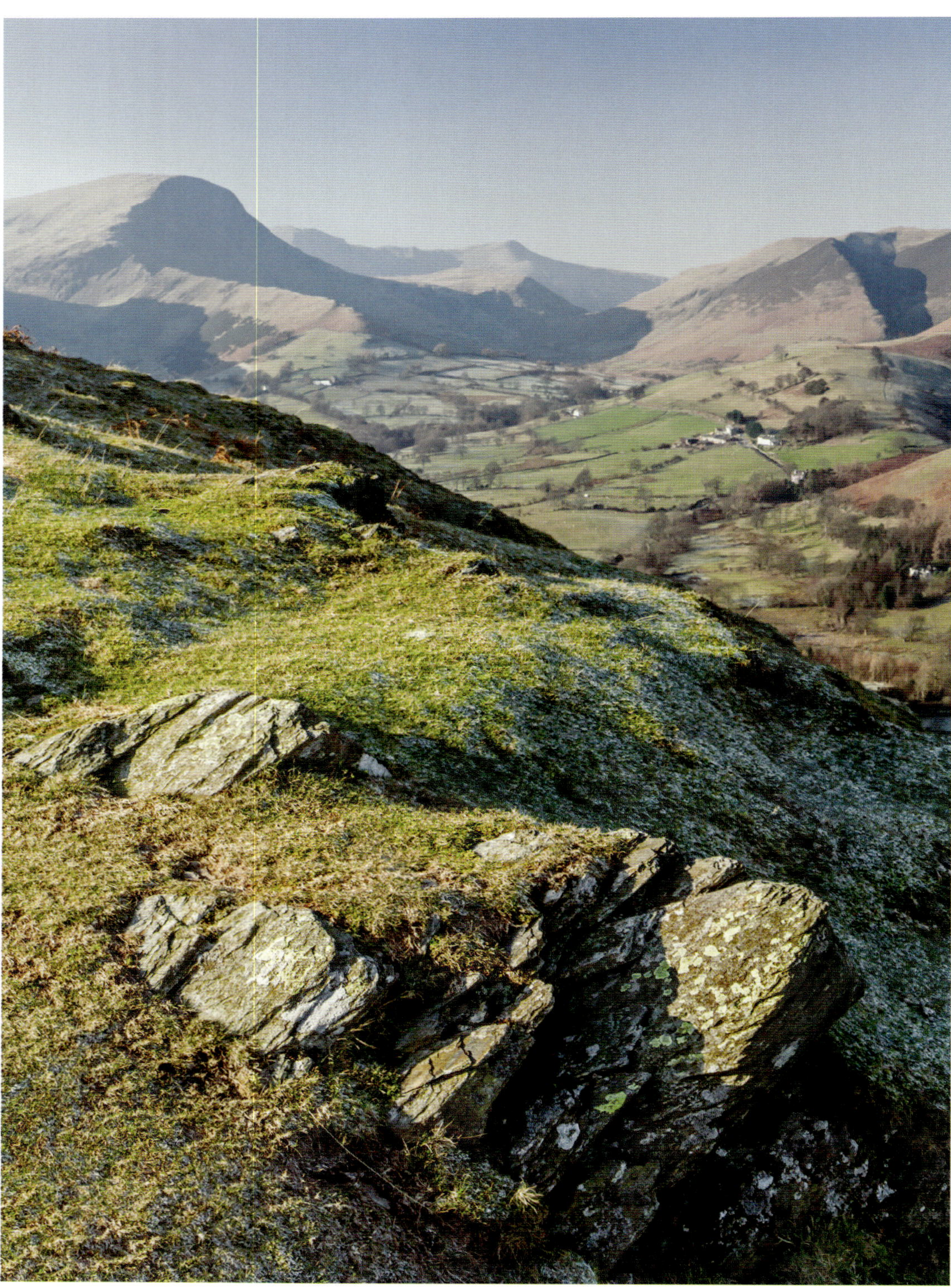

Right: Aerial perspective forms another depth cue, as color saturation and contrast is reduced by distance. The effect is seen most strongly on misty days, and while it's not as strong a depth cue as perspective, it is still effective at conveying a sense of distance.

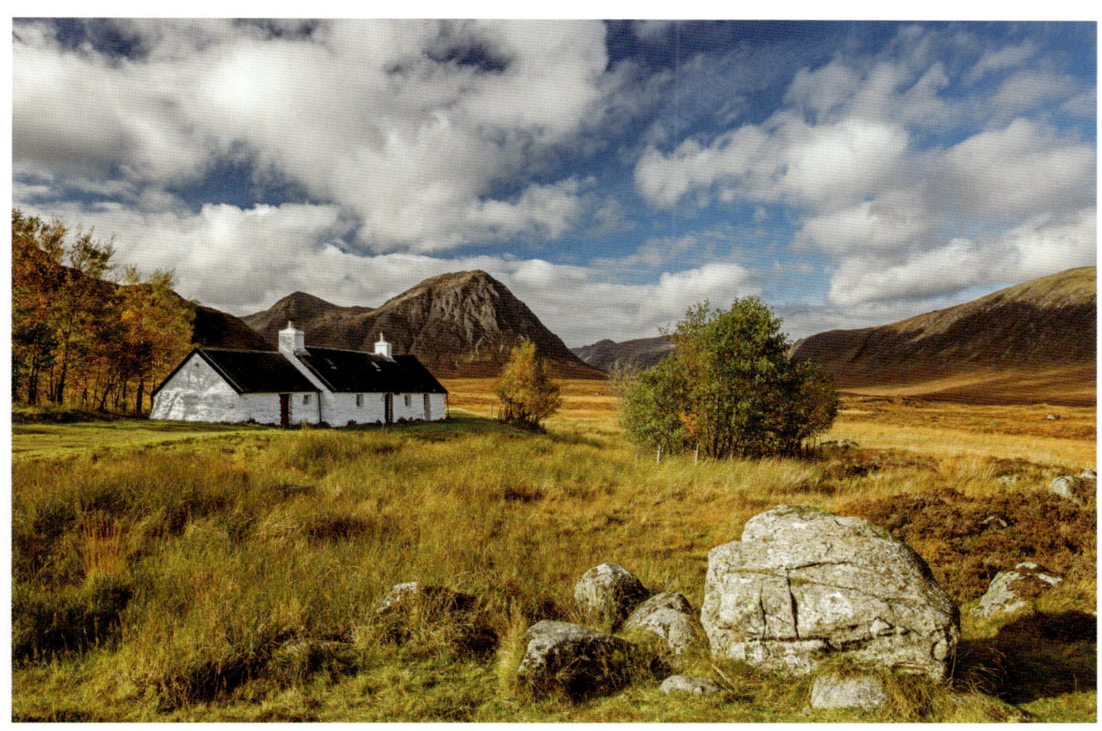

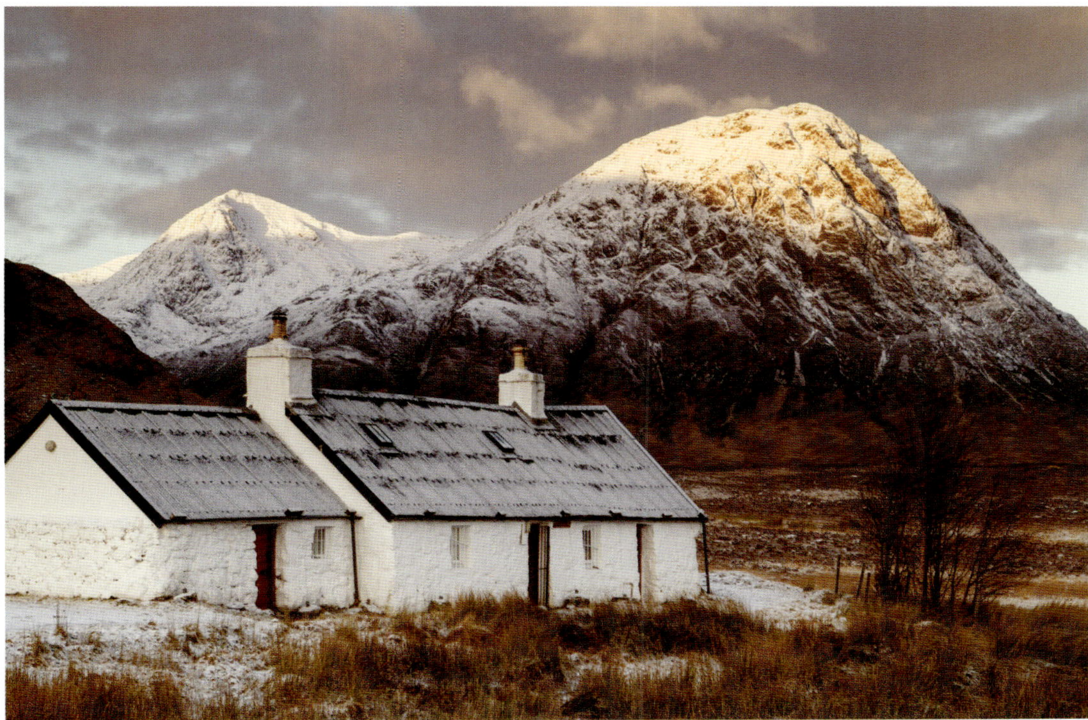

Top left & Left: Wide-angle lenses exaggerate spatial relationships, making distant objects appear further back from your shooting position than they are in reality. Telephoto focal lengths have the opposite effect, appearing to pull elements in a scene closer together, creating a closer spatial relationship. Compare the two shots here, both photographed from roughly the same position: which of them creates a greater sense of depth?

Minimalism

The natural world can be a visually complex place and the temptation is to try and include everything you see: after all, more is better.

Or is it? In many ways, all photography is a process of simplification. The edges of the frame mark the boundary between what's included in an image and what's left out. Minimalism takes this process to its logical conclusion by reducing an image to its simplest possible form. This usually means a single element against a background.

The danger of minimalism is that it's all too easy to produce boring images. It's important therefore to think carefully about how your subject is placed within the image space: strong lines add interest, as do bold colors and texture.

With imagination, minimalist images can be very compelling. The lack of obvious reference points or a sense of scale can make them slightly harder to read without careful study. Trying to work the puzzle out can make them more rewarding to study than complex photographs.

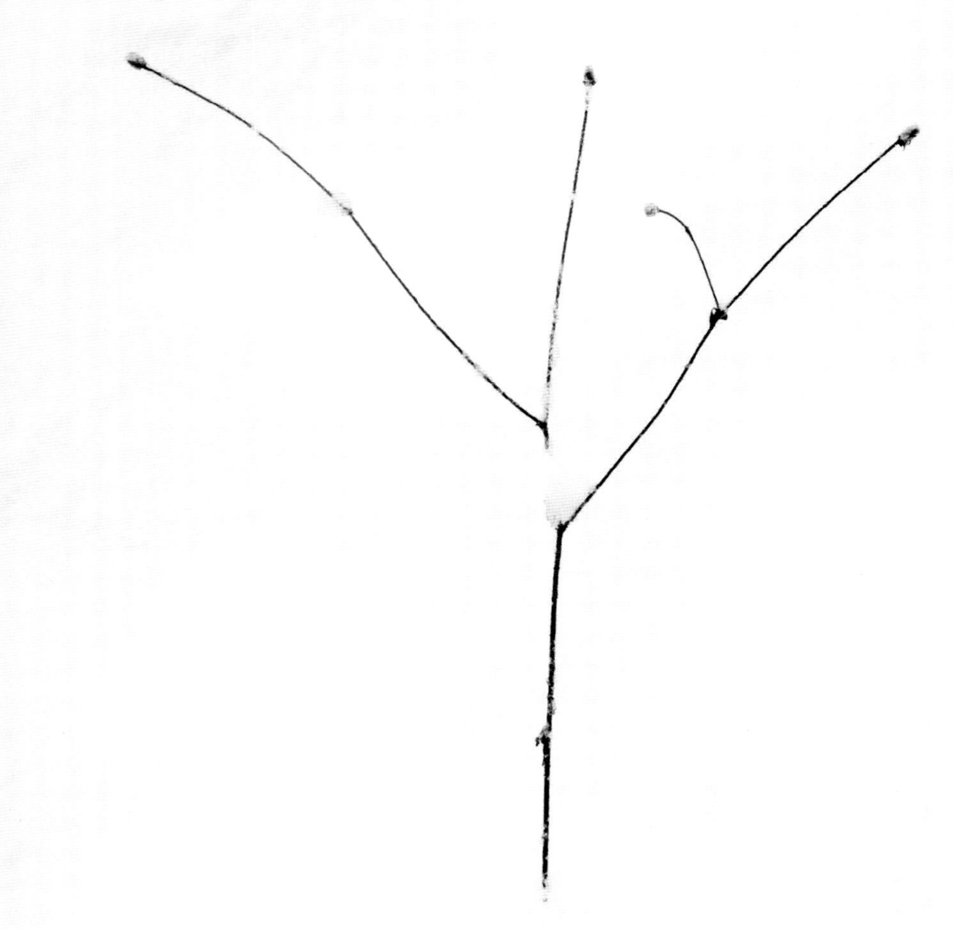

Right: Snow or fog will naturally simplify the landscape, making it easier to create minimalist compositions.

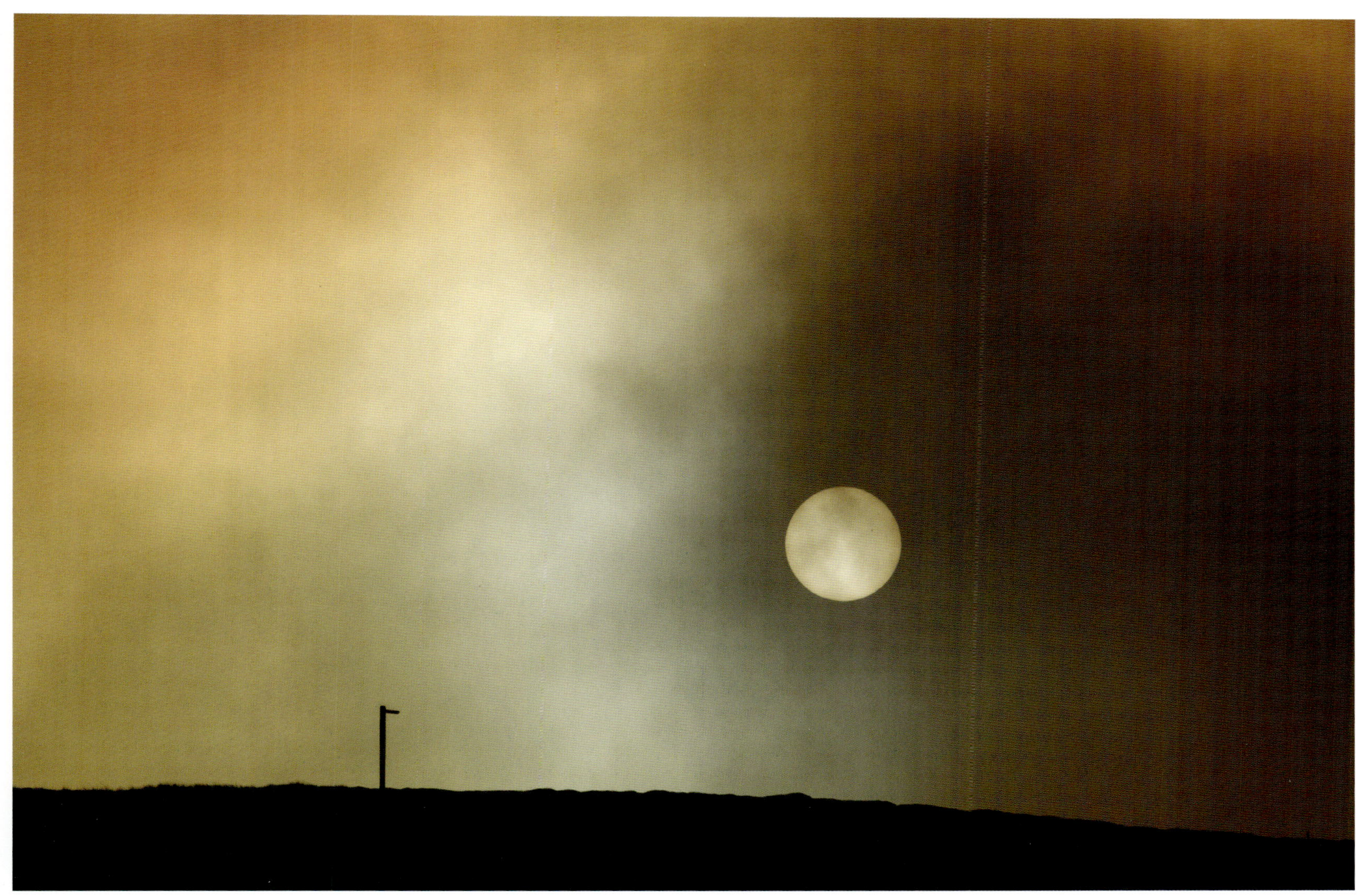

Above: It's easier to create minimalist images with a standard or telephoto lens. Wide-angle lenses require you to get in close in order to exclude elements, which means that the perspective often isn't as aesthetically pleasing.

Right: Run your eye around the edge of the frame when composing a minimalist image to check that nothing is entering the image space that detracts from the subject.

Chapter 7
Filters

Filters are sheets of glass or optical resin that affect the light that passes through them in a specific way. This can be a subtle change or something more dramatic, but there's a good argument to be made that an image that looks as though a filter has been used has failed in some way. This is particularly true of landscape photography if the aim is to represent the scene in as truthful a way as possible.

Right: To create the right effect it's often necessary to use multiple filters. This image required the use of an ND filter to reduce the shutter speed to 1.6 sec., plus a 2-stop graduated ND filter to retain detail in the sky.

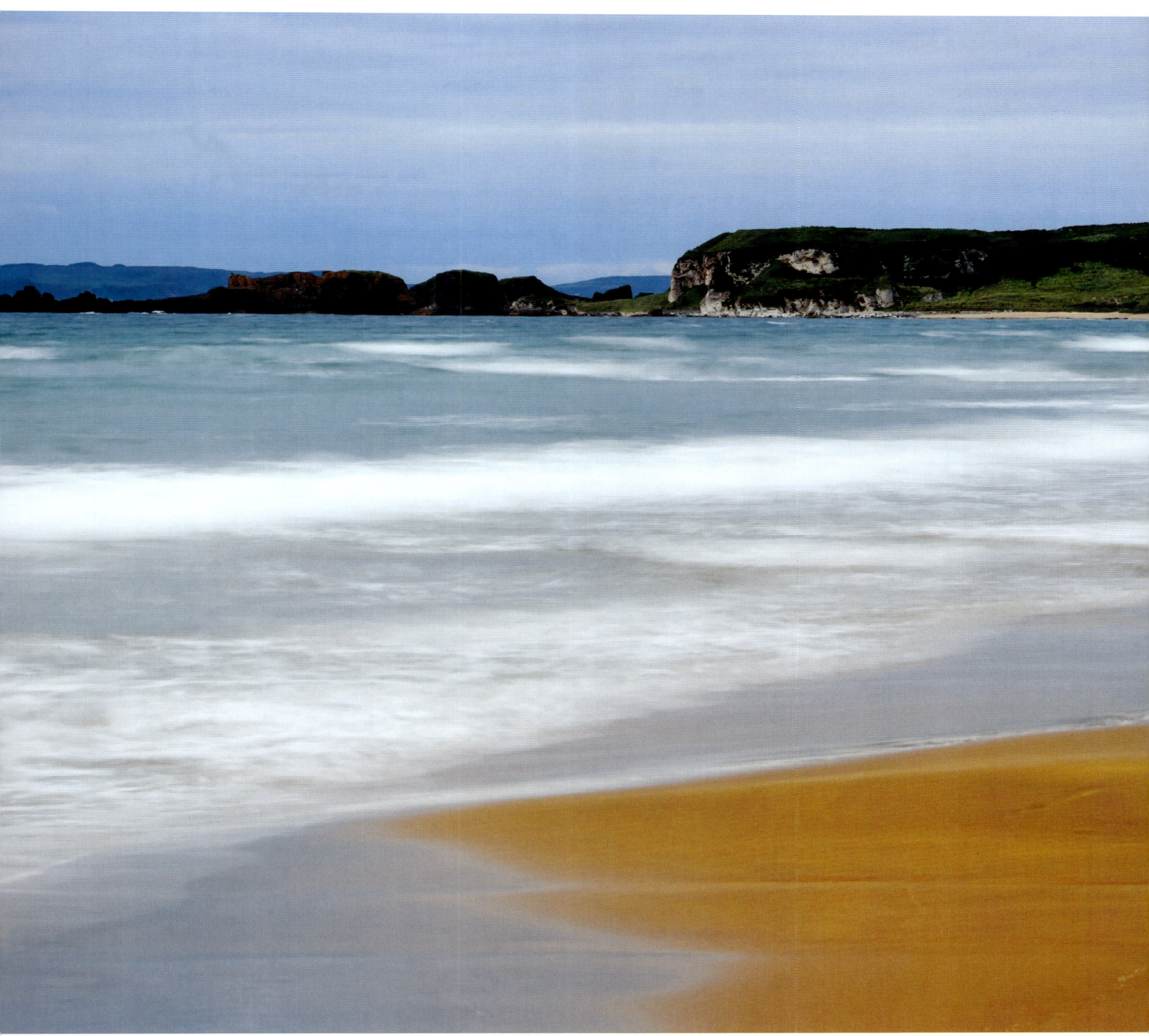

Using Filters

Filters in landscape photography are often used as a way of controlling exposure. This is generally because a camera does not have the built-in capability of recording the scene as desired. However, techniques such as HDR have arguably made the use of filters less necessary, and this is even more pertinent given that filters degrade image quality to some degree.

At the same time, there are certain filters that cannot be replicated using software, as well as those that are very hard to emulate. So, if your preference is to avoid extensive postproduction in favor of achieving the correct results at the moment of exposure, a filter over the lens can still be a useful tool.

Filters are manufactured in two basic forms: threaded or system. A threaded filter is round and is designed to be screwed onto the front of a lens. The advantage of threaded filters is that they tend to be relatively inexpensive.

Unfortunately, there is no one standard lens thread size, so it's common to own lenses each with a different thread size. One solution is to buy a filter that fits the largest thread size you own, and then use a step-up ring to convert the filter for use on a smaller lens. This is not ideal, but it works.

System Filters

An arguably better solution is to use system filters. These are either square or rectangular and are designed to slot into a holder. The holder clips to an adapter ring, which is screwed to the lens. If you want to use the holder on lenses with a different thread size you need only buy the relevant adapter ring to do so. To save time it's possible to leave an adapter ring permanently attached to a lens so that all you have to do is clip the holder on whenever a filter is required.

Of course, nothing is ever simple and system filters also have disadvantages. The first is cost.

Filter type	Filter factor	Exposure increase
UV/Skylight	1x	None
Polarizing filter	Up to 4x	Up to 2 stops
ND 0.1 filter	1.3x	$^{1}/_{3}$ stop
ND 0.3 filter	2x	1 stop
ND 0.6 filter	4x	2 stops
ND 0.9 filter	8x	3 stops
ND 3.0 filter	1000x	10 stops

FILTER EXPOSURE COMPENSATION TABLE

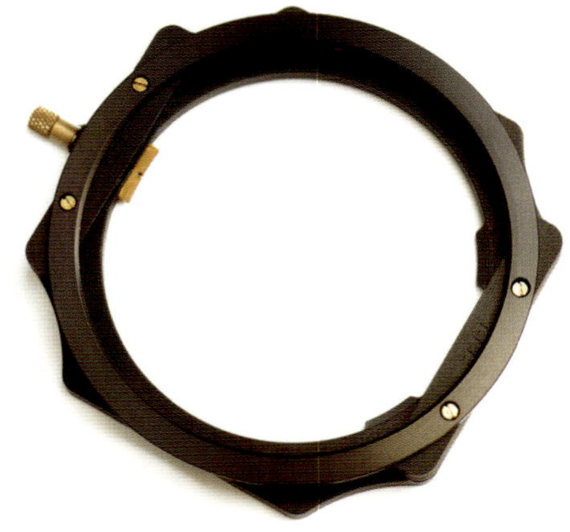

Above: Lee 100mm system filter holder.

By the time you've bought a holder, adapter rings, and filters the cost will be greater than it would be for an equivalent set of threaded filters.

The second disadvantage is that filter systems come in different sizes. Once you've bought a holder you're effectively locked into that system, as it's expensive to change. There are currently three popular filter system sizes on the market: 67mm (Cokin A-system); 84/85mm (Cokin P-system); and 100mm (produced by a number of manufacturers including Cokin, Lee Filters, and Hitech).

If you mainly use wide-angle lenses (which are almost essential for landscape photography) it's not worth considering the two smaller systems. This is because wide-angle lenses invariably have large front elements (particularly fast, wide-angle zooms), which means that the two smaller filter holders may not fit. Even if they do fit, the holder may be visible in the corners of your images, due to the lens' wide angle of view. Consequently, a 100mm filter system is the most versatile option, and the best long-term investment. However, it is also the most expensive of the three.

Tips

The more threaded filters you fit to a lens, the greater the risk of unacceptable image quality degradation. "Stacked" filters also increase the risk of vignetting, especially when using wide-angle lenses.

Threaded filters can often become stuck to the front of a lens, making them difficult to remove. You can buy tools to remove stubborn filters, but a cheaper alternative is to wrap a thick rubber band around the edge of the filter to help you turn it more easily.

UV & Skylight Filters

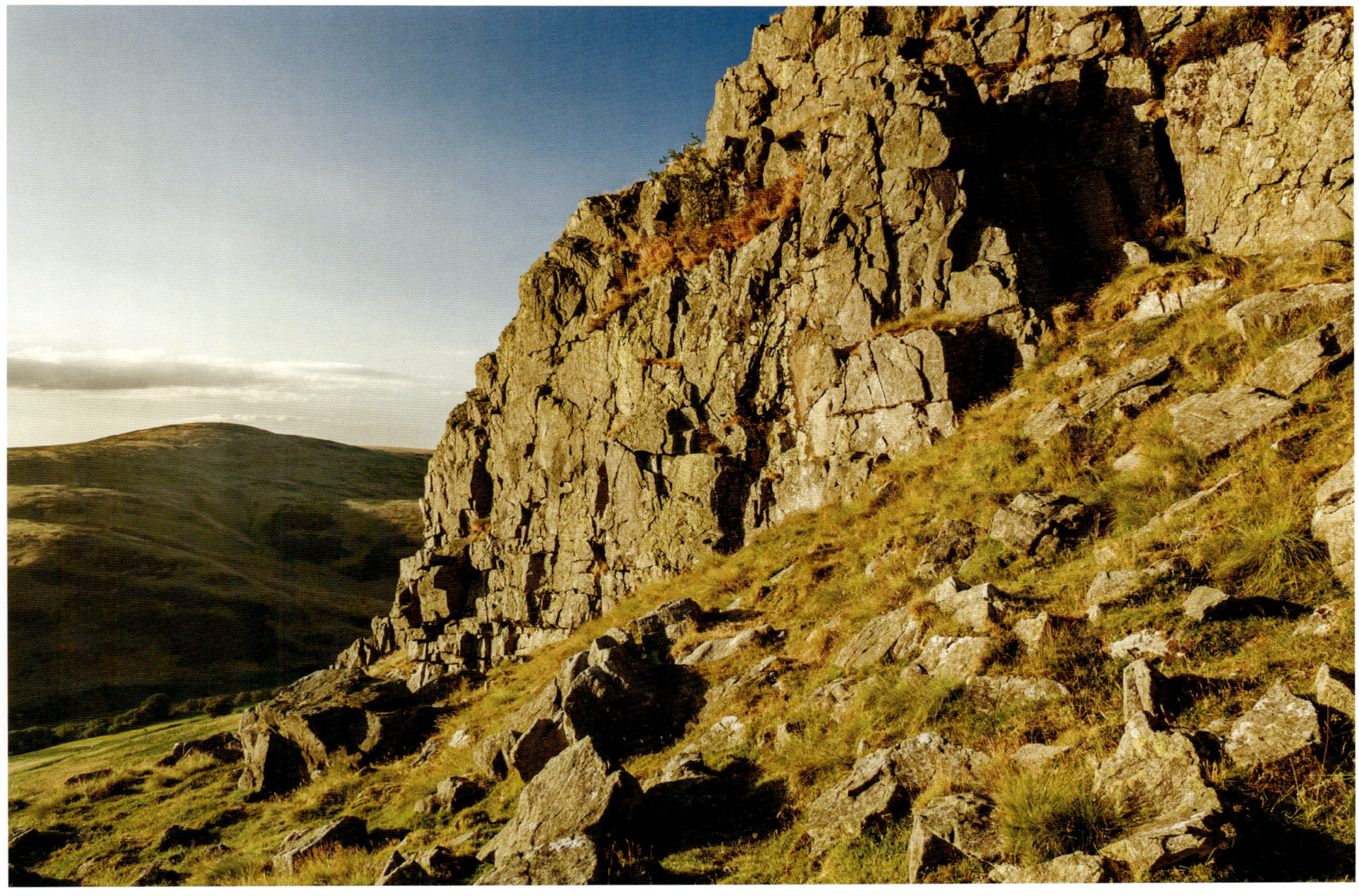

Although the human eye can't see ultraviolet (UV) light its effects are often noticeable in photographs, particularly snow scenes and those shot at high altitude. UV light tends to reduce contrast and can add a purple-blue tint to images.

UV and skylight filters absorb ultraviolet light, correcting these faults and making images crisper than they would otherwise have been. Of the two filters, a UV filter is more neutral than a skylight filter. There are also two different strengths of skylight filter—1A and 1B—with a 1B being slightly stronger and warmer.

Although UV and skylight filters are available for slotting into filter holders, most are sold in threaded form and attached permanently to a lens to protect the front element from damage (the logical reasoning being that it's less expensive to replace a scratched filter than a scratched lens). This is eminently sensible as long as you don't end up with too many other filters attached to the lens.

Above: Skylight filters help to cut down distant haze, adding clarity to an image.

ND Filters

There will be times when you can't set the exposure you want. In low-light conditions it may be that increasing the ISO will allow you to use a faster shutter speed or a smaller aperture, but what if you want to extend the shutter speed or use a wider aperture in bright conditions? Once your camera is set at its lowest possible ISO it can be difficult to achieve this without overexposing an image.

Fortunately, there's a simple solution: a neutral density (or ND) filter. As the name suggests, an ND filter is "neutral" in color and is designed to absorb a certain amount of light as it passes through it. This effectively "tricks" your camera into thinking the light levels are lower than they actually are, allowing a slower shutter speed and/or wider aperture setting to be used. Because ND filters are neutral, all wavelengths of light are absorbed equally so the image remains free from color casts.

The darker an ND filter, the greater its light absorption and the more the exposure is affected. Filter manufacturers show the strength of an ND filter using one of two systems. The most common system uses a value of 0.1 to represent a ⅓-stop light loss. A 1-stop ND filter is therefore 0.3; a 2-stop filter 0.6; a 3-stop filter 0.9, and so on.

The other method uses filter factors to show a filter's strength. Using this system a filter providing 1 stop of light reduction would be 2x; a 4x filter is equivalent to 2 stops; 8x equivalent to 3 stops, and so on. It's rare for a filter manufacturer to use both systems, so sometimes a little mental agility is required to know that you're comparing like with like.

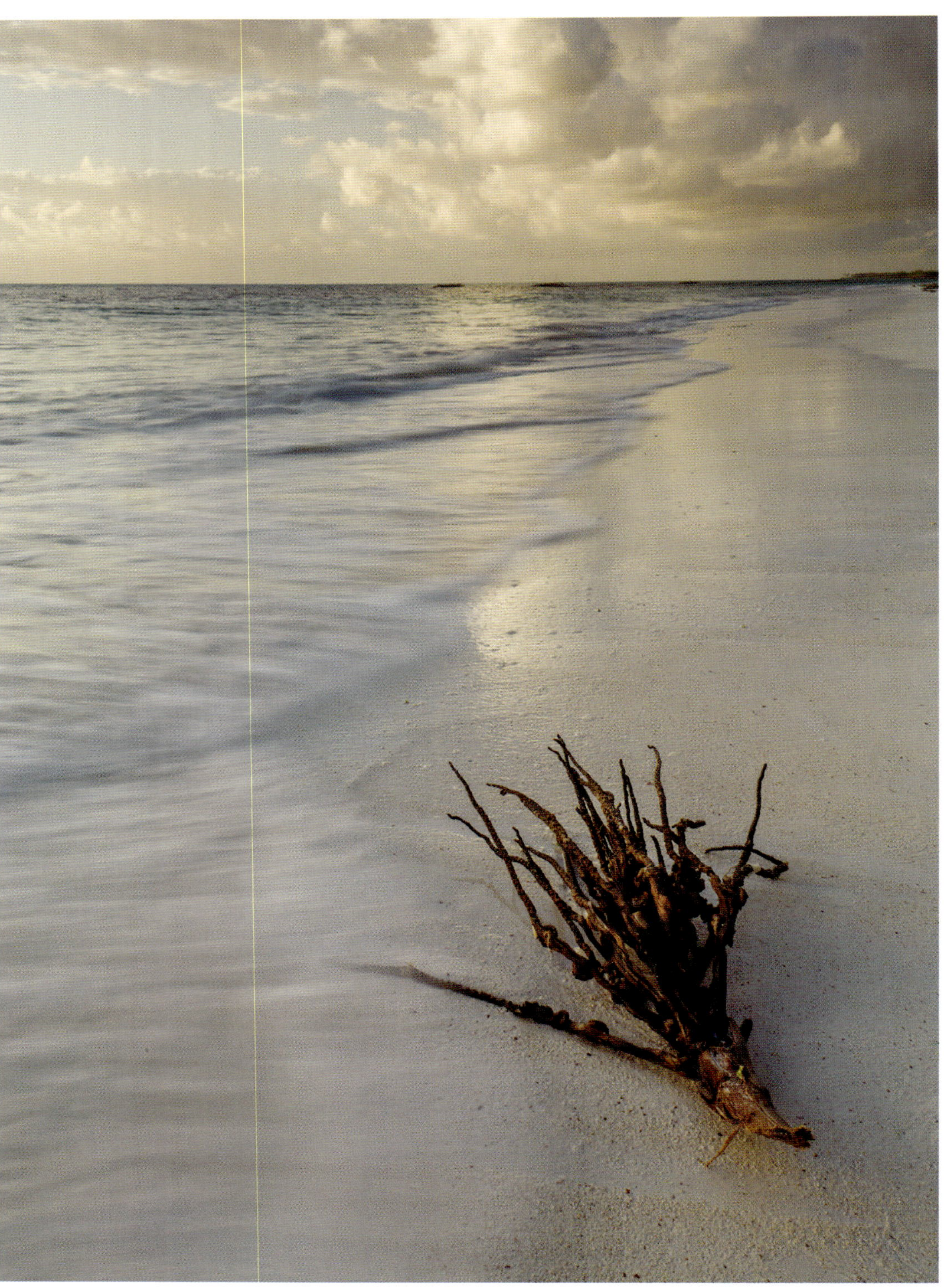

Right: ND filters aren't usually needed in low light, as it's relatively easy to use longer shutter speeds or larger apertures. They're more useful in bright conditions when there's too much light.

Extreme ND Filters

If 3 stops of filtration isn't enough then you need to invest in an "extreme" ND filter. The most common example of this type of filter is the 10-stop ND filter made by companies such as Lee Filters (which refers to its extreme ND filter as the "Big Stopper"), B+W, and Hoya. These filters are highly opaque, and they're also never strictly neutral, adding either a cool or blue cast to an image. This is not important if you plan to convert your images to black and white, and it can usually be compensated for by a custom white balance when shooting color.

Extreme ND filters are available as both screw-on and slot-in types, but as you probably won't want to fit other filters at the same time the threaded form is a good option. A screw-on extreme ND filter is also more light-tight than the filter holder equivalent, unless the latter type has a foam gasket to prevent light leaks. Even then you will need to fit the filter into the slot closest to your lens.

Because an extreme ND filter is so opaque you'll need to frame your shot and focus before it's fitted (although sometimes Live View can still function remarkably well). To calculate the exposure, first meter without the filter in place. Note the shutter speed and then use the grid at the right to determine the shutter speed you will require with the filter in place.

It's better to shoot using Manual exposure mode to give you greater control over the shutter speed (you may even have to switch to Bulb and time the shutter speed yourself if it exceeds 30 seconds). As the exposure time will be extremely long, a tripod is essential. It's also a good idea to cover the (optical) viewfinder of your camera during the exposure to stop light leaks from affecting the final image.

EXTREME ND FILTER EXPOSURE COMPENSATION

Shutter speed without filter	Shutter speed with 5-stop ND	Shutter speed with 8-stop ND	Shutter speed with 10-stop ND
1/8000 sec.	1/250 sec.	1/30 sec.	1/8 sec.
1/4000 sec.	1/125 sec.	1/15 sec.	1/4 sec.
1/2000 sec.	1/60 sec.	1/8 sec.	1/2 sec.
1/1000 sec.	1/30 sec.	1/4 sec.	1 sec.
1/500 sec.	1/15 sec.	1/2 sec.	2 sec.
1/250 sec.	1/8 sec.	1 sec.	4 sec.
1/125 sec.	1/4 sec.	2 sec.	8 sec.
1/60 sec.	1/2 sec.	4 sec.	15 sec.
1/30 sec.	1 sec.	8 sec.	30 sec.
1/15 sec.	2 sec.	15 sec.	1 min.
1/8 sec.	4 sec.	30 sec.	2 min.
1/4 sec.	8 sec.	1 min.	4 min.
1/2 sec.	15 sec.	2 min.	8 min.
1 sec.	30 sec.	4 min.	16 min.
2 sec.	1 min.	8 min.	32 min.
4 sec.	2 min.	16 min.	64 min.
8 sec.	4 min.	32 min.	128 min.
15 sec.	8 min.	64 min.	256 min.
30 sec.	16 min.	128 min.	512 min.
1 min.	32 min.	256 min.	1024 min.

Tip

When using an extreme ND filter it's better to shoot under constant lighting conditions. Overcast days—particularly when there's cloud in the sky—are ideal.

Graduated ND Filters

A graduated ND filter is a close cousin to the ND filter. The main difference is that only one half of the filter is semi-opaque; the other half is completely transparent. Graduated ND filters are used to balance the exposure between two areas of an image when one area is far brighter than the other. In landscape photography it's usually the sky that's brighter than the foreground, particularly when there's no direct light on the foreground. As with ND filters, graduated ND filters are sold in different strengths: most commonly as 1-stop, 2-stop, and 3-stop filters. The greater the difference in exposure between the two areas of an image, the stronger the required graduated ND filter.

Another way that graduated ND filters can differ is in the way that the semi-opaque area shades to clear. This can either be soft, hard, or very hard. Soft graduated ND filters are most useful when the horizon isn't perfectly straight. If you use a hard graduated filter on a mountainous horizon, for example, the peaks of the mountains will be unnaturally darkened compared to the unfiltered foreground. Hard graduated ND filters are better suited to seascapes or relatively flat landscapes.

The key to using graduated ND filters is placement. You don't want the filter to be too high or there will be a bright, possibly overexposed, strip in the sky close to the horizon. You also don't want to place it too low so that it darkens a strip along the foreground.

It's easier to see the effect when using a stronger filter than a weaker one, so if in doubt, fit your strongest graduated ND filter into one slot of your filter holder and position it so it creates the look you are after. Then, fit the correct filter into another slot, aligning it with the first filter. Once you're happy with the position remove the stronger filter and take your shot.

Above: Hard ND filters (left) have a more abrupt transition than soft ND filters (right).

Using Graduated ND Filters

When using a graduated ND filter you set the correct exposure for the foreground (or the darkest part of the image) without any filters in place. The exposure shouldn't change once the filter has been fitted as the foreground will be within the clear part of the filter. You then use the correct strength graduated ND filter to change the exposure of the sky (or the brightest part of the image) so that the sky is approximately 1-stop brighter. A very quick method to judge whether a graduated ND filter is needed is to squint at the scene. If you can clearly see detail in both the sky and foreground you probably don't need a filter. If the sky is bright, but you can no longer see detail in the foreground it's likely that you'll need a filter.

NOTE

Graduated ND filters are available in threaded form, but as the transition zone between semi-opaque and clear is essentially fixed into position, they are less useful than slot-in filters.

METERING METHOD #1

1 Switch your camera to Manual and select center-weighted metering.

2 Take a meter reading from the foreground and set the required aperture and shutter speed combination for the foreground.

3 Aim the camera at the sky and take another meter reading (but don't alter the shutter speed or aperture settings). Make a note of the difference and fit a graduated ND filter that reduces this difference to 1 stop.

4 Compose the shot, and without adjusting the exposure, fit your graduated ND filter. You are now ready to shoot.

METERING METHOD #2

1 Switch your camera to Manual exposure and select spot metering (or you can use a handheld spot meter).

2 Take a meter reading from a midtone in the foreground. This could be green grass, a rock, or a gray card placed temporarily in the foreground. Manually set the exposure to the metered value.

3 Take a meter reading from the brightest part of the sky (excluding the sun and its immediate area—don't point your camera or spot meter toward the sun). If the meter reading is more than 2 stops brighter than the foreground exposure, fit a graduated filter that will reduce these bright areas to approximately 1 stop more than the foreground exposure.

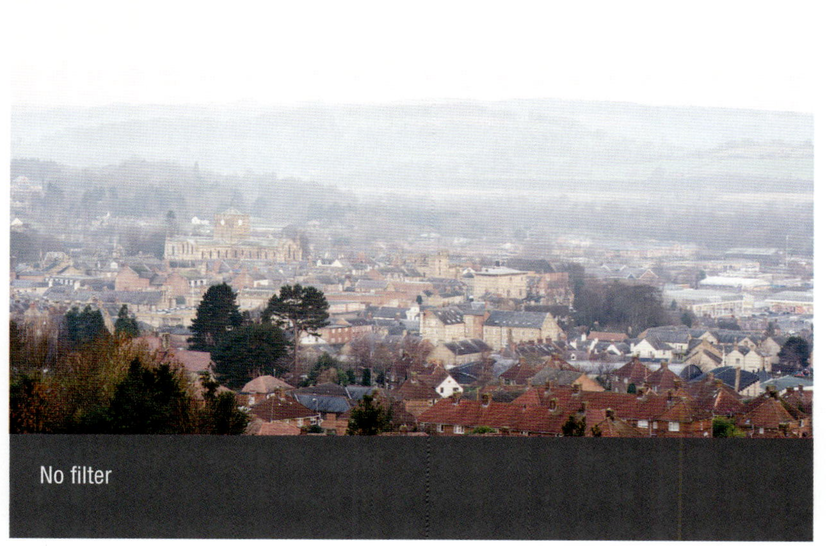

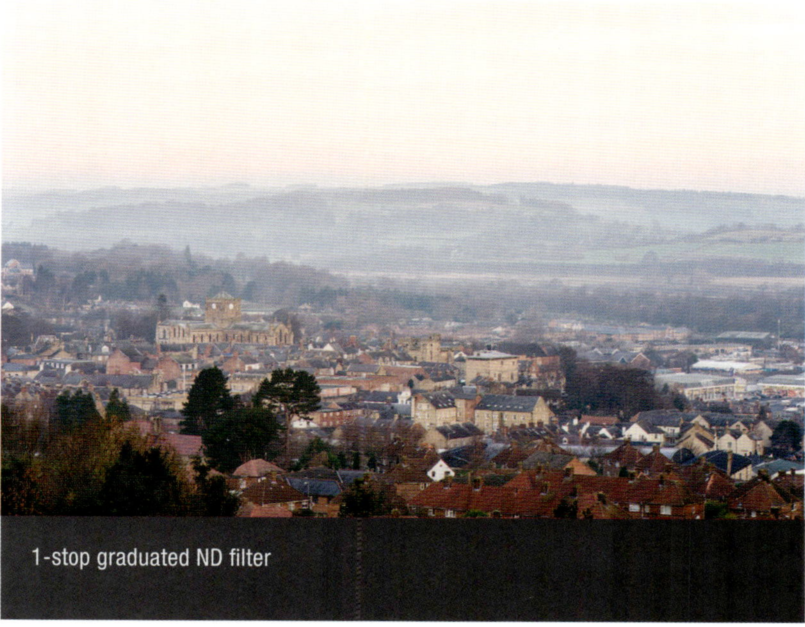

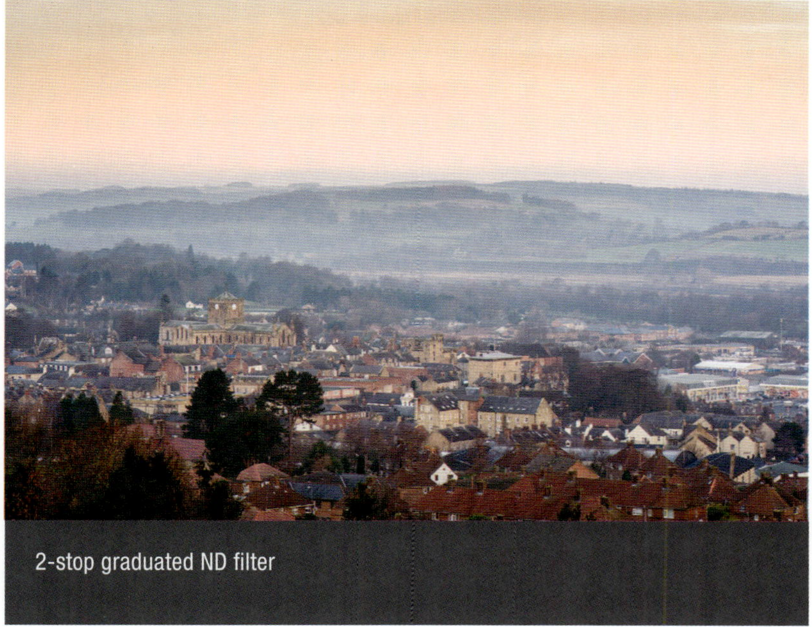

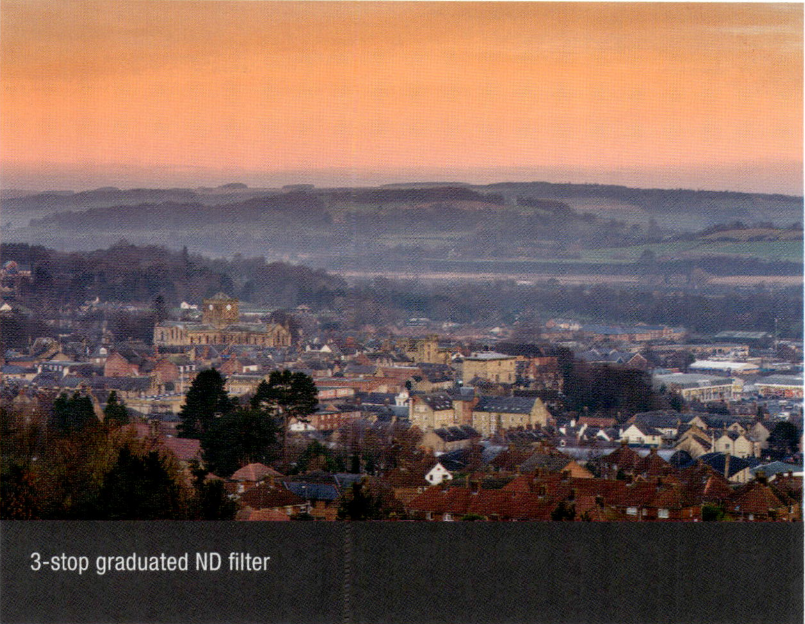

Above: When the landscape isn't lit directly there will be an exposure difference between the land and the sky: the greater the difference, the stronger the ND filter required. In this sequence, the exposure (0.6 seconds at f/13) remained constant—it's just the use of (or lack of) a graduated ND filter that has affected the amount of detail recorded in the sky. The use of a 2-stop graduated ND filter has produced an acceptable result that could be adjusted further in postproduction if necessary. The 3-stop filter has produced the most dramatic result, although it is arguably too strong and unnatural.

Polarizing Filters

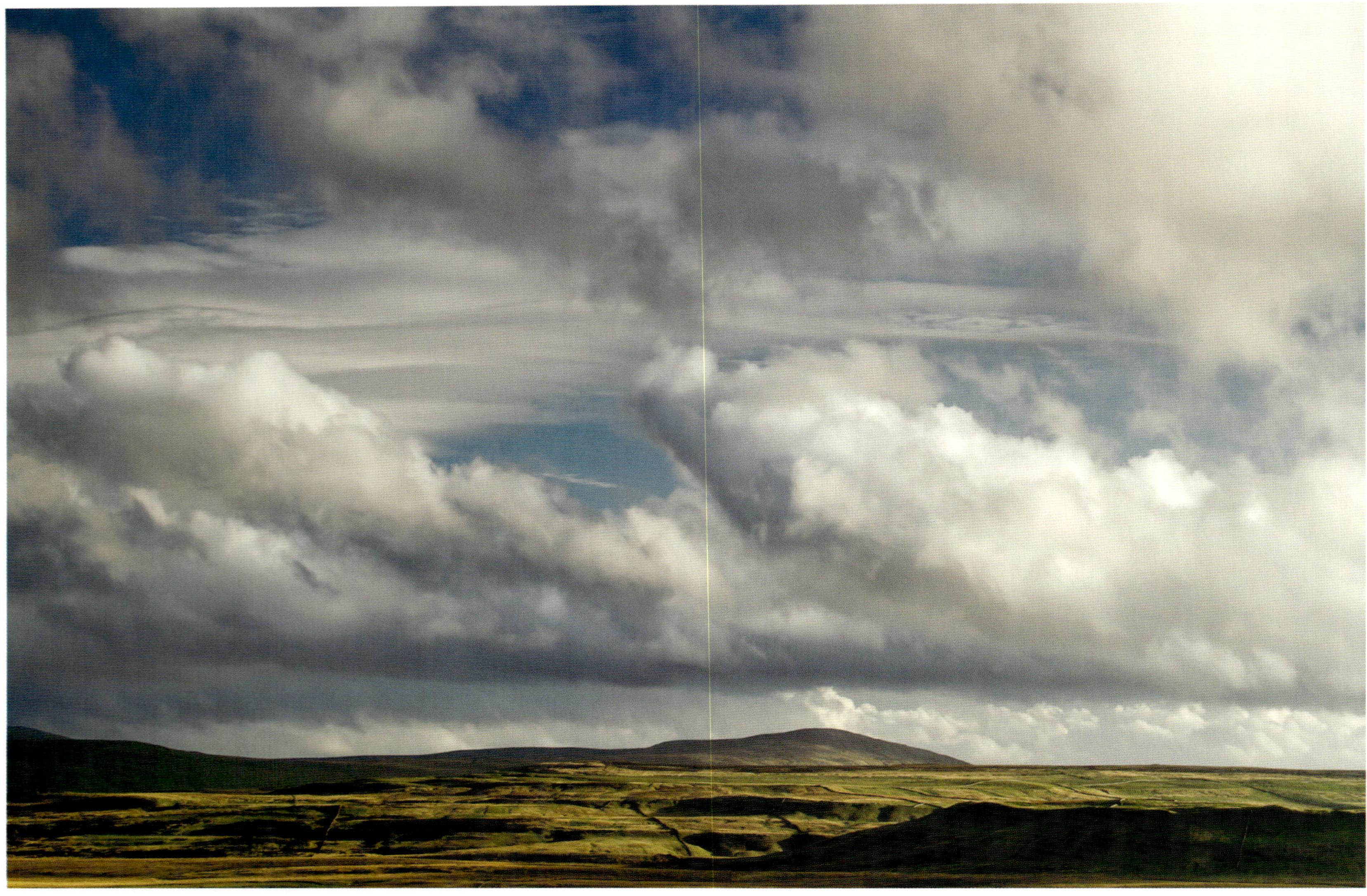

A polarizing filter has two main uses in landscape photography: cutting out glare from non-metallic surfaces, and deepening the intensity of a blue sky. A polarizer is also the only filter that cannot be replicated in postproduction, so if you're only going to invest in one filter, a polarizing filter is the one you should go for.

There are two types of polarizing filter: linear and circular. This isn't a reference to the shape, but to the way that the filter polarizes light. If you're using a DLSR (or any camera that uses phase-detection autofocus) you'll need to buy a circular polarizing filter.

Using a Polarizing Filter

Polarizing filters are made of glass mounted in a ring that can be rotated through 360°. By turning the ring you vary the strength of the polarizing

Above: Using a polarizing filter on a cloudless sky can make the sky appear "overcooked" and unnatural. However, used on a cloudy sky, the polarizing effect can help clouds stand out dramatically from the blue sky behind.

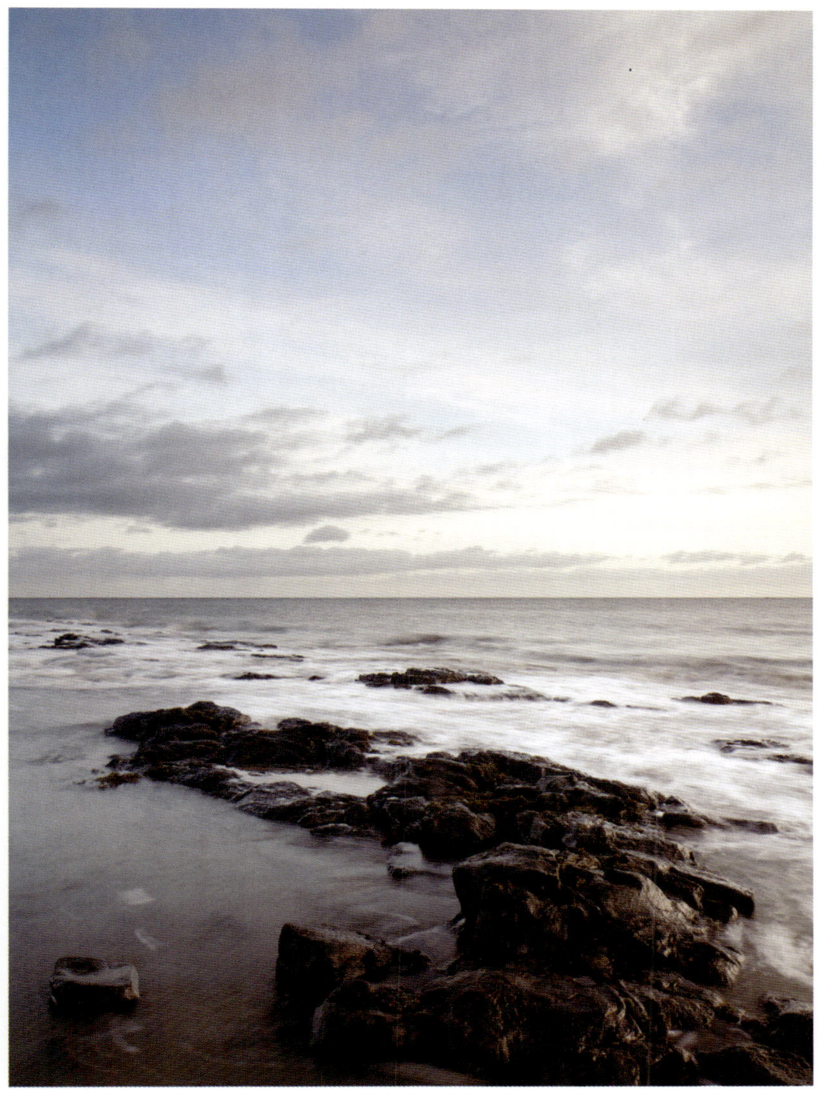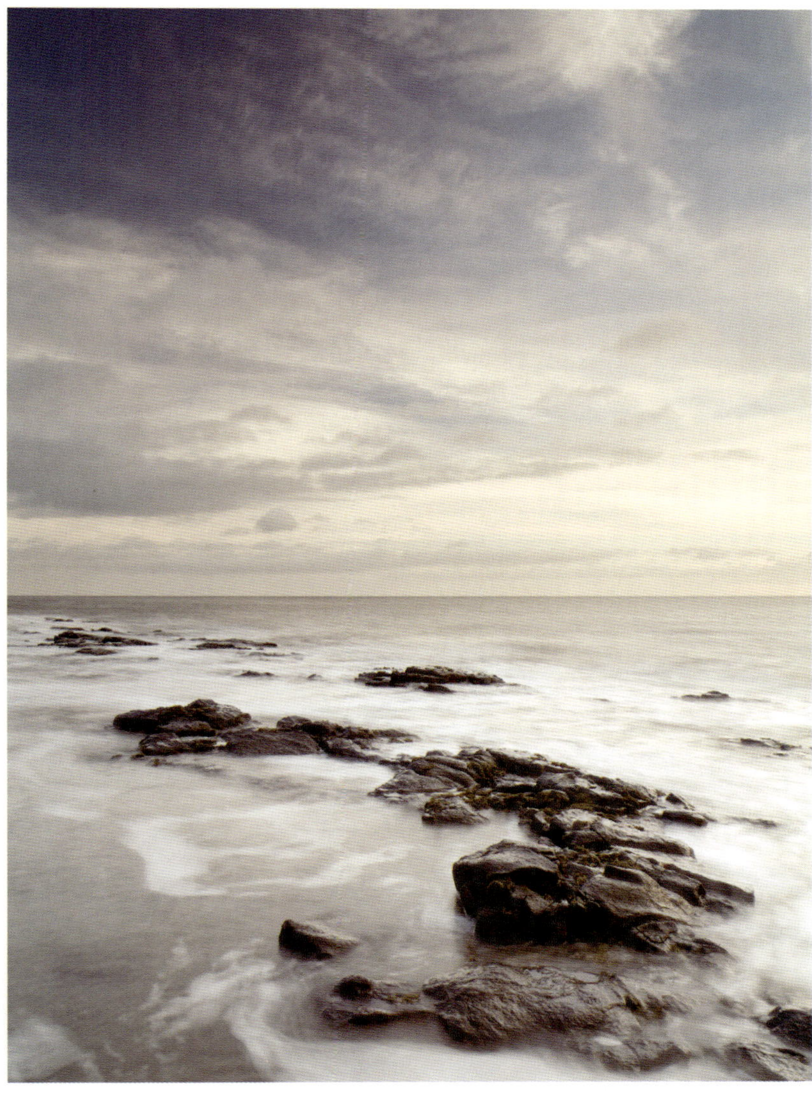

filter's effect. However, these filters only work their magic under certain conditions. The classic deepening of a blue sky only works when the polarizing filter is pointed at 90° to the sun, for example, with the effect diminishing notably away from this angle. For this reason polarizing filters should be used with care on very wide-angle lenses as they can cause an unnatural dark blue band across the sky. The height of the sun will also affect how strongly the polarizing filter works.

A similar restriction applies when a polarizing filter is used to reduce glare on non-metallic surfaces. In this instance the optimum angle is approximately 56° from the vertical. A common use for this effect is increasing the apparent transparency of water. However, polarizing filters are also useful for increasing the color saturation of wet leaves by reducing glare. The effect is noticeable even on overcast days, not just when the sun is shining.

Above left & Above: Used correctly a polarizing filter can have a dramatic effect on an image. The first image (above left) was shot without a polarizing filter, while the second image (above right) was shot just a few seconds later with a polarizing filter fitted.

Chapter 8
Postproduction

If you shoot Raw, you commit yourself to working on your images after they've been exposed. However, postproduction shouldn't be seen as an onerous task that has to be got through as quickly as possible—rather it's a chance to refine and polish your images so that you make the most of their potential. Postproduction can be as simple as a few tweaks to color and contrast, or it could be as involved as blending exposures. This chapter is a short guide to the possibilities available.

Right: Successful landscape photography is often a combination of good shooting technique and sympathetic postproduction. This image required the use of a dense ND filter to achieve a long exposure followed by conversion to black and white in postproduction.

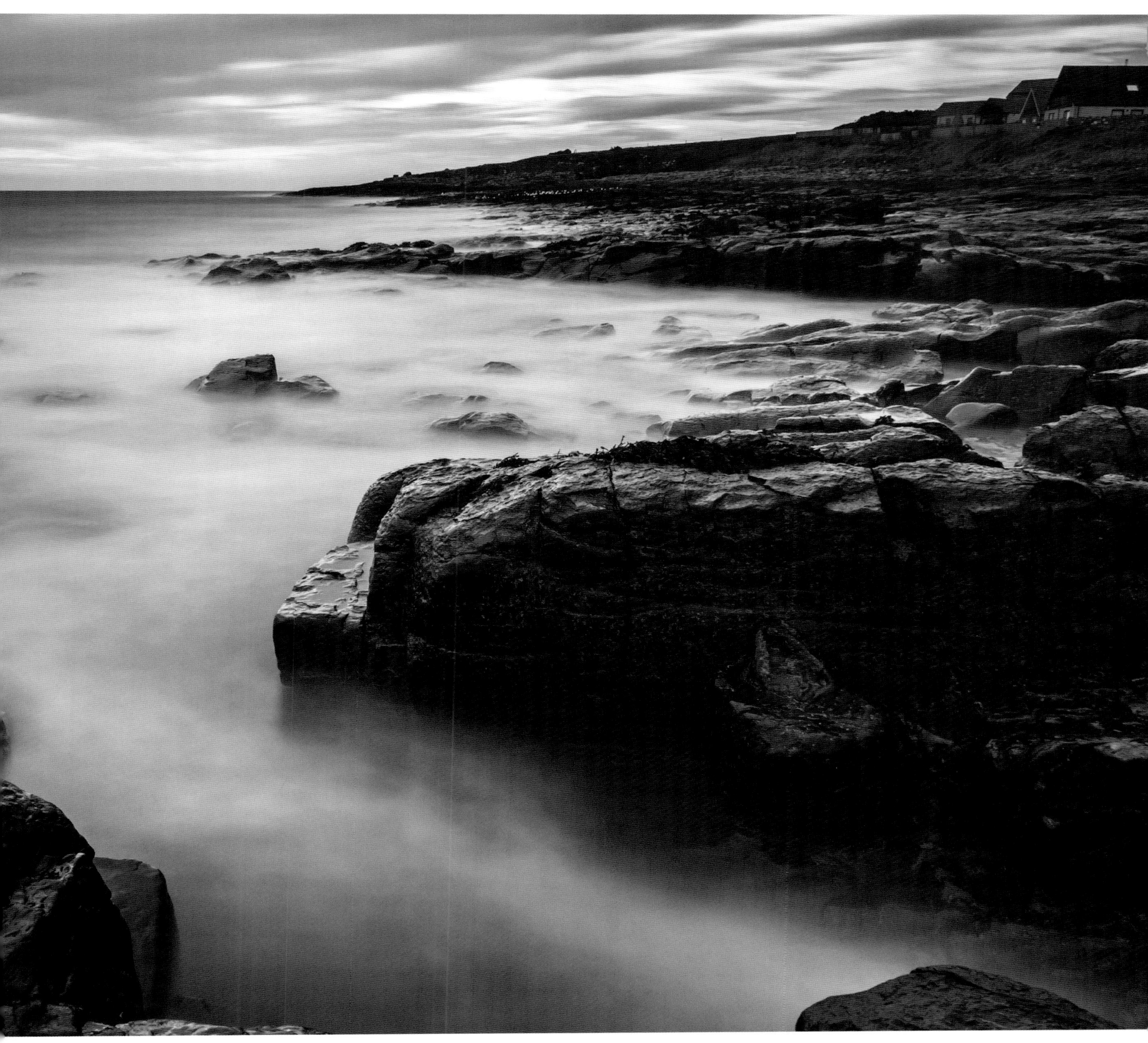

Postproduction Fundamentals

After shooting comes the postproduction process. How taxing you find this will largely depend on your attitude toward editing image files. Disciplined shooting will cut down on the number of files that need to be assessed, sorted, and edited, while getting fundamentals such as white balance right when shooting will also save precious time later. However, if you shoot using Raw there will inevitably be some editing and polishing of your images required.

Raw Converters

There are numerous Raw converters available, and the most obvious one to use is the one that came with your camera. However, it's fair to say that the offerings that come with most cameras are often lacking compared to third-party alternatives.

Good Raw conversion software should allow you to do more than just tweak the look of your images—it should also be capable of Digital Asset Management (DAM). It's all too easy to be swamped with digital images, even after a week or so of shooting. DAM allows you to keep track of your images through folder and file name management, adding keywords and descriptions to image metadata, and allowing you to quickly search for, view, and edit specific images or those that match specified criteria.

There are several Raw conversion packages that feature DAM, but arguably the best known is Adobe Lightroom. However, Capture One Pro produced by Phase One is highly regarded and is worth considering (both Lightroom and Capture One are available on a 30-day trial basis). Mac users also have the choice of Apple Aperture.

Choosing Raw conversion software is partly down to whether you like how the software works, and if you like the way in which Raw files are rendered. There's no right way to extract the information from a Raw file: it's achieved in different ways by different software, making choosing software a very personal business.

Workflow

A slightly underrated aspect of photography is the need for an efficient, but easy-to-follow, workflow. Again, there is no right or wrong way of working, but there are certain fundamentals that you need to think about in a certain order (see below). Get it wrong and you store trouble up for yourself. Before too long it will become a monumental task to sort the situation out.

Task	Sub-tasks
Importing images	• *Import to computer* • *Rename* • *Back-up images to DVD or external hard drive* • *Assess, rate, and delete if applicable*
Editing	• *Apply white balance corrections* • *Correct for lens aberrations* • *Rotate, straighten, or crop if necessary* • *Remove dust spots or blemishes* • *Noise reduction* • *Adjust exposure if required* • *Basic image adjustments (such as altering contrast)* • *Other image adjustments (such as converting to black and white)*
Exporting images	• *Convert to 8-Bit (if shooting Raw) and save as either JPEG or TIFF* • *Update digital asset management (DAM) database*
Printing	• *Open and duplicate image (close original image)* • *Resize duplicate as required* • *Sharpen duplicate as required* • *Print* • *Close duplicate without saving*

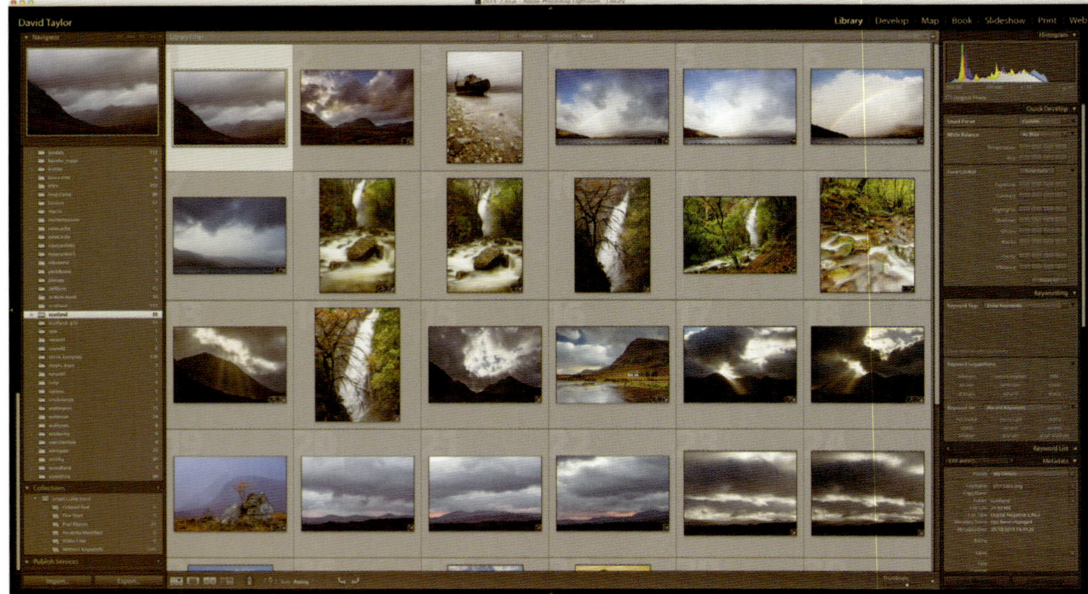

Above: Adobe Lightroom is essentially Adobe Photoshop refashioned to more closely suit the needs of photographers.

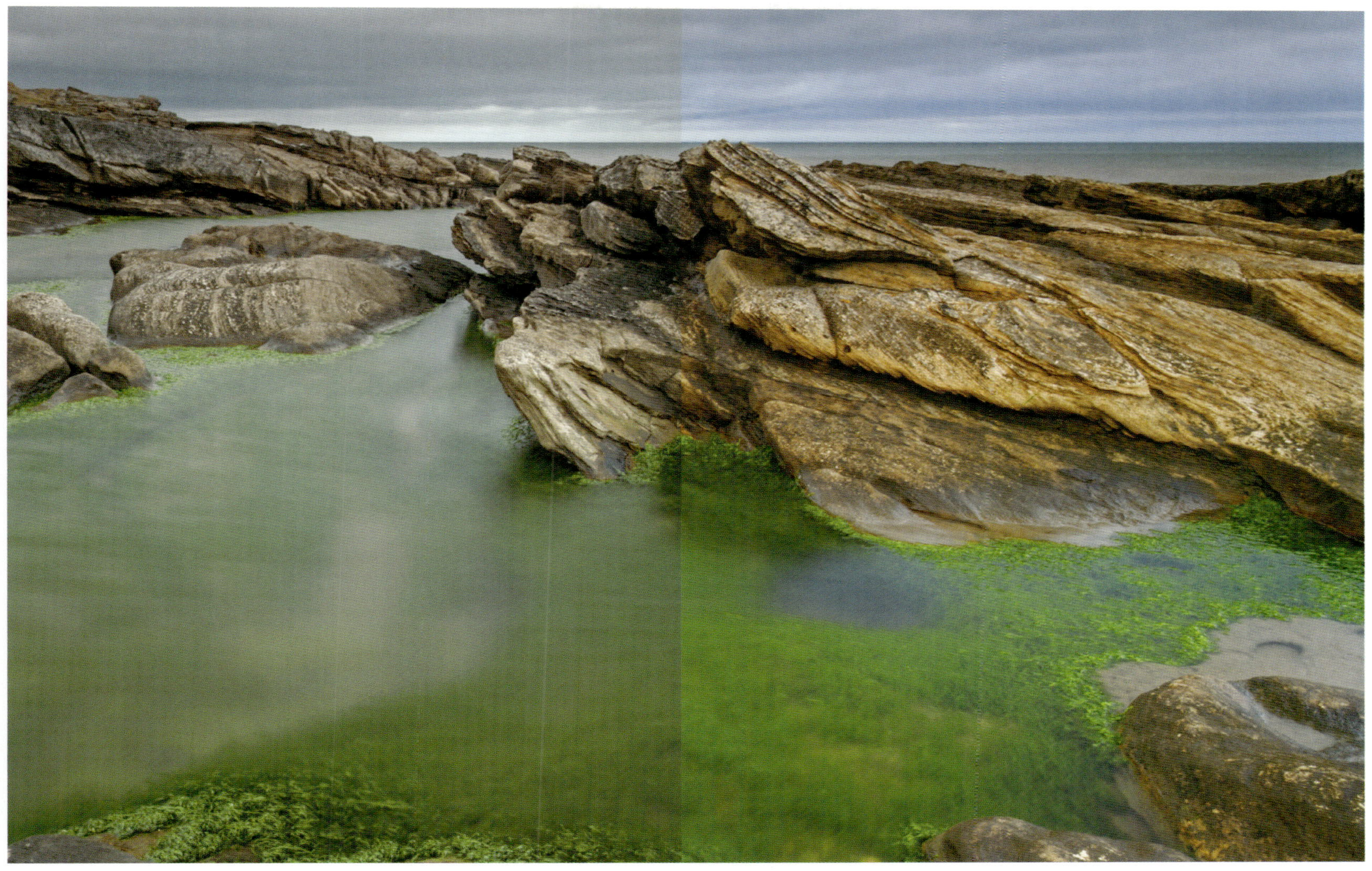

Unprocessed

Processed

Above: Raw files often appear disappointing when first viewed. The key is to see the latent potential in the image. It's also a good idea to assess an image properly and determine what changes are needed. Although any alteration to a Raw file can be unpicked, it saves time to have a clear vision to start with.

Importing

The import process—copying images from your memory card to your computer's hard drive—will vary according to the Raw conversion software you use. At a basic level the software should allow you to decide where on the hard drive the images are stored, whether you want to rename them, and whether you want to add descriptions and keywords to those photographs.

Setting up a sensible folder structure is important, but how you do this is very much a personal choice. Using categories to divide your work into different folders (by date or by subject) is a good starting point. The use of folders within folders will allow you to refine your categorization into more specific subsets.

It is also important to rename your images. Cameras assign file names based on a four-digit numbering system, so if you shoot more than 10,000 images the file names will start to repeat. This won't make it easy to find specific photographs. Again, how you name your photos is a personal decision. My system is to rename images according to the year and month they were shot (so 1407 would be for an image shot in July 2014) followed by a unique four digit number.

Finally, descriptions and keywords will help you search for images within your Raw software. A description is just that—a brief description of the subject—while keywords are individual words that refer to some aspect of the image. Keywords should be specific: the name of the location, state, and country, for example. They should also refer to elements within the image, such as the weather or time of day, and could be more conceptual, using descriptive words such as light, airy, dark, moody, and so on.

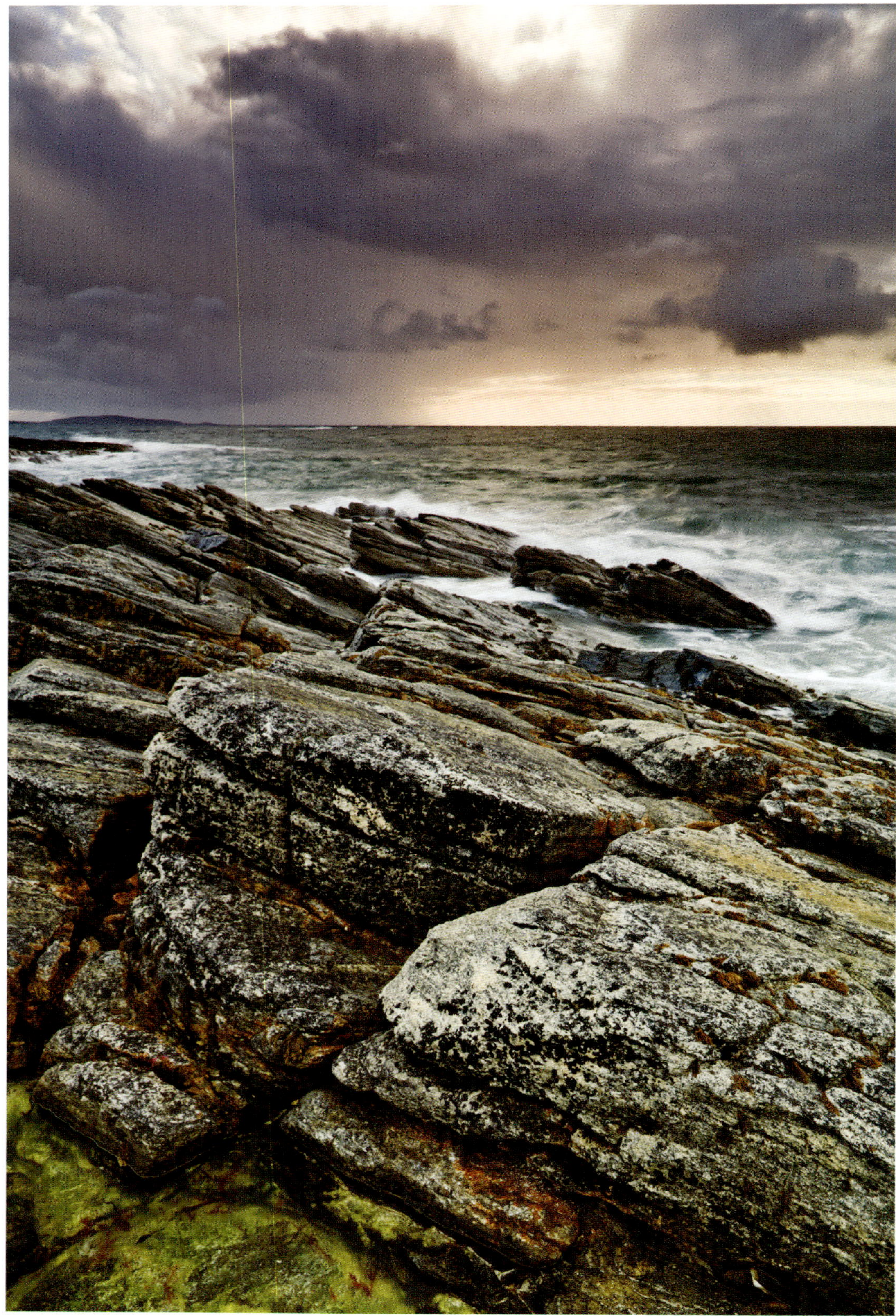

Right: This is file number 0708_0034. At a glance I can tell it was shot in August 2007. It was shot on the island of North Uist in the Outer Hebrides. It's therefore stored in a nested folder under Landscape > United Kingdom > Scotland > Outer Hebrides > North Uist > Coast. Although this may seem long-winded it makes specific images very easy to find.

Rating

Once your images have been imported into your computer you'll need to decide which ones are worth keeping to work on and which are only suitable for the trash. However, this isn't a process that should be rushed—some may immediately stand out as "keepers," while others may take time to grow on you.

Using a rating system will help you sort your images. Photographs that will definitely be kept could have five stars, those that are deficient for some reason could be given one star, and those that are more ambiguous could have three stars. Once I've rated my images in this way I will often leave them for a day or so, then come back with fresh eyes to make a final decision.

Tip

You should back-up your images once they've been imported—external hard drives are cheap, whereas your images may be irreplaceable. If possible, use two hard drives and keep one at a relative or friend's house, swapping over every so often so that you always have a reasonably up-to-date back-up in another location.

Right: The description embedded in the metadata for this image is "Summer evening light on an arable farm field overlooking the village of Wylam and the Tyne Valley, Northumberland, England." This contains the basic information needed to identify the location and subject.

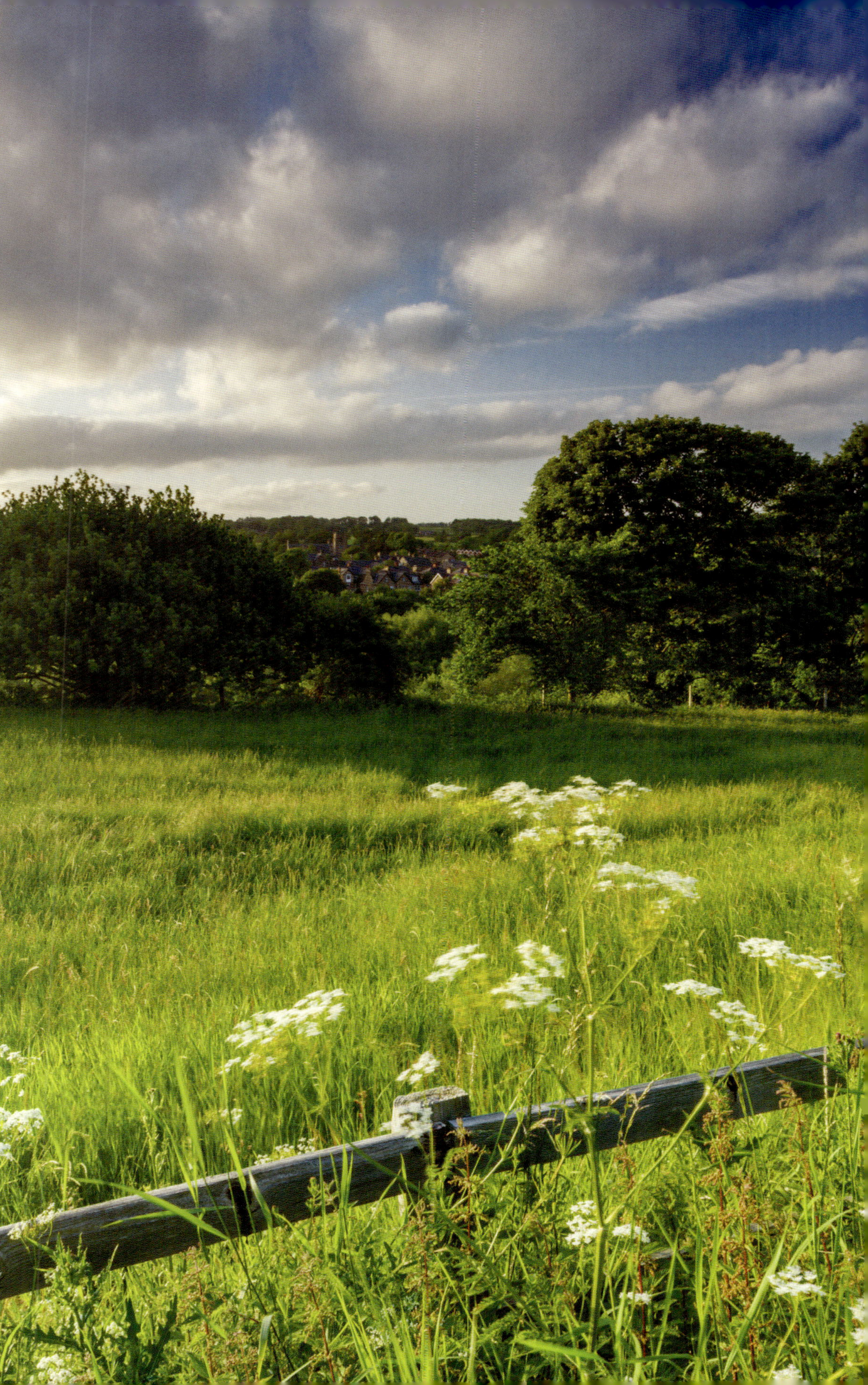

Basic Image Corrections

Once you've imported your images you will need to adjust them. Certain adjustments, such as white balance, can usually be set for one image and then applied automatically across a range of photographs. This is particularly useful when it comes to eliminating repetitive and time-consuming corrective tasks. Ultimately, however, each image will require a certain amount of individual care and attention.

There are two types of adjustment you can make to an image: global adjustments and local adjustments. A global adjustment affects the image as a whole (changing the white balance is typically a global adjustment), while local adjustments are made to a specific area of an image, often using a brush that can be altered in size.

The order in which adjustments are made is largely a matter of preference, but it often pays to make global adjustments first and then work toward fixing specific (local) problem areas last.

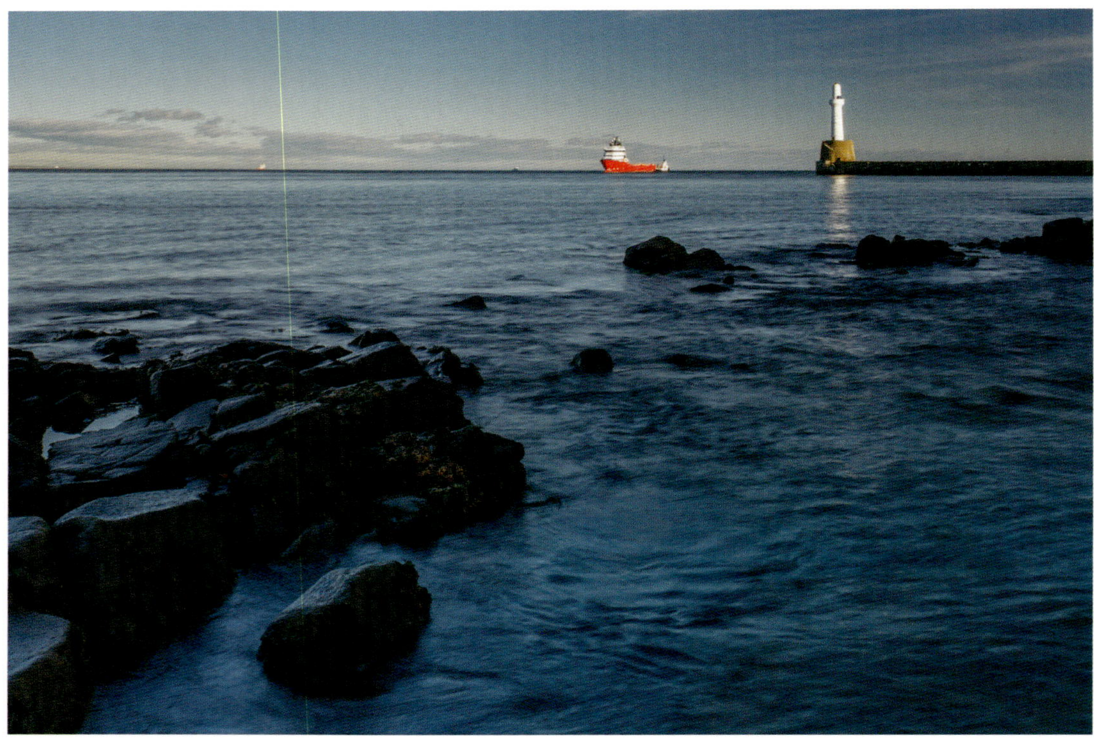

Above: Generally, artificial subjects make better white balance targets than natural ones. The white balance for this image was set by using the lighthouse on the pier as a target. Midday clouds make a good natural white balance target. However, don't use sunrise or sunset clouds as this will remove any warmth from the image.

White Balance

You may have got the white balance exactly right in camera, in which case this is a step you can miss out. However, it's generally the case that a small white balance tweak is necessary for all images. This is achieved either by using a preset similar to those found on your camera, or by selecting a specific Kelvin value (and then refining this by adjusting the magenta/green bias).

Some software features a color picker that allows you to select a neutral area of an image as a basis for the white balance. At the shooting stage it's worth exposing a test image using a gray target in the same light as your scene. In postproduction you can then use this image to set the white balance and apply the same setting to other images shot under the same light.

Exposure

The Exposure tool mimics exposure compensation on a camera (to the extent that it works in stops, just like a camera), so it can be used to lighten or darken an image very intuitively. However, unless you've shot your image "exposed to the right" (see page 50), the Exposure tool shouldn't be used too excessively: lightening an image is particularly destructive, as it increases the likelihood of noise appearing in the shadow areas.

Contrast

Raw files can often look disappointingly flat at first, particularly if you're using a picture parameter with the contrast turned down. The quickest way to add punch to an image is to increase its contrast. Most image-editing software has numerous ways of achieving this.

The simplest method is a Contrast slider that allows you to increase or decrease contrast, while a more sophisticated tool—Curves—allows you to adjust specific parts of an image's tonal range. The simplest curve is an "S-curve" that lightens highlights and darkens shadows, immediately boosting the contrast in an image.

Color Adjustments

As well as a lack of contrast, Raw images can also appear flat in terms of color saturation. Again, most software offers multiple ways of correcting this, with the simplest being a Saturation slider. This global adjustment boosts all colors equally, but needs to be used carefully, as it's easy to make an image garish.

Slightly more subtle is Vibrance, which initially boosts the least saturated colors in an image. It's only when you increase Vibrance to its maximum level that more heavily saturated colors are affected as well.

Good Raw conversion software should also allow you to adjust the saturation (luminance and hue) of individual colors in an image. This is useful for altering the color of sky without affecting the foreground areas of an image.

Highlights & Shadows

One of the major benefits of shooting Raw is that there's often more detail in the highlights and shadows than you'd think (although this is dependant on the dynamic range of your camera). Raw software with Highlights and Shadows sliders allows you to adjust these specific tonal areas without affecting the midtones in an image.

Dust Spotting

Before digital cameras had built-in dust removal systems, cloning out dust from digital images could be a laborious process. It's generally less necessary now, but it's still important to check for dust and other blemishes. Software dust removal generally clones one area of an image to remove dust from another (with you controlling both the "from" and "to" points). Theoretically, dust-busting is a task that can be done once and then applied automatically to other images in a sequence—after all, the dust will always be in the same place in each image. Unfortunately, life isn't so simple and you may find that the specified "clone from" area isn't ideal for every image.

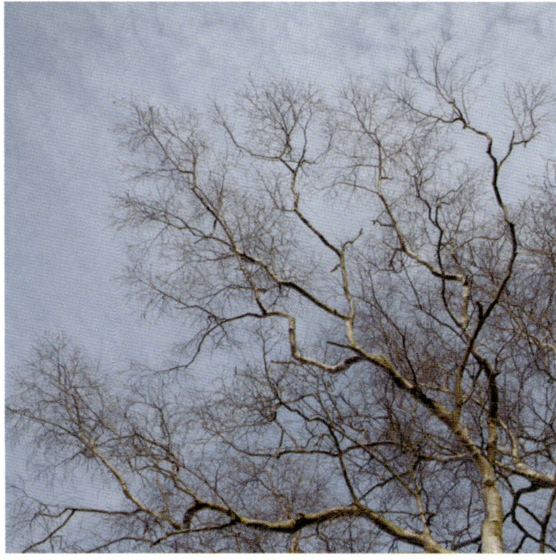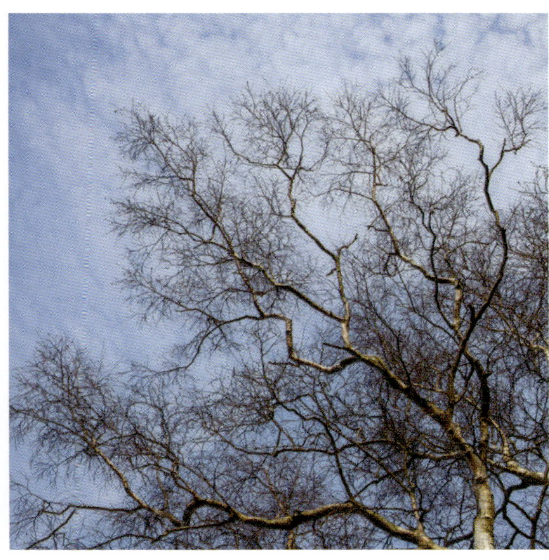

Above & Above right: A simple contrast adjustment is often all that's needed to immediately add bite to an image.

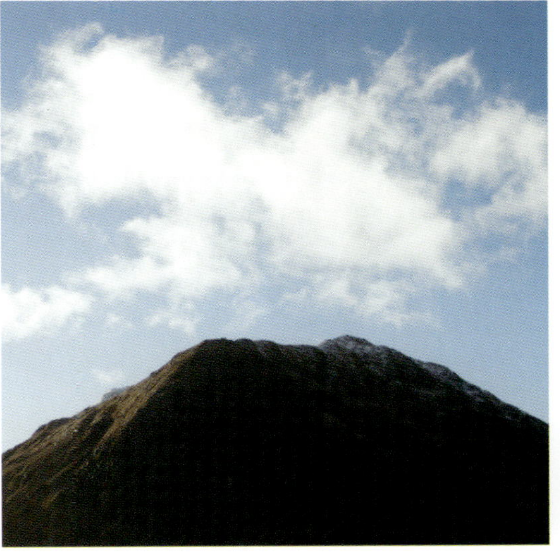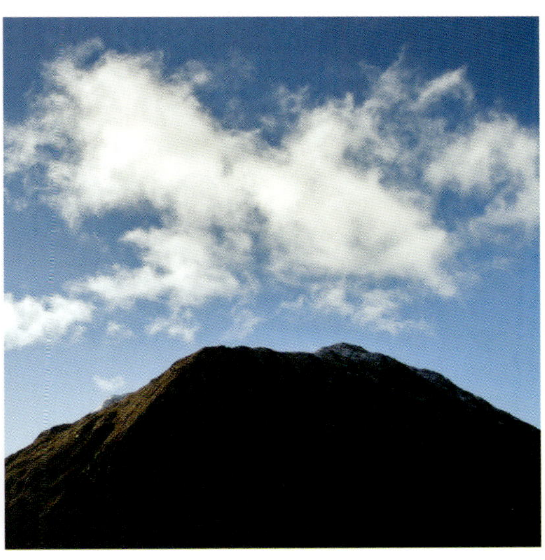

Above & Above right: Highlight is a useful tool to extract hidden image detail within the brightest parts of an image.

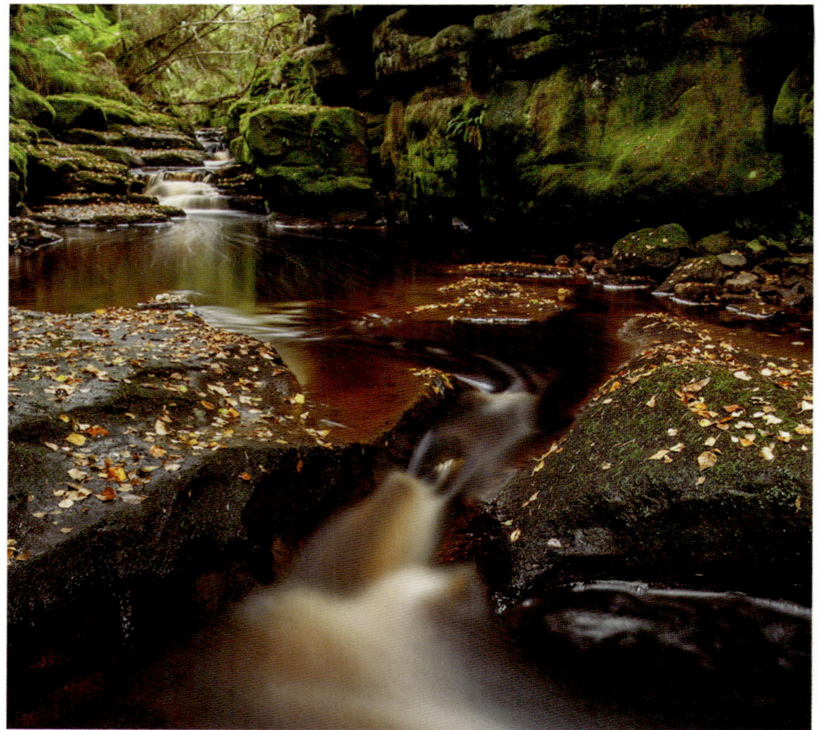 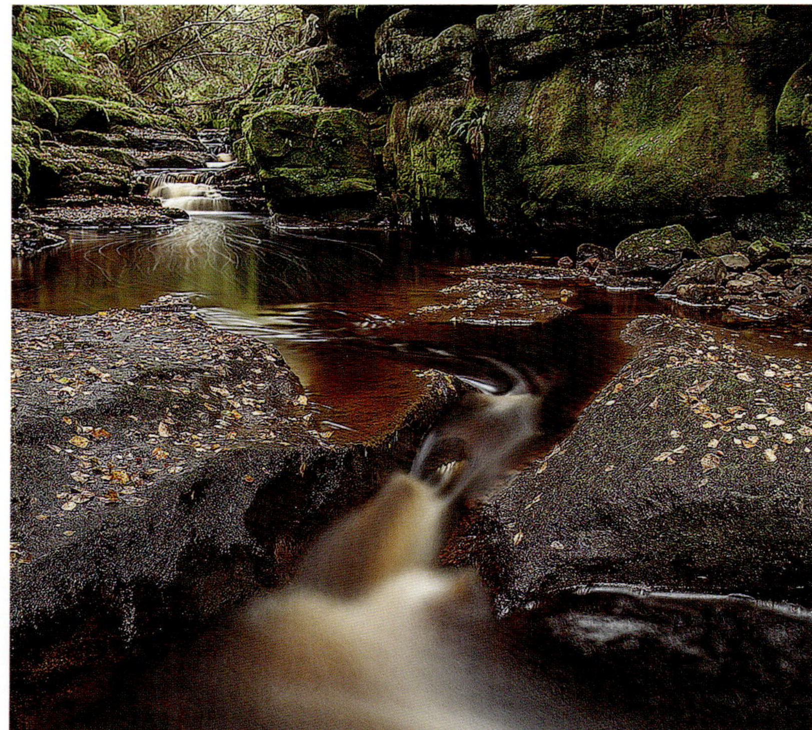

Sharpening

How sharp an image is depends on a number of factors, including how well (or otherwise) you focused and whether you handheld the camera correctly (assuming you didn't use a tripod). However, sharpness can also be measured at a pixel level. This is dependant on the quality of the lens used and whether or not the sensor features an optical low-pass or anti-aliasing filter. These filters sit in front of a digital sensor and deliberately soften an image very slightly to reduce the problem of moiré. This is a shimmering effect in images of tightly textured subjects such as fabric.

There's currently a vogue to produce sensors without optical low-pass filters, to maximize sharpness. Even so, most digital images will benefit from a small amount of sharpening in postproduction. This is often referred to as "capture sharpening."

Additional sharpening may be required when you output an image, especially if the photograph is going to be printed. This is known as "output sharpening." To complicate matters, an image should be sharpened less when output for use on screen (such as for a web site) than when printing, and the size of the output image also plays a part in how much (or how little) sharpening it needs.

Sharpening in postproduction is slightly misnamed; the process could more accurately be described as "edge contrast enhancement." By increasing edge contrast an image immediately appears sharper (or, to put it another way, the image's acutance has increased). However, there's a definite art to sharpening—if an image is over-sharpened it's possible to see ugly halos around edges in the image.

Above left & Above: The image above left has had no sharpening applied; the photograph above has clearly been over-sharpened.

Noise Reduction

An image should need very little noise reduction if you've used the camera's base ISO setting, which is a good thing, as reducing noise inevitably means losing some fine detail. However, if you've used a particularly long exposure or a higher ISO setting then some noise reduction will be necessary. Good Raw conversion software should allow you to tackle luminance and chroma noise separately—if you have to remove just one, chroma noise is generally more objectionable.

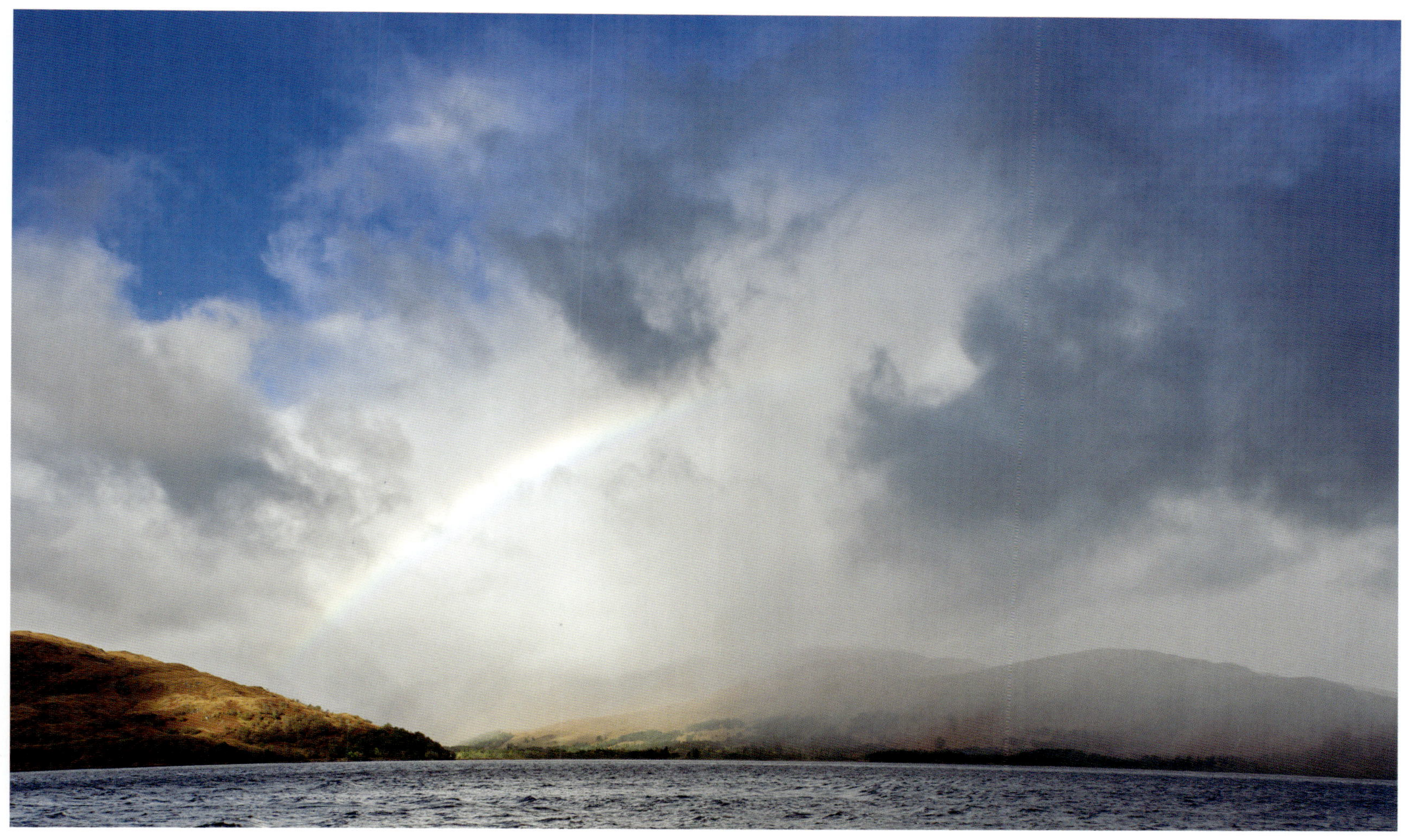

Lens Correction

No lens is perfect, but slight flaws can be quantified and corrected during postproduction. There are three main flaws that a lens can suffer from to one degree or another: chromatic aberration, vignetting, and distortion.

There are two types of chromatic aberration: axial and transverse. Axial chromatic aberration is typically seen across an image when a lens is used at maximum aperture, but is reduced and eventually disappears once the aperture is stopped down. Transverse chromatic aberration is seen only at the edges of an image, usually on high-contrast edges as red/green or blue/yellow fringing. Transverse chromatic aberration is not reduced by stopping the aperture down.

Vignetting is seen as a darkening around the edges of an image when a lens is used at maximum aperture. It usually reduces to insignificance once the aperture is set just a few stops from maximum. If you generally use small apertures for depth of field reasons you're unlikely to see vignetting.

Finally, distortion is a description of how a lens can bend an image out toward the edges (known as barrel distortion) or in toward the center (pincushion distortion). It can be particularly noticeable if there are straight lines in an image. In landscape photography this is often seen when shooting seascapes.

Above: A banana-shaped horizon is a good indication that the lens you've used suffers from distortion—in this instance strong pincushion distortion.

Black & White

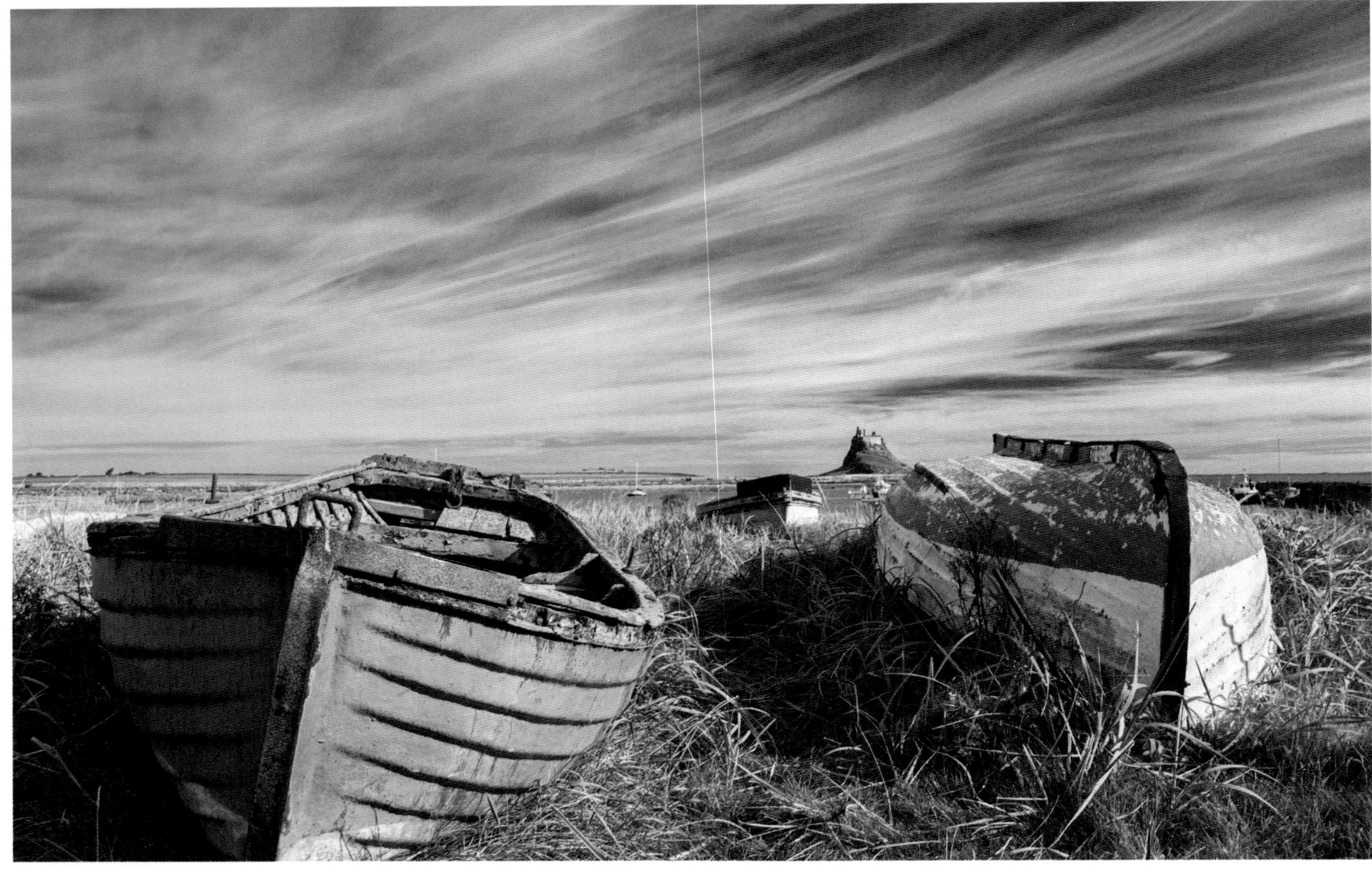

You'd be forgiven for thinking that black and white would have been consigned to history's dustbin once color photography took hold. However, black-and-white imagery has a unique power that is far different to color work. Black-and-white landscape photography has a long pedigree that virtually stretches back to the dawn of photography. The advantage of digital capture is that the decision to shoot black and white can be made either at the time of capture or in postproduction, giving you the best of both worlds.

Above: This image was shot as a Raw file. Raw files contain color information, but my camera allows me to view a black-and-white image as I shoot (essentially this is the camera showing a preview of the Raw file after processing). This means I can easily assess an image in monochrome when I'm shooting, but still have the option of processing it in either color or black and white later.

Filtration

A successful black-and-white image isn't just a color image that's been desaturated—how colors are translated into shades of gray is a key part of the process.

How dark or light a gray tone is in an image is usually determined by a subject's reflectivity. A subject that reflects an average amount of light would be converted to mid-gray in a simple black-and-white conversion. However, this applies to subjects that may be radically different in color: if a green subject and a red subject reflect the same amount of light they will be seen as very similar shades of gray. This can make images appear flat and dull.

When shooting with black-and-white film the solution is to use colored filters. A colored filter blocks the wavelengths of light on the opposite side of the color wheel, so a red filter blocks green-blue, for example. This has the effect of darkening anything in an image that's green-blue and lightening anything that's red—separating these colors tonally in the black-and-white image.

It's still possible to use colored filters with digital cameras, but it's easier to mimic their effects in postproduction (or in-camera if you're shooting JPEG images). Lightroom, for example, has sliders for individual colors to give you far greater control over the black-and-white conversion process than a set of lens filters ever could.

Right: A red filter strongly affects the blue sky here, almost turning the deepest blue areas black. This can produce very bold images, especially when there's cloud in the sky to add contrast. Unfortunately, the blue channel is the noisiest of the RGB channels and this can cause problems when extreme adjustments are made to blue areas of an image. For this reason I often simulate the use of a green filter instead of red, as this has less effect on the blue channel.

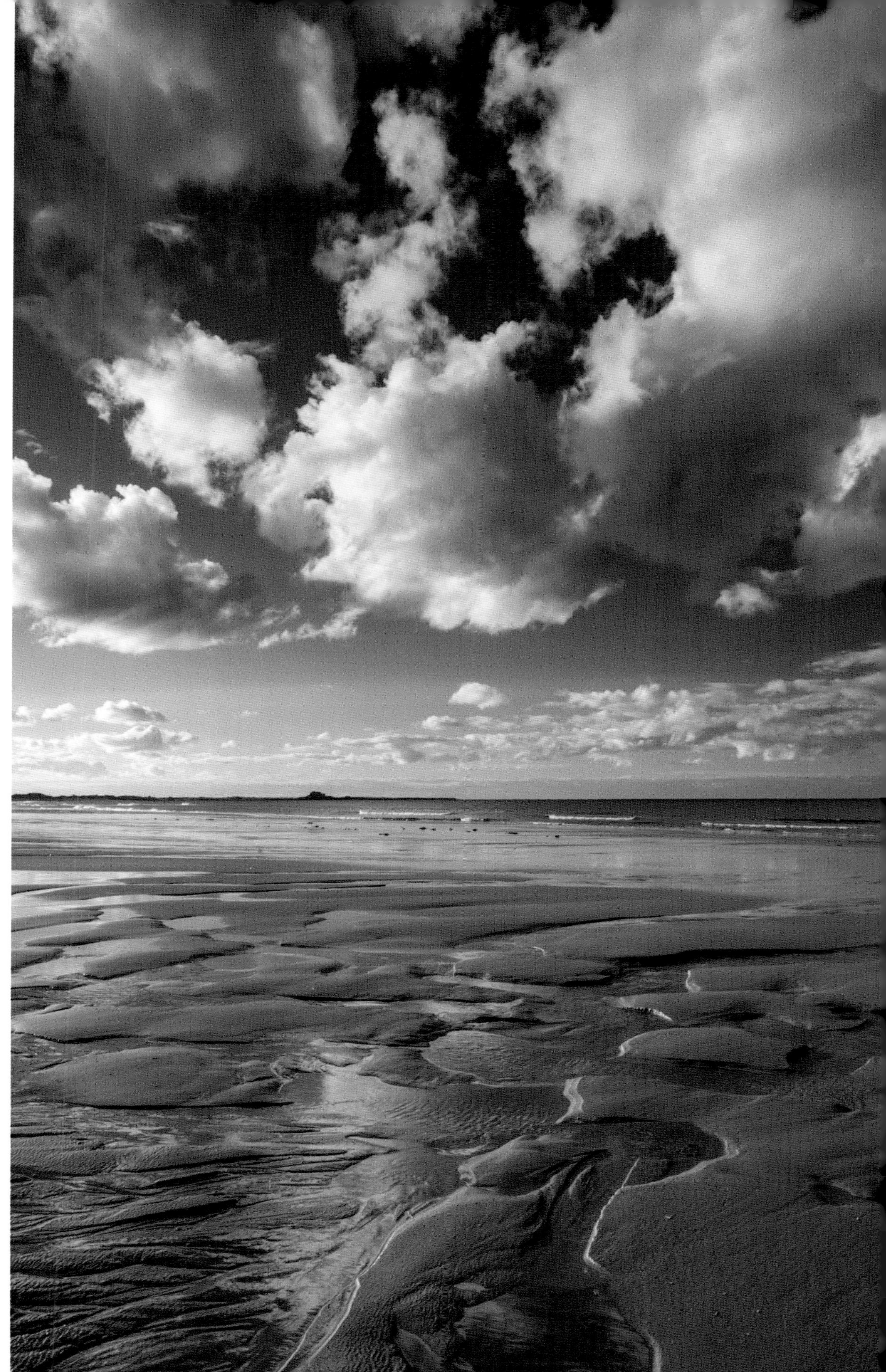

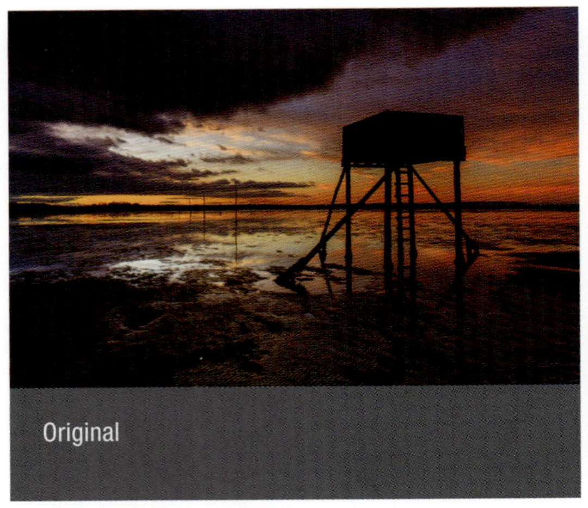

Original

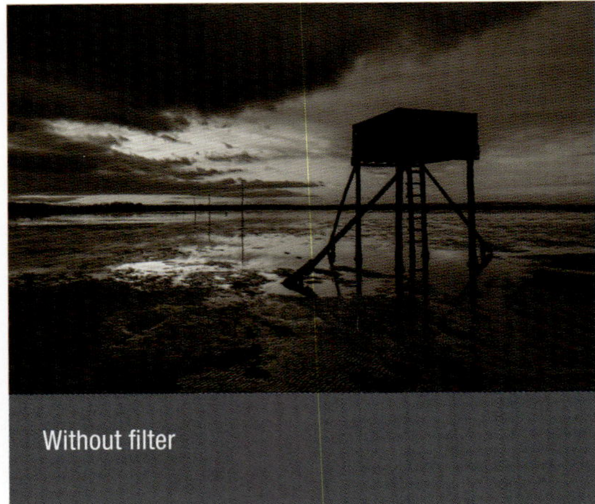

Without filter

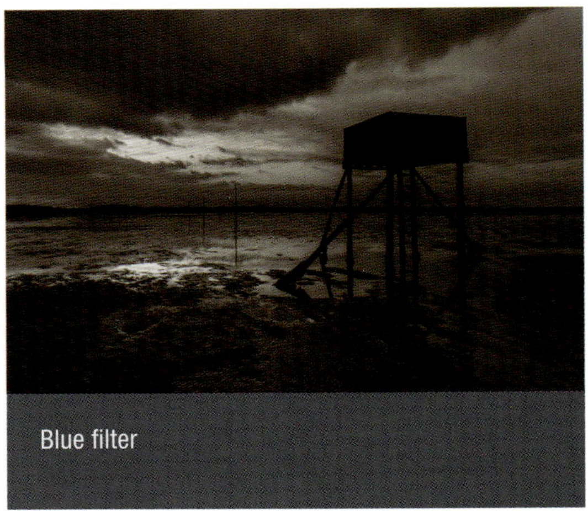

Blue filter

Green filter

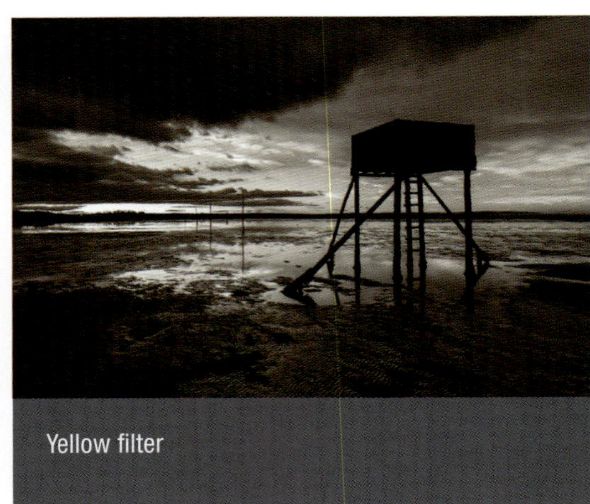

Yellow filter

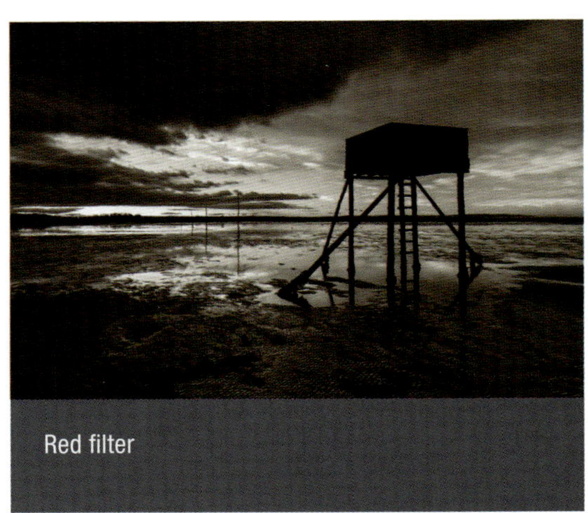

Red filter

Above: Colored filters have a dramatic effect on how colors are rendered in a black-and-white image. Physical filters need to be fitted to the lens at the time of exposure when shooting with monochrome film. This approach can still be taken when shooting black-and-white JPEG images, but most cameras have the option to simulate colored filters. Raw images need to be converted to black and white in postproduction: good conversion software will allow you to simulate the use of filters.

Right: Black-and-white imagery is more open to a variety of postproduction interpretations than color. The contrast in this image has been increased to produce a stark, minimalist effect. However, I could equally have lowered the contrast and lightened or darkened the image in order to create a different mood.

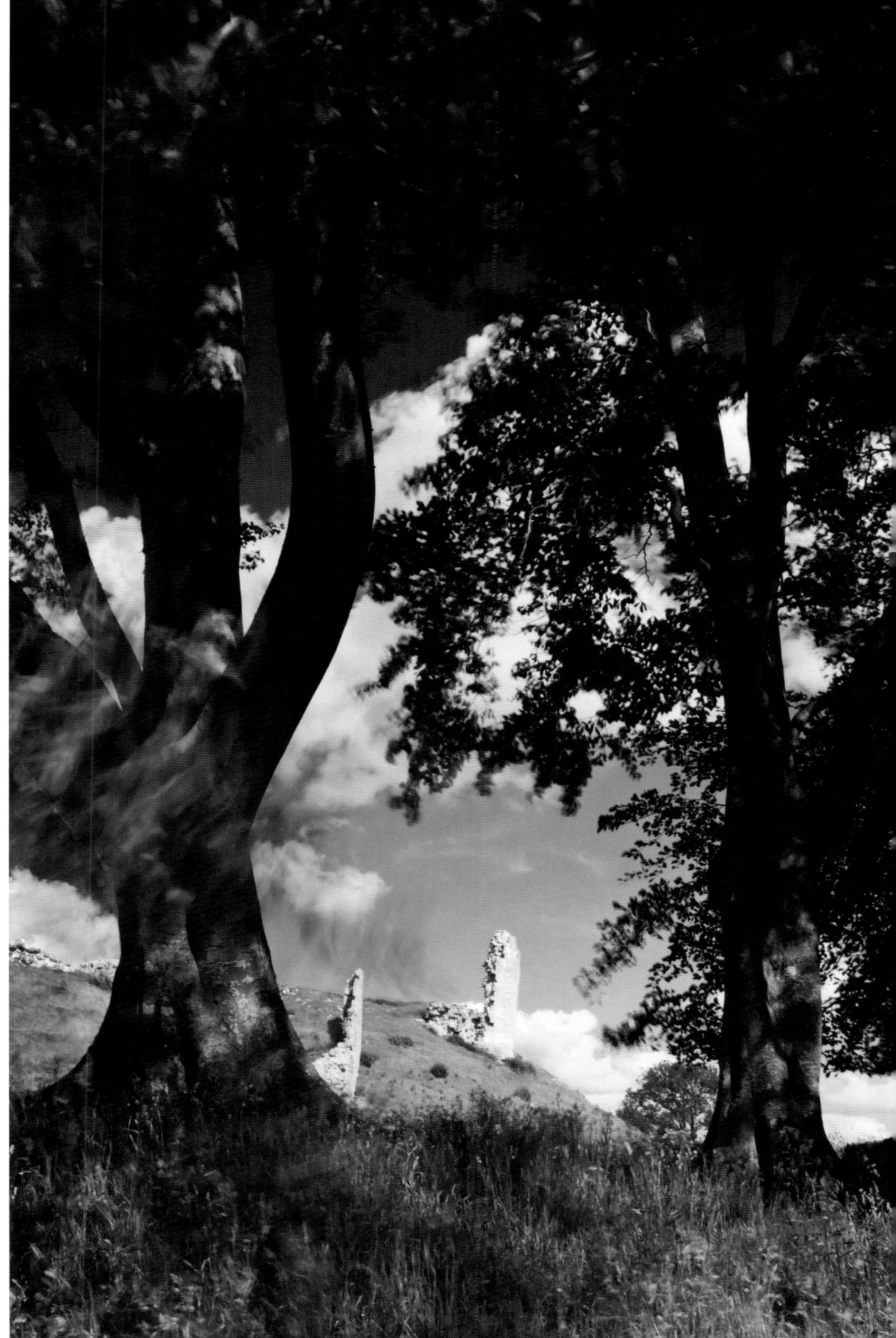

Right: Black and white is arguably better suited to
techniques such as using long shutter speeds: we can
accept less naturalistic effects more readily with black and
white as it is inherently less "realistic" than color.

Output

Although it's recommended that you shoot Raw to achieve the best result, you will eventually need to export the Raw file as a more usable format. Raw conversion software will typically give you several options to choose from—which you choose will depend on how "finished" your image is.

If you intend to work on the image further, in software such as Photoshop, then export the Raw file as a 16-bit TIFF or PSD file initially. This will maintain image quality when the file is imported into Photoshop, although TIFF and PSD files take up a large amount of hard drive space.

If the image is in a finished state, and no further work is envisaged, then export it as an 8-bit JPEG file at maximum quality to produce a file that takes up less space on your hard drive.

Another option when exporting a file is the image color space. There are several options, but the two that are most commonly encountered are Adobe RGB and sRGB. Of these, Adobe RGB is the option to choose if you intend to submit your images to photo libraries or to work further on your images. The sRGB color space is a smaller color space than Adobe RGB, but it's the standard for web use and when sending your images for printing to a commercial lab. It produces images that look bolder than Adobe RGB, but actually have slightly less accurate color information.

A third option is ProPhoto RGB. This is a bigger color space than Adobe RGB, making it a good option when you want to maximize the color information in images on your own system. However, you'll need to convert your images to Adobe RGB when sending them to third-parties.

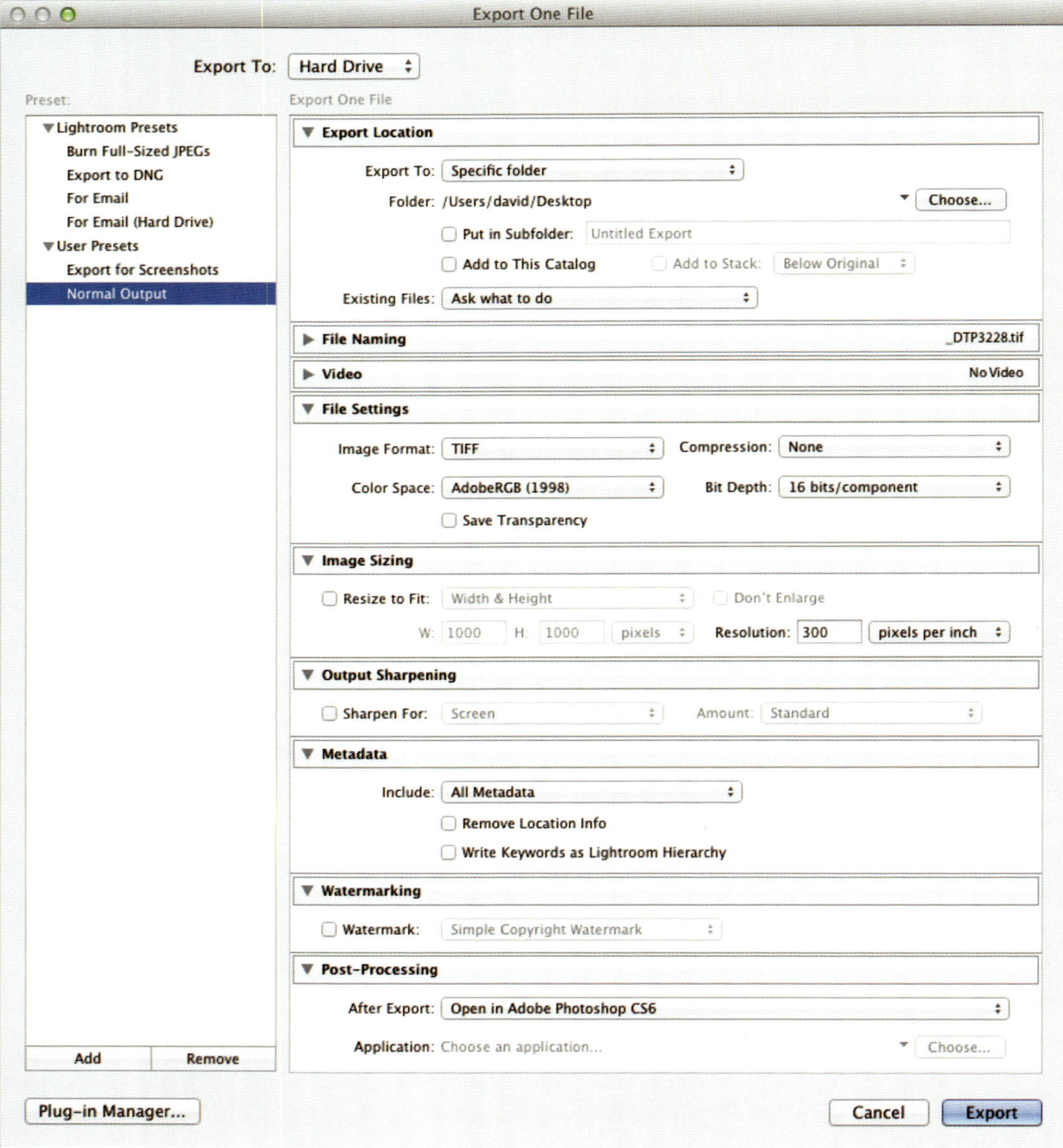

Above: Adobe Lightroom's Export dialog box. A useful aspect of Lightroom's Export function is that you can save presets so that images can be exported in a number of different ways, depending on how they will be used.

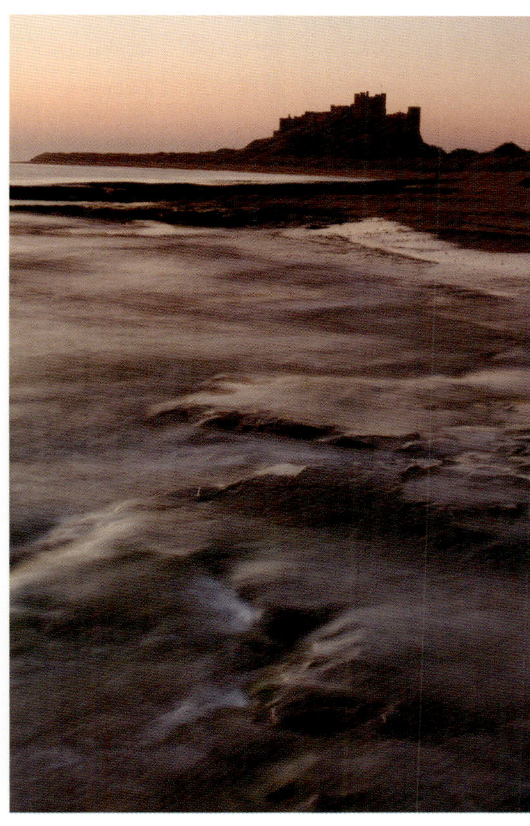

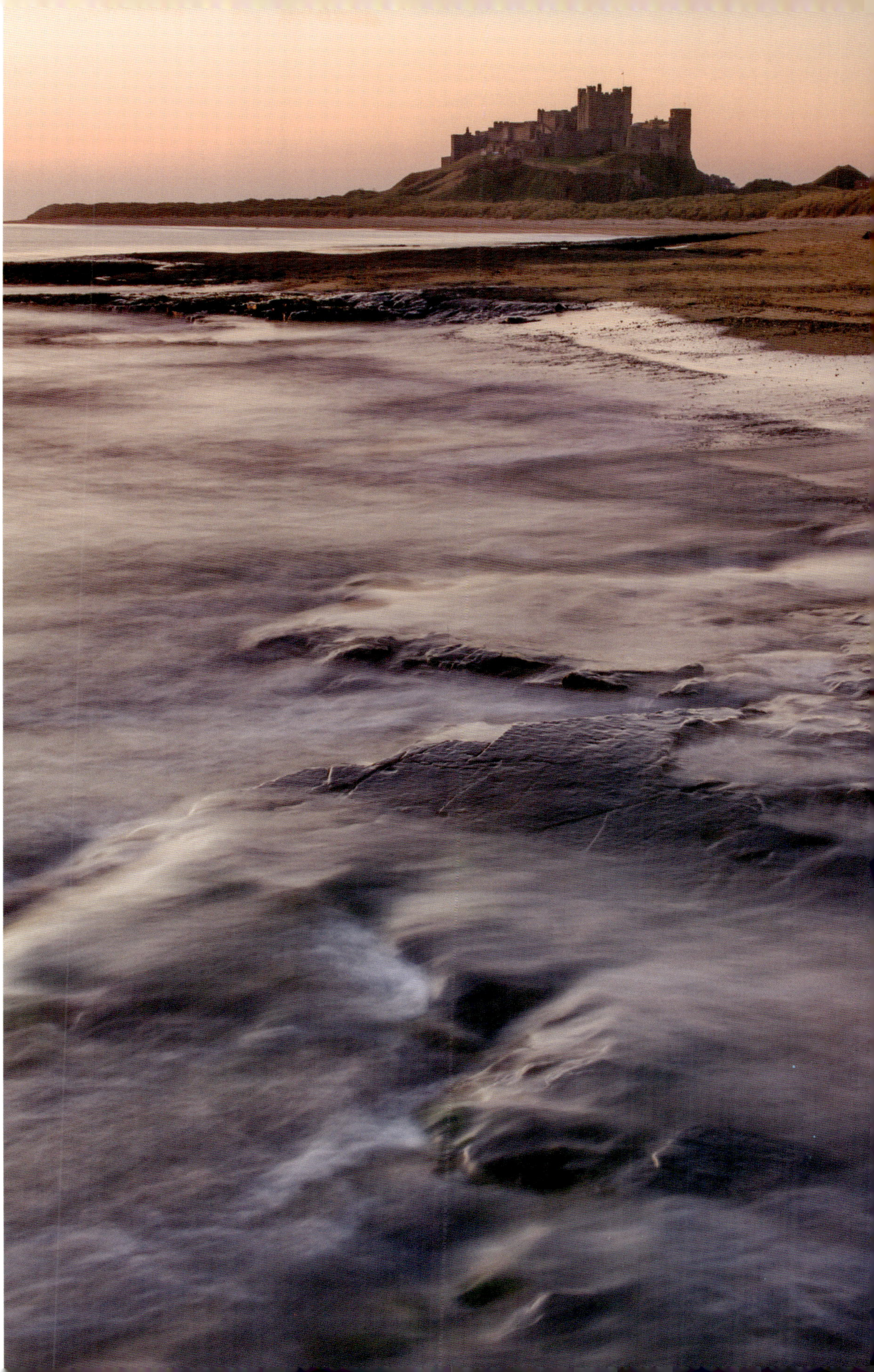

Above & Right: A well-exposed Raw file (above) is the starting point for the creation of an image (right). The beauty of Raw files is that they can be interpreted over and over again in a number of different ways. Personal tastes change and Raw software improves, so there's no reason not to revisit old images from time to time.

Preparing to Print

Viewing a well-shot image on a computer screen is rewarding, but it's even more satisfying to see the image printed out, mounted, framed, and then displayed. Preparing an image for print requires an understanding of a few simple concepts.

Calibration

Digital devices all display or output color in different ways, which can potentially make it impossible to match colors between devices. This can be a big problem when printing, as an image seen on an RGB monitor needs to be translated so that it prints accurately on a CMYK printer. This is unlikely if the two devices don't speak the same language.

The solution is a "profile," which is a file that describes how a device handles color. With accurate profiles for your monitor and your printer's ink/paper combination, your computer can provide a translation service between the two devices.

To create a profile for your monitor and printer you need hardware calibrators. Screen calibrators are far more reasonably priced than they once were and are available from most good electrical or photographic retailers. Print calibrators are slightly more specialized (and therefore more expensive), but most paper manufacturers supply ready-made profiles for popular printers. However, a specially created profile for your personal printer and paper combination will be far more accurate.

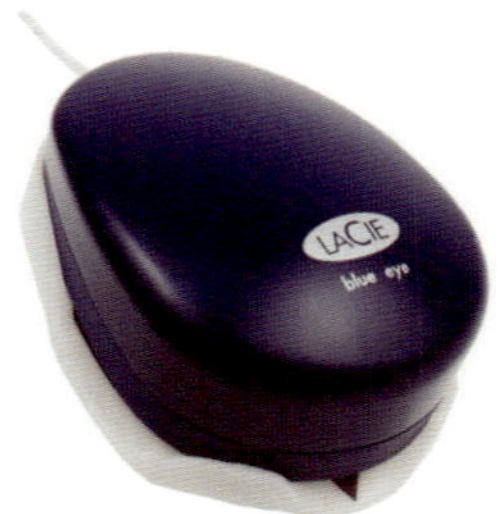

Above: LaCie Blue Eye Pro Hardware Monitor Calibrator.
© LaCie

Resolution

Making a print means converting an image from pixels into ink. One of the first decisions involved in this process is to determine how the pixels in your image will equate to one inch (or one centimeter) in your print. The generally accepted standard for printing is 300 pixels per inch (ppi)/118 pixels per centimeter (ppc). Using this standard, an image that is 3000 pixels wide could be printed 10 inches across (3000/300=10).

However, 300ppi is actually rather generous, as perfectly acceptable prints can be made at 200ppi. In this instance, a 3000-pixel wide image could be printed at 15 inches across. There will be some loss of quality at 200ppi compared to 300ppi, as the pixels are spread more thinly across the print, but this is offset by the fact that you tend to view bigger prints from further away. As a result, you don't notice the quality loss as readily.

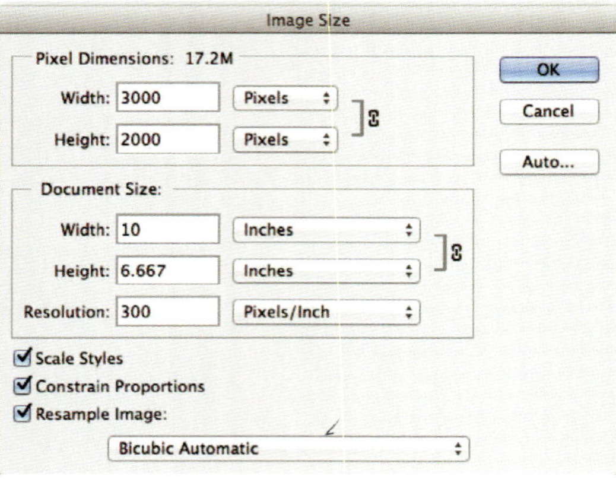

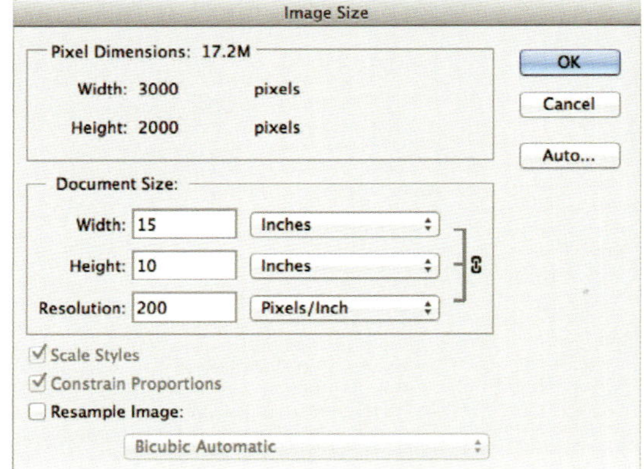

Above & Above right: In Photoshop, an image's size in pixels and its print size are both controlled using Image > Image Size. If you alter the Document Size values with Resample Image checked, the pixel size of the image is adjusted. Pixels are either removed if the image is made smaller or added if it's made bigger (using a process known as interpolation). You don't necessarily need to do this in order to resize an image for printing, though—if you uncheck Resample Image you can change the Resolution of the image, which will only alter the size the image will be printed at.

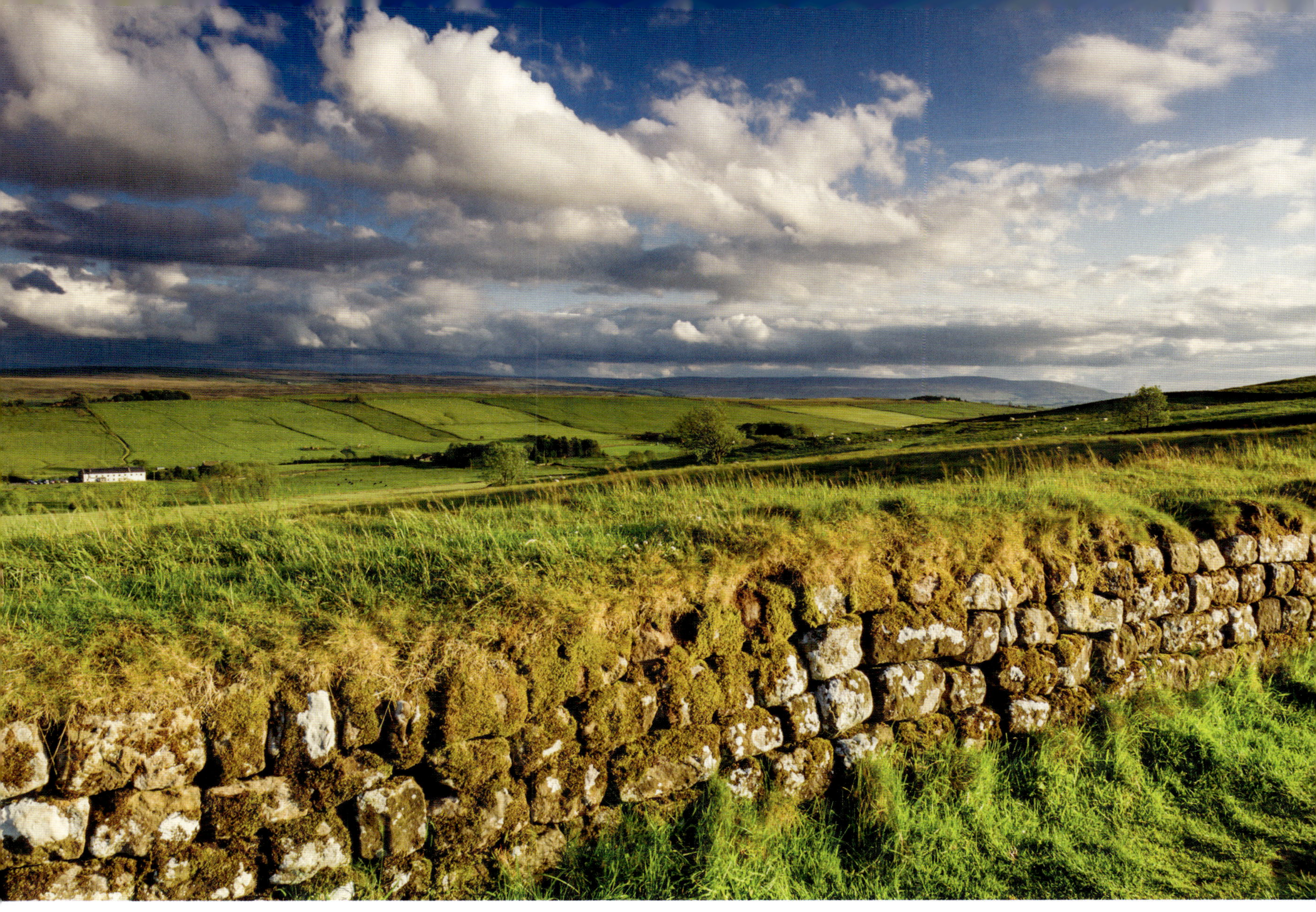

Soft Proofing

Calibration and the use of accurate profiles takes some of the guesswork out of printing, but there's nothing like making a test print to make sure that everything is as it should be. Unfortunately, this can get expensive in terms of paper and ink if you keep needing to make small changes to your images to ensure the perfect print.

One way to keep the cost down is not to print full-size initially, but to use smaller pieces of paper to produce test prints (on the same paper type that you intend to use for your final print).

This has a lot to recommend it, but it still uses (expensive) ink. A method that's far less wasteful is "soft proofing." Essentially, this is an on-screen simulation of what your image would look like when printed on a particular paper (a hard proof is a print made actually using the paper). When you create a soft proof the software temporarily alters the colors and brightness of the image on screen using the relevant printer profile. Soft proofing therefore requires relevant (and accurate) monitor and paper profiles installed on your computer.

Above: Printers tend to have the greatest problems when it comes to reproducing highly saturated colors accurately. A color that can't be reproduced accurately is referred to as being 'out of gamut." Soft proofing allows you to see potential problems and take remedial action. This often requires a reduction in color saturation.

Choosing a Paper

The paper type you choose to print an image on is a very personal decision. There are essentially three different types of finish to choose from: gloss, semi-gloss, or matte.

It's probably fair to say that gloss is by far the most popular type of paper. It has a highly smooth finish that's usually robust and hardwearing. Of the three types of paper it's generally possible to achieve the highest contrast and color saturation with gloss paper.

Images will also appear sharper in a gloss print, particularly in comparison with matte paper. This is largely because ink spread is less on gloss paper. However, there are downsides to using gloss paper. For a start, it's highly reflective, so it doesn't suit images that will be displayed where there are a number of point light sources. It is also arguably less subtle than semi-gloss or matte paper.

Semi-gloss paper is quite often seen as a compromise between the stridency of gloss paper and the more muted qualities of matte.

Matte paper is, of course, entirely non-reflective. This makes it a good choice for display in areas where lighting could be a problem. The big disadvantage is that the surface of matte paper tends to be less robust than gloss or semi-gloss papers. It's very easy to scratch a matte print, particularly when a textured watercolor paper is used. The color and contrast of matter paper is also lower than gloss paper so prints don't have as an immediate an impact. Conversely, black-and-white imagery works really well with matte.

However, there are no rules: experimenting and finding a paper that suits your photographic style and making successful prints is almost as rewarding as making the original photos.

Paper Sizing

Paper is usually sold in set sizes. There are two main systems that determine these set sizes: the ISO 216 standard and the ANSI system. The ISO 216 standard is used internationally, ANSI mainly in North America.

The ISO 216 standard uses a prefix A followed by a number to define the size of the paper: starting from A0 (the largest size) through to A10 (the smallest). The proportions of all ISO 216 paper is 1:1.41, with each paper size in the sequence created by halving the previous size along its longest side to create a sheet that's half the size. The only anomaly is A3+ or Super A3 size, which isn't part of the ISO 216 standard, but is commonly supported by printer and paper manufacturers such as Epson and Canon.

The ANSI system is based around the standard North American Letter size of 8.5 x 11 inches (or ANSI A, roughly equivalent to A4). A letter, starting with A and ending with E, defines the sequence of different sizes in the series. Unlike the ISO 216 standard the aspect ratio is not constant through the ANSI series. It alternates between 1:1.29 (so that the height of the paper is 1.29 times longer than the width) and 1:1.54 (when the height of the paper is 1.54 times longer than the width).

Paper Format	Size (mm)	Size (inches)
A0	841 x 1189	33.1 x 46.81
A1	594 x 841	23.39 x 33.11
A2	420 x 594	16.54 x 23.39
A3+	330 x 483	13 x 19
A3	297 x 420	11.69 x 16.54
A4	210 x 297	8.27 x 11.69
A5	148 x 210	5.83 x 8.27
A6	105 x 148	4.13 x 5.83
A7	74 x 105	2.91 x 4.13
A8	52 x 74	2.05 x 2.91
A9	37 x 52	1.46 x 2.05
A10	26 x 37	1.02 x 1.46

Paper Format	Size (mm)	Size (inches)
ANSI A	216 x 279	8.5 x 11
ANSI B	279 x 432	11 x 17
ANSI C	432 x 559	17 x 22
ANSI D	559 x 864	22 x 34
ANSI E	864 x 1118	34 x 44

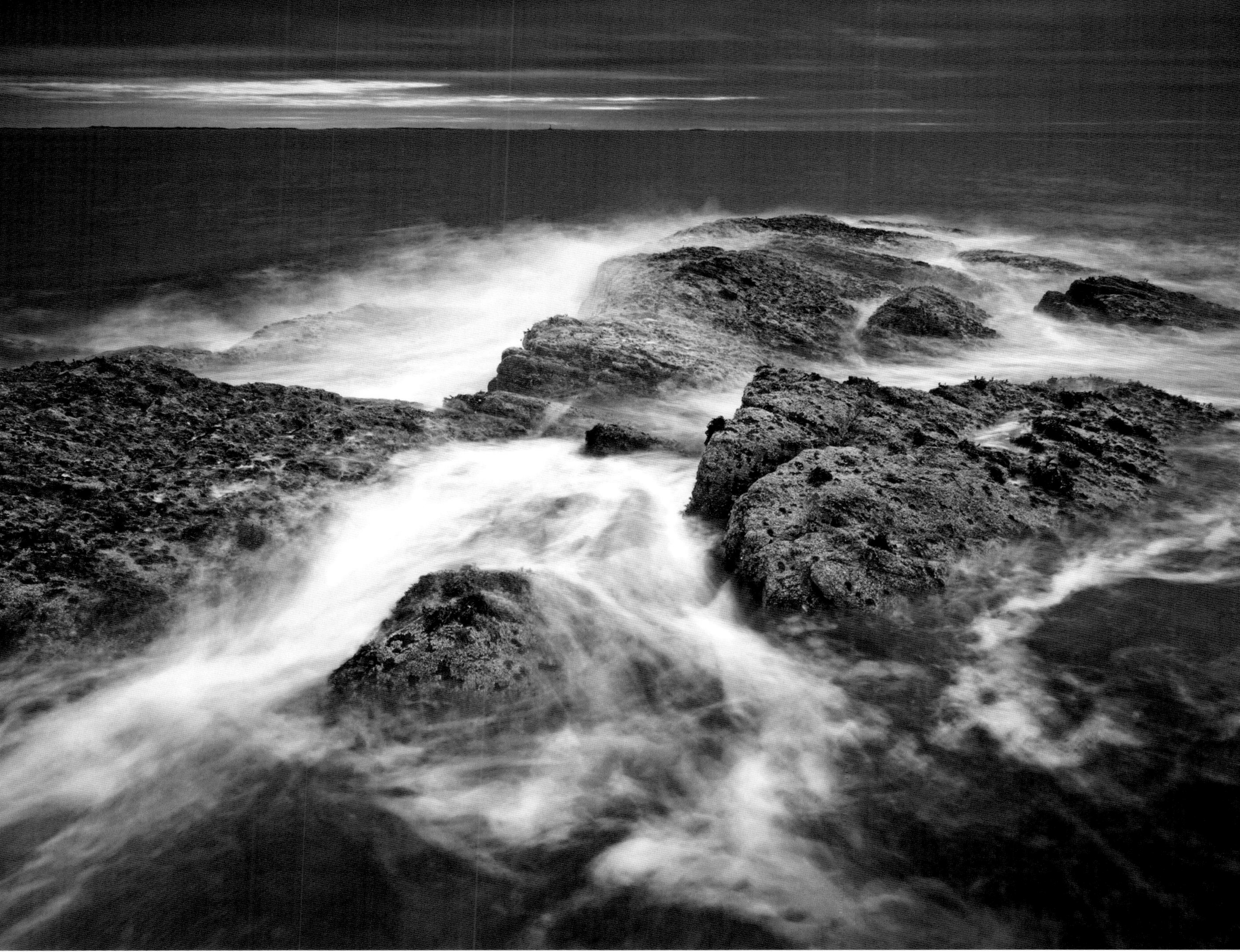

Above: There is a bewildering number of paper manufacturers, each producing papers with different finishes, weights, and textures. If you're unsure about what paper to use it's worth buying a sample pack, which will usually include samples of each type of paper that a manufacturer produces.

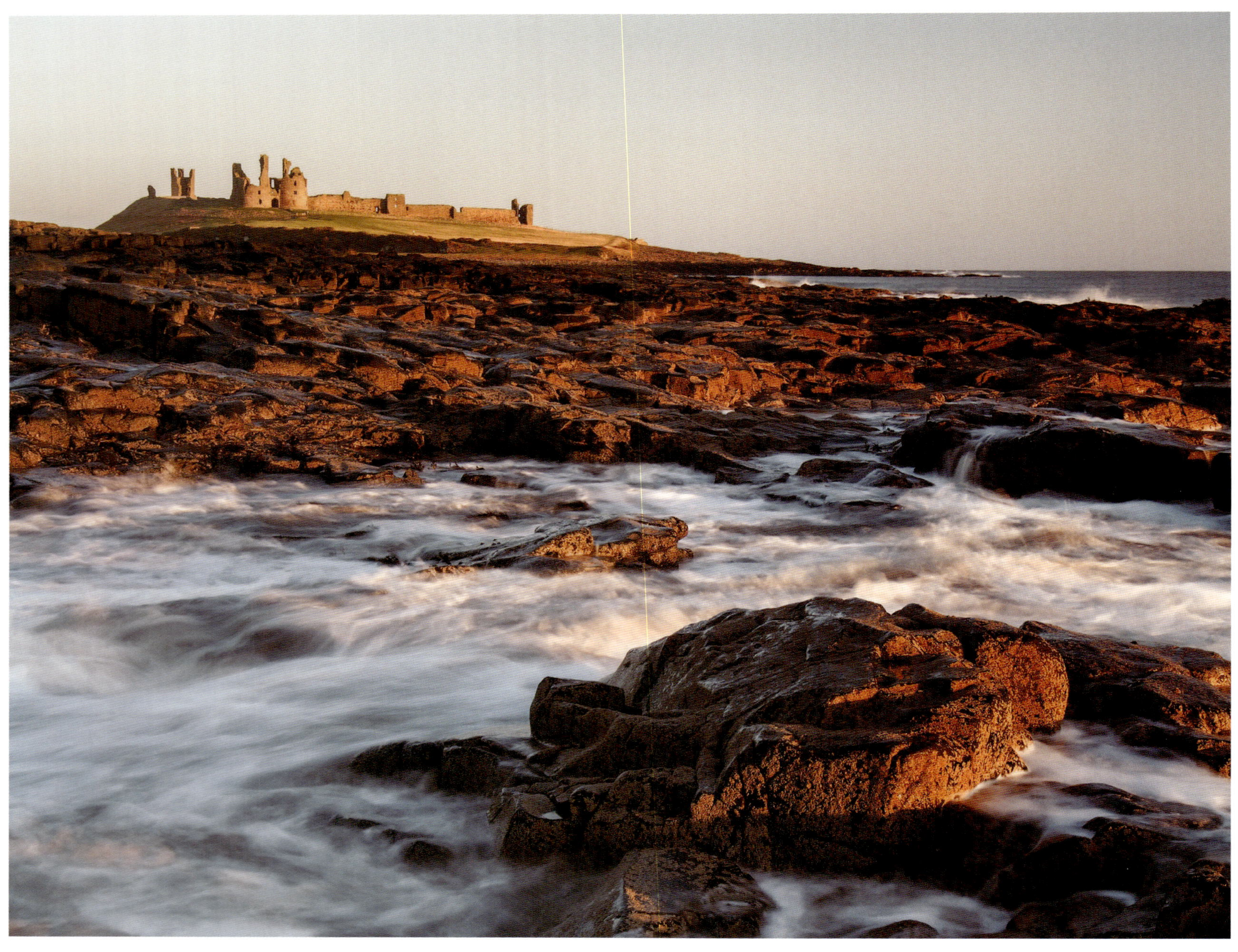

Above: Some locations work better as summer subjects, others as winter subjects. This is the south-facing aspect of the castle shown on page 72. The image was shot in late winter when the sun rose in the south east, arguably the ideal time for this particular viewpoint.

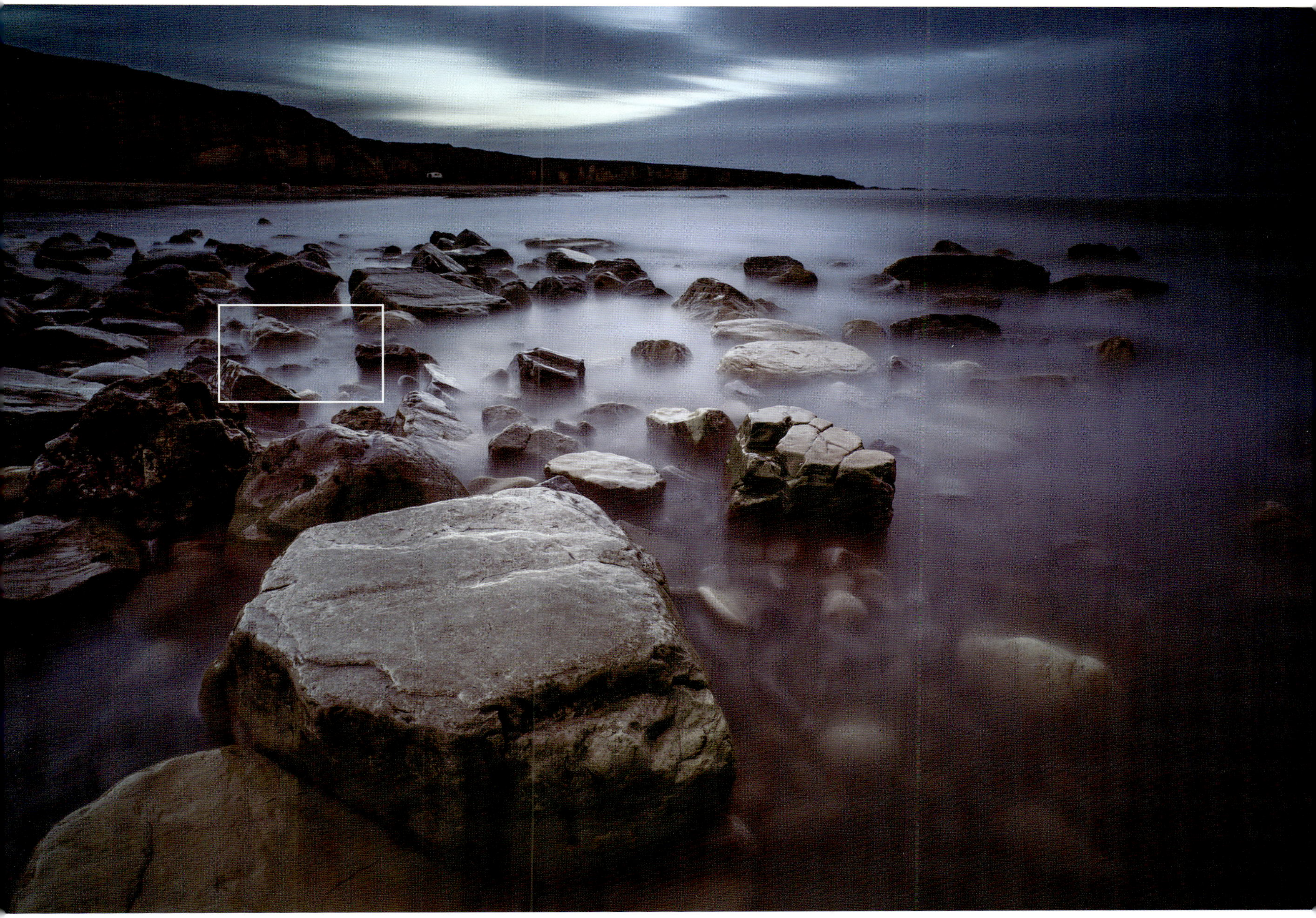

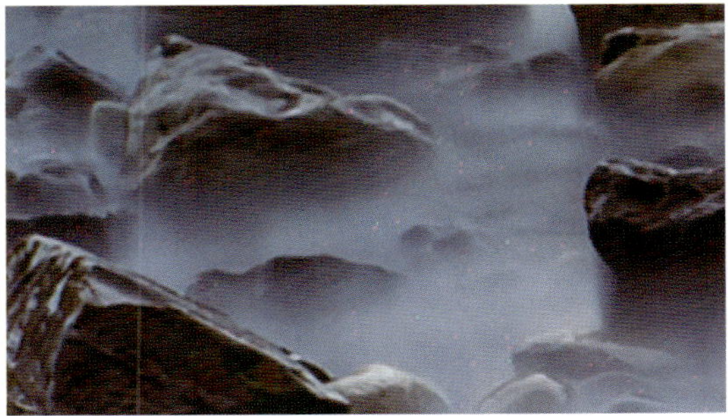

Above: Exposures longer than 30 seconds can produce a phenomenon known as "hot pixels." These are seen as red or cyan spots scattered randomly across an image (as shown in the enlarged portion, left). Not all sensors suffer from this problem, so it's a case of experimenting to see if your camera does. The solution is to switch on Long Exposure Noise Reduction and accept the necessary increased exposure time.

Glossary

Aberration An imperfection in a photograph, usually caused by the optics of a lens.

AEL (Automatic Exposure Lock) A camera control that locks in the exposure value, allowing a scene to be recomposed.

Angle of view The area of a scene that a lens takes in, measured in degrees.

Aperture The opening in a camera lens through which light passes to expose the sensor. The relative size of the aperture is denoted by f-stops.

Autofocus (AF) A reliable through-the-lens focusing system allowing accurate focus without the photographer manually turning the lens.

Bracketing Taking a series of identical pictures, changing only the exposure, usually in ⅓-, ½-, or 1-stop increments.

Buffer The in-camera memory of a digital camera.

Camera shake Image fault caused by camera movement during exposure.

Center-weighted metering A metering pattern that determines the exposure by placing importance on the lightmeter reading at the center of the frame.

Chromatic aberration The inability of a lens to bring spectrum colors into focus at a single point.

Color temperature The color of a light source expressed in degrees Kelvin (K).

Compression The process by which digital files are reduced in size. Compression can retain all the information in the file, or "lose" data for greater levels of file-size reduction.

Contrast The range between the highlight and shadow areas of a photo, or a marked difference in illumination between colors or adjacent areas.

Depth of field (DOF) The amount of an image that appears acceptably sharp. This is controlled primarily by the aperture: the smaller the aperture, the greater the depth of field.

Digital sensor A microchip consisting of a grid of millions of light-sensitive cells. The more cells, the greater the number of pixels and the higher the resolution of the final image. The two most commonly used types of digital sensor are CCD (Charge-Coupled Device) and CMOS (Complementary Metal-Oxide Semi-conductor).

Diopter Unit expressing the power of a lens.

Distortion A lens fault that causes what should be straight lines in an image to bow outward from the center (referred to as barrel distortion) or inward (referred to as pincushion distortion).

dpi (dots per inch) Measure of the resolution of a printer or scanner. The more dots per inch, the higher the resolution.

DPOF Digital Print Order Format.

Dynamic range The ability of the camera's sensor to capture a full range of shadows and highlights.

Evaluative metering A metering system where light reflected from several subject areas is calculated based on algorithms.

Exposure The amount of light allowed to hit the digital sensor, controlled by aperture, shutter speed, and ISO. Also, the act of taking a photograph, as in "making an exposure."

Exposure compensation A control that allows intentional over- or underexposure.

Fill-in flash Flash combined with daylight in an exposure. Used with naturally backlit or harshly side-lit or top-lit subjects to prevent silhouettes forming, or to add extra light to the shadow areas of a well-lit scene.

Filter A piece of colored or coated glass, or plastic, placed in front of the lens.

Focal length The distance, usually in millimeters, from the optical center of a lens to its focal point.

fps (frames per second) A measure of the time needed for a digital camera to process one photograph and be ready to shoot the next.

f/stop Number assigned to a particular lens aperture. Wide apertures are denoted by small numbers (such as f/1.8 and f/2.8), while small apertures are denoted by large numbers (such as f/16 and f/22).

HDR (High Dynamic Range) A technique that increases the dynamic range of a photograph by merging several shots taken using different exposure settings.

Highlights The brightest part of an image.

Histogram A graph representing the distribution of tones in a photograph.

Hotshoe An accessory shoe with electrical contacts that allows synchronization between a camera and a flash.

Hotspot A light area with a loss of detail in the highlights. This is a common problem in flash photography.

Incident-light reading Meter reading based on the light falling onto the subject.

Interpolation A way of increasing the file size of a digital image by adding pixels, thereby increasing its resolution.

ISO The sensitivity of the digital sensor measured in terms equivalent to the ISO rating of a film.

JPEG (Joint Photographic Experts Group) JPEG compression can reduce file sizes to about 5% of their original size, but uses a lossy compression system that degrades image quality.

LCD (Liquid Crystal Display) The flat screen on a digital camera that allows the user to compose and review digital images.

Macro A term used to describe close focusing and the close-focusing ability of a lens.

Megapixel One million pixels is equal to one megapixel.

Memory card A removable storage device for digital cameras.

Metering Act of measuring the amount of light falling on a scene to determine the required exposure.

Mirrorless Common name given to a camera that doesn't have a reflex mirror (*see* SLR). The photographer views a live image streamed from the digital sensor to an LCD.

Monochrome A synonym for black-and-white photography.

Noise Interference visible in a digital image caused by stray electrical signals during exposure.

Overexposure A result of allowing too much light to reach the digital sensor during exposure. Typically, the highlights in an overexposed image will be burnt out to pure white and the shadows unnaturally bright.

PictBridge The industry standard for sending information directly from a camera to a printer, without the need for a computer.

Pixel Short for "picture element"—the smallest bit of information in a digital photograph.

Predictive autofocus An AF system that can continuously track a moving subject.

Raw A file format in which the raw data from the sensor is stored without permanent alteration.

Red-eye reduction A system that causes the pupils of a subject's eyes to shrink, by shining a light prior to taking the main flash picture.

Remote switch A device used to trigger the shutter of the camera from a distance, to help minimize camera shake. Also known as a "cable release" or "remote release."

Resolution The number of pixels used to capture or display a photo.

RGB (red, green, blue) Computers and other digital devices understand color information as combinations of red, green, and blue.

Rule of Thirds A rule of composition that places the key elements of a picture at points along imagined lines that divide the frame into thirds, both vertically and horizontally.

Shadows The darkest part of an image.

Shutter The mechanism that controls the amount of light reaching the sensor, by opening and closing.

SLR (Single Lens Reflex) Describes a camera that allows a photographer to see the image projected through the lens by directing the image to the viewfinder using a reflex mirror.

Soft proofing Using software to mimic on screen how an image will look once output to another imaging device. Typically this will be a printer.

Spot metering A metering pattern that places importance on the intensity of light reflected by a very small portion of the scene, either at the center of the frame or linked to a focus point.

Teleconverter A supplementary lens that is fitted between the camera body and lens, increasing its effective focal length.

Telephoto A lens with a large focal length and a narrow angle of view.

TIFF (Tagged Image File Format) A universal file format supported by virtually all relevant software applications. TIFFs are uncompressed digital files.

TTL (Through The Lens) metering A metering system built into the camera that measures light passing through the lens at the time of shooting.

Underexposure The result of allowing too little light to reach the digital sensor during exposure. Typically, the highlights in an underexposed image will be muddy and the shadows dense and lacking in detail.

USB (Universal Serial Bus) A data transfer standard, used by most cameras to connect to a computer.

Viewfinder An optical system used for composing and sometimes for focusing the subject.

White balance A function that allows the correct color balance to be recorded for any given lighting situation.

Wide-angle lens A lens with a short focal length and, consequently, a wide angle of view.

Zoom A lens with a variable focal length.

Useful Web Sites

General

Digital Photography Review
www.dpreview.com

On Landscape
www.onlandscape.co.uk

Photographers

David Taylor
www.davidtaylorphotography.co.uk

Photographic Equipment

www.canon.com DSLRs, CSCs, compact cameras, and proprietary lenses; Printers; Photographic paper

www.fujifilm.com CSCs, compact cameras, and proprietary lenses; Photographic paper; Film products

www.leica-camera.com Digital and film rangefinder cameras, medium-format DSLRs, and proprietary lenses

www.nikon.com DSLRs, CSCs, compact cameras, and proprietary lenses

www.olympus-global.com CSCs, compact cameras, and proprietary lenses

www.panasonic.com CSCs, compact cameras, and proprietary lenses

www.ricoh-imaging.com DSLRs, CSCs, compact cameras, and proprietary lenses

www.sigma-photo.com DSLRs, compact cameras, and proprietary lenses; Third-party lenses for Canon, Micro Four Thirds, Nikon, Pentax, and Sony mounts

www.sony.com DSLRs, CSCs, compact cameras, and proprietary lenses

www.tamron.com Third-party lenses for Canon, Nikon, Pentax, and Sony mounts

www.tokinalens.com Third-party lenses for Canon, Nikon, and Sony mounts

www.zeiss.com Third-party lenses for Canon, Fujifilm, Nikon, and Sony mounts

Photography Publications

Ammonite Press
www.ammonitepress.com

Black & White magazine
www.blackandwhitephotographymag.co.uk

Outdoor Photography magazine
www.outdoorphotographymagazine.co.uk

Printing

www.epson.com Inkjet printers; Photographic paper

www.hahnemuehle.de Fine-art photographic paper

www.harmantechnology.com/inkjet Fine-art photographic paper

www8.hp.com Inkjet printers; Photographic paper

www.ilford.com Photographic paper

www.kodak.com Inkjet printers; Photographic paper

www.lexmark.com Inkjet printers; Photographic paper

www.marrutt.com Third-party inks; Continuous ink systems; Photographic paper

Software

www.adobe.com Standalone imaging software (Photoshop, Lightroom, plus others)

www.alienskin.com Standalone imaging software; Photoshop and Lightroom plugins

www.apple.com Mac/iPad tablets; Standalone imaging software (Aperture, plus others)

www.corel.com Standalone imaging software (PaintShop Pro, plus others)

www.dxo.com Standalone imaging software (Optics Pro, plus others)

www.phaseone.com Medium format digital backs; Standalone imaging software (Capture One Pro, plus others)

www.hdrsoft.com Standalone HDR software (Photomatix Pro); Photoshop and Lightroom plugins

www.photopills.com iOS landscape photography app

Index

Acknowledgments

No one is an island and it would be impossible to develop both as a person and as a photographer without the support and influence of others. There are innumerable photographers who I've met that have encouraged me to continue in my chosen field. In no particular order I'd like to thank Colin Dixon, David Noton, Joe Cornish, and Lee Frost. Particular thanks, however, must be given to Andy Stansfield who introduced me to Ammonite Press. On the subject of which, I wouldn't have got past my first book without the patience of Richard Wiles and Jonathan Bailey at Ammonite, and Chris Gatcum.

Friends and family may be puzzled at my need to wield a camera in all weathers, but that doesn't mean they aren't important too. I'd like to thank Jim and Sheilah Parr for being there; my parents Bill and Carol for getting it right; my in-laws Brian and Sue for their support; and last, but not least, my wife Tania who doesn't mind me being out at odd hours of the day, and to whom this book is dedicated.

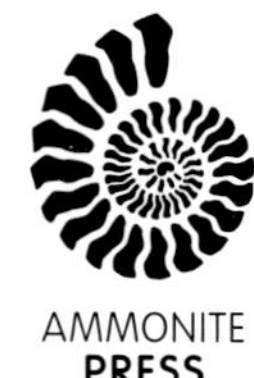

AMMONITE
PRESS

To place an order, or request a catalog, contact:
Ammonite Press
GMC Publications Ltd, Castle Place, 166 High Street, Lewes, East Sussex, BN7 1XU, United Kingdom
Tel: +44 (0)1273 488006
www.ammonitepress.com